Introduction to Professional Policing

Policing is a dynamic profession with increasing demands and complexities placed upon police officers, staff and volunteers who provide a 24-hour service across a diverse range of communities. Written by experts in policing higher education from across both academic and professional practice, this book equips aspiring or newly appointed police officers, staff and volunteers with the knowledge and understanding to deal with the significant and often complex challenges they face daily.

This second edition of *Introduction to Professional Policing* explores a number of the core underpinning knowledge requirements identified as themes within the ever-evolving National Policing Curriculum (NPC) and Police Constable Entry Routes (PCER), while also informing those embarking on leadership development. These include:

- Community and neighbourhood policing
- Counter-terrorism
- Digital policing
- Ethics, equality, diversity and inclusion
- Evidence-based policing
- Maintaining professional standards
- Police leadership
- Problem solving and problem-oriented policing
- Victims and protecting the vulnerable
- Volunteers in policing

This edition has been reviewed and significantly updated in line with the dynamic and ongoing demands faced by operational policing and therefore the associated knowledge requirements for policing education and training. The book is refocused on the learning requirements contained within the range of entry routes now available in to policing, as well as the professional development of those serving as police staff and volunteers. This includes new chapters providing insights into community and neighbourhood policing, problem solving and volunteers in policing.

At the end of each chapter the student finds a case study, reflective questions and an extensive reference list, all of which reinforces students' knowledge and furthers their professional development. Written in a clear and direct style, this book supports aspiring police officers, newly appointed police officers, direct entry detectives, community support officers, special constables and police staff. It will also be of interest to those embarking on a leadership journey within policing and anyone wanting to learn more about the profession of policing. It is essential reading for students taking a professional policing degree or commencing any of the police constable entry routes.

Ian Pepper is a professor in policing at the International Centre for Policing and Security, University of South Wales, and an advisor on higher education within policing nationally. Ian is a former principal lecturer in policing, senior lecturer in crime scene and forensic science, police trainer, crime scene investigator (CSI) and fingerprint officer. He has been a team leader at the National Training Centre for Scientific Support to Crime Investigation and has designed and delivered education and training to crime scene investigators and police officers worldwide. Ian has undertaken additional academic roles including chair of the QAA/College of Policing subject benchmark statement for policing, visiting professor in professional practice at the University of Sunderland and invited visiting scholar at the University of Central Florida, USA. With research interests focused on policing higher education, police leadership and volunteering in policing, Ian has authored and edited a range of journal articles and policing publications.

Ruth McGrath teaches on the BSc Crime and Investigation course at Teesside University, and more recently became course leader of the BSc Professional Policing. Before this Ruth served with Cleveland Police where she experienced a range of operational roles, including uniformed policing, investigation, roads policing and custody officer. As a detective she was engaged in major crime investigations and completed a six-month secondment to a national unit based at New Scotland Yard. During her service she was also a police trainer and an A1 NVQ Assessor. Ruth has taught and managed numerous policing programmes at Teesside University including the Police Foundation Degree. With a special interest in policing higher education, Ruth has authored several journal articles and contributed to a published volume.

Introduction to Professional Policing

Examining the Evidence Base

Second edition

Edited by
Ian Pepper and Ruth McGrath

Routledge
Taylor & Francis Group

LONDON AND NEW YORK

Designed cover image: Shutterstock

Second edition published
by Routledge
4 Park Square, Milton Park, Abingdon, Oxon OX14 4RN

and by Routledge
605 Third Avenue, New York, NY 10158

Routledge is an imprint of the Taylor & Francis Group, an informa business

© 2025 selection and editorial matter, Ian Pepper and Ruth McGrath; individual chapters, the contributors

The right of Ian Pepper and Ruth McGrath to be identified as the authors of the editorial material, and of the authors for their individual chapters, has been asserted in accordance with sections 77 and 78 of the Copyright, Designs and Patents Act 1988.

All rights reserved. No part of this book may be reprinted or reproduced or utilised in any form or by any electronic, mechanical, or other means, now known or hereafter invented, including photocopying and recording, or in any information storage or retrieval system, without permission in writing from the publishers.

Trademark notice: Product or corporate names may be trademarks or registered trademarks, and are used only for identification and explanation without intent to infringe.

British Library Cataloguing-in-Publication Data
A catalogue record for this book is available from the British Library

ISBN: 978-1-032-79599-7 (hbk)
ISBN: 978-1-032-79514-0 (pbk)
ISBN: 978-1-003-49294-8 (ebk)

DOI: 10.4324/9781003492948

Typeset in Sabon
by Taylor & Francis Books

Dedicated to all police officers, staff and volunteers, past, present and future

Contents

List of illustrations   ix
List of contributors   x
Foreword   xvii

Introduction   1
IAN PEPPER AND RUTH MCGRATH

1 Ethics, equality, diversity and inclusion   8
EIFION SWINNERTON-GISMONDI

2 Maintaining professional standards and reflective practice   26
DOMINIC A. WOOD

3 Criminology and criminal justice   42
ANNE LODGE

4 Public protection: The role of the police as a public authority   65
ANGELA KING AND ANNABELLE JAMES

5 Evidence-based policing   82
HELEN SELBY-FELL AND IAN PEPPER

6 Communication skills, decision-making and managing conflict   98
RUTH MCGRATH, IAN PEPPER AND MARK THORNTON

7 Problem solving and problem-oriented policing   112
JANE BAXENDALE

8 Community and neighbourhood policing: The shifting sands   127
MOLLIE RENNOLDSON

9 Policing vulnerability attrition, rape and domestic abuse   145
EMMA WILLIAMS, JENNIFER NORMAN AND KATY BARROW-GRINT

10 Counter-terrorism: The front line   168
    PETER WILLIAMS

11 Digital policing   186
    BENJAMIN FINDLAY, SHAWN ROBERTSON AND HARRY STEWART

12 Volunteers in policing   201
    COLIN ROGERS

13 An introduction to coaching and mentoring   214
    DAVID TAYLOR

14 Leadership in policing: An international comparison   229
    IAN PEPPER, RICK RUDDELL, ROSS WOLF AND CHRISTOPHER D. O'CONNOR

    Index   248

Illustrations

Figures

I.1	Percentage comparison of policing workforce roles in England and Wales, 31 March 2024	1
1.1	Behavioural chart	17
5.1	A hierarchy of research evidence	86

Tables

4.1	Human Rights Act 1998, Schedule 1	67
6.1	Level of resistance, likelihood of harm and person's behaviour	104
9.1	Withdrawal of complaints	159

Contributors

Katy Barrow-Grint joined Thames Valley Police in 2000 having studied sociology at the London School of Economics and has worked in a variety of roles and ranks including uniform patrol, CID, neighbourhood policing, child abuse investigation, surveillance and strategic development. She became assistant chief constable in 2023 overseeing the Crime and Criminal Justice Portfolio and was the force lead for violence against women and girls. In November 2024 Katy became interim deputy chief constable for Gloucestershire Constabulary.

Jane Baxendale is a national senior educational advisor in policing, with considerable experience in higher, further and primary education. A role as a mentor for new teachers led to a career in higher education as a programme lead and external examiner. Jane has a special interest in the areas of problem-solving, evidence-based practice, public protection and safeguarding. She has a masters in education focusing on leadership skills in the education sector and was a member of the QAA working group which set the first benchmark statement for policing in the UK. Jane has contributed to the working group on learning and development for the national problem-solving programme to set up workshops, guidance and practice advice to support forces on problem solving projects and learning. The programme revived the Tilley awards, the UK version of the international Goldstein awards, where she has been a sift judge since its inception.

Benjamin Findlay is a senior lecturer at Teesside University and the course leader for the BSc (Hons) computer and digital forensics and MSc digital forensics and cyber investigation programmes. He also teaches on the MSc crime intelligence and data analytics programme. During his previous career in law enforcement, Ben worked for North Yorkshire Police (NYP) as an investigator within the force's digital forensic unit (DFU). He has investigated a wide variety of cases, including murder, large scale fraud, child abuse, grooming, online harassment, missing persons, infanticide, dangerous driving and some internal investigations. He also worked actively on the DFU's ISO/IEC 17025 accreditation, fulfilling the role of Acting Technical Manager for the final six months of his time with the force. Ben has a BSc (Hons) in applied science and forensic investigation and an MSc in digital forensics, both from Teesside University. His research interests include forensic artefacts, mobile forensic investigations, cloud forensics and child protection.

Dr Annabelle James is a principal lecturer at Teesside University, currently responsible for recruitment across all provision in the School of Social Sciences, Humanities and Law and the School of Arts and Creative Industries. She holds an undergraduate law degree and master's in criminal justice, both from the University of Leeds, a doctorate in education from Teesside University and is currently undertaking an MBA with psychology at Wrexham University. She is a senior fellow of the Higher Education Academy. She has 25 years' experience of working in Higher Education across a variety of different roles including subject group lead for Law and Policing and head of Department for Criminology, Law and Policing. Her main teaching interests lie in human rights and criminal justice which she currently teaches across Teesside's Law and Policing provision, and she has published on these areas. Her current research is in the field of legal education.

Angela King is head of Department for Law, Policing and Investigation at Teesside University and, as such, has been involved in the cross-disciplinary delivery of contemporary police practice and policy. Angela is interested in the role of the police as a public authority, tasked with the responsibility to exercise powers in conformity with the fundamental human rights of the citizens living within the state, and criminal evidence and procedure. Angela is involved with the policing portfolio within the department, most recently supporting the development of the DHEP provision. Angela is also actively engaged in research in this area and has recently contributed to an article focussed on confession evidence obtained from vulnerable defendants in the criminal law review and currently working towards a PhD from Northumbria University, exploring the role of cross examination in criminal trials.

Dr Anne Lodge is a senior lecturer in law at Teesside University. She graduated with first-class honours LL.B. (Hons) law in 2003 and completed her PhD in Criminal Law at Durham University in 2009. Anne's primary research interests lie in criminal law, criminal law theory, and criminal justice, with a particular focus on criminal law defences, homicide offences, and legal responses to domestic abuse. In addition to her research, Anne is passionate about legal education. She has held various teaching and administrative roles throughout her career in higher education and was recently awarded a senior fellowship from the Higher Education Academy. Currently, she serves as the course leader for the LL.B. programme at Teesside University and brings extensive interdisciplinary teaching experience to students in law, criminology, and policing as part of their respective programmes of study.

Dr Ruth McGrath is a principal lecturer (learning & teaching) at Teesside University. She is course leader of the BSc professional policing and the graduate diploma in professional policing courses and teaches on the BSc Crime and

Investigation course. Before this Ruth served with Cleveland Police where she experienced a range of operational roles, including uniformed policing, investigation, roads policing and custody officer. As a detective she was engaged in major crime investigations and completed a six-month secondment to a national unit based at New Scotland Yard. During her service she was also a police trainer and an A1 NVQ assessor. Ruth has taught and managed numerous policing programmes at Teesside University including the police foundation degree. With a special interest in policing higher education, and the professionalisation of policing, she has had a number of published journal articles and has contributed to several textbooks.

Dr Jennifer Norman is the head of policing at the Open University. She has long-standing experience of delivering policing qualifications to policing practitioners via several undergraduate and post-graduate programmes and at different universities. Her academic background is in policing and criminology, and she has a keen interest in social research methodologies, given her experiences of conducting a longitudinal study for her PhD research. Her research interests are in police professionalisation with an emphasis on police education. Prior to joining academia, Jennifer worked as a strategic researcher for the Metropolitan Police Service (MPS) for 13 years which became the foundation of her operational knowledge of policing, as well as the driver to research more about the complexities in policing.

Dr Christopher D. O'Connor is an associate professor of criminology at Ontario Tech University. His primary research areas include policing, youth participation in crime, rapid growth communities, and emerging/disruptive technologies. He has researched public perceptions of a range of issues including crime, disruptive technologies, and attitudes toward the police. More recently, his research has examined police data quality and collection techniques and data modernisation within policing. He is currently a co-investigator on a SSHRC-funded partnership development grant examining facial recognition use by the police which involves working with a range of multi-disciplinary stakeholders to examine the viability of the technology for police use. His work appears in a number of peer reviewed journals.

Dr Ian Pepper is a professor in policing at the International Centre for Policing and Security, University of South Wales, and an advisor on higher education within policing both nationally and internationally. Ian is a former principal lecturer in policing, senior lecturer in crime scene and forensic science, police trainer, crime scene investigator (CSI) and fingerprint officer. He has been a team leader at the National Training Centre for Scientific Support to Crime Investigation and has designed and delivered education and training to crime scene investigators and police officers worldwide. Ian has undertaken additional academic roles including chair of the QAA/College of Policing subject benchmark statement for policing, visiting professor in professional practice at the University of Sunderland and invited visiting scholar at the University of Central Florida, USA. Ian is a senior fellow of the Higher Education Academy. He has research interests focused on policing higher education, evidence-informed practice, police leadership and volunteering in policing. Ian has authored, contributed to and edited a range of books, journal articles, policing and professional publications, including the text *Crime Scene Investigation: Methods and Procedures*, 2nd edition.

Mollie Rennoldson, a senior lecturer in policing and course lead for Teesside University's police constable degree apprenticeship, holds a BSc (Hons) in criminology and sociology and an MSc in criminal investigation. She retains experience in empirical research with police practitioners, with research interests centred on community engagement, mental health, county lines, organised crime, and other vulnerability-related issues. As a dedicated policing practitioner, Mollie has served as a special constable with Northumbria Police for over five years, contributing to both response and community-based policing teams. Additionally, she has held various roles within the criminal justice system (CJS), including work with NEPACS and supporting young people with special educational and mental health needs (SEMH). In her higher education career, Mollie has lectured on a wide range of policing programmes, such as MSc criminal investigation, BSc (Hons) crime and investigation, BSc (Hons) professional policing, and the BSc (Hons) professional policing practice (PCDA), as well as the Degree Holder Entry Programme (DHEP) in collaboration with Cleveland Police. Recently, Mollie earned fellowship status with the Higher Education Academy and is involved in local research aimed at improving police practice relating to individuals missing from home.

Shawn Robertson is lecturer at Teesside University for the computer and digital forensics bachelor's degree programme. During his previous career in law enforcement, Shawn worked for Greater Manchester Police (GMP) as a Digital Forensic Investigator and a digital forensic evidence examiner within the force's digital forensic unit (DFU). He has investigated a wide variety of cases, including murder, large scale fraud, child abuse, grooming, online harassment, missing persons, infanticide, dangerous driving and some internal investigations. Shawn has taught and managed multiple modules within the computer and digital forensic courses at Teesside University and provided drop-in sessions for other Police related modules and programmes. Shawn has BSc (Hons) in computer and digital forensics from Teesside University. His research interests include forensic artefacts, mobile forensic investigation, cloud forensics and information of things devices.

Dr Colin Rogers is emeritus professor of policing and security at the International Centre for Policing and Security, the University of South Wales. A former police practitioner of 30 years' service, he has researched and advised policing agencies across the world, including such countries as Australia, Uruguay, Abu Dhabi, and Brunei as well as European police agencies. A keen advocate of research into policing he has published numerous articles

xiv *List of contributors*

and books on such topics as police education, crime prevention, police organisation and volunteers as well as police legitimacy.

Professor Rick Ruddell, the Law Foundation of Saskatchewan Chair in Police Studies, joined the Department of Justice Studies at the University of Regina in September 2010. Prior to this appointment he served as director of operational research with the Correctional Service of Canada and held faculty positions at Eastern Kentucky University and the California State University, Chico. Prior to his academic career, he served with the Saskatchewan Ministry of Corrections, Public Safety and Policing as a supervisor and manager. Professor Ruddell's research has focused upon policing, criminal justice policy and youth justice.

Dr Helen Selby-Fell holds a senior lectureship in policing and is deputy director of SCiLAB (the Scholarship Centre for Innovation in Online Legal and Business Education) in the Faculty of Business & Law (FBL) at the Open University. Helen has 15 years' experience working in the police service, where she held the roles of head of corporate analysis & research at Merseyside Police and director of commissioning, policy & research at the Office of the Police & Crime Commissioner for Merseyside. Helen has a PhD from the Applied Criminology Centre at the University of Huddersfield, which explored the challenges and opportunities associated with embedding 'evidence based policing' (EBP) in the police service. Helen has wide ranging research interests including the conceptualisation and implementation of EBP, decision making, crime analysis, and forensic psychology in policing.

Harry Stewart is a lecturer at Teesside University teaching on BSc (Hons) computer and digital forensics and MSc digital forensics and cyber investigation degree programmes. He also module leads several modules across these and other courses. Previously Harry spent 5 years as a digital forensic investigator for North Yorkshire Police (NYP) as part of the forces digital forensic unit (DFU). During this time, he worked on a wide variety of cases and investigated all types of digital device specifically taking the lead on mobile devices. He is experienced at giving evidence in crown court and has live crime scene and incident response experience. He also worked as an active trainer in the department training a wide range of new staff. Harry was also involved in the creation and maintenance of procedures as part of the departments ISO/OEC 17025 accreditation.

Eifion Swinnerton-Gismondi is a former member of the Royal Military Police and a retired Cleveland Police officer. During his time as a police officer, Eifion worked in many areas of policing and was involved in some of the most significant changes to the police service in modern history, not least in respect to ethics, equality and diversity. In the early 1990s he sat on the National Steering Group for the policing of LGBT communities and the ACPO committee for the policing of Gypsy and Traveller communities, assisting in the development of policy and guidance to bring about the ethical and equitable policing of communities, in addition to working as a minorities group liaison office. With a passion for the field of equality and diversity, both for the communities he served and those he worked alongside, Eifion fulfilled many additional roles in the advancement of equality and developing legislation: former secretary of Cleveland AIDS Support, committee member Victim Support Scheme, chair of Cleveland LGBT Policing Forum, first contact officer, equality advisor and equality lead for the Cleveland Police Federation. Eifion went on to serve as a trainer both at a national level and within his home force working on many training programmes and initiatives from student officer training to the development of equality and diversity training programmes for the force, in line with national policy, guidance and legislation. Eifion latterly worked on the College of Policing Initial Police Learning and Development Programme as it moved towards policing apprenticeships.

David Taylor joined Cleveland Police in 1990 and early in his career became interested in how police officers were trained and developed on live incidents. Key aspects of coaching and assessment together with the experiences of integrating officers into existing and changing police cultures motivated him to take further opportunities to train and develop officers. This included training officers on their initial training, coaching and mentoring, CPD for existing officers and the Special Constabulary. Alongside this commitment, David developed teacher training courses with partner colleges and Teesside University. Since leaving the police, David has worked as a senior lecturer in education studies at Teesside University and works with students to help develop their research projects.

Mark Thornton joined Cleveland Police in 1989 and rose through the ranks reaching superintendent in 2013. A uniformed officer though-out his career he has spent most of his time in operational postings while also enjoying various training roles. He has held strategic responsibility in areas of public order, CBRN and search. Outside of these roles Mark was an accredited Firearms Silver Commander for ten years and is a post incident manager. An accredited Public Order Public Safety (Gold) Commander, he has delivered public order command training to senior police officers including some in Tanzania. Mark now runs his own business, he is married with two successful daughters, enjoys exercise, the outdoors and the opportunity to socialise with friends and family.

Professor Emma Williams is the director of the Centre of Excellence in Equities in Uniformed Public Services (CEEUPS) at Anglia Ruskin University. She recently led one of the key research streams for Operation Soteria - a national Home Office funded project exploring rape investigation. Emma led the strand on learning and development and officer wellbeing. Her research interests are police professionalism, organisational justice and policing VAWG. Emma was the academic director of the Centre for Policing

Research and Learning (CPRL) at the Open University and the director of the Canterbury Centre for Policing Research at CCCU. Prior to that she was a principal researcher at the Metropolitan Police Service for 12 years and at the Ministry of Justice for two years where she worked on the criminal justice reform agenda. She has experience in operational and action research focused on the needs of the practitioner. Emma sits on the executive board for the Society of Evidence Based Policing.

Peter Williams is a senior lecturer at the Liverpool Centre for Advanced Policing Studies, Liverpool John Moores University and presents modules in terrorism, counter terrorism and intelligence at both undergraduate and postgraduate levels. Previously, he was a senior lecturer in policing at Teesside University and delivered programmes to West Mercia Police, the Royal Military/RAF Police, Rwandan National Police, in addition to distance-learning modules in policing, terrorism and counter terrorism. Prior to working in higher education he served with Merseyside Police, retiring as an inspector in 2005. He is a regular contributor to local, national and international media as a subject-matter expert in policing, terrorism and counter terrorism and has been involved in a number of written publications in these areas.

Dr Ross Wolf serves as professor of criminal justice and associate provost for UCF Downtown at the University of Central Florida in Orlando, Florida. He has over three decades of experience in policing in both full-time and volunteer roles, and has worked in patrol, criminal investigations and a plainclothes tactical unit with the Orange County (Florida) Sheriff's Office, where he currently serves as reserve chief deputy. He is an active member of the International Association of Chiefs of Police, the National Sheriffs' Association and the Volunteer Law Enforcement Officer Alliance. In addition to his work with police agencies throughout the United States, he has worked with the police in and from the Caribbean, the United Kingdom, Saudi Arabia, Dubai, Russia, Hong Kong and Singapore.

Dr Dominic A. Wood is professor of ethical policing at Canterbury Christ Church University. He has worked with police for 30 years designing bespoke professional degrees for police employees and was formerly the chair of the Higher Education Forum for Learning and Development in Policing. Dominic is a lead editor, author and contributor to a number of textbooks and has published papers on different aspects of police work.

Foreword

As the complexities of policing in the twenty-first century grow, police officers, staff and volunteers, regardless of the time of day or night, provide an uninterrupted policing response and an essential service to all our communities. Professional development that ensures they are empowered to deal with the challenges they face is vital.

Led and informed by the professional body for the service, the College of Policing, what was the Policing Education Qualifications Framework has now evolved into a range of police constable entry routes, which seek to embed professionalism within the service. Additional programmes for leaders, staff and specialist roles continue to evolve based on the national policing curriculum. A professional policing degree also develops aspiring police officers, preparing them to join the service.

Policing is complex and the range of education and training programmes available are focused on developing new officers, staff and volunteers, and equip them with the knowledge and understanding they require to analyse and interpret the growing evidence-base that is necessary to inform effective practice. Further in such a complex environment staff must strive to be innovative, to continually improve, lead cultural change and enhance our communities' trust in policing … quite an ask!

The national policing vision for 2030 aims to develop an effective, inclusive and trusted police service. Investing in and supporting the professional development of the current and future workforce will go a long way in the desire to achieve such a vision for policing.

This second edition assists newly appointed or aspiring police officers, staff and volunteers to develop their knowledge and understanding of the evidence-base that underpins their professional development, the national policing curriculum and professional policing practice.

Professor Peter Vaughan, QPM, CStJ, director of the International Centre for Policing and Security, University of South Wales

Introduction

Ian Pepper and Ruth McGrath

Ultimately responsible for keeping citizens of the United Kingdom safe, the Home Office (2024) report how a multi-faceted workforce exceeding over 236,000 police officers, police staff, police community support officers (PCSOs) and designated officers, are supported by over 13,000 volunteer special constables and police support volunteers, serving in a variety of frontline and supporting roles across the 43 territorial police forces in England and Wales.

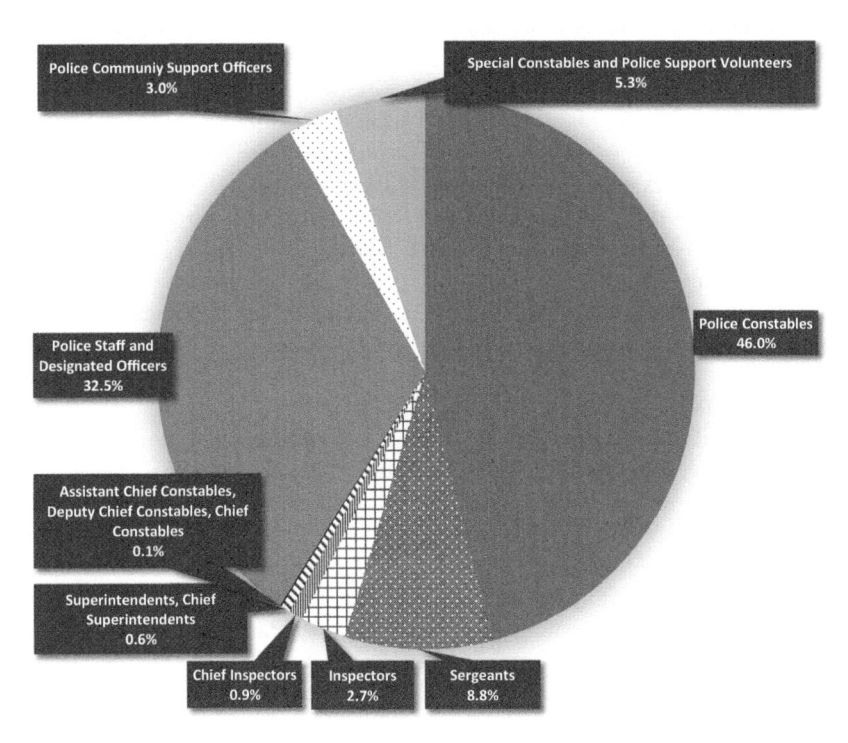

Figure I.1 Percentage comparison of policing workforce roles in England and Wales, 31 March 2024.
Source: Home Office (2024)

DOI: 10.4324/9781003492948-1

In addition, Police Scotland (2024) has slightly over 16,300 police officers and 5,800 police staff, while the Police Service of Northern Ireland (PSNI) report slightly over 6,700 police officers and 200 part-time reserve officers (Northern Ireland Policing Board, 2023), with these forces (and others such as the States of Jersey Police and the Royal Gibraltar Police) operating under different Governmental jurisdictions.

The figures above do not include a number of other role specific policing agencies with over 10,000 officers and staff serving across the United Kingdom: the British Transport Police (BTP), Civil Nuclear Constabulary (CNC) and Ministry of Defence Police (MDP). Other law enforcement organisations with specific responsibilities, such as the National Crime Agency (NCA), National Police Air Service (NPAS) and the National Counter Terrorism Security Office (NaCTSO), also have significant numbers of staff operating within the policing environment regionally, nationally and even internationally.

Whether serving as a member of the Metropolitan Police, the police force in the county with the largest number of police officers at over 34,000, or within a smaller force such as Warwickshire, with slightly over 1,100 officers or City of London with fewer than 1,000 officers (Home Office, 2024), those on the frontline of policing provide the daily 24-hour responses to the needs of the public they serve.

The expectations for professional policing practice were set by the College of Policing (2018) as fundamental to an officer's performance as an effective police officer, these are the ability to operate as a response officer, work within community policing and roads policing, and being able to handle both information and intelligence, along with conducting investigations. This must also include the ability to work in partnership and solve problems. The Competency and Values Framework (CVF) sets the values and competencies expected of all working and volunteering within policing (College of Policing, 2024).

Numerous policing authorities in Europe, North America and Australia continue to discuss the impact, or otherwise, of police officers engaging in formal post-compulsory education (Punch, 2007). Across the UK a recurring solution suggested for improving police performance and culture is to enhance the educational qualifications of those in policing (Punch, 2007). Supporting what Sherman (1978) describes as a vision to use the intellectual rigour and broad conceptual understanding offered by education to reform policing, the principal aim of the national policing curriculum (NPC) and the police constable entry routes (PCER) – previously known as the policing education qualifications framework (PEQF) – is to standardise and develop a learner's underpinning knowledge, understanding, behaviours and transferrable skills relating to their professional performance as an aspiring or newly appointed police officer. Recognising the profession of policing and the ability of its officers and staff is an important, and well overdue, positive leap forward for the service. Punch (2007) advocates how the increasing number of police officers with higher and/or further educational experience and qualifications has had a positive influence on the evolution of policing organisations and their culture. Palmer et al. (2019) rightly suggests that the adoption of evidence-based policing is also intrinsically linked to both the cultural and organisational reform of the police service. Such transition to a policing culture which values and embeds an evidence-based approach has some way to go yet (Pepper et al. 2020).

Written by experts in policing higher education from across both academic and professional policing practice, this core textbook explores key learning for aspiring police officers, newly appointed police officers, direct entry detectives or those aspiring to work as staff or volunteer across policing. This textbook explores in greater depth some of the core underpinning knowledge requirements identified as themes within the national policing curriculum (NPC). It is impossible in one core textbook to cover the vast array of contemporary and future requirements for knowledge identified within the evolving NPC upon which the standardised national PCER are based. However, the themes have been chosen to support aspiring or new police officers' professional education as they commence this fascinating career and progress towards achieving both independent patrol status (IPS) and then full occupational competence (FOC), along with the development of those who would like to work as staff or volunteer within policing in a range of roles. Throughout the chapters, case studies, reflective questions and further reading assist an individual's personal and professional development as a police constable, staff member, community support officer or volunteer.

The police officer

In 1829, the then Home Secretary, Sir Robert Peel, worked alongside the first commissioners of the newly established Metropolitan Police to formalise the principles by which the police service should operate ethically and with the consent of the public. The so called 'Peelian Principles' included the requirement for the police to prevent crime and public disorder, operate with the approval of the public, impartially applying the law and only using the necessary physical force (College of Policing, 2014). Success in policing is measured not by the visible presence of officers enforcing the law, rather the absence of crime and disorder itself (College of Policing, 2014).

Acknowledging the shortcomings in policing identified by, among others, the Baroness Casey Review (2023), everyone within the police service must act with honesty, integrity, fairly and impartially at all times both on and off duty; they should never discriminate but respect individuals and their varied backgrounds and beliefs, the ethical policing principles must be adhered to (College of Policing, 2023). All police officers, regardless of rank or role, must be fit to perform their duties at all times, only issue and complete lawful orders and adhere to the expected standards of dress and overall behaviour. those in policing must never bring discredit upon themselves or the service; such incidents will be investigated internally by the professional standards department in line with the Police (Complaints and Misconduct) Regulations 2020 and the associated statutory guidance. More serious and sensitive cases are referred to and investigated by the Independent Office for Police Conduct (IOPC).

In the twenty-first century, the principles of policing still hold true and have been reaffirmed by the Select Committee (2008) as the 'Statement of Common

Purpose and Values for the Police Service'. This has been reinforced by the National Police Chiefs' Council (2023) vision for policing which emphasises a commitment to ensure that all communities served trust the police to keep them safe, as the service strives to strengthen such trust through meaningful and respectful engagement. Police and crime commissioners (PCCs) reflect the voice of the community they represent and hold chief constables to account for the effective and efficient policing within their force. Within the Metropolitan Police Service a similar function is performed by the Mayor's Office for Policing and Crime (MOPAC), while the National Police Chiefs' Council (NPCC) works across police leaders to agree, co-ordinate and make changes transforming policing (National Police Chiefs' Council, 2018).

With national agendas set for policing, such as a focus on violence against women and girls (VAWG), the rejuvenation of approaches, such as a refocus on neighbourhood policing, the evolution of complex crime types, the globalisation of communities along with huge expansion in digital enabled crime, careers in policing are many, varied, evolving and often challenging. As a new officer it is likely that response (or incident) policing will be the first position, then perhaps later specialising within criminal investigations, counterterrorism, firearms, air support, digital investigations, public protection etc., as well as opportunities to share knowledge and experience as a mentor or seek promotion taking on new leadership challenges as a first line leader (police sergeant) or mid-level leader (police inspector). A review of frontline policing by the Home Office (2019) highlighted the ongoing and changing nature of the demands placed upon policing and the importance of embedding the support available to ensure the well-being of police officers, staff and volunteers.

The police service should be representative of those policed and professionally recognised, while working with educational and developmental frameworks to ensure such a workforce is equipped with the best knowledge, understanding skills and potential to police the challenges faced as the twenty-first century progresses. The College of Policing, first established in 2012, is the professional body for the police service across England and Wales. The College aims to support the development of members of, and for, the profession of policing through training, education, setting standards and improving evidence-based practice through identifying what works (College of Policing, 2017).

Focusing on the training and/or education of new police officers (sometimes referred to as police constables) through the PCER, two initial entry routes for new police officers recruited in England and Wales were introduced in 2018 and a further route in 2024. The programmes introduced in 2018 were built upon a policing vision which intended to improve the capability of the police service and recognise learning through academic accreditation (Association of Police and Crime Commissioners/National Police Chiefs' Council, 2015). This approach has been further developed as a vision for the service to embrace a learning culture which is evidence informed and ensures a workforce which is talented and innovative (National Police Chiefs' Council, 2023).

The two work-based programmes linked directly to higher education are the police constable degree apprenticeship (PCDA) and degree holder entry program (DHEP). These work-based programmes are studied by new police officers in an established partnerships between a police force and a higher education provider. The PCDA is a blend of three-years study and work-based practice, it is fee free for the police officer (who is salaried) and is for those who do not already hold a degree. During this work-based programme new police officers must spend a minimum of 20% of their time 'off the job' learning in an educational setting. Successful completion of all work-based and academic assessments leads to confirmation as a police officer and the award of a higher education degree.

While for new police officers who have already successfully completed a degree prior to joining, the DHEP is studied in the workplace for two years at no financial cost for the police officer (who is salaried). There is also a DHEP detective route of initial entry which follows a similar pathway for learning. Successful completion of all work-based and academic assessments of the DHEP leads to confirmation in post as police officer and the award of a graduate diploma. Placing graduates on a par with graduates of the PCDA.

In 2024, an additional route of training was introduced for new police officers, whether they hold a degree or not. This Police Constable Entry Program (PCEP) is taught 'in-force' by police trainers with no formal academic involvement or recognition through an award. This PCEP is mapped to the first two years of the PCDA and is still of no cost to the new salaried police officer. The PCEP has been welcomed by some and challenged by others, who raise issues with the potential for a lowering of the standard for training and an unfair two-tier policing system (Police Federation, 2023).

Opportunities also exist in some forces to apply for the Detective Constable Entry Programme (DCEP). Whether a graduate or not, studying DCEP means completing an intensive two-year programme of study and practical specialist experience linked to being a detective, during which time competence must be demonstrated in the detective role and the National Investigators Exam (NIE) must be successfully completed.

For traditional undergraduate students who aspire to join the police service but have not yet been recruited by a force, there is the higher education taught Professional Policing Degree (PPD). The student is not employed in policing (although some volunteer), they pay traditional university fees to their higher education provider and study a programme that still covers both the knowledge and understanding contained within the PCDA through attending a traditional model of university-based education. However, the practical work-based components contained within the PCDA, DHEP and PCEP initial entry routes are not taught. Following graduation, a graduate who aspires to be a police officer must then successfully apply through a national recruit assessment centre to join their chosen police force. If recruited, the practical components are then taught and assessed by the recruiting force.

As well as the PCDA, DHEP, PCEP and PPD being licensed and quality assured by the College of Policing, there is also a national Quality Assurance

Agency for Higher Education subject benchmark statement for policing that programme designers and deliverers can refer to as the statement describes the nature of study and academic standards expected of policing graduates (QAA, 2022). Also across Europe, law enforcement organisations are benefiting from establishing formal partnerships with higher education, making the best use of academic expertise in curriculum development, teaching, learning and research in support of policing (López, 2022).

Continuing the valued traditions of policing, the future for the police service across England and Wales is a culturally evolving, motivated, skilled and professionally recognised workforce aligned to the professional standards of the service, which is underpinned by evidence-based professional practice, operating within the parameters of the national code of ethics and CVF providing an inclusive and unparalleled service to the public.

References

Association of Police and Crime Commissioners/National Police Chiefs' Council. (2015). *Policing Vision 2025*. London: Association of Police and Crime Commissioners/National Police Chiefs' Council. https://assets.college.police.uk/s3fs-public/policing_vision_2025.pdf.

Baroness Casey Review. (2023). Final Report: An Independent Review into the Standards of Behaviour and Internal Culture of the Metropolitan Police Service. [online]. www.met.police.uk/SysSiteAssets/media/downloads/met/about-us/baroness-casey-review/update-march-2023/baroness-casey-review-march-2023a.pdf (31 August 2024)

College of Policing. (2014). The Code of Ethics Reading List. [online]. www.college.police.uk/What-we-do/Ethics/Ethics-home/Documents/Code_of_Ethics_ReadingList.pdf (20 February 2019).

College of Policing. (2017). About Us. [online]. www.college.police.uk/About/Pages/default.aspx (2 July 2019).

College of Policing. (2018). *Police Education Qualifications Framework: National Pre-join Degree in Professional Policing*. Ryton: College of Policing.

College of Policing. (2023). Code of Practice for Ethical Policing. [online]. www.college.police.uk/ethics/code-of-practice (14 October 2024).

College of Policing. (2024). Competency and Values Framework (CVF). [online]. www.college.police.uk/career-learning/competency-and-values-framework (31 August 2024).

Home Office. (2019). *The Front Line Review: Recommendation Report*. London: Home Office. https://assets.publishing.service.gov.uk/media/5d25bb0aed915d69895f3190/FLR_Recommendations_report_sent_V2.pdf.

Home Office. (2024). National Statistics, Police Workforce, England and Wales: 31 March 2024. [online]. www.gov.uk/government/statistics/police-workforce-england-and-wales-31-march-2024/police-workforce-england-and-wales-31-march-2024 (11 September 2024).

López, M. (2022). Executive Director's Prologue. *European Law Enforcement Research Bulletin*. [online]. www.cepol.europa.eu/publications/european-law-enforcement-research-bulletin-issue-22 (21 November 2024).

National Police Chiefs' Council. (2018). Workforce Transformation in the Police Service: An Introduction. [online]. www.college.police.uk/About/Workforce-Transformation/Documents/COP_workforce_transformation.pdf (26 October 2019).

National Police Chiefs' Council. (2019). Our Work. [online]. www.npcc.police.uk/NPCCBusinessAreas/Default.aspx (2 August 2019).

National Police Chiefs' Council. (2023). Policing Vision 2030. [online]. www.npcc.police.uk/publications/policing-vision-2030/ (26 October 2024).

Northern Ireland Policing Board. (2023). What Are the PSNI Officer Numbers, Year on Year, since 2001? [online]. www.nipolicingboard.org.uk/questions/what-are-psni-officer-numbers-year-year-2001 (21 September 2024).

Palmer, I., Kirby, S. & Coleman, R. (2019). Assessing the Appetite for Evidence Based Policing: A UK Based Study. *International Journal of Police Science and Management*, 21(2). https://doi.org/10.1177/1461355719838930.

Pepper, I., Rogers, C. & Martin, H. (2020). Evidence Based Policing: A View on its Development within the Police Service. *Journal of Work-Applied Management*, 12(1), 91–96. https://doi.org/10.1108/JWAM-01-2020-0001.

Police Federation. (2023). Why the Proposed Fourth Entry Route into Policing Won't Work. [online]. www.polfed.org/news/blogs/2023/why-the-proposed-fourth-entry-route-into-policing-wont-work/ (24 October 2024).

Police Scotland. (2024). Police Scotland Officer Numbers. [online]. www.scotland.police.uk/about-us/how-we-do-it/police-scotland-officer-numbers/ (21 September 2024).

Punch, M. (2007). Cops with Honours: University Education and Police Culture. *Sociology of Crime, Law and Deviance*, 8, 105–128. https://doi.org/10.1016/S1521-6136(07)08004-08009.

QAA. (2022). Subject Benchmark Statement for Policing. [online]. www.qaa.ac.uk/the-quality-code/subject-benchmarkstatements/policing#:~:text=Policing%20as%20a%20subject%20is,and%20bringing%20offenders%20to%20justice (23 September 2024).

Select Committee. (2008). Home Affairs Seventh Report. [online]. https://publications.parliament.uk/pa/cm200708/cmselect/cmhaff/364/36402.htm (21 February 2019).

Sherman, L. (1978). *The Quality of Police Education*. San Francisco, CA: Jossey-Bass.

1 Ethics, equality, diversity and inclusion

Eifion Swinnerton-Gismondi

Introduction

Members of the police service are rigorously selected from their communities and are by virtue of their appointment elevated to a position of trust to safeguard their communities. The public service of policing requires police officers, staff and volunteers, to think beyond their own needs and personal, moral values, in the process of providing an ethical service to all members of the public. This relates to any circumstances they encounter, decisions they make, both within their work and personal lives. The right to private and family life (Human Rights Act 1998: article 8) is limited to those aspects that would not reasonably impact undermine or discredit the police service (i.e. anything posted on a social media site or group chat would not attract the protection of article 8).

To deliver this service there is a need for diversity within policing, which includes an understanding of equality, acknowledging and recognising the different needs that may arise from the diversity of people encountered. This in turn will foster greater inclusion, encompassing a range of people who have previously felt excluded from joining the police or assisting the police service, or from calling upon the police service in times of need.

If it is to be accepted that the concept of ethics is based on the thought processes of decision making and therefore manifests itself in how people *behave* towards each other, equality and diversity are terms concerned with how we *treat* each other. These areas meet in a way that demands they should be considered at all times to maintain the trust of the public and the unique principles of British Policing, particularly that of 'policing by consent'.

Historical context

Sir Robert Peel, a former Home Secretary between 1822–1827 and 1828–1830, is widely recognised for the introduction of the first full-time, professional police force in England and Wales, for the Greater London area (Reith, 1952). Together with the first police commissioners, Charles Rowan and Richard Mayne, a philosophy of policing by public consent was developed, as opposed to a militia governed by power of the state or wealthy landowners.

Ethics, equality, diversity and inclusion 9

The philosophy was supported by nine principles, often attributed solely to Peel (Lentz and Chaires, 2007) and considered to have formed the ethical backbone of policing for more than 180 years.

These principles are summarised as:

1 The purpose of the police is to prevent crime and disorder,
2 The police need the approval and respect of the public to perform their duties,
3 The public must be willing to cooperate in observing the law, in order for the police to secure the respect of the public,
4 The co-operation of the public reduces in proportion to the use of physical force,
5 The police must demonstrate absolute impartiality toward the law in order to maintain public support,
6 The police should use only as much physical force as is necessary to maintain the law or to restore order; only resorted to when persuasion, advice and warnings given fail,
7 The police should always maintain a relationship with the public that reinforces the traditional basis of the police service, that the police are the public and the public are the police. This reinforces the fact that the police are members of the public paid to undertake duties which are incumbent on every citizen in the interests of community welfare and existence,
8 Police should always carry out their required functions and never appear to usurp the powers of the judiciary,
9 The absence of crime and disorder is the measure of police efficiency rather than the visible police action.

(Based on Reith, 1952)

These principles formed the foundations of modern policing. Remnants of them are contained within laws that have come into being since their inception, for example, sec. 3 of the Criminal Law Act 1967 (relating to the reasonable use of force) and article 7 of the Human Rights Act 1998 (no punishment without Law), however some aspects, such as principle 5, have perhaps now been updated by the introduction of the updated College of Policing Code of Ethics (College of Policing, 2024a, 2024b).

It should be recognised that both the law of the land and the governance of the police service upholding those laws is, and has been, an organic development. Ethics and equality continued to evolve within the process, as is evident when comparing the oath officers swore out to become a constable from the inception of the Police Act 1996, and the attestation, which was introduced in the Police Reform Act 2002 and is still in use today. One of the purposes of the change was to allow non-UK subjects to be able to join the police force of England and Wales. The following extracts from the legislation enable a comparison:

The Police Act 1996, Schedule 4, as enacted:

> I, … … … … of … … … … do solemnly and sincerely declare and affirm that I will well and truly serve Our Sovereign Lady the Queen in the office of constable, without favour or affection, malice or ill will; and that I will

to the best of my power cause the peace to be kept and preserved, and prevent all offences against the persons and properties of Her Majesty's subjects; and that while I continue to hold the said office I will to the best of my skill and knowledge discharge all the duties thereof faithfully according to law.

Section 83 of the Police Reform Act 2002 (wording referring to the sovereign has been updated following the 2023 Coronation):

I … … of … … do solemnly and sincerely declare and affirm that I will well and truly serve the King in the office of constable, with fairness, integrity, diligence and impartiality, upholding fundamental human rights and according equal respect to all people; and that I will, to the best of my power, cause the peace to be kept and preserved and prevent all offences against people and property; and that while I continue to hold the said office I will to the best of my skill and knowledge discharge all the duties thereof faithfully according to law.

The police service has always purported to act ethically, in accordance with the wording of the principles and the attestation. Despite this, however, history shows that many key decisions have been compounded by moralistic not ethical behaviours and decision making, further confused by loyalty to the service over service to the public. This is highlighted in reports into the Hillsborough disaster (College of Policing, 2023). Historically, the service has predominantly been made up of a narrow niche of society, white, Christian, heterosexual males, therefore moral decisions made potentially came from a narrow field of values that would provide a preferential treatment to those with similar characteristics than those who don't. This is evidenced by some of the reports into the policing of black communities leading up to the Brixton riots of 1981 (Scarman, 1982), the police protecting itself from criticism around the Hillsborough disaster (Home Office, 1990, 2012) and the inquiry into the police handling of the murder of Stephen Lawrence which led to the condemnation of both individual and organisational actions and the introduction of the term 'institutional racism' (Macpherson, 1999).

Despite endeavours to broaden representation of the service and keep pace with changing societal attitudes (i.e. Black Lives Matter, Me Too, violence against women and girls; see Chapter 9) there is much evidence to support a reticence for changing attitude and culture within the service, with misogyny and a lack of candidness when things go wrong continuing to damage public trust and confidence. This is demonstrated in the following reports: Operation Hotton Learning Report (IOPC, 2022), Baroness Casey Review Final Report (Casey, 2023), and An inspection of the Metropolitan Police Service's response to lessons from the Stephen Port murders (HMICFRS, 2023). These all demonstrate where the attitudes and behaviour of individuals in the service have fallen well below what should reasonably be expected by the codes of conduct and the prevailing ethical framework of the day.

The police service has also been positioned outside of developments within the field of employment rights and legislation governing the provision of goods and services, primarily because police officers are 'servants of the crown' rather than 'employees'. Therefore, most provisions of employment legislation were not applied to the service until the introduction of the Equality Act 2010. The police service, however, has acted with due regard to such developments and has, generally, adhered to their principles, most forces having adopted equal opportunity policies by the mid-1990s.

Despite its, on occasion, very public failings, the police service, as a whole, has endeavoured to advance and develop through learning the lessons of its past failings and the development and sharing of best practice across all forces (HMIC, 1997, 1999, 2000a, 2000b).

The introduction of the Human Rights Act 1998 certainly helped to raise the profile of ethical public authorities and accountability; it should be recognised that many aspects of the treatment of suspects and victim/witnesses were already well governed through the Police and Criminal Evidence Act 1984.

Current professional practice

The police service endeavours to acknowledge and promote the rights and responsibilities of all those working within the organisation, and/or who may have cause to work with or use the organisation. This is achieved through developing knowledge and understanding of ethics and equality and valuing diversity, while encouraging mutual respect through confidentiality of information and being proactive in eliminating discrimination in all its manifestations.

Success requires staff to be able to reflect upon their own attitude and behaviour to recognise those traits which positively or adversely impact upon others, often referred to as 'unconscious bias', 'stereotypes' and 'prejudice' (Stout, 2010) and adjust behaviour as appropriate.

The police service is required to be able to actively promote a non-discriminatory working environment for everyone and all service users based upon mutual respect. This includes eliminating inappropriate behaviour and discrimination within the workplace, creating a climate which encourages the challenging of such behaviour and which is supportive of those doing so.

Ethics is the means by which personal values (Massey, 1972) and concepts of right and wrong are moderated, adjusted or overridden with a concept of professional shared values which would reflect those organisational and societal expectations.

A value can be defined as a fundamental, and sometimes more complex, principle or ideal which is considered important within human existence. This could be conscious or sub-conscious. Examples include the principle of queueing, or common courtesies of saying 'please' and 'thank you' and extend to the right to life and freedom of speech. A value system is a set of values adopted by individual, personal values (i.e. guidelines by which we would choose to live our life, or societal values by which the majority of people adjust and compromise their personal values to be able to live in a collective).

Value systems can also be taken from a plethora of other sources, including:

- Economic values – money, stable economy, private property, pride of ownership, etc.
- Political values: national welfare state, public service, voting, civic responsibility, loyalty to country, etc.
- Religious values: belief in a supreme being, worship, good and evil, etc.

The adoption of a code of ethics removes the optional and aspirational concept of ethics and replaces it with a firm commitment to operate within the boundaries of the code. The decisions taken by members of the police service can then be rightly held to account against the code and the public can take greater confidence in the service delivery being provided.

Ethics has been viewed from three main strands:

1. Character (attributed to Socrates) and formed through the practicing of good habits; members of the service historically trained in good habit, therefore are professional and can be trusted.
2. Consequence (attributed to Niccolò Machiavelli): getting the right outcome for the greater good despite the means used.
3. Absolute rule of law, without discretion, not concerned with circumstance and variables.

It would be fair to say that these all have their shortfalls; repetition of good habit with a poor outcome is unacceptable, achieving good outcomes despite the harm done or illegal practice would be intolerable as would law applied without common sense or discretion. This has been influential in the development of the National Decision Model (NDM) (Flanagan, 2008) (Chapter 6) and the introduction of the Code of Ethics (College of Policing, 2014, 2023). This also builds on the behavioural standards within the discipline governance (Police Conduct Regulations 2012; Police Staff Council, 2008).

The first Code of Ethics for policing across England and Wales was introduced by the College of Policing in 2014 and was based on 'Principles of Public Life' published by the Committee on Standards in Public Life in 1995 (cited in College of Policing, 2014), enhanced to incorporate the additional areas of 'fairness' and 'respect':

- *Accountability* You are answerable for your decisions, actions and omissions
- *Fairness* You treat people fairly
- *Honesty* You are truthful and trustworthy
- *Integrity* You always do the right thing
- *Leadership* You lead by good example
- *Objectivity* You make choices on evidence and your best professional judgement

- *Openness* You are open and transparent in your actions and decisions
- *Respect* You treat everyone with respect
- *Selflessness* You act in the public interest(College of Policing, 2014, p. 3)

However, these were so reflective of the Codes of Professional Conduct that the concept of 'ethics' became focused on behaviours within disciplinary matters, rather than being fundamental to the functioning of the service. The introduction of the revised Code of Ethics has a much clearer purpose of being embedded in the hearts and minds of the service, from which ethical behaviour will be a natural consequence, 'Doing the right things, in the right way, for the right reasons' (College of Policing, 2024a). It rightly builds on the Policing Principals, but has simplified it into three core areas required of ethical policing:

- *Courage*
- *Respect and empathy*
- *Public service.*

Understanding of these core areas is achieved more readily by examining the Code of Ethics policing principles and aligning them to each of the core areas:

- *Courage* – draws on the Policing Principles of Accountability, Honesty and Integrity, Objectivity and Openness, Fairness and Respect, developing their use to explain this core area in respect of the making and communication of decisions, being accountable for those decisions and standing against anything that could bring the profession into disrepute. It is noted that The Code of Ethics still underpins the use of the National Decision-Making Model.
- *Respect and empathy* – draws on the Policing Principles of Objectivity, Openness, Selflessness, Fairness, and Respect, using them to explain this core area which encompasses those served by the police, who should be encouraged to communicate, knowing they will be listened to, and attempts made to understand their views. This will be further supported by seeking to recognise and respond to the physical, mental, and emotional challenges faced by everyone.
- *Public service* – this area draws on the Policing Principles of Accountability, Honesty, Integrity, Leadership, Objectivity, Openness, Selflessness, and Respect. These are developed to explain this core area critical to policing and continue to embed those Peelian principals in respect of working in the public interest, fostering public trust and confidence, and taking pride in providing an excellent service to the public (College of Policing, 2024b). It is important to note that taking the right and ethical approach to resolving an issue is not always the most comfortable route to a resolution.

The Code also includes a statutory Code of Practice, The Code of Practice for Ethical Policing' to compliment the non-statutory Code of Ethics, which aims to provide a more consistent approach to professional policing. This also emphasises the need for the presence of public trust and confidence to underpin effective policing and draws attention to the need for the police service to include respect of, listening and responding to the public, and improving and serving the public.

The new Code of Ethics now sits alongside the Police Conduct Regulations 2020 (relating to police officers) and the Police Staff Council Joint Circular 54 (relating to police staff), to create a standardised approach which is relevant to all staff (College of Policing, 2014).

When discussing ethical behaviour consider this example. You find £1,000 in a carrier bag; what would you do if no one saw you? Would your decision be different if other people were about at the time? In either circumstance, what would the public expect of you? Think about your personal accountability and professional accountability.

As seen, across the codes and the regulations there is an ongoing strand referring to the need for fairness, respect, equality and diversity and challenging improper conduct. These are further supported by the Equality Act 2010 and the equality duties for public authorities such as the police service. Thus it is important that those wishing to join the service in any role have an understanding of unconscious bias; this could best be described as the internal thoughts (stereotypes) and feeling (prejudices) of bias that we are unaware of being triggered by an external stimulus, which can, if not recognised and countered by balanced objective thought, lead to actions which may be discriminatory (Luft & Ingham, 1955). The concept of fairness and ethical policing has been the subject of research by Myhill and Quinton (2011) and also Quinton et al. (2015), together with guidance developed by the College of Policing (2024c). The fact this topic is the subject of regular research demonstrates the significance of this as a topic to the police service.

The ethical/equality test

A good indicator of when you are about to do something which is potentially unethical is if you immediately think 'I can justify this (divergence from the required standard)' as opposed to an action being justifiable within the ethical standard. When this occurs try considering a comparator at the opposite end of a spectrum you consider may be causing your behaviour or decision making to be questionable.

Would you treat a man differently from a woman, i.e. if you stopped a young male driver for failing to give way and nearly causing an accident, would you deal with him the same way as a young female driver or an elderly male driver?

Stereotyping and prejudice can also be conscious thought processes which again need to be recognised by individuals if we are to work towards greater inclusion within the workplace and with community and public participation with the service. Police officers are expected to engage in reflective practice throughout their service to create a culture of self-development to provide an ethical and equitable service.

Members of the service need to be able to identify when and how they use stereotypes, to actively reduce any detrimental impact that these may have on other people, by discounting the stereotype and working off objective facts available to arrive at ethical decision making and behaviours. This has been extensively discussed in Parliament and the media in relation to the police's use of the power to stop and search (Equality and Human Rights Commission, 2010).

What is stereotyping?

Stereotyping is a natural function of the brain and the way in which we can assimilate vast amounts of information received. The brain takes images and creates patterns (stereotypes) against which those images can be matched. An example of this is that you may have seen hundreds of different styles of seating, but you might categorise or stereotype them generally as being 'chairs' without having to think about it for any length of time. This can also be done with sounds, vocabulary and intonation of voice etc.

Once a stereotype has been developed, an individual may attach a value to it, which could be positive or negative. If applied to the stereotyping of people, it is more likely to attach a positive value to those who are most like us, who share the same values, beliefs etc. Equally we are more likely to attach negative values to those who are least like us. This then leads to the creation of a prejudice. This is not a function that can simply be 'turned off'.

What is a prejudice?

Our values cause us to rate and scale other people, pre-judging them (prejudice), often based on little or no known fact. This can result in both positive or negative assumptions. If a prejudice is not recognised as such, it could be described as an unconscious bias. It is often the case that we focus on the negatives, an example being a focus on those people who we believe don't appear to share our values. In effect we create 'out groups' rather than 'in groups' (Charman, 2017).

This leaves us surrounded by those who share our values or feel they can't challenge our value for fear of reprisal or exclusion, which can have a detrimental impact to the creation of an inclusive workplace and service where people feel valued for who they are, not for who they can pretend to be like.

As you may be realising, everyone has personal biases. These can lead to us stereotyping others, who we consider belong to a range of 'out groups', often in a negative manner. Stop and think for a few minutes about your beliefs in relation to people who have different values to yourself. How does this make you feel about those people? Awareness of your own biases is a strength as it can help you to ensure you do not treat people unfairly, which may then lead to discriminatory behaviour.

What is discrimination?

If stereotyping is linked to our thoughts, and prejudice linked to our feelings, discrimination occurs when we undertake actions which involve treating someone less favourably than others or omitting to do something you should. While the Equality Act 2010 makes it unlawful to discriminate against certain people based upon what is referred to as a protected characteristic, rules of discipline extend the protection to cover everyone against bullying, harassment and discrimination where it cannot be justified on reasonable grounds.

To better understand discrimination in general terms, Allport's Scale of Discrimination and responses to dominance (Rogers & Lewis, 2013) provides a stark insight into discrimination when it goes unchecked, particularly when it is viewed with his responses to dominance, which explains how members of minority groups may react to discrimination. These models help to put in context how the police service may be seen, or perceived to be seen, by minority groups often based on the historical treatment of such groups by the service. This can restrict communication with the community as people can be reluctant to engage with the police or sceptical as to benefits from doing so. That is why it is not enough to have changed as an organisation, the police service must take positive steps to engage and improve its service to the public across all sections of society.

Language and our use of it has the potential, if not used with care, to be one of our biggest barriers to inclusion and creating a feeling of being harassed, bullied or discriminated against. Therefore, it is important that staff try to ensure that their communications are sensitive, respectful and appropriate (SRA):

- *Sensitive* to someone else's feelings.
- *Respectful* to their difference (religion, background, sexuality, culture, etc.).
- *Appropriate* given the position they hold within the service.

SRA can also assist in challenging inappropriate comments by explaining how it fails against the three strands. Challenging using this model allows for dialogue to better understand why someone has found a comment or word/phrase offensive and allows for the person using it to apologise and explain what it was they were trying to express; this works on the assumption it was not their intent to cause offence.

Some may feel the phrase 'man overboard', referring to someone having fallen into water, is sexist and dismissive of women involved in shipping and sailing (insensitive and disrespectful), however it is an internationally recognised phrase around lifesaving and would be appropriate and unavoidable.

If the phrase 'coloured' was used, referring to someone who is black, some may feel it is racist due to its historical use in slavery and segregation (insensitive and disrespectful); it serves no purpose as a descriptive term and would therefore be inappropriate and avoidable. Some people hold on to the fact that they never meant to cause offence and feel they can just keep using language

Ethics, equality, diversity and inclusion 17

that has been pointed out to them as failing against the model, however once you use it with such knowledge it moves from innocently offensive to purposefully offensive, which can be viewed as active harassment or discrimination.

The behavioural chart in Figure 1.1 may assist to further promote understanding; this can be linked to the duties under the Equality Act 2010, covered later.

A member of the public can be indifferent in their attitude, such as ignoring or not acknowledging someone, simply not showing them any consideration or care. This may fall below the cultural concept of good manners but is not unlawful.

A member of the public can demonstrate unacceptable behaviour, below the prevailing societal standard and be offensive; this might be in the form of low-level swearing, vulgar language, tasteless jokes, poking fun at people in jest, wearing a Tee shirt with a British National Party logo on, etc. Being rude towards someone may be unpleasant but in itself may not be an offence, however if this moves into

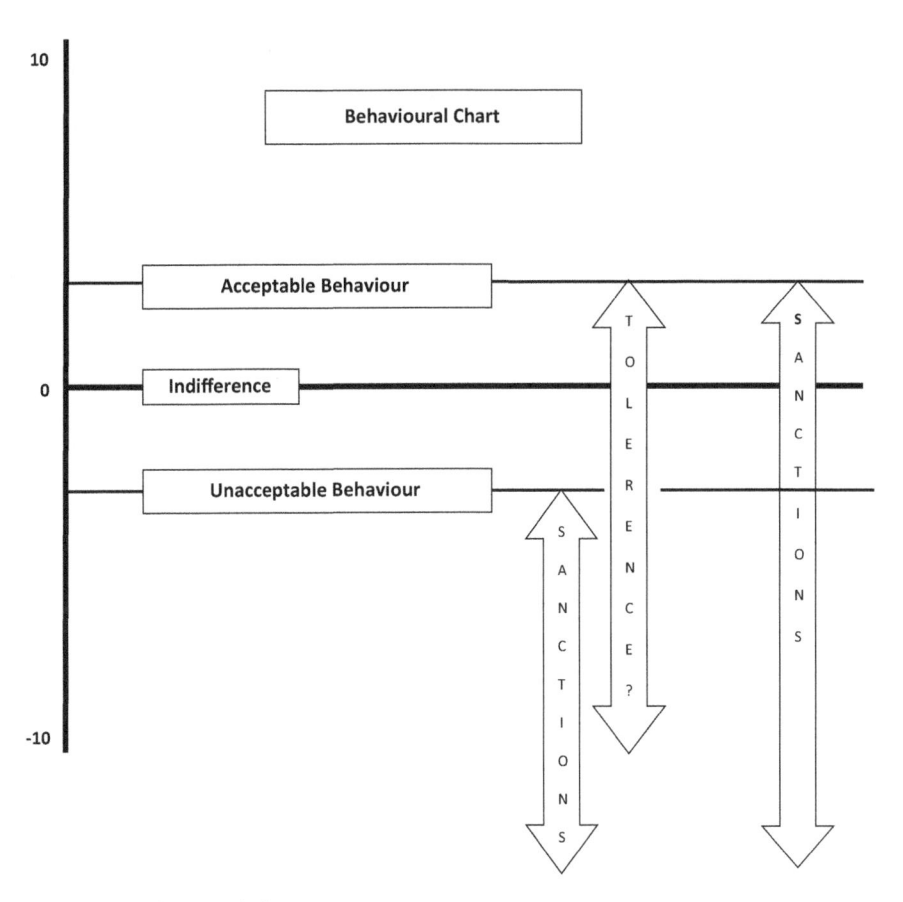

Figure 1.1 Behavioural chart.

the realms of causing harassment, alarm or distress to the target, this behaviour would be considered against the standards of a reasonable person and if the individual could not reasonably avoid being the subject of the behaviour, then it is possible that Public Order Act 1986 offences may be invoked.

An example to illustrate this may be seen where a person swearing within a jovial conversation with a group of friends may be unpleasant and inappropriate, but not an offence, but if they were shouting and swearing in a crowded place in a way that would cause other people alarm then it would be an offence.

On joining the service, the standard of behaviour expected is set above indifference, into what would be considered acceptable behaviour for an employee, servant of the crown, a professional public service, which mirrors the original requirements of the Statement of Common Purpose and Values for the Police Service introduced by the Association of Chief Police Officers (ACPO, 1990).

In a work context, some behaviour which falls short of the required standards, and moves towards being unacceptable, may be tolerated and explained as being a result of police sub-culture, often used as an explanation of beliefs and values within the police service (Cockroft, 2013). Alternative explanations of 'high spirits', or even 'canteen culture', are also used. The concept of 'canteen culture' is explored by Waddington (1999) when discussing police sub-culture. Waddington notes that comments between staff privately, e.g. while in the canteen, might be representative of their personal values, and be used to explain inappropriate behaviour within the public domain. He uses the example of the expression of racist views in the privacy of the police station (the canteen), which could be used to explain subsequent racist behaviour when dealing with the public, which might then be explained as the result of 'canteen culture', although there appears to be limited evidence to support this (Waddington, 1999).

It might be suggested that tolerance of, for example, racist comments itself leads to the lowest level of behaviour tolerated in the organisation being the demonstrated accepted level of behaviour, which is falling short of the legal standard required and would be viewed as the reality, if subject to disciplinary action, litigation or employment tribunal.

Consider: would the public want a police officer or member of staff to be ignorant towards them, or rude or swearing at them? Would those joining the service want to work with colleagues who use vulgar language, telling offensive jokes etc?

Everyone has a right to work in an environment, or to be provided with a service, with dignity and respect, and everyone in the organisation has a responsibility to ensure that this happens. Performing to a higher standard may be worthy of praise and sometimes welcome, but equally those trying to impose 'higher' standards, above the 'acceptable standard', placing upon themselves or others a greater expectation than that required by law, contract or task may fail to perform their duties appropriately or create an environment which may be perceived as bullying or discriminatory.

An example might be that of a supervisor who could place an expectation that staff will come in an hour early before their shift starts (without pay or time back) to be briefed and do administrative work, so they can hit the ground running, because they feel that this is professional. This would have an adverse impact on those who could not meet the demand and would be deemed unreasonable and unjustifiable.

Being a member of the police service also encompasses behaviours and expressions of opinion that are outside of the scope of duty time but would have the potential to impact upon how the service is viewed. It would do little to advance the ethics and equality of the organisation if its staff only behave appropriately while on duty but act unethically in their dealings with others or post things on social media which are offensive or discriminatory.

It is worthy of note that in joining the service, your life in essence is lived in a bubble for all the world to see (Skolnick, 1966). This may not be a problem for the many already in the organisation and those wishing to join who share the common values of the organisation. For some it is a less than welcome reality, one which is perpetually running in the mind of those who serve the public (i.e. will this action or expression of opinion etc., bring me or the organisation into disrepute?).

Professionally, when relating to people, the service's primary concern must be with behaviour rather than with the underlying attitude, as this is the physical manifestation that is observable. As studies show that whether or not people disclose their attitudes or act upon them depends on the situation, their personal stress level, their cultural views and their general expression of feeling, it is imperative that members of the service use reflective practice to self-challenge their own attitudes and moderate their behaviours to fall within the reasonable and acceptable boundaries of equitable and ethical behaviour.

The framework of the Equality Act 2010 (explained by ACAS, 2022), creates positive obligations for public authorities, which includes the police and those organisations that perform duties of a public nature for or on behalf of a public authority, known as the General Duties, which are:

1 The promotion of equal opportunities.
2 The removal of unlawful discrimination.
3 The promotion of good relationships between those who share protected characteristics and those who don't.

All staff have responsibilities under the General Equality Duties in addition to the requirements placed upon them to challenge inappropriate behaviour under the codes of conduct. Staff are the organisation and therefore they have organisational responsibilities, thus needing to be part of the culture of change, not accepting of the unacceptable, or waiting for someone else to change it.

These duties require a more positive and proactive approach to how the police service undertakes its duties of public service. Policies and guidance documents are regularly reviewed by equality impact assessment to ensure the anticipation of adverse impact and promote positive outcomes. As individuals, all members of staff should be considering all their actions while providing service in all forms, whether it is dealing with a missing person or considering arresting someone. In terms of arrest the equality and human rights are supported by the considerations within the Police and Criminal Evidence Act 1984, Code G (2022).

The Equality Act 2010 provides a legislative framework to protect the rights of individuals and advance equality of opportunity for all. The Act simplifies and brings into one act existing discrimination legislation, making it clearer to understand and easier to comply with.

It outlaws discrimination on grounds of certain protected characteristics (replacing what were previously referred to as the strands of diversity) within areas including employment and the provision of goods and services. These protected characteristics have been identified over time due to the historical injustices people have faced on such a scale it has been felt necessary to introduce protective legislation to bring about a social change in attitude and provide people who share a characteristic equitable treatment with those who don't. The protected characteristics within the legislation are:

- Age
- Disability
- Gender reassignment
- Marriage and civil partnership
- Pregnancy and maternity
- Race (Including: colour, nationality, ethnic or national origin)
- Religion or belief
- Sex (Gender, male or female)
- Sexual orientation(Equality Act 2010)

Under the Act, the types of discrimination and consideration which are covered are:

- Direct discrimination
- Indirect discrimination
- Discrimination by perception
- Discrimination by association
- Discrimination arising from disability
- Make reasonable adjustment
- Harassment
- Victimisation
- Positive action
- Genuine Occupational Requirements (GOR)(Equality Act 2010)

Changing organisational or social attitudes can take a long time, due to the layers of generations and ingrained attitudes. Examples of discrimination headline news, despite legislation being in place to make it unlawful for over 50 years. This is why there is such a strong drive on proactively promoting positive attitudes and behaviours.

The legislation referred to in this chapter is designed to protect people in their treatment within work, and in the provision of lawful goods and services, however the very nature of policing means the police service deals with matters outside of normal governance and the rule of law, i.e. criminal behaviour. If a person does not comply with the law, they may be subject to punishment by law if found guilty. There is much legislation in place to govern the fair treatment of people under investigation (Police and Criminal Evidence Act 1984; Human Rights Act 1998; Criminal Procedure and Investigations Act 1996). By comparison, the provision for victims may be considered scant. The Code of Practice for Victims of Crime, when published in 2015 (Ministry of Justice, 2015, 2024) went some way towards providing entitlements for victims, and its 2024 update (Ministry of Justice 2024) enhanced the earlier code, showing greater awareness of individual needs of victims. While it does not specifically refer to victims of 'hate crimes', it does indicate referral to services able to offer services and support tailored to the needs of the individual. But does this go far enough?

Hate incidents and hate crimes are identified often by how the victim was selected, i.e. based on some aspect of their identity. Often the actions applied are motivated by a hatred, hostility, dislike or intolerance of the chosen victim based upon a real or perceived difference. They are distinctive for not only the greater potential for violence towards the victim but also for their acute impact on the individual concerned and the ripple effect upon others who share the characteristic and the increased fear they may feel of being a victim.

The victims of hate crime may be vulnerable and lack capacity to report what is taking place to them or are not taken seriously, in cases of disability hate crime, for example (Equality and Human Rights Commission, 2011), or as discussed earlier the victim may not trust the police, lacking confidence in them based on past failings, such as the Stephen Lawrence murder inquiry (Macpherson, 1999). The victim may have to face the difficult decision of disclosing personal information about themselves in order to make the report, i.e. someone who is gay and has been targeted because of this, but is not open about being gay with friends, family or work colleagues, followed by the fear of being 'outed' if they report.

It should not be underestimated that such vulnerabilities may play a part in victim selection. For these reasons it adds greater weight to the fact we need to build links with all communities, to foster trust in the service, ahead of any need for the service arising. The police service works hard with many other agencies to promote reporting of hate crimes and third-party reporting, which can raise awareness of the true scale of the problem, potentially allow for investigation or actions to be taken to prevent further occurrence and provide much needed support to the victim.

There are many other types of crime where victims are targeted due to their diversity/difference which brings with them their own vulnerability, such as honour-based violence, child sexual exploitation, modern-day slavery, drug selling, such as that of County Lines activities, and Organised Crime Groups.

To understand the nature of these and emerging crime trends where victims are targeted because of their difference and/or vulnerability, it is imperative that the police service constantly looks to maintain and develop open channels of communication to gain the necessary intelligence to prevent and tackle such crimes while providing appropriate support and encouraging inclusion within society and service use.

Future development

The police service will endeavour to recruit from a broad section of society to better reflect the communities it serves, but in working towards this it requires every serving member and those joining to aspire to and adopt such working practices that embodies the principles of the Code of Ethics and the equality general duties. To further advance this, the College of Policing has developed the police constable entry routes (PCER), which incorporate entry routes into the police service. These fundamentally alter the process of recruitment to the service, providing alternative entry processes and which are designed to meet the needs of each force's academic demographic.

Ultimately this will work towards every officer being appropriately trained for their role, with the potential to achieve a qualification, on the courses delivered in collaboration with educational providers, creating recognised transferable skills outside of policing and benchmarking, to ensure individuals meet the standards required and expected.

The police service in collaboration with other agencies will continue to seek proactive ways to engage with people in its communities, to better identify those who are vulnerable and require greater and differing levels of support to enable them, their best chance of achieving justice through providing their best evidence or minimise the risk of them becoming a victim or repeat victim of crime.

His Majesty's Inspectorate of Constabulary Fire & Rescue Services (HMICFRS), in conjunction with the College of Policing, will continue to quality assure, visit and assess forces against the required standards and share evidence of good practice for the benefit of all forces.

Conclusion

In conclusion it can be seen that the Code of Ethics is a fundamental foundation of professional policing, befitting and recognising the proud history of policing and advancing it to a position where it remains at the forefront of modern policing. The unique nature of policing by consent, which exists within the United Kingdom, is to be both heralded and upheld.

To continue this, it is important that the service draws its staff, volunteers and officers from a broad section of society and that it is able to reach out to and be called upon by anyone. This requires everyone within the organisation to believe in the need for the Code of Ethics and to embrace its principles within all their actions, expressions of opinion and decision making. There is also an expectation of understanding that they have a right to be treated equitably, with dignity and respect and this must be actively given to everyone the police service encounters, whether colleagues, members of another organisation, victims, witnesses or someone suspected of a crime.

Ethics, equality, diversity and inclusion 23

> **Evidence-based case study illustrating professional practice**
>
> A group of police officers and special constables are out for the evening socialising. During the evening one of them shows you a WhatsApp group message which contains comments relating to another member of the team, with some cartoons. When you view the content you consider them to be inappropriate and discriminatory towards the member of staff.
>
> When you challenge the inappropriate nature of the message and cartoons, the group member laughs and tells you not to be so sensitive, and proceeds to forward the message to someone else. At this point you make your excuses and leave the gathering; at the earliest opportunity you make a few notes of what you have read and seen.
>
> The next day you are working an early shift and, being concerned about the target of the discrimination and feeling uncomfortable about the reaction, you decide to be courageous, drawing on the policing principles, to report the matter to your supervisor and share your notes.

Reflective question

A long-term friend, who now lives in another county, posts a homophobic joke and tags you into it. How would you react to this, and why?

References

ACAS. (2022). Discrimination at Work: Discrimination and the Equality Act 2010. [online]. www.acas.org.uk/index.aspx?articleid=3017 (12 September 2024).

ACPO. (1990). *Statement of Common ~ Purpose and Values*. London: ACPO.

Casey, L (2023). Baroness Casey Review Final Report: An Independent Review into the Standards of Behaviour and Internal Culture of the Metropolitan Police Service. [online] www.met.police.uk/SysSiteAssets/media/downloads/met/about-us/baroness-casey-review/update-march-2023/baroness-casey-review-march-2023a.pdf (3 November 2024).

Charman, S. (2017). *Police Socialisation, Identity and Culture: Becoming Blue*. Basingstoke: Palgrave Macmillan.

Cockroft, T. (2013). *Police Culture: Themes and Concepts*. Abingdon: Routledge.

College of Policing. (2014). Code of Ethics: A Code of Practice for the Principles and Standards of Professional Behaviour for the Policing Profession of England and Wales. [online]. https://assets.publishing.service.gov.uk/media/5a7d867140f0b65084e75b94/Code_of_Ethics_2014_Web_Accessible.pdf (3 September 2024).

College of Policing. (2023). National Police Response to the Hillsborough Families Report. [online] https://assets.college.police.uk/s3fs-public/2023-01/National-police-response-to-the-Hillsborough-Families-Report.pdf (3 November 2024).

College of Policing. (2024a). Code of Ethics. [online]. www.college.police.uk/ethics/code-of-ethics (3 September 2024).

College of Policing. (2024b). Ethical Policing Principles. [online] (4 September 2024).

College of Policing. (2024c). Perceptions of Police Fairness. [online]. www.college.police. uk/app/engagement-and-communication/engagement#perceptions-of-police-fairness (4 September 2024).

Criminal Law Act (1967). [online]. www.legislation.gov.uk/ukpga/1967/58/section/3 (23 October 2024).

Criminal Procedure and Investigations Act. (1996). [online]. www.legislation.gov.uk/ukpga/1996/25/contents (23 September 2024).

Equality Act. (2010). [online]. www.legislation.gov.uk/ukpga/2010/15/contents (23 September 2024).

Equality and Human Rights Commission. (2010). *Stop and Think: A Critical Review of the Use of Stop and Search Powers in England and Wales*. Manchester: Equality and Human Rights Commission.

Equality and Human Rights Commission. (2011). *Hidden in Plain Sight: Inquiry into Disability-Related Harassment*. Manchester: Equality and Human Rights Commission.

Flanagan, R. (2008). The Review of Policing: Final Report. [online]. www.justiceinspectorates.gov.uk/hmicfrs/publications/flanagan-review-of-policing/ (23 September 2024).

HMIC. (1997). *Winning the Race: Policing Plural Communities*. London: Home Office.

HMIC. (1999). *Winning the Race: Policing Plural Communities Revisited*. London: Home Office.

HMIC. (2000a). *Policing London: Winning Consent*. London: Home Office.

HMIC. (2000b). *Winning the Race: Embracing Diversity*. London: Home Office.

HMICFRS. (2023) An Inspection of the Metropolitan Police Service's Response to Lessons from the Stephen Port Murders. [online] https://hmicfrs.justiceinspectorates.gov.uk/publications/inspection-of-the-metropolitan-police-services-response-to-lessons-from-the-stephen-port-murders/ (2 November 2024).

Home Office. (1990). *The Hillsborough Stadium Disaster: 15 April 1989, Inquiry by the Rt Hon Lord Justice Taylor, Final Report*. London: HMSO.

Home Office. (2012). *The Report of the Hillsborough Independent Panel*. London: TSO.

Human Rights Act. (1998). [online]. www.legislation.gov.uk/ukpga/1998/42/schedule/1 (23 September 2024).

IOPC. (2022). Operation Hotton: Learning Report. [online] www.policeconduct.gov.uk/publications/operation-hotton-learning-report-january-2022 (3 November 2024).

Lentz, S. A. & Chaires, R. H. (2007). The Invention of Peel's Principles: A Study of Policing 'Textbook' History. *Journal of Criminal Justice*, 35(1), 69–79. https://doi.org/10.1016/j.jcrimjus.2006.11.016.

Luft, J. & Ingham, H. (1955). *The Johari Window: A Graphic Model of Interpersonal Awareness. Proceedings of the Western Training Laboratory in Group Development*. Los Angeles, CA: University of California.

Macpherson, W. (1999). *The Stephen Lawrence Inquiry: Report of an Inquiry*. London: HMSO.

Massey, M. (1972). *What You Are Is Where You Were When*. Lakewood, WA: Richardson Co.

Ministry of Justice. (2015). *The Code of Practice for Victims of Crime*. London: HMSO.

Ministry of Justice. (2024). The Code of Practice for Victims of Crime in England and Wales (Victims' Code). [online] www.gov.uk/government/publications/the-code-of-practice-for-victims-of-crime/code-of-practice-for-victims-of-crime-in-england-and-wales-victims-code (23 September 2024).

Myhill, A. & Quinton, P. (2011). It's a Fair Cop? Police Legitimacy, Public Co-operation and Crime Reduction: An Interpretive Evidence Commentary. [online]. www.resea

rchgate.net/profile/Paul_Quinton/publication/265889188_It's_a_Fair_Cop_Police_Legit imacy_Public_Cooperation_and_Crime_Reduction_An_Interpretative_Evidence_ Commentary/links/55b40a6908aed621de0112f5.pdf (6 September 2024).

Police Act. (1996). [online]. www.legislation.gov.uk/ukpga/1996/16/schedule/4 (12 October 2024).

Police and Criminal Evidence Act. (1984). [online]. www.legislation.gov.uk/ukpga/1984/60/contents (23 September 2024).

Police and Criminal Evidence Act 1984, Code G. (2022). [online]. www.gov.uk/government/publications/pace-code-g-2012 (23 September 2024).

Police Conduct Regulations. (2012). [online]. www.legislation.gov.uk/uksi/2012/2632/contents/made (12 September 2024).

Police Conduct Regulations. (2020). [online]. www.legislation.gov.uk/uksi/2020/4 (03 October 2023).

Police Reform Act. (2002). [online]. www.legislation.gov.uk/ukpga/2002/30/section/83 (12 October 2024).

Police Staff Council. (2008). Joint Circular No 54: Standards of Professional Behaviour. [online]. www.local.gov.uk/sites/default/files/documents/workforce%20-%20Police%20-%20PSC%20handbook%20-%20Guidance%20Note%209%20-%20Standards%20of%20Professional%20Behaviour.pdf (23 October 2024).

Public Order Act. (1986). [online]. www.legislation.gov.uk/ukpga/1986/64/section/5 (5 September 2024).

Quinton, P., Myhill, A., Bradford, B., Fildes, A. & Porter, G. (2015). Fair Cop 2: Organisational Justice, Behaviour and Ethical Policing, an Interpretive Evidence Commentary. [online]. https://assets.college.police.uk/s3fs-public/2022-04/Fair-cop-2-%20organisational-justice-behaviour-and-ethical-policing.pdf (3 September 2024).

Reith, C. (1952). *The Blind Eye of History*. London: Faber & Faber.

Rogers, C. & Lewis, R. (eds). (2013). *Introduction to Police Work*. Cullompton: Willan.

Scarman, L. G. (1982). *The Scarman Report: The Brixton Disorders 10–12 April 1981. Report of an Inquiry by the Rt Hon The Lord Scarman*. Harmondsworth: Penguin.

Skolnick, J. H. (1966). *Justice Without Trial*. New York: Wiley.

Stout, B. (2010). *Equality and Diversity in Policing*. Exeter: Learning Matters.

Waddington, P. A. J. (1999). Police (Canteen) Sub-Culture: An Appreciation. *The British Journal of Criminology*, 39(2), 287–309. https://doi.org/10.1093/bjc/39.2.287.

2 Maintaining professional standards and reflective practice

Dominic A. Wood

Introduction

The landscape of policing is a dynamic and ever-changing environment. Over the past ten years we have seen a concerted effort to take seriously how higher levels of knowledge and understanding can enhance police officer performance and the professional standards expected within policing. The College of Policing (CoP) has promoted the idea that all aspects of policing are underpinned by knowledge, which is reinforced by the adoption of evidence-based policing (EBP) (Chapter 5). There has been a growing recognition that establishing and maintaining professional standards in policing requires police officers to be able to reflect upon their duties and obligations within changing social contexts, and in the light of a growing evidential base. Moreover, this requires police organisations to encourage, enable and ensure such reflection is embedded within the idea of what it means to be a police officer, staff member or volunteer. Broader society also needs to allow policing organisations to be reflective practices. These different layers of reflective practice are the focus of this chapter. However, the author argues that the aspirational tone of the College's earlier approach to driving up professional standards in policing has not been universally accepted or supported in practice, and this has been evidenced by the extent to which the College's Policing Education and Qualifications Framework (PEQF) has stalled, and its scope diminished. Even more damning, the HMICFRS (2022) inspection of vetting, misconduct, and misogyny in the police service, and the Baroness Casey Review (2023) final report on the standards of behaviour and internal culture of the Metropolitan Police Service, have shown that in practice, the espoused values of police leaders (Chapter 14) are not reflected across important aspects of police work. Establishing what reflective practice should look like in policing and ensuring that the mechanisms are in place to address and remove the cultural toxicity described in the above reports, is the focus of this revised chapter.

It is important, notwithstanding just how damning the Baroness Casey Review (2023) and HMICFRS (2022) are, that there remains a focus on the positive approach taken from a reflective practice perspective to the issue of professional standards. Professional standards are understood as aspirational markers linked to professional pride and a sense of vocational purpose rather than mechanisms solely for combatting police corruption (Waddington, 2013). The assumption here is that professional standards represent much more than simply being lawful and meeting minimum levels of performance criteria. Embracing a culture of reflective practice encourages the police to approach professional standards by enhancing the police's ability to meet the growing expectations of the people they serve, rather than simply reducing incidents of bad policing. As such, the author uses reflective practice as a means of articulating professional policing values as they relate to the moral agency required of officers, staff and volunteers operating within the ethical contexts of policing practice, which require high levels of emotional intelligence alongside the need to demonstrate commitment to principles of diversity, equality and inclusion, in accordance with an evidence-based approach to police work.

Historical context

The seminal text in this area of study is Schön's (1983) *The Reflective Practitioner: How professionals think in action*. This publication built upon Schön's earlier work with Argyris from the 1970s, which focused on the development of knowledge within organisational practices (Argyris & Schön, 1974, 1978). This work was important in breaking down the division between theory and practice, building upon the earlier philosophical perspectives of Dewey (1904, 1916) and Piaget (1977) that had challenged traditional ways of understanding how people learn. Schön's (1983) approach also draws upon a model of reflection found within later works by Dewey (1933).

The backdrop to Schön's reflective practitioner is thus one that emphasises active over passive learning, and at the same time stresses the importance of experience and practice as stimuli for learning. Moreover, the organisational contexts within which professionals learn are important factors in shaping knowledge acquisition and development. From this backdrop, Schön (1983) develops a theory of knowledge that places the reflective practitioner at its heart. This practitioner centred understanding of knowledge is recognised by Kinsella (2007) when arguing that Schön's (1983) articulation of the reflective practitioner draws heavily on the philosophical insights of Polanyi (1967) and Ryle (1949). Kinsella (2007) continues to argue that Schön (1983) offers important insights into understanding the idea of reflection as it is conceived within professional life. The important point is that reflection ceases to be simply a detached moment of contemplation but is rather embodied within the physical actions of the practitioner in practice.

In relation to different modes of thinking that relate to reflection (Danielson, 2008), places the reflective police practitioner primarily operating, for most of the time, beyond technological thinking, which relies on reference to external authorities for routine matters. It requires situational, deliberate and dialectical thinking, which progress reflections respectively through contextual, more complex and ultimately transformative thinking. However, as Danielson (2008) stresses, it is important that this progression in terms of depth of thought is not treated in an overly hierarchical manner. The importance is to stress which mode of thinking is most appropriate to the situation at hand. Danielson (2008) also stresses that reflection should not be restricted to responding to problems; it should also be utilised in understanding things that went, and are going, well.

A primary motivation for Schön (1983) was a growing concern that professional life was in a state of moral crisis and, in particular, he felt there was a growing perception of irrelevancy with certain aspects of education for professionals. The idea of the reflective practitioner is presented as an alternative to what he presents as the 'Technical Rationality' model of professional knowledge, which involves the use of theory based on scientific principles (Schön, 1983). Schön (1983) also challenges the idea that knowledge is established in the abstract, and then applied in practical contexts. Instead, he argues that there is something called knowing-in-action. Kinsella (2007) links this idea of knowing-in-action to Polanyi's notion of tacit knowledge.

The important point is that knowledge and understanding is gained from doing things, although it is not easy to articulate what this knowledge and understanding is. This is what makes it tacit knowledge: practitioners know without knowing how they know. There are limits to the usefulness of tacit knowledge. It will have a practical use to some extent but cannot go beyond the immediacy of a given situation. To the extent that tacit knowledge can be developed, it is a slow-moving development. The important step in Schön's thinking is to move from the idea that practitioners can know in action, to the idea that practitioners can also reflect in action. Reflecting in action becomes a deliberate and conscious effort to recognise that individuals know in action, thereby transforming the tacit knowledge into something that is more mindful. The reflective practitioner is aware that tacit knowledge is known and by reflecting on what this is, transforms it into something more powerful.

Schön (1983) develops thinking further by situating knowing and reflecting in action within a concept of professional practice. This is an important step in understanding what a reflective practitioner is, as opposed to someone who is simply a reflective person. Again, it is important to note the purposeful intention of the reflection here. It is not abstract contemplation for its own sake, but rather a deliberate and conscious effort to improve professional understanding and practice. The knowing and reflecting is occurring within a professional context and this is what shapes reflective practice.

At this point Schön's earlier work with Argyris (Argyris & Schön, 1974, 1978) is informative. The reflective practitioner needs to be set within the context of a learning organisation, one that supports reflective practice. Reflective practice thus understood requires not only reflective practitioners, but also that the professional practice itself is reflective. An important point is that reflective practice could be rather narrowly framed if the reflection is limited to the specific tasks performed by a professional. This is recognised by Schön (1983) when noting that a practice involves repetition and therefore a practitioner can easily fail to recognise the *frame* within which a practice is performed. In other words, a practitioner can reflect on their own practice without questioning or reflecting more deeply on the purpose of the professional practice with which they are engaged. Awareness of frames is important in developing the critically reflective capacity of practitioners (Kinsella, 2007) and this allows for a greater reflexive capacity to transform a professional practice. The reflective practitioner understood in this way is not only changing their own performance, but also the contribution made by their profession to the wider society. This in turn adds a further dimension regarding the relationship between a professional practice and society, and in many respects, the development of reflective practice is dependent upon the degree of reflexivity permitted and tolerated within the profession at a societal level.

Schön's (1983) idea of reflective practice has been widely established within different professional areas (Staller & Koerner, 2023), in particular within education and the health professions. As Rhodes (2016) notes, nursing established a professional body nearly 100 years before the police service, and reflective practice features prominently within its professional code (NMC, 2018) and documents relating to learning within the nursing profession (RCN, 2019). Indeed, its influence has been perceived as being so widespread in some professional areas that it is deemed to be accepted uncritically (Halpin, 2015). This is not the case in policing.

Current professional practice

Reflective practice has been less prominent in the policing literature (Christopher, 2015a), but this is changing. The College of Policing's (2024a) revised *Code of Ethics,* which has in turn led to a revision of its *Competency and Values Framework* (CVF) (College of Policing, 2024b), promoting reflection and the sentiments of reflective practice. The CVF and the Code of Ethics emphasise the importance of values, critical thinking, responsibility and professional development through reflection (Chapter 1). The College of Policing (2022) also promotes the use of a reflective approach to the supervision of colleagues and the Independent Office for Police Conduct (IOPC) has developed a reflective practice approach to investigating complaints into police misconduct, with an emphasis on learning (IOPC, 2022a, 2022b). These are positive steps in the right direction, although it appears to the author that the current debate about professional standards within policing is too narrow and it lacks the kind of moral depth that comes from reflective practice (Wood, 2020). In particular, the guidance for the College of Policing can focus too much on reflection at the individual level, for example promoting Gibbs's Reflective Cycle and the Betari's Box Framework (College of Policing, 2023). Similarly, the College of Policing can oversimplify what reflective practice is, in its attempt to promote reflection. For example, the College suggest that reflecting is thinking about things, which everyone does, and that reflective practice is just doing this well (College of Policing, 2020). Reflective practice is not simple, and as Staller and Koerner (2023) note, there are different levels of reflection. The aim of developing reflexivity, what Staller and Koerner (2023) present as applying reflection on reflection, is to go beyond the immediate assumptions of a situation, which is not necessarily achieved from an individual's use of a reflective tool.

Promoting Schön's (1983) concept of reflective practice is an important component in establishing what it means to be a good police officer, staff member or volunteer. The emphasis being on establishing what good policing is. For example, on the one hand, police officers demonstrate Schön's (1983) understanding of knowing-in-action and that the move towards EBP offers opportunities to strengthen this, but this also develops the ability of an officer to reflect-in-action. The idea that knowledge shapes policing in particular also provides a mechanism to allow for a greater degree of reflecting-in-practice by making the professional intentions of policing more explicit and high profile to both those within police organisations, and to external stakeholders and society more broadly. However, at the same time, in order to realise these aspirations, there is a need to go beyond a narrow focus on professional standards.

Simmons (1979) sees a distinction between positional duties and legal obligations on the one hand, and moral obligation on the other hand. Positional duties and legal obligations are more or less clearly defined constraints that demand compliance. They are in many respects essential aspects of professional practice. However, adherence to positional duties and legal obligations will not necessarily result in the kind of reflecting-in-practice demanded of the reflective practitioner. Moral obligation, on the other hand, requires a deeper understanding of the applicability of positional duties and legal obligations within any given context. Moral obligation is more ambiguous and less clearly defined than positional duties and legal obligations, and therefore demands a more critically reflective engagement with them in practice. What Simmons (1979) defines as moral obligation is thus embedded within the ideals of reflective practice at the level of the individual officer but also at the police organisational level.

When reflecting upon what the police do in society, it seems that there is a strong moral basis to what police officers do. Others may disagree, but what seems abundantly clear is the argument that a focus on professional standards, understood narrowly as the negation of bad policing, emphasises what Simmons (1979) defines as positional duties and legal obligations (MacVean et al., 2013). The focus on reflective practice, on the other hand, emphasises much more the need to establish moral obligation at the heart of good policing (Wood, 2020). A focus on reflective practice is a means of achieving truly professional standards, beyond what the focus on professional standards alone can achieve. The narrow focus on professional standards alone does not engender the kind of ethical reasoning that is implicit within the concept of reflective practice. This is illustrated by Hughes (2013) when noting in a balanced and insightful contribution to MacVean et al. (2013), that ethical behaviour cannot alone be attributed to the use of professional standards. Hughes (2013) notes that other factors inform and shape professional standards, and that practitioners need to engage ethically to ensure professional standards. Despite these qualifications, and a cautionary approach to the linking of professional standards to ethical policing, Hughes (2013) nonetheless acknowledges the benefits of professional standards guiding practice and as a means of encouraging ethical behaviour, to some extent the author agrees. It should not be underestimated how difficult it is to change the values within large public institutions, such as the police service. A narrow focus on professional standards may well reinforce a technical approach to professional standards, rather than encourage a more reflective approach, as it is much easier to establish and maintain professional standards than it is to develop ethical behaviour or critically reflective practice.

This problem is discussed by Waddington (2013) when noting that professional standards deal with unethical behaviour but do little to promote ethical behaviour, noting that such standards set only minimum expectations. Indeed, it could be argued that professional standards normalise and legitimise behaviours that fall short of what we might consider to be ethical. Negating unethical behaviour does not in itself produce ethical behaviour, nor does it promote reflective practice.

Waddington (2013) highlights the imbalance currently found within our approach to improving policing. Continuing to suggest that there is far too much emphasis on uncovering unethical behaviour and punishing with severity officers found guilty of wrongdoing, and conversely, too little emphasis on rewarding and promoting the heroic endeavours routinely performed by many officers.

The author suggests that Waddington (2013) articulates a strong sense of moral purpose for policing, which in turn delivers a far more appropriate, meaningful and ultimately effective guide to police officers than is provided through a narrow focus on professional standards. If policing is to be conceptualised as ethical, officers need to be inspired, supported and motivated to act with moral purpose and to make ethical judgements. The focus on professional standards encourages not ethically informed decision making, but rather compliance with minimal standards, risk aversion and a cautionary approach that falls short of the noble calling emphasised by Waddington (2013). Rather than seeing professional standards as an impetus towards ethical policing, there is a need to focus on what makes policing ethical in order to inform better what is understood to be appropriate professional standards in policing. This needs to be at the core of any understanding of policing as a reflective practice.

It is here that reflective practice offers a more appropriate focus for maintaining, and indeed enhancing, the professional standards within policing. There are a multitude of considerations arising from an officer's positional duties and legal obligations that shape their responses to given situations. These can be defined and articulated through policies and legislation. They can be learnt and adhered to, but such compliance does not in itself produce good policing. The officer's moral obligations are manifested in the decisions made when considering the totality of the appropriate positional duties and legal obligations that apply in each situation. An officer's reflexivity improves the more they reflect upon a wide range of variables when dealing with policing matters. This includes reflecting upon past experiences and performance, but also legal knowledge, awareness of force policy, appreciation of socio-economic and demographic circumstances, and other factors that frame the professional practice contexts in which the officer is operating. It also includes addressing the democratic deficit within policing, in terms of both the internal organisation of police services (Sklansky, 2008) and the broader question of the police's democratic mandate within society (Manning, 2010; Reiner, 2013). The more reflective officers are in these processes, and the more conscientious officers are in their reflecting-in-practice, the more they discharge their moral obligations.

Reflective practice understood in this way challenges any idea that posits experience against education in establishing how police officers become good at their jobs. Reflective practice, as we have seen, is developed from earlier ideas about active learning and learning through experiential engagement. It is also grounded in professional practice in a way that demands both educational and experiential endeavours to operate in a mutually reinforcing manner. Reflexivity understood in this way draws upon a quality identified by Aristotle as *phronesis* (Grint, 2007). Phronesis draws upon both technical and academic understandings to produce a third kind of understanding, which is manifested as a practical wisdom that informs the kind of professional decision making required of police officers (Wood & Tong, 2009). Avoid viewing experience as better than education or vice versa and focus rather on experience as an integral part of learning processes that produce practical wisdom within professional contexts (Wood & Tong, 2009).

It is also important to stress that positional duties and legal obligations are not in opposition to moral obligations within policing. The point is that adhering to positional duties and legal obligations is necessary but not sufficient in establishing good policing. Moral obligations require the officer to understand positional duties and legal obligations fully and indeed more deeply. For an officer to meet their moral obligations they must have also complied with their positional duties and legal obligations, not in a perfunctory manner, but in a way that understands fully not only the wording of policies and legislation, but also the reasoning that gives rise to the policies and legislation in the first instance.

Of course moral obligations are much more difficult to define than positional duties and legal obligations. This is made difficult within policing by the fact that establishing what it means to be a good police officer is complex. Policing, as Reiner (2015) notes, is what Gallie (1956) describes as an essentially contested concept. There are, and always will be, very different ideas of the purpose of policing and what police officers should be doing routinely. The moral obligations of the police are in this respect fluid. However, this is precisely why moral obligation is such an important component of good policing. Police officers are routinely placed in nuanced and complex situations that require professional judgement, interpretation and reflection (Christopher, 2015b). This makes policing a necessarily reflexive occupation and is reflected in the focus on discretion within the police ethics literature (Kleinig, 1996; Davis, 2002; Delattre, 2011). The ideal of autonomous police officers empowered to make discretionary, professional judgements is expressed within the concept of the office of constable (Police Federation, 2008), and is reaffirmed within the Policing Protocol 2011 (Winsor, 2013).

This is also underpinned by the notion of the moral agent found within the contexts of professional ethics (Hill et al., 1978). A police officer would not be performing professionally if they failed to act simply on the grounds that acting was outside of their defined positional duties and/or legal obligations. There are times when the expectation would be for a police officer to act simply because it is the right thing to do, even if that right thing is not defined explicitly within legislation and/or the job description, and notwithstanding how difficult it is to define or agree upon what the right thing to do is. Nonetheless, of most importance here is the expectation that the police officer will take moral responsibility in all situations, irrespective of whether that means they act in this way or that, or indeed not at all. Such an officer fits the description of what MacIntyre (2004) refers to as a moral agent.

A narrow focus on professional standards tends to situate responsibilities *exclusively* in clearly defined documents. It encourages minimal responsibility taking and within clearly contracted roles. A focus on reflective practice on the other hand demands that an officer not only considers such documents but also reflects more broadly on all aspects of a situation. This approach encourages officers to take greater levels of responsibility and to make judgements about how best to carry out their professional responsibilities.

Understanding the reflective practitioner as a moral agent requires the idea of police discretion to be taken seriously. This does not mean allowing police officers to simply act as they see best. Police discretion should be understood as the burden of professional responsibility (Davis, 2002). Police discretion does not allow officers to ignore professional standards as defined within positional duties and legal obligations, but rather requires them to understand more deeply about the purpose of professional standards and their respective appropriateness in given situations. There is a need to recognise that police work can be a highly emotional labour (Rhodes, 2016) and the investment made by officers in this way needs to be understood as a core component of police discretion. The notion of emotional labour (Hochschild, 1983) emphasises a truly human dimension within policing that is at the heart of reflective practice. Officers need to be supported within the force and appreciated more widely within society to ensure that there is adequate space for officers to reflect in meaningful ways to ensure the human dimension of police work is not lost, both in the sense of how officers treat others, but also in how they are treated by their own organisations.

One feature of the emotional labour conducted by officers is the need to make moral judgements. The moral agent, defined by MacIntyre (2004), is continuously engaged in critical conversations. These conversations need to be such that they hold all participants to account in a way that gives objective meaning to judgements made by moral agents. To be clear, the idea of moral agency is not to give licence to the subjective preferences of officers. There needs to be ways of assessing moral judgements, such that they have meaning beyond the perspective of the moral agent; the moral agent needs to provide all reasons for their decisions (Beardsmore, 1969).

In practice an officer's power to exercise discretion of any kind, good or bad, is increasingly curtailed. This is especially true at the rank of constable (Rowe, 2015), when considered against the dominance of risk aversion (Westera et al.,

2014) and the presentation of professional standards narrowly framed within the contexts of positional duties and legal obligations. Indeed Sklansky (2008) argues that reflexivity is discouraged by top-down regulation, which emphasises compliance and consistency. Moral obligation is, however, embedded within the ideal of policing even if it is not expected, encouraged or promoted currently in policing practice.

Understanding the police role through the discourse of the reflective practitioner as moral agent, with a focus on moral obligation, reflects actual good policing practice. It therefore promotes, encourages and incentivises good police practice and, conversely, it challenges, discourages and impedes bad policing. Understanding policing on the other hand through the professional standards discourse, with a focus on positional duties and legal obligations, does little to promote good policing in practice, indeed quite the reverse. The focus exclusively on positional duties and legal obligations does not reflect or capture what police officers do, and certainly not to the extent this is achieved through an emphasis on the moral obligations of a police officer.

Rowe (2015) introduces the concept of accurate misrepresentations to define situations in which police officers are recording an event accurately, in terms of the required paperwork, but in such a way as to misrepresent what actually occurred. The police officer does not deliberately or consciously misrepresent what happened, but the forms they are required to complete constrain what is captured in the reporting of the incident. The police officer answers the questions asked of them on the form accurately and honestly, but the questions fail to engage with important aspects of an encounter. Rowe (2015) describes, for example, a routine instance of police practice he observed as part of an ethnographic research project. He reports seeing officers carry out a stop and search that was in full accordance with force policy. The appropriate paperwork was completed, which in turn provided an accurate account of the event.

However, Rowe (2015) was left feeling that this account was nonetheless a misrepresentation of what happened. The officers had performed the stop and search in accordance with their positional duties and legal obligations, and this is recorded on forms that are designed to ensure that positional duties and legal obligations are discharged appropriately. However, what is not captured through this accountability mechanism is a true representation of whether the stop and search has made a positive or negative impact overall. There is no scope within the process for measuring the decision-making capacity of the officer. Instead, the officer simply provides documentation to show that procedures have been followed. But a more representative account of the stop and search encounter, which would enable a much richer measurement of the officer's ability to assess a situation and respond in an appropriate and proportionate manner, is lost.

Increasingly such examples simply lead to further attempts by governments, policy makers and police leaders to curtail the discretion of front-line police officers even further. Officers are given even more precise directives to follow. In other words, their positional duties and legal obligations are defined more tightly and there is a greater emphasis placed on them having to follow prescribed instructions. They are trusted less to make professional decisions and their moral agency is diminished. Constraining police officers in this way is counter-productive and diminishes what is demanded of the police today. Indeed, rather than burdening the police officer with more responsibilities, they are being absolved of moral obligation. Allowing them to do what the moral agent is not permitted to do: allowing officers to offload responsibilities on to others higher in the hierarchy, or to shelter in the precise wording of their job description. Perfunctory performance is encouraged rather than aspiring to the kind of professional excellence identified and referred to by Waddington (2013).

This becomes more problematic the more policing is considered in terms of the societal aspirations espoused through the concepts of democracy and human rights. Society demands more of the police; democratic sensibilities create expectations among the policed, and human rights require the police to consider the specifics and particularities of incidents. Manning (2010) critically notes that policing is not formally judged against democratic norms or values, but it should not ignore the extent to which the increasingly democratic sensibilities of the age transform the conceptualising of policing (Wood, 2014). Likewise, Manning (2010) correctly questions why the police are not assessed in terms of the extent to which they have upheld, or indeed advanced, human rights. But at the same time the extent to which human rights increasingly inform and impact all aspects of social life should not be underestimated. At the very least, there are forceful arguments promoting a greater embedding of democracy and human rights within policing ideals (Manning, 2010; Reiner, 2013). This demands of police officers a high degree of reflexivity and above all else, moral obligations. The police officer, understood as a reflective practitioner with moral agency, is an inescapable reality of an increasingly democratic society that values human rights. It is the contention of this chapter, that the move towards EBP and the recognition that knowledge is an important component of policing will create different expectations in society, and indeed that this has already begun to happen. The focus on reflective practice allows policing to be established as a reflective practice, which in turn places moral obligation as a defining feature of the good police officer.

As suggested earlier, reflective practice is dependent not only on having reflective practitioners, but also on having reflective organisations. For MacIntyre (2004) moral agents need to be engaged in social relationships between colleagues within supportive institutional settings that foster discussion in order to be able to make judgements with a rationally justifiable confidence. As suggested elsewhere (Wood & Williams, 2016) this is a particularly pressing issue within policing. Police services are seen to fall short of what is expected in terms of how they are organised internally (Sklansky, 2008). The fostering of reflective practitioners within policing demands democratic structures that allow for appropriate levels of dissent, diversity of thought and questioning. Villiers and Adlam (2004) are not overly confident in being able to claim this happens within policing.

For policing to become a reflective practice, police services need to find better ways of handling their well-defined and authoritative rank structure. While it has merit in many circumstances, there is a danger of exaggerating the importance of hierarchical necessity within policing and, in particular, of insisting that this is a consistent feature across all aspects of police work. In particular, it is important that the rank structure does not obstruct critical reflexivity that challenges unexamined assumptions and/or promotes innovative ways of working.

A final consideration is that reflective practices need to be trusted within society. High-profile cases that highlight serious deficiencies in policing, such as the Hillsborough disaster in 1989 and the investigation into the murder of Stephen Lawrence in 1993, undermine trust in the police. The Baroness Casey Review (2023) and the fallout from the murder of Sarah Everard by a serving police officer (HMICFRS, 2022) have only exacerbated the difficulties confronting policing today. However, the more the police are mistrusted, the more difficult it is for them to be reflective. Across society we need to find opportunities to give policing the space to experiment and innovate, to try new ways of working and to trust that such experimentation is being done with good intentions. The move towards EBP and the focus on meaningful learning must be appreciated not only as important internally within police organisations, but also as mechanisms that can significantly increase trust in the police, in ways that allow for greater reflexivity and the development of policing as a truly reflective practice.

It is worth remembering that policing is still very much in its infancy with regards to establishing the importance of knowledge and understanding at the heart of its professionalism (Wood and Bryant, 2015). It takes time for a learning culture to be developed and it will not happen overnight. As Rury (1986) discusses in a review of an early publication by the American educational philosopher John Dewey, at the beginning of the twentieth century Dewey was very much in a minority of people seeing the need for teacher education to be anything more than practical skills in the classroom. Dewey was also swimming against the tide of received wisdom that saw a clear distinction between experiential, practical skills on the one hand, and contemplative, scholarly reflection on the other. The concept of reflective practice provides a theoretical and pragmatic framework through which higher level, experiential learning can be attained and recognised, which seems highly appropriate for policing today.

Future developments

As Bacon (2021) notes, there is a well-established argument that police culture prevents change in policing. Furthermore, considering the findings in the Baroness Casey Review (2023) and HMICFRS (2022), it would be understandable to be pessimistic about the prospects for reflective practice in policing. However, there are positive developments that counterbalance the persistence of the kind of toxicity identified by the Baroness Casey Review (2023). For a starter, the College of Policing's (2024a) revised Code of Ethics is much improved from the 2014 iteration in that it places much more focus on the reasoning and reflexivity of officers, staff and volunteers. It provides a more than useful starting place for responding to the challenges captured in the

Baroness Casey Review (2023) and HMICFRS (2022). There are also positive signs emerging from the focus on reflexivity in police training. Bacon (2021) and Hillen et al., (2024) report positively on changing attitudes among police officers following training in relation to different aspects of drugs policing. Likewise, the number of officers completing a police constable degree apprenticeship (PCDA), degree holder entry programme (DHEP) or other policing course over the past few years is also helping to develop a more reflective and critically minded cadre of officers.

The more that knowledge and a reflective frame of mind can become routine policing activities, the more the opportunities for developing reflective practice in policing will increase. The gains made by the College of Policing's promotion of EBP and knowledge bases for policing, e.g. through its Authorised Professional Practice guidance, need to be encouraged, sustained and defended. Importantly, the professionalisation agenda within policing should not be reduced to a focus on defining the positional duties and legal obligations of the police. The real strength of the reflective practice approach is that it establishes a sense of purpose within policing and focuses attention on the moral obligations of police officers.

Such aspirations should be maintained, particularly as and when economic, political, social and internal obstacles make its realisation difficult. Perhaps the greatest obstacle and challenge to realising reflective practice in policing is establishing a sufficient level of trust across society and among the various stakeholders with a view on policing, to allow the police the space to be reflective, experimental and innovative. This does not require giving the police the freedom to do whatever they like, but it does mean recognising the differences between on the one hand corrupt behaviour and poor performance, and on the other hand genuine mistakes and failed initiatives that nonetheless provide useful lessons. Society needs to allow the police to become a learning organisation if the principles of reflective practice are to flourish and the utilisation of a reflective practice approach by the IOPC is a positive development.

Conclusion

This chapter has argued in favour of reflective practice being the means by which professional standards can be achieved within policing. The chapter is necessarily presented as an argument because of the extent to which reflective practice is still largely in its infancy within policing. Reflective practice is needed in policing today more than ever. Trust and confidence in policing is at a low ebb (HMICFRS, 2024), understandably given the seriousness of the shortcomings identified by the Baroness Casey Review (2023) and HMICFRS (2022). To take policing seriously as a profession and give the warranted police officer the recognition that its status surely deserves, reflective practice is a necessity. This means recognising the warranted officer as a moral agent, an individual with moral obligations beyond their positional duties and legal obligations. Importantly, though, there is the need to recognise that establishing policing as a reflective practice requires not only reflective practitioners as moral agents, it also entails policing services adapting their internal hierarchical structures to ensure there is a greater level of support given to reflective practitioners engaged in problem solving and critical discussions about their profession. This will only really happen if and when there are appropriate levels of support and trust across society to allow the police the space to be reflective and experimental, and when society has a sufficient level of tolerance towards genuine mistakes within policing to enable it to become a learning organisation.

> **Evidence-based case study illustrating professional practice**
>
> Officers Patel and Smith attend a domestic incident following a call from a concerned neighbour who has reported hearing shouting over a sustained period followed by the sound of glass smashing. On arrival at the address, an elderly woman answers the door. Her name is Beryl and she is 82 years old. She invites the officers into the house. In the living room, sitting on the sofa, is Frank, Beryl's husband. Frank is 84 years old and he has been married to Beryl for 55 years. Both Frank and Beryl seem calm but there is clear evidence of a disturbance in the living room. A number of figurines are broken on the floor and it appears a vase with flowers in it had been thrown against the wall in the corner of the living room. There are no obvious signs of physical harm to Beryl or Frank. Beryl offers the officers a cup of tea and Frank seems confused as to why the officers are in the house.

Reflective questions

In the given scenario, consider what is the relevance of the couple's age. What other factors are of immediate importance within the information provided? What would be the most pressing actions for officers Patel and Smith to conduct? How important would the ethnicity of the couple be in the given scenario? How should officers Patel and Smith make sure that they are considering legislation, force policies and EBP appropriately?

References

Argyris, C. & Schön, D. (1974). *Theory in Practice: Increasing Professional Effectiveness*. San Francisco, CA: Jossey Bass.

Argyris, C. & Schön, D. (1978). *Organisational Learning: A Theory of Action Perspective*. Reading, MA: Addison Wesley.

Bacon, M. (2021). Desistance from Criminalisation: Police Culture and New Directions in Drugs Policing, *Policing and Society*, 32(4), 522–539. https://doi.org/10.1080/10439463.2021.1920587.

Baroness Casey Review. (2023). Final Report: An independent review into the standards of behaviour and internal culture of the Metropolitan Police Service. [online]. www.

met.police.uk/SysSiteAssets/media/downloads/met/about-us/baroness-casey-review/up date-march-2023/baroness-casey-review-march-2023a.pdf (13 August 2024)

Beardsmore, R. (1969). *Moral Reasoning*. London: Routledge & Kegan Paul.

Christopher, S. (2015a). The Police Service Can Be a Critical Reflective Practice … If It Wants. *Policing*, 9(4), 326–339. https://doi.org/10.1093/police/pav007.

Christopher, S. (2015b). The Quantum Leap: Police Recruit Training and the Case for Mandating Higher Education Pre-entry Schemes. *Policing. A Journal of Policy and Practice*, 9 (4), 388–404. https://doi.org/10.1093/police/pav021.

College of Policing. (2020). Continuing Professional Development. [online]. www.col lege.police.uk/career-learning/career-development/CPD (accessed 10 July 2024).

College of Policing. (2022). Supporting the Delivery of Good Service. [online]. www.col lege.police.uk/guidance/effective-supervision/supporting-delivery-good-service#reflecti ve-supervision (accessed 10 August 2024).

College of Policing. (2023). Making Good Decisions. [online]. www.college.police.uk/ guidance/conducting-effective-investigations/making-good-decisions (accessed 10 July 2024).

College of Policing. (2024a). Code of Ethics. Revised 2024. [online]. www.college.police. uk/ethics/code-of-ethics (accessed 10 July 2024).

College of Policing. (2024b). Competency and Values Framework (CVF). Updated May 2024. [online]. www.college.police.uk/career-learning/competency-and-values-fram ework (accessed 10 July 2024).

Danielson, L. (2008). Making Reflective Practice More Concrete Through Reflective Decision Making. *The Educational Forum*, 72(2), 129–137https://doi.org/10.1080/ 00131720701805009.

Davis, M. (2002). *Profession, Code, and Ethics: Towards a Morally Useful Theory of Today's Professions*. Aldershot: Ashgate.

Delattre, E. (2011). *Character and Cops. Ethics and Policing*, 6th ed. Lanham, MD: Rowman & Littlefield.

Dewey, J. (1904). The Relation of Theory to Practice in Education. In, *Third Yearbook of the National Society for the Scientific Study of Education* (pp. 9–30). Chicago: University of Chicago Press.

Dewey, J. (1916). *Democracy and Education*. New York: Macmillan.

Dewey, J. (1933). *How We Think: A Restatement of the Relation of Reflective Thinking to the Educative Process*. New York: Heath.

Gallie, W. B. (1956). Essentially Contested Concepts. *Proceedings of the Aristotelian Society*, 56(1), 167–198. www.jstor.org/stable/4544562.

Grint, K. (2007). Learning to Lead: Can Aristotle Help Us Find the Road to Wisdom? *Leadership*, 3(2), 231–246. https://doi.org/10.1177/1742715007076215.

Halpin, D. (2015). Essaying and Reflective Practice in Education: The Legacy of Michael de Montaigne. *Journal of Philosophy of Education*, 49 (1), 129–141https://doi.org/10. 1111/1467-9752.12098.

Hill, P., Bedau, H., Chechile, R., Crochetiere, W., Kellerman, B., Ounjian, D., Pauker, S. G., Pauker, S. & Rubin, J. (1978). *Making Decisions. A Multidisciplinary Introduction*. Reading, MA: Addison-Wesley.

Hillen, P., Speakman, E., Jamieson, M., Dougall, N., Heyman, I., Murray, J., Aston, E. & McAuley, A. (2024). Police officer knowledge of and attitudes to opioid overdose and naloxone administration: an evaluation of police training in Scotland. *Policing and Society*, 1–16. https://doi.org/10.1080/10439463.2024. 2367142.

HMICFRS. (2022). An Inspection of Vetting, Misconduct, and Misogyny in the Police Service. [online]. https://hmicfrs.justiceinspectorates.gov.uk/publications/an-inspection-of-vetting-misconduct-and-misogyny-in-the-police-service/ (accessed 13 August 2024).

HMICFRS. (2024). State of Policing: The Annual Assessment of Policing in England and Wales 2023. [online]. https://hmicfrs.justiceinspectorates.gov.uk/publication-html/state-of-policing-the-annual-assessment-of-policing-in-england-and-wales-2023/ (accessed 10 August 2024).

Hochschild, A. (1983). *The Managed Heart: Commercialization of Human Feeling*. Berkeley, CA: University of California Press.

Hughes, J. (2013). Theory of Professional Standards and Ethical Policing. In A. MacVean, P. Spindler & C. Solf (eds), *Handbook of Policing, Ethics and Professional Standards* (pp. 7–16). Abingdon: Routledge.

IOPC. (2022a). Reflective Practice Review Process: Summary Report. [online]. www.policeconduct.gov.uk/sites/default/files/documents/RPRP-summary-report.pdf (accessed 10 July 2024)

IOPC. (2022b). Reflective Practice. [online]. www.policeconduct.gov.uk/sites/default/files/documents/IOPC-Focus-21-RPRP.pdf (accessed 10 July 2024)

Kinsella, E. A. (2007). Embodied Reflections and the Epistemology of Reflective Practice. *Journal of Philosophy of Education*, 41(3), 395–409. https://doi.org/10.1111/j.1467-9752.2007.00574.x.

Kleinig, J. (1996). *The Ethics of Policing*. Cambridge: Cambridge University Press.

MacIntyre, A. (2004). Social Structures and Their Threat to Moral Agency. In P. Villiers & R. Adlam (eds), *Policing a Safe, Just and Tolerant Society: An International Model for Policing* (pp. 36–54). Winchester: Waterside Press.

MacVean, A., Spindler, P. & Solf, C. (2013). *Handbook of Policing, Ethics and Professional Standards*. Abingdon: Routledge.

Manning, P. (2010). *Democratic Policing in a Changing World*. Boulder, CO: Paradigm Publishers.

NMC. (2018). *The Code. Professional Standards of Practice and Behaviours for Nurses, Midwives and Nursing Associates*. London: Nursing and Midwifery Council.

Piaget, J. (1977). The Role of Action in the Development of Thinking. In W. F. Overton & J. M. Gallagher (eds), *Knowledge and Development* (pp. 17–42). Boston, MA: Springer.

Polanyi, M. (1967). *The Tacit Dimension*. London: Routledge.

Police Federation. (2008). *The Office of Constable. The Bedrock of Modern Day British Policing*. Leatherhead: Police Federation of England and Wales.

RCN. (2019). Revalidation Requirements: Reflection and Reflective Discussion. [online]. www.rcn.org.uk/professional-development/revalidation/reflection-and-reflective-discussion (accessed 6 June 2019).

Reiner, R. (2013). Who Governs? Democracy, Plutocracy, Science and Prophecy in Policing. *Criminology and Criminal Justice*, 13(2), 161–180https://doi.org/10.1177/1748895812474282.

Reiner, R. (2015). *Utopia in One Institution? Can Policing be Democratic in an Unjust Society?* Presented at Policing and Democracy in the 21st Century, International Criminological Research Unit, Liverpool University, 17 September.

Rhodes, A. (2016). The Professionals. 8 January. [online]. www.college.police.uk/News/College-news/Pages/the_professionals.aspx (accessed 25 June 2019).

Rowe, M. (2015). *Police! Camera! Lay Observation!* Presented at Policing and Democracy in the 21st Century, International Criminological Research Unit, Liverpool University, 17 September.

Rury, J. (1986). Book Review of John Dewey's 1904 'The Relation of Theory to Practice in Education'. *Journal of Teacher Education*, 37(4), 57–61.

Ryle, G. (1949). *The Concept of Mind*. London: Hutchinson.

Schön, D. (1983). *The Reflective Practitioner. How Professionals Think in Action*. New York: Basic Books.

Simmons, A. J. (1979). *Moral Principles and Political Obligations*. Princeton, NJ: Princeton University Press.

Sklansky, D. A. (2008). *Democracy and the Police*. Stanford, CA: Stanford University Press.

Staller, M. S. & Koerner, S. (2023). A Case Example of Teaching Reflective Policing to Police Students. *Teaching Public Administration*, 41(3), 351–366. https://doi.org/10.1177/01447394211067109.

Villiers, P. & Adlam, R. (2004). *Policing a Safe, Just and Tolerant Society: An International Model for Policing*. Winchester: Waterside Press.

Waddington, P. A. J. (2013). Introduction. In P. A. J. Waddington, J. Kleinig & M. Wright (eds), *Professional Police Practice: Scenarios and Dilemmas* (pp. 3–24). Oxford: Oxford University Press.

Westera, N., Kebbell, M., Milne, B. & Green, T. (2014). The Prospective Detective: Developing the Effective Detective of the Future. *Policing and Society: An International Journal of Research and Policy*, 26(2), 197–209. https://doi.org/10.1080/10439463.2014.942845.

Winsor, T. (2013). Operational Independence and the New Accountability of Policing [online]. www.hmic.gov.uk/media/hmcic-tom-winsor-john-harris-memorial-lecture.pdf (accessed 20 March 2014).

Wood, D. A. (2014). The Importance of Liberal Values within Policing: Police and Crime Commissioners, Police Independence and the Spectre of Illiberal Democracy. *Policing and Society: An International Journal of Research and Policy*, 26(2), 148–164https://doi.org/10.1080/10439463.2014.922086.

Wood, D. A. (2020). *Towards Ethical Policing*. Bristol: Policy Press.

Wood, D. A. & Bryant, R. P. (2015). Researching Police Professionalism. In M. Brunger, S. Tong & D. Martin (eds), *Introduction to Policing Research: Taking Lessons from Practice*. Abingdon: Routledge.

Wood, D. A. & Tong, S. (2009). The Future of Initial Police Training: A University Perspective. *International Journal of Police Science & Management*, 11(3), 294–305. https://doi.org/10.1350/ijps.2009.11.3.131.

Wood, D. A. & Williams, E. (2016). The Politics of Establishing Reflexivity as a Core Component of Good Policing. In S. Armstrong, J. Blaustein & A. Henry (eds), *Reflexivity and Criminal Justice. Intersections of Policy, Practice and Research* (pp. 215–236). London: Palgrave Macmillan.

3 Criminology and criminal justice

Anne Lodge

Introduction

Criminal behaviour is a significant and inescapable feature of everyday life. For this reason, an understanding of the nature of crime, its causes and consequences, and of established systems for dealing with crime, is essential for anyone wishing to pursue a career in policing and criminal justice. This chapter aims to assist readers to make the links between their vocational aspirations as policing practitioners and the academic disciplines of criminology and criminal justice. It is important for reflective police officers, staff and volunteers to have an awareness of some foundational issues within contemporary criminology to develop a better understanding of criminal behaviour and the societal responses to crime. An increased focus on rooting policing practices in an evidence-base means that criminological research (in collaboration with academic or other partners) can be used to enable officers, staff and volunteers to make informed decisions, challenge existing practices and innovate in the public interest. While it is not possible within the confines of this chapter to address every aspect of the vast enterprise that constitutes 'criminology', the aim is to demonstrate the way in which key criminological theories, research and debates can inform and influence the practice of those working in the criminal justice sector, particularly in the context of contemporary policing.

The theoretical context

The relationship between criminology, a multifaceted academic discipline, and policing has become increasingly important. Though often used interchangeably, the terms 'criminology' and 'criminal justice' have distinct meanings. Criminology is the study of the anatomy of crime, explanations for criminal behaviour and consequences of criminality; in contrast, criminal justice is primarily concerned with societal responses to crime, including the purpose and function of agencies operating within the criminal justice system, the objectives of punishment, crime prevention and community safety strategies, and the ways in which the system accommodates victims (Joyce & Laverick, 2022). While the scope of this introductory text precludes any detailed discussion of these complex issues, some significant criminological debates are introduced to encourage aspiring criminal justice practitioners to engage with relevant literature. Understanding crime, criminal behaviour and its impacts is crucial for informed decision-making in often operational policing environments.

The nature of crime: what is crime?

Given that the focus of criminology as an academic discipline is on 'crime', it is important to consider what constitutes criminal behaviour. A simplistic view would be that a crime occurs when the letter of the law is broken; but if criminal behaviour is defined as being that which is contrary to law, questions arise as to the content and appropriate boundaries of the criminal law (Zedner, 2004). Some argue that criminal prohibitions reflect a common social morality about right and wrong which can vary depending on prevailing social attitudes (Wood et al., 2024). However, there is not always a consensus about what conduct should be deemed 'criminal'; reasonable people may disagree, for example, about the criminalisation of certain drugs, the utility of criminalising sex work, or the extent to which online harms should be prohibited. It could also be argued that because criminal laws are established by people occupying powerful societal positions, members of the judiciary and parliament determine the boundaries of the law according to their own standards, which may not always reflect broader societal views. Political considerations also significantly influence criminal law boundaries (Herring, 2024). There is substantial debate about how the contours of the criminal law are determined; the only thing that is certain is that a person may be described as a 'criminal' if their conduct is proscribed by rules set out either in legislation passed by Parliament or in court decisions.

The nature of crime: why do people commit crime?

Criminologists are concerned with examining the underlying causes of crime, using theories to explain why people engage in criminal behaviour. It is important to reflect on key theories in outline to understand how they might inform criminal justice policy, and to appreciate their influence on policing.

One such theory is derived from 'classical' criminology, which counts philosophers such as Jeremy Bentham and Cesare Beccaria as chief proponents (Joyce & Laverick, 2022). This explanation is premised on the idea that crime occurs because criminals make conscious choices to commit it; offenders are seen as rational, calculating individuals, exercising free will (Cornish & Clarke, 2014). Consequently, the primary aim of state intervention, through the mechanism of the criminal law, is to deter criminals from making bad choices; any resulting punishment must therefore be uniform and consistent, proportionate, and swiftly administered. Theories emerging from this classical school of thought – such as 'rational choice' theory (Cornish & Clarke, 2014) and 'routine activities' theory (Cohen & Felson, 1979) – focus on human agency and choices to offend and presuppose that if crime is chosen based on a cost/benefit analysis by the offender, tough punishments counter or deter criminal behaviour. Routine-activities theory emphasises that opportunities for criminality arise where there is a motivated offender, a suitable target, and the absence of a capable guardian (Cohen & Felson, 1979). To demonstrate the influence of this theory on criminal justice policy and practice, the police have adopted crime prevention strategies that reduce opportunities for criminal situations to arise, thereby enabling them to more effectively allocate crime reduction resources (College of Policing, 2021a). So-called 'hot spot' policing (Chapter 7) involves the mapping of crime, and targets particular areas that are prone to crime and anti-social behaviour, resulting in uneven crime distribution (Sherman et al., 1989; Weisburd et al., 2015), 'hot offenders' (prolific or high volume offenders responsible for a majority of crimes; Farrington et al., 2006), 'hot victims' (prone to repeat victimisation, often by the same perpetrator; SooHyun et al., 2017), and 'hot products' (prone to being stolen by offenders; Wood et al., 2024). Understanding what is causing high volume offending or problems in 'hot spots', and developing specific solutions or initiatives allows the police to drive down crime (College of Policing, 2021a). Examples include removing suitable targets ('target hardening' through the installation of anti-theft devices or additional surveillance measures such as CCTV to prevent situational crime), increasing visible police patrols to act as 'suitable guardians' in crime hotspots at specified times, and engaging problem-solving and community-based approaches to help reduce crime in the longer term, such as Neighbourhood Watch schemes (Braga et al., 2019). This 'hot' model of crime therefore forms part of problem-oriented policing strategies (Chapter 7), is linked to the National Intelligence Model, and is a core aspect of the neighbourhood policing strategy (Wood et al., 2024) (Chapter 8).

Critics argue that the classicist/neoclassicist focus on rationality does not account for offenders lacking the mental capacity to make rational choices to commit crime, does not sufficiently explain what leads people to exercise their rationality in radically different ways, and does not afford sufficient weight to environmental and social pressures influencing criminal behaviour (Steinmetz & Pratt, 2024). For these reasons, alternative accounts of criminal behaviour have been developed.

An alternative influential exposition of the reasons why crime is committed was proffered by 'positivists', emerging in the nineteenth century. In essence, positivists argue that crime results from factors beyond individual control (Joyce & Laverick, 2022). Positivist theorists are divided as to whether criminality should be attributed to the offender's biological, psychological or sociological dispositions. Some positivist theories suggest that criminality is dictated by an individual's biological make-up. Lombroso was a chief proponent of this school of thought; inspired by Darwin's theory of evolution, in his early work he concluded that criminals are essentially 'born criminal', in the sense that they were primitive beings who were biologically predisposed to crime and could be identified by distinct physical features (Lombroso, 1876). Despite subsequent discrediting of Lombroso's conclusions (Rock 2007), his work shifted the focus to the individual dispositions as a way of explaining offending, which marked a move away from approaches that focused on the free will and personal responsibility of the offender. More recent biological research explores the link between biological and social factors, focusing on finding possible genetic explanations for criminal behaviour (Brunner et al., 1993), locating biochemical explanations (such as hormonal explanations, or links to poor diet) and establishing intelligence-based or neurophysiological explanations (e.g. learning disabilities caused by brain damage) (Raine, 2008). Interesting though this research is, it remains difficult to determine the extent to which predisposition to crime is the result of biological characteristics (Newburn, 2017).

With these limitations in mind, others prefer to root their explanations of crime in the psychological make-up of the offender. The pioneering work of Sigmund Freud suggested that human behaviour, including criminality, is shaped by underlying forces, revealed through a process of psychoanalysis, proposing that personality, and thereby propensity to criminal behaviour, was influenced by childhood experiences (Newburn, 2017). This work paved the way for other psychological explanations of criminal behaviour, based on, for example, cognition, personality, parenting and trauma, but these explanations have often faced criticism for focusing on the psychological profile of the offender at the expense of broader social considerations that may impact criminal behaviour (Hollin, 2012).

In response to criticisms of alternative theories, numerous sociological explanations for crime have developed which emphasise social factors influencing criminal behaviour, such as poverty, unemployment, and familial or peer influences. One important theoretical approach emerged from research conducted by sociologists at the University of Chicago (the 'Chicago School') in the 1920s and 1930s, which sought to explain crime as a product of the environment. The concept of 'social disorganisation' was developed predominantly by Shaw and McKay (1942), whose research on the spatial pattern of crime suggested that criminal activity is a product of neighbourhood dynamics. They suggested that patterns of delinquency were higher in areas beleaguered by socio-economic disadvantage, poor housing, poor health, and transient populations. Several policing strategies and models of crime prevention have emerged, underscored by these theoretical advancements. For example, grounded in the suggestion advanced by 'broken windows' theory, that early intervention in low-level crime prevents escalation (Kelling & Wilson, 1982), 'zero-tolerance' approaches have garnered favour in certain forces at times in the UK, following successful strategies employed in New York in the 1990s (Squires, 2017). There is evidence to suggest, however, that policing low level disorder aggressively is not always an effective crime reduction strategy (Braga et al., 2019), with community-based policing approaches perhaps holding more promise to strengthen social control (Lombardo & Lough, 2007).

Other sociological research links crime to social upheaval. Durkheim's concept of 'anomie' describes a breakdown of social norms and an associated rise in criminal activity as an accompaniment to rapid social change (Durkheim, 1970). In essence, the suggestion is that when collective conscience is diminished, people feel socially disconnected (or less integrated) and are therefore more likely to offend. Building on this idea, Merton's 'strain theory' posits that a more constant social inequality, and the gap between cultural aspirations and the structural means to achieve them cause frustration and resentment, drives criminal behaviour (Merton, 1938). Modern sociological theorists continue to explore 'strains' (e.g. familial, economic, peer groups) that influence criminality (Agnew & Brezina, 2019).

Indeed, a variety of subcultural theories have developed, which focus on group responses to the inability to achieve societal goals. Criminologist Cohen coined the term 'status frustration' to describe the situation where working-class youths, unable to attain the middle-class values dominating society, engage in delinquent behaviour that leads to the emergence of a deviant subculture, chiefly concerned with achieving status within the peer group (Cohen, 1955). Other social learning theories are predicated on the premise that crime is a learned behaviour, an idea underpinned by 'differential association' theory (Sutherland et al., 1992) which asserts that criminality is developed through association with criminals or people who deem criminal activity acceptable. These theories underscore policies that acknowledge criminal behaviour could potentially be countered by creating social environments in which it is deemed unacceptable, and can be used as a basis for imposing less punitive, more supportive and preventative approaches to crime e.g. to divert young people away from offending, working with youth offending teams, and engaging communities (Hobson et al., 2021). Explanatory models of criminality may therefore inform the contemporary policing of gang-related culture and crime, encouraging collaboration with stakeholders (e.g. social workers, schools, parents) to divert potential offenders and disrupt associations (for examples of initiatives, see College of Policing, 2024).

Other contemporary criminological theories focus on state agents that control deviant behaviour, rather than the individual offender. Becker's 'labelling theory' asserts that the stigmatisation of offenders encourages continued deviance, suggesting that state action (especially from the police) can amplify criminal behaviour (Becker, 1963). Although often criticised for being vague and simplistic (Bernburg, 2019), this theory has been central to, for example, diversion interventions, where adults and children committing low level crime are diverted away from formal criminal justice processes to avoid stigmatisation (Centre for Justice Innovation, 2024). Labelling theory also has implications for police treatment of communities and individual offenders. To illustrate, the College of Policing emphasise 'procedural justice' approaches to policing, advocating the need for 'fair decision-making and respectful treatment' to avoid labelling and its negative effects on respect for, and compliance with, authority, and to enhance police legitimacy in the eyes of the public (College of Policing, 2021b). Ensuring that individuals feel valued and respected, in turn, promotes individual responsibility and may ultimately lead to crime reduction. However, the efficacy of procedural justice approaches, particularly for individuals or communities with negative past experiences with police, is arguably under-researched (Nagin and Telep, 2020).

This outline synopsis of some important theoretical accounts of criminal behaviour highlights complex factors leading to crime. While criminal justice practitioners (including the police) may not be able to change the deep-seated conditions that lead to crime, awareness of criminological theories can positively influence policy and practice. This is especially important in the context of policing, given the increased momentum towards developing policing strategies and approaches that are based on evidence of what works and what does not. The subsequent section examines the role various criminal justice agencies, alongside the police, in securing justice.

The current professional practice of delivering criminal justice

The criminal justice system is composed of various institutions with the primary aim of upholding the law and bringing perpetrators of crime to justice, which is achieved through enforcement (largely the task of the police and prosecuting agencies), by determining the guilt of the defendant and the appropriate sentence (the domain of the criminal courts), by engaging the penal system where appropriate (e.g. through the prison and probation service), and finally through crime prevention (involving a variety of public and private agencies, including the police). The overarching objectives of the system within which each individual agency operates include public protection, promoting the rule of law by ensuring due process and procedural safeguards are adhered to, maintaining public order, denouncing criminal behaviour through social disapproval, delivering appropriate punishments, providing services for victims of crime, and inspiring public confidence in the justice system (Davies, Croall and Tyrer, 2015). However, these goals are often in conflict with one another, and the prioritisation of a particular aim is often dependent on the political concerns of the day, with successive governments struggling to achieve a satisfactory balance.

Understanding the role of the police in this wider context requires knowledge of key institutions within the criminal justice system, such as the Crown Prosecution Service, the courts and the prison and probation services. This chapter proceeds with a brief commentary on the historical context, current structure, organisation, and the processes and procedures practiced therein. Current approaches to punishment, youth justice and victim support also warrant some consideration. In addition to the primary agencies considered in the following subsections, several smaller organisations play important roles in criminal justice delivery in England and Wales. These include coroners, the Criminal Injuries Compensation Authority, His Majesty's Inspectorate of Constabulary and Fire & Rescue Services and the Parole Board. The effective operation of the criminal justice system also relies on the involvement of lay people as volunteers, such as magistrates and victim support volunteers, and private sector agencies, such as private security providers, detectives and bailiffs.

The police

Those working and volunteering within policing have varied roles and responsibilities including maintaining order, law enforcement, public protection, crime investigation and crime prevention. The specific roles and responsibilities of the police, and the nature and extent of police powers and processes, are considered in more detail in other chapters.

The Home Office oversees the 43 territorial police services in England and Wales. Except for the Metropolitan Police Service, each force is headed by a chief constable, whose work is directed by a police and crime commissioner (PCC). The PCC role, introduced in 2012 by the Police Reform and Social Responsibility Act 2011, replaced the now abolished police authorities to enhance accountability. PCCs are elected to secure efficient and effective policing in their areas; this is achieved by the production, implementation and monitoring of a police and crime plan which includes details of policing objectives, resource allocation from the police fund, and performance measurement. By the authority of the Policing and Crime Act 2017, some PCCs also have responsibility for fire and rescue service governance (titled police, fire and crime commissioners, or PFCCs).

The twenty-first century has seen dramatic societal changes, particularly driven by technological advancements and the impact of the COVID-19 pandemic, with the consequence that offending is evolving. The complexity of modern crimes such as counter-terrorism, cybercrime and violence against women and girls, present significant challenges for policing (College of Policing, 2020). The continued growth of more diverse communities means that to maintain legitimacy and increase public confidence, police personnel must reflect the diversity of the communities they serve. Simultaneously, public spending cuts have also impacted the police force's ability to respond effectively to contemporaneous demands. It is against this backdrop that efforts to modernise and professionalise the police service have gained momentum, the ambition being to transform policing into a reflective, enquiring and trustworthy profession, where officers can use discretion, make decisions and public finances are used wisely (Knutsson & Tompson, 2017).

It is clear that policing is at a critical juncture in its history, and the challenges and opportunities for policing are explored further throughout this textbook. For now, it is important to recognise the central role that the police play as 'gatekeepers' of the entire criminal justice system, working alongside a variety of other agencies in the pursuit of justice. As often the first point of contact with the criminal justice system for both offenders and victims, the police are usually involved in the initial investigation of the alleged offence(s). If a prosecution is subsequently pursued, this is usually either police-led (in respect of less serious, summary or lower level either-way crimes) or initiated by the Crown Prosecution Service (CPS) (who prosecute on behalf of the Crown in respect of more serious, indictable or higher-level either-way offences) (Crown Prosecution Service, 2020). Since 2010, and the decision to increase responsibility for the police to make charging and prosecution decisions, the number of police-led prosecutions has grown significantly; but since the CPS retains responsibility for more complex and serious cases, it is therefore central to the operation of the criminal justice system.

The Crown Prosecution Service

The Crown Prosecution Service (CPS), created by the Prosecution of Offences Act 1985, is an independent body that prosecutes criminal cases on behalf of the state, independently from the police. It operates through 14 regional teams, each led by a Chief Crown Prosecutor, working alongside local police forces and other criminal justice partners to ensure the delivery of justice. The Director of Public Prosecutions is the head of the CPS and is accountable to the Attorney General, who is ultimately responsible to Parliament for the conduct and performance of the service (Crown Prosecution Service, 2018a).

The CPS advises the police on potential prosecutions, reviews cases that have been investigated by the police, and decides whether to prosecute, guided by the Code for Crown Prosecutors (Crown Prosecution Service, 2018b). In essence, the prosecutor must be satisfied that there is sufficient evidence to provide a realistic prospect of conviction, and that pursuing a prosecution is in the public interest. If these conditions are satisfied, the CPS then decides which specific charge should be laid against the accused person. Alongside this role, the CPS is also responsible for preparing cases for prosecution in court and instructing appropriate advocates (solicitors and barristers acting as Crown prosecutors) to present the cases and is also tasked with supporting victims and witnesses to assist their effective participation in the criminal justice process (Crown Prosecution Service, 2018a). Central to any successful prosecution is the preparation of accurate case files which provide key evidence and relevant information to the prosecutor, defence, and the court (subject to the National File Standard; Crown Prosecution Service, 2020), and in order to effect a fair trial, the prosecution has a duty to ensure that all relevant evidence is disclosed (i.e. material is provided to the defence that may assist them in defending themselves, in accordance with the Criminal Procedure and Investigations Act 1996).

In the years since the CPS was formed, the process for progressing a case to court has become increasingly inefficient. While the police and the CPS have a shared desire to achieve a high standard of casework, and there are examples of very effective partnership working, it is evident that the pursuit of high-quality prosecutions is often hindered by cultural and communication barriers that ultimately fail victims of crime, with the two agencies often reportedly working in silos. Disclosure issues are deep-rooted, and the way in which both the police and the CPS exercise their duties in this regard has been the subject of intense criticism (Bowcott, 2018), resulting in the production of a National Disclosure Improvement Plan 2018, to encourage more effective joint working (Crown Prosecution Service, 2018c). More recently a joint inspection report suggested that ongoing challenges are derived from differing priorities, overly bureaucratic systems and processes and the lack of data sharing, not to mention resource constraints that impact the time taken to charge suspects, with a knock-on effect on victims (Criminal Justice Joint Inspection, 2024a). The relationship between the police and the CPS has come under further strain against a backdrop of other challenging circumstances, particularly evident since the COVID-

19 pandemic, including a significant backlog of cases in the courts (Ministry of Justice, 2024a), and the fact that the prison population is almost full (Ministry of Justice, 2024b).

Despite these challenges, it is clear that the CPS plays a crucial role in progressing deserving cases to court, and the maintenance of an effective working relationship between the police and the CPS is vital for ensuring justice. Once it has been determined that a prosecution is warranted, and the suspect is formally charged, they become a 'defendant' and the criminal case will proceed to court, where guilt will be determined; the criminal court process is examined in the next section.

The criminal courts – establishing criminal liability

The court system in England and Wales operates on an adversarial basis, whereby two 'adversaries' (one acting for the prosecution, the other for the defence) work in opposition to determine the defendant's guilt, which must be established beyond reasonable doubt (Gillespie & Weare, 2023).

Given that the standard of proof in criminal cases is so high, it is important to understand how criminal liability is established in the first instance. Although laws relating to specific criminal offences are many and varied, most criminal offences (with the exception of strict liability offences) require two elements to be proven before guilt can be established: that the defendant has engaged in proscribed conduct (known as the '*actus reus*' of the offence); and that the defendant also has an accompanying guilty state of mind (known as the '*mens rea*' of the offence). Each offence has its own unique *actus reus* and *mens rea* elements, which are expressed in either decided cases (thereby constituting 'common law' offences), or in statutory provisions (thereby constituting 'statutory' offences; Herring, 2024). As part of the process of determining the defendant's culpability, the defence may also contest guilt by raising one of the established defences (e.g. self-defence, duress or insanity) if there are circumstances that furnish the offender with a justification or excuse for what would otherwise be deemed criminal conduct. If the requirements of any proposed defence are satisfied, the defendant may be absolved of criminal responsibility, either completely or partially, depending on the nature of the defence being raised (Herring, 2024).

Classification of offences and the criminal court process

All criminal cases start in a magistrates' court, with subsequent case progression depending on the severity of the offence. If charged with a summary offence (that is, a minor criminal offence), the case will usually be determined in a magistrates' court, which has limited penalties at its disposal if guilt is proven (Magistrates' Court Act 1980, as amended). If charged with an indictable offence (that is, a more serious criminal offence such as murder or rape), the case will be referred to a Crown Court. If charged with an offence that is 'triable either way' (an offence that can be more or less serious, depending on the circumstances), the defendant can opt for their case to be tried in the magistrates' court or in the Crown Court (Criminal Procedure Rules 2020, in particular part 9). If a case is tried summarily in the magistrates' court, it may be presided over by either a bench of three lay magistrates (known as 'justices of the peace') or a district judge, a qualified lawyer, sitting alone. Magistrates are lay volunteers who receive appropriate training and are assisted by legally qualified court clerks. If the case falls to be determined in a Crown Court, and no guilty plea is entered, a jury will decide guilt or innocence (Gillespie & Weare, 2023). In addition to the role of the police in investigating and charging a defendant, officers may also sometimes be required to give evidence during these court proceedings, usually as an 'officer in the case' (OIC); hence familiarisation with court procedures and processes is essential.

It is important to note that there are a range of other courts operating within the criminal justice arena that may need to be engaged as part of the process of bringing perpetrators of crime to justice (for example, specialist domestic violence or youth courts). If either the prosecution or defence appeal the defendant's conviction or ensuing sentence, there are appeal courts that will determine the outcome. The most prominent of these appellate courts are the Court of Appeal (the Criminal Division of which presides over criminal appeals from the Crown Court) and the Supreme Court (the highest court in the United Kingdom, which is the final appeal court for both criminal and civil cases; Courts and Tribunals Judiciary, 2024).

Sentencing

Following a guilty verdict, judges in the criminal court will determine the appropriate sentence. Various sentences can be imposed, including discharges (absolute or conditional), fines, community sentences (which place particular requirements on an offender, e.g. to serve the community by clearing overgrown areas or engaging in a drug treatment programme), and prison sentences (which can be suspended, determinate or indeterminate). When determining an appropriate and proportionate sentence, consideration must be given to the nature of the offence and its severity, and the circumstances within which it was committed. For instance, any admission of guilt, any criminal history and the personal and financial circumstances of the defendant may be considered. Relevant sentencing guidelines must also be consulted; these guidelines are produced by the Sentencing Council, created by the Coroners and Justice Act 2009, with the aim of ensuring consistency in sentencing (see www.sentencingcouncil.org.uk). Prior to 2024, the focus on imposing tougher sentences, without prioritising the speed and certainty of sentencing, led to debates about the efficacy of sentencing practices (Tony Blair Institute for Global Change, 2023). Ensuring timely and certain sentencing is essential for maintaining public confidence in the justice system and achieving the desired deterrent effect.

As alluded to above, sentences are administered either in prisons or in the community, and therefore joint responsibility for punishing and rehabilitating offenders lies with prison and probation services; it is to these institutions we now turn.

The penal system: prison and probation

The purpose of punishment

Before outlining the purpose and function of prison and probation services, attention must be drawn to the significant body of academic literature devoted to the scientific study of punishment, known as 'penology'. While any detailed discussion of this topic is not possible here, it is important to identify key objectives underlying penal strategies for criminal behaviour to understand why certain punishments are, or have been, preferred and to evaluate their effectiveness.

There is a significant body of literature devoted to developing an understanding of what penal responses are designed to achieve. Simply put, penal strategies have either reductivist or retributivist aims (Joyce and Laverick, 2022). Reductivist strategies are forward-looking and seek to prevent future criminal behaviour through deterrence (general or individual), incapacitation (restricting the ability of the offender to reoffend) and rehabilitation (to encourage behavioural change). Retributivist strategies, conversely, focus on the justifications for punishment of criminal conduct that has already taken place; in short, criminals should be punished because they deserve it. According to this strategic approach, public condemnation of the crime is an important aspect of punishment. Governmental policies have historically placed different emphases on these objectives, swayed by prevailing political inclinations and public attitudes (Joyce & Laverick, 2022). Recently, restorative or reparative approaches to justice, focused on repairing harm through dialogue between offenders and victims, have gained significant attention in criminological research (O'Mahony & Doak, 2017). Restorative justice is reductivist in nature, but its primary focus is not on punishment; it is designed to aid the reintegration of the offender into the community and can arguably be more beneficial to victims than more traditional criminal justice responses.

Imprisonment is the harshest sanction available to the courts on conviction of the offender, and much of the discussion concerning the objectives of punishment outlined above is particularly pertinent to the debate about the efficacy of the prison and probation systems. In an effort to reform and rehabilitate offenders, and with a view to discouraging reoffending, it was decided that a joined-up approach was required to support offenders both within prison and on subsequent release. His Majesty's Prison and Probation Service (2024a) (formerly the National Offender Management Service) was therefore created and is responsible for the running of both prison and probation services in England and Wales. It comprises both His Majesty's Prison Service and the Probation Service; the purpose and function of each of these services, and their relevance to policing, is considered in the following sections.

The prison service

According to its statement of purpose, His Majesty's Prison Service (HMPS) is charged with keeping offenders who have been sentenced to prison in custody and, therein and on subsequent release, helping them to lead law-abiding and useful lives (His Majesty's Prison Service, 2024). The extent to which the service achieves this laudable aim is a topic of great debate.

The prison system has been through several significant developments, with its evolution reflecting changing penal rationales. According to a useful historical summary provided by Davies et al., (2015), prisons have changed from being places where suspects were held while awaiting trial or punishment in the sixteenth and seventeenth centuries, to the eighteenth century era of imprisonment with hard labour (or, alternatively transportation to British colonies), to the emergence of the first state prison in the early nineteenth century. All the while, the rationale for imposing custodial sentences on criminals was shifting. In the late eighteenth century, prisons were viewed as institutions aimed at deterring future criminal behaviour by offering opportunities for criminals to reform; but the nineteenth century saw a shift to a rationale based on deterrence through the imposition of harsh conditions, thereby discouraging future criminal conduct. By the end of the nineteenth century, in large part due to the Gladstone Report of 1895, rehabilitation was emphasised as a primary objective of custodial sentences. Although rehabilitative functions were not subsequently abandoned altogether, the approach of the twentieth-century Conservative governments to prisons gave rise to a more retributivist approach that appealed to penal populism and prioritised the punishment of wrongdoers who chose to break the law. The 'prison works' movement emerged in the 1990s; this phrase alluded to the increasing prison population at the time, which the Conservative government applauded as demonstrative of the success of their robust, retributive policies with respect to custodial sentences (Davies et al., 2015).

In more recent years, the numbers of offenders residing in prisons has steadily risen and the political rhetoric that 'prison works' has, in reality, foundered against a background of economic austerity, and growing recognition that increasing numbers of incarcerated people is not necessarily a marker of success. Currently 123 prisons operating across England and Wales, housing over 87,000 inmates, with 109 managed by HMPS, the remaining 14 by private companies (Ministry of Justice, 2024b). The effectiveness of the prison system has long been contentious (Chamberlen and Carvalho, 2019). Recent reports have highlighted the consequences of years of underinvestment: a growing prison population serving increasingly longer sentences, significantly reduced staff numbers, and prison estates not fit for purpose, with overcrowding and squalid conditions rife (Taylor, 2024). There is a continuing rise in violence, drug abuse and self-harm in prisons, as confirmed by recent figures released by the Ministry of Justice (2024b). Stubbornly high reoffending rates also persist, especially amongst those serving short term sentences, with concerns raised about the ability of prisons to engage prisoners in meaningful rehabilitative activity which actively supports them to reduce their reoffending risk (Taylor, 2024). Intense political debates are ongoing, and measures are being introduced by the newly elected Labour government to replace short-term prison sentences with community orders to address the root causes of criminality, with many arguing that prison should be a weapon of last resort reserved only for those who have committed the most serious and dangerous offences (Ministry of Justice, 2024c).

Despite these challenges, the prison system remains a pivotal cog in the machinery of criminal justice. The success of any potential future shift in focus from prison to community sentences in respect of lower risk offenders to ensure the smooth transition of offenders back into communities is dependent on the effective operation of, and collaboration with, the probation service.

The probation service

The Probation of Offenders Act 1907 established the first formal statutory probation service which permitted courts to appoint probation officers to guide offenders on release from prison. Significant transformation followed including, in more recent history, the creation of the National Probation Service for England and Wales in 2001 (established by the Criminal Justice and Court Services Act 2000). In 2007, the Offender Management Act introduced further structural changes to this service, including the creation of Probation Trusts which supervised activities required under community orders, but these Trusts were later abolished by the Offender Rehabilitation Act 2014. In place of the Trusts, a new National Probation Service (NPS) was established in 2014, against a backdrop of significant criticisms of probation services, with governmental promises to transform rehabilitation. Operating in partnership with the NPS (who were responsible for managing high risk offenders), were 21 privately run community rehabilitation companies (CRCs) charged with managing low and medium risk offenders (Joyce and Laverick, 2022).

Despite some valuable work undertaken by the NPS, there was concern that offenders were not being properly supervised or supported in their rehabilitation, largely due to restricted budgets, leading to staff shortages, heavy caseloads and communication systems that were not fit for purpose, problems recognised by the Probation Inspectorate, which described the 'Transforming Rehabilitation' model as 'fundamentally flawed' (Her Majesty's Inspectorate of Probation, 2017). There were concerns that the CRCs, in particular, were not operating effectively and that some medium-to-low risk offenders were committing more serious crimes on release as levels of communication with the probation staff were sometimes negligible. As a direct result of sustained criticisms, a new unified public sector Probation Service was created in 2021, merging the NPS divisions and the private CRCs to enhance service effectiveness.

The Probation Service supervises offenders released into the community and aims to protect the public. It has responsibility for sentence management, along with Accredited Programmes, Unpaid Work and Structured Interventions. Other rehabilitative and resettlement needs are delivered by Commissioned Rehabilitative Service providers, who provide vital support services, such as employment, education and training, accommodation, well-being and women's services (Probation Service, 2024). The Probation Service also provides pre-sentence reports to courts to support them to make informed, appropriate, and proportionate sentencing decisions, and it plays an important role in monitoring compliance with sentences post-release. In the case of those convicted of violent, sexual and terrorism offences who are living in the community, the probation service works closely with the police and prison service, via multi-agency public protection arrangements (MAPPA) provided for in the Criminal Justice Act 2003, to manage offender risk and provide public protection in a co-ordinated way (His Majesty's Prison and Probation Service, 2024b).

When functioning effectively the probation service, which has both punitive and rehabilitative functions, is vital for public protection and reducing reoffending. Sustained investment, settled offender management structures, and effective collaboration with other agencies (including the police), is essential for improving offenders' lives and fulfilling the mission of the service.

The youth justice system

While the introductory nature of this chapter precludes any detailed analysis of the youth justice system, it is important for aspiring police officers to be aware that the criminal justice system affords different treatment to children and young people (defined respectively by the Children and Young Persons Act 1933 as a person under the age of 14, and someone who has attained the age of 14 and is under 18). A brief synopsis of some key policies, laws and processes, designed to ensure the criminal justice system acknowledges disparities in levels of maturity and understanding between adult and young offenders is required.

The range of measures available to deal with young offenders has varied over time. This variance is broadly reflective of two divergent approaches to achieving youth justice: one focuses on the reasons why the crime was committed and prioritises the welfare of young people by, for example, promoting diversion and rehabilitation; the other concentrates on the crime committed and encourages accountability through the implementation of punitive sanctions. These competing priorities affect the way in which 'youth justice' is perceived, and therefore delivered, by the various criminal justice agencies.

The law, somewhat controversially (McDiarmid, 2013), requires that only children aged ten years and over can be criminally responsible for their conduct (Children and Young Persons Act 1933, section 50 as amended). The age of the accused will also determine their subsequent treatment by the justice system in terms of trial and punishment. Youth Courts, established by the Criminal Justice Act 1991, handle the majority of offences committed by young offenders aged 10–17 (with a minority of trials for the most serious offences taking place in adult courts, often with special adaptations made). The sentence imposed on a convicted young offender varies depending on the court in which they are tried, but there is a range of specific sentencing options at the courts' disposal, including discharges (absolute or conditional), referral orders, reparation orders, Youth Rehabilitation Orders or custodial sentences (always used as a last resort; Sentencing Council for England and Wales, 2024).

The Youth Justice Board (YJB), established by the Crime and Disorder Act 1998, oversees the youth justice system in England and Wales, supervising multi-disciplinary youth offending teams (YOTs) in every local area. YOTs operate independently of the police and the courts with the aim of preventing children and young people offending and reoffending (Ministry of Justice, 2024d). Each team consists of personnel from a range of agencies, including representatives from social services, the police, probation, education and health services, drug and alcohol misuse teams and housing authorities. YOTs are often contacted by the police and become involved with young people who are either arrested, charged, or convicted of a crime and given a sentence. Key YOT interventions, engaged at various stages of the criminal justice process, include the delivery of crime prevention programmes, assisting young people at the police stations and courts, supervising young people with a community sentence, and keeping in touch with a young person sentenced to a period of imprisonment (Ministry of Justice, 2024d). YOTs therefore play a significant role in achieving justice for young offenders and the victims of their crimes.

The treatment by the criminal justice system of victims impacted by the crimes of both young and adult offenders is considered in the subsequent section.

Victims of crime

An awareness of the impact that crime can have on victims, and of academic research in respect of victims, is also essential to a broader understanding of criminal justice. Although historically side-lined by a system whose adversarial model of justice focused almost exclusively on the perpetrator of crime (Davies et al., 2015), there is now greater acknowledgement that victims are a crucial part of the criminal justice system, often initiating the criminal justice process by reporting crimes in the first instance.

In recognition of the previously peripheral position of victims in the criminal justice process, in the last few decades successive governments have committed to providing increased support for victims through the introduction of a range of practical measures. For example, the police automatically pass on the victim's information to Victim Support, an independent charity that seeks to ensure the needs of victims are met in the criminal justice system (see www.victimsupport.org.uk). A Code of Practice for Victims of Crime (the 'Victims' Code') was also introduced by the Domestic Violence, Crime and Victims Act 2004, and the recently enacted Victims and Prisoners Act 2024 confirms that adherence to the Code is now mandatory - victims *require* protection of the rights contained therein, with consequences for criminal justice agencies, including the police, for non-compliance. This statutory code proscribes the minimum level of service that victims should receive from each of the criminal justice agencies they encounter. Perhaps most significantly, the Code stipulates that victims must be kept informed about the progress of the case by the police and must be informed when a suspect is arrested, charged, bailed, or sentenced. Particularly vulnerable victims can also apply for additional help (known as 'special measures') when giving evidence in court. The Victim Personal Statement Scheme permits victims of crime the opportunity to make a statement detailing how the crime has affected them, which may be read out in court. As already mentioned earlier, victims may also access restorative justice activities, where the victim can explain to the offender the impact of their criminal behaviour and secure an apology or explanation for the behaviour from the offender (Ministry of Justice, 2024e).

Although victim-centric procedures have now been strengthened by the Victims and Prisoners Act 2024, it will be important to carefully monitor whether the measures are being put into practice, with important implications for operational policing. Prior to the legislative change in 2024, it was reported that there were high levels of dissatisfaction with support mechanisms and routine failures to adhere to the Code in respect of the police, the CPS and the Probation Service (Criminal Justice Joint Inspection, 2024b). For example, the police were criticised for omitting to pass on victim information to support services, failing to inform victims of developments with investigations, and failing to offer victims a chance to make a personal statement (Dearden, 2018). The experience of female victims of rape, sexual offences and domestic abuse were reportedly often even more negative, with many victims citing long delays, case mishandling, poor levels of support and victim-blaming during police interactions (Victim Support, 2018; Baroness Casey Review, 2023). It is evident, therefore, that concentrated efforts to improve victim support mechanisms are required to meet newly imposed statutory obligations and to increase confidence in the system.

As part of this agenda, the Victims' Commissioner will continue to advocate for, and represent the interests and views of, victims and witnesses. This role was created by the Domestic Violence, Crimes and Victims Act 2004, and operates independently of the government and criminal justice agencies to ensure that the concerns of victims and witnesses are voiced and that the various criminal justice organisations take their responsibilities to victims seriously. The Victims' Commissioner seeks to achieve this by, for example, listening to the concerns of victims and witnesses, engaging in research about victims' services to recommend positive changes, sharing good practice across criminal justice agencies and monitoring the implementation of the Victims' Code. The Commissioner also campaigns for positive changes to the support mechanisms in place for victims and witnesses, playing an instrumental role in driving recent changes to victim protections (see https://victimscommissioner.org.uk).

It is clear, then, that there is a commitment to ensuring that the people most directly affected by criminal behaviour can benefit from an improved criminal justice response, which, if delivered effectively, consults, informs and encourages victim input from first contact with the police through to the sentencing stage. Victim-focused innovations and a continuing commitment to championing the rights of victims and witnesses will remain an important part of the criminal justice system in the future.

Future developments and contemporary challenges

The criminal justice systems are dynamic, responding to evolving crimes, societal changes, and operational demands. The performance of the various criminal justice agencies has provoked much debate in recent years, with widespread reports of failures. It has been suggested that the system is locked in a cycle of decline; while the current crisis was no doubt exacerbated by the Covid-19 pandemic, the issues are longstanding. Complex police investigations and charging processes lead to delays and increased victim attrition, leaving the courts with a seemingly insurmountable backlog of cases. Judicial overreliance on prisons due to a lack of confidence in alternatives has resulted in overcrowded and increasingly dangerous prisons. The probation service is accused of offering ineffective supervision which jeopardises public protection and results in recidivism. These system-wide challenges stem from technological, environmental, and social transformations, policy shifts, and financial austerity, leaving the criminal justice system at a decisive point in its history (Tony Blair Institute for Global Change, 2023).

In terms of significant social transformation in the post-pandemic era, technological advances have begun to have a significant impact on criminal justice and will continue to do so in the future. Digital developments can be harnessed to promote efficiency through, for example, virtual court hearings, AI-enhanced crime prevention and investigation strategies, and better inter-agency collaboration (College of Policing, 2020). However, these advancements are also transforming the composition of crime and present novel problems for the delivery of justice. For instance, the system is responding to new forms of criminal activity (such as online fraud, cybercrime, and serious and organised crime that transcends geographical boundaries), and online disinformation that presents a threat to both individuals and communities, complicating justice delivery and demanding more effective responses (College of Policing, 2020).

At the centre of much of the unrest about the current state of the criminal justice system is a deep concern about the long-lasting impact of austerity measures introduced by the Conservative government between 2010 and 2017. Reduced staffing levels and increasing skills gaps heighten anxiety amongst professionals working within the system, for whom the appeal of such work is to deliver an effective public service that achieves justice. Within a policing context, austerity impacts have also prompted debate about the precise remit of the police, with the erosion of neighbourhood policing resulting in a more reactive police force focused on emergency response rather than crime prevention.

Aside from the direct impact of financial austerity on the practical workings of the criminal justice agencies, financial strain precipitated by austerity and a cost-of-living crisis also has broader societal impacts. Although the criminological research is ambiguous, it is at least conceivable that crime trends and rates are impacted in a climate of economic austerity. Depleted public sector spending on social and welfare provision may also result in a downturn in funding for allied services (e.g. relating to mental health, community safety, social services and social housing) which, in turn, places greater demands on criminal justice practitioners to respond to the associated needs of citizens (Barber, 2022).

It would seem, then, that the most significant future challenge is maintaining a fair and efficient criminal justice system, that promotes public trust and confidence, against a backdrop of substantial social, environmental, and technological transformation. The quality of processes and agencies delivering justice cannot be further compromised, and a sustained and collective effort from all the criminal justice agencies is required to deliver justice efficiently. The new Labour government's promise to 'reform the justice system to put the needs of victims first, tackle the prisons crisis and cut reoffending' (Labour Party Manifesto, 2024) signals a potential shift towards further transformation.

Conclusion

It is without doubt that justice is fundamental to the successful functioning of any civilised society, and the central purpose of the criminal justice system is to deliver a fair, effective, efficient and accountable process which brings offenders to justice. To assist with the implementation of the desired aims, criminal justice practitioners should develop an understanding of relevant criminological theories about the nature of crime and its underlying causes, in order to improve responses to crime. Knowledge and understanding of important criminological debates can benefit operational policing and decision making in a variety of different ways, not least because it encourages innovative problem-solving, provokes debate about the efficacy of pre-determined concepts (such as policing models), and provides evidence-based justifications for decision making. Indeed, criminological research has yielded some very robust evidence about crime, its causes and consequences that has been used to develop effective policies and practices within the criminal justice system.

There are several key agencies involved in the delivery of criminal justice, including the police, the CPS, the criminal courts, the prison service and the probation service. While the overarching aims of these agents of the state are laudable, each institution has attracted criticism on account of various failings; the extent to which the main agencies are achieving their objectives is therefore disputed, especially considering prevailing social and economic circumstances. There are certainly challenges ahead as the criminal justice system attempts to allay fears that it is amid a crisis and pursue its goals of maintaining the rule of law and creating a safer society for everyone. The police service, especially those officers and staff who interact daily with offenders, victims, and witnesses, are at the forefront of this mission.

> **Evidence-based case study illustrating professional practice**
>
> This case study highlights the collaboration between the key criminal justice agencies involved in the investigation, prosecution, and punishment of serious offences. Dom, a gang member, is arrested for allegedly stabbing and

killing a rival gang member in his local area. Although Dom claims innocence, on the basis that he was not in the vicinity when the incident took place, there is substantial evidence linking Dom to the crime. The police play a key role in investigating the incident; they collect relevant evidence and witness statements, which leads to Dom's arrest. The Crown Prosecution Service (CPS) subsequently reviews the case, determining that there is sufficient evidence and a public interest in prosecuting Dom for murder.

After being formally charged, Dom's initial hearing takes place in the magistrates' court, where it is determined that he should remain in custody until trial. Because it involves a serious, indictable-only offence, Dom's case moves to the Crown Court, where it is tried by a judge and jury. The prosecution presents evidence linking Dom to the crime, while Dom's defence counsel challenges it, maintaining that he was not present. Following a protracted trial, the jury unanimously find Dom guilty of murder. The judge imposes a mandatory life sentence, with a minimum term of 25 years before parole eligibility.

After sentencing, given the serious nature of his offending, Dom serves his time in a high-security prison. Upon completing the minimum term, he may apply for parole, which, if granted, would be subject to strict monitoring by the Probation Service. If released, he would remain on life licence, subject to recall if he violates conditions or commits further offences.

Reflective question

To what extent is it true to say the criminal justice system is a system in crisis? Explain your answer with reference to the various stages of the criminal justice process.

References

Agnew, R. & Brezina, T. (2019). General Strain Theory. In M. Krohn, N. Hendrix, G. Hall & A. Lizotte (eds), *Handbook on Crime and Deviance* (pp. 145–160). Cham, Switzerland: Springer.

Barber, M. (2022) The Final Report of Strategic Review of Policing in England and Wales: A New Mode of Protection – Redesigning Policing and Public Safety for the 21st Century. [online]. https://policingreview.org.uk/wp-content/uploads/srpew_final_report.pdf (accessed 15 September 2024).

Baroness Casey Review. (2023). Final Report: An Independent Review into the Standards of Behaviour and Internal Culture of the Metropolitan Police Service. [online]. www.met.police.uk/SysSiteAssets/media/downloads/met/about-us/baroness-casey-review/update-march-2023/baroness-casey-review-march-2023a.pdf (accessed 11 September 2024).

Becker, H. S. (1963). *Outsiders: Studies in the Sociology of Deviance*. New York: Free Press.

Bernburg, J. G. (2019). Labelling Theory. In M. Krohn, N. Hendrix, G. Hall & A. Lizotte (eds), *Handbook on Crime and Deviance* (pp. 179–196). Cham, Switzerland: Springer.

Bowcott, O. (2018). Failure to Disclose Evidence in Rape Trials a Sign of 'Dystopian Disaster' Engulfing Courts. *The Guardian*, 29 January. [online]. www.theguardian.com/law/2018/jan/29/underfunded-justice-system-crumbling-top-criminal-barrister-says (accessed 15 July 2024).

Braga, A., Turchan, B., Papachristos, A. & Hureau, D. (2019). Hot Spots Policing of Small Geographic Areas Effects on Crime. *Campbell Systematic Reviews*, 15(104). https://doi.org/10.1002/cl2.1046.

Brunner, H., Nelen, M., Breakefield, X., Ropers, H. & Van Oost, B. (1993). Abnormal Behaviour Associated with a Point Mutation in the Structural Gene for Monoamine Oxidase. *Science*, 22(262), 578–580, https://doi.org/10.1126/science.8211186.

Centre for Justice Innovation. (2024). Pre-court Disposals. [online]. https://justiceinnovation.org/areas-of-focus/pre-court-disposals (accessed 15 September 2024).

Chamberlen, A. & Carvalho, H. (2019). The Thrill of the Chase: Punishment, Hostility and the Prison Crisis. *Social & Legal Studies*, 28(1), 100–117https://doi.org/10.1177/0964663918759820.

Cohen, A. (1955). *Delinquent Boys: The Culture of the Gang*. Glencoe IL: The Free Press.

Cohen, L. & Felson, M. (1979). Social Change and Crime Rate Trends: A Routine Activity Approach. *American Sociological Review*, 44(4), 588–608.

College of Policing. (2020). Policing in England and Wales Future Operating Environment 2040 – Part 3, Future Challenges. [online]. https://assets.college.police.uk/s3fs-public/2020-08/Future-Operating-Environment-2040-Part3-Challenges.pdf (accessed 10 September 2024).

College of Policing. (2021a). People and Places – How Resources Can Be Targeted. [online]. www.college.police.uk/research/what-works-policing-reduce-crime/people-and-places (accessed 15 July 2024).

College of Policing. (2021b). What Stops People Offending. [online]. www.college.police.uk/research/what-works-policing-reduce-crime/what-stops-people-offending (accessed 15 August 2024).

College of Policing. (2024). Vulnerability and Violent Crime Interventions. [online]. www.college.police.uk/research/vulnerability-violent-crime-interventions (accessed 15 October 2024).

Cornish, D. & Clarke, R. (eds). (2014). *The Reasoning Criminal: Rational Choice Perspectives on Offending*. New Brunswick, NJ: Transaction Publishers.

Courts and Tribunals Judiciary. (2024). Structure of Courts and Tribunals System. [online]. www.judiciary.uk/structure-of-courts-and-tribunals-system/ (accessed 15 September 2024).

Criminal Justice Joint Inspection. (2024a). Joint Case Building by the Police and Crown Prosecution Service Interim Findings from Phase 1 of a Joint Inspection by HMCPSI and HMICFRS of Case Building by the Police and Crown Prosecution Service. [online]. www.justiceinspectorates.gov.uk/cjji/wp-content/uploads/sites/2/2024/01/Joint-case-building-by-the-police-and-Crown-Prosecution-Service-7.pdf (accessed 15 September 2024).

Criminal Justice Joint Inspection. (2024b). Meeting the Needs of Victims in the Criminal Justice System: An Inspection of How Well the Police, the CPS and the Probation Service Support Victims of Crime. [online]. www.justiceinspectorates.gov.uk/cjji/wp-content/uploads/sites/2/2023/12/meeting-needs-of-victims-inspection-police-cps-and-probation-1.pdf (accessed 15 July 2024).

Crown Prosecution Service. (2018a). About CPS. [online]. www.cps.gov.uk/about-cps.

Crown Prosecution Service. (2018b). Code for Crown Prosecutors. [online]. www.cps.gov.uk/publication/code-crown-prosecutors (accessed 15 September 2024).

Crown Prosecution Service. (2018c). National Disclosure Improvement Plan, 26 January 2018. [online]. www.cps.gov.uk/publication/national-disclosure-improvement-plan (accessed 15 September 2024).

Crown Prosecution Service. (2020). Director's Guidance on Charging, sixth edition, December 2020, incorporating the National File Standard. *The Crown Prosecution Service*. [online] www.cps.gov.uk/legal-guidance/directors-guidance-charging-sixth-edition-december-2020-incorporating-national-file (accessed 15 September 2024).

Davies, M., Croall, H. & Tyrer, J. (2015). *Criminal Justice*, 5th edition. Harlow: Pearson Education.

Dearden, L. (2018). Victims 'Increasingly Failed by Authorities' as Confidence in Criminal Justice System Falls, Research Shows. *The Independent*, 3 August. [online]. www.independent.co.uk/news/uk/crime/police-victims-failed-confidence-reporting-dangerous-support-criminal-justice-system-a8476811.html (accessed 15 July 2024).

Durkheim, E. (1970). *Suicide*. London: Routledge & Kegan Paul.

Farrington, D., Coid, J. W., Harnett, L. M., Jolliffe, D., Soteriou, N., Turner, R. E. & West, D. J. (2006). *Criminal Careers up to Age 50 and Life Success up to Age 48: New Findings from the Cambridge Study in Delinquent Development* (2nd edition). London: Home Office.

Gillespie, A. & Weare, S. (2023). *The English Legal System*, 9th edition. Oxford: Oxford University Press.

Herring, J. (2024). *Criminal Law: Text, Cases and Materials*, 11th edition. Oxford: Oxford University Press.

Her Majesty's Inspectorate of Probation. (2017). Annual Report. [online]. www.justiceinspectorates.gov.uk/hmiprobation/corporate-documents/annualreport2017/ (accessed 15 September 2024).

His Majesty's Prison and Probation Service. (2024a). About Us. [online]. www.gov.uk/government/organisations/hm-prison-and-probation-service/about (accessed 15 July 2024).

His Majesty's Prison and Probation Service. (2024b). *MAPPA Guidance*. London: HM Prison and Probation Service.

His Majesty's Prison Service. (2024). About Us. [online]. www.gov.uk/government/organisations/hm-prison-service/about (accessed 15 July 2024).

Hobson, J., Lynch, K., Payne, B. & Ellis, L. (2021). Are Police-Led Social Crime Prevention Initiatives Effective? A Process and Outcome Evaluation of a UK Youth Intervention. *International Criminal Justice Review*, 31(3), 325–346. https://doi.org/10.1177/1057567718814891.

Hollin, C. (2012). *Psychology and Crime*, 2nd edition. London: Routledge.

Joyce, P. & Laverick, W. (2022). *Criminal Justice: An Introduction*, 4th edition. London: Routledge.

Kelling, G. & Wilson, J. (1982). Broken Windows: The Police and Neighbourhood Safety. *Atlantic Monthly*, 249 (3). www.theatlantic.com/magazine/archive/1982/03/broken-windows/304465/.

Knutsson, J. & Tompson, L. (2017). *Advances in Evidence-Based Policing*. New York, NY: Routledge.

Labour Party Manifesto. (2024). Take Back our Streets. [online]. https://labour.org.uk/change/take-back-our-streets/ (accessed 15 August 2024).

Lombardo, R. & Lough, T. (2007). Community Policing: Broken Windows, Community Building, and Satisfaction with the Police. *Police Journal*, 80(2), 117–140https://doi.org/10.1350/pojo.2007.80.2.117.

Lombroso, C. (1876). L'Uomo Delinquente. [online]. www.bl.uk/collection-items/luomo-delinquente (accessed 15 July 2024).

McDiarmid, C. (2013). An Age of Complexity: Children and Criminal Responsibility in Law. *Youth Justice*, 13(2), 145–160 https://doi.org/10.1177/1473225413492056.

Merton, R. (1938). Social Structure and Anomie. *American Sociological Review*, 3. 672–682. https://doi.org/10.2307/2084686.

Ministry of Justice. (2024a). Courts Data: Criminal Courts. [online]. https://data.justice.gov.uk/courts/criminal-courts (accessed 15 July 2024).

Ministry of Justice. (2024b). Prisons Data. [online]. https://data.justice.gov.uk/prisons (accessed 15 July 2024).

Ministry of Justice. (2024c). Lord Chancellor Sets Out Immediate Action to Defuse Ticking Prison Time Bomb. [online]. www.gov.uk/government/news/lord-chancellor-sets-out-immediate-action-to-defuse-ticking-prison-time-bomb (accessed 15 July 2024).

Ministry of Justice. (2024d). Youth Justice Board: About Us. [online]. www.gov.uk/government/organisations/youth-justice-board-for-england-and-wales/about (accessed 12 September 2024).

Ministry of Justice. (2024e). Code of Practice for Victims of Crime in England and Wales. [online]. www.gov.uk/government/publications/the-code-of-practice-for-victims-of-crime/code-of-practice-for-victims-of-crime-in-england-and-wales-victims-code (accessed 15 August 2024).

Nagin, D. & Telep, C. (2020). Procedural Justice and Legal Compliance: A Revisionist Perspective. *Criminology and Public Policy*, 19, 761–786. https://doi.org/10.1111/1745-9133.12499.

Newburn, T. (2017). *Criminology*, 3rd edition. London: Routledge.

O'Mahony, D. & Doak, J. (2017). *Reimagining Restorative Justice: Agency and Accountability in the Criminal Process*. London: Bloomsbury Publishing.

Probation Service. (2024). About Us. [online]. www.gov.uk/government/organisations/probation-service/about (accessed 15 September 2024).

Raine, A. (2008). From Genes to Brain to Antisocial Behavior. *Current Directions in Psychological Science*, 17(5), 323–328. https://doi.org/10.1111/j.1467-8721.2008.00599.x.

Rock, P. (2007). Caesare Lombroso as a Signal Criminologist. *Criminology and Criminal Justice*, 7(2), 117–133. https://doi.org/10.1177/1748895807075565.

Sentencing Council for England and Wales. (2024). Sentencing Children and Young People. [online]. www.sentencingcouncil.org.uk/overarching-guides/magistrates-court/item/sentencing-children-and-young-people/ (accessed 15 July 2024).

Shaw, C. & McKay, H. (1942). *Juvenile Delinquency and Urban Areas*. Chicago: University of Chicago Press.

Sherman., Gartin, P. & Buerger, M. (1989). Hots Spots of Predatory Crime: Routine Activities and the Criminology of Place. *Criminology*, 27(1), 27–56. https://doi.org/10.1111/j.1745-9125.1989.tb00862.x.

SooHyun, O., Martinez, N., Lee, Y. & Eck, J. E. (2017). How Concentrated Is Crime among Victims? A Systematic Review from 1977 to 2014. *Crime Science* 6(9). https://doi.org/10.1186/s40163-017-0071-3.

Sutherland, E., Cressey, D., & Luckenbill, D. (1992). *Principles of Criminology*. Philadelphia, PA: Lippincott.

Steinmetz, K. & Pratt, T. (2024). Revisiting the Tautology Problem in Rational Choice Theory: What it Is and How to Move Forward Theoretically and Empirically. *European Journal of Criminology*, 21(4), 513–532. https://doi.org/10.1177/14773708241226537.

Squires, P. (2017). Anti-social Behaviour. In A. Brisman, E. Carrabine & N. South (eds), *The Routledge Companion to Criminological Theory and Concepts*. London: Routledge.

Taylor, C. (2024). Improving Behaviour in Prisons: A Thematic Review. 11 April 2024. https://hmiprisons.justiceinspectorates.gov.uk/hmipris_reports/improving-behaviour-in-prisons-a-thematic-review/ (accessed 15 July 2024).

Tony Blair Institute for Global Change. (2023). A Plan to Reform the Criminal Justice System 23 October 2023. [online]. www.institute.global/insights/public-services/a-plan-to-reform-the-criminal-justice-system (accessed 15 August 2024).

Victim Support. (2018). Survivor's Justice: How Victims and Survivors of Domestic Abuse Experience the Criminal Justice System. [online]. www.victimsupport.org.uk/wp-content/uploads/documents/files/VS_Survivor%E2%80%99s%20justice.pdf (accessed 15 August 2024).

Weisburd D. (2015). The Law of Crime Concentration and the Criminology of Place. *Criminology*, 53(2), 133–157. https://doi.org/10.1111/1745-9125.12070.

Weisburd, D., Davis, M. & Gill, C. (2015). Increasing Collective Efficacy and Social Capital at Crime Hot Spots: New Crime Control Tools for Police. *Policing: A Journal of Policy and Practice*, 9(3), 265–274. https://doi.org/10.1093/police/pav019.

Wood, D., Bradshaw, S., Dickens, T. & Parker-McLeod, J. (2024). *Blackstone's Handbook for Policing Students*. Oxford: Oxford University Press.

Zedner, L. (2004). *Criminal Justice*. Oxford: Oxford University Press.

4 Public protection
The role of the police as a public authority

Angela King and Annabelle James

Introduction

The introduction of the Policing Education Qualifications Framework (PEQF) in England and Wales reinvigorated discussions as to the relationship between public authorities exercising power under the direction of the executive government and the citizens residing in the governed state. This chapter seeks to explore some of the key issues underpinning the relationship between the citizen and the state and will consider the role of the police as a public authority in ensuring a balance between state security and the protection of fundamental human rights. The focus will be on the impact of two important rights-based documents: the European Convention on Human Rights and Fundamental Freedoms of 1950 (ECHR) and the Human Rights Act 1998 (HRA), with particular consideration given to how they impact upon the practical role of the police officer in the exercise of powers under a variety of provisions.

The Police and Criminal Evidence Act 1984 (PACE) and its Codes of Practice provide the police with a broad and diverse set of powers including stop and search of a person or vehicle, the treatment of suspects in police custody and the extraction of confession evidence. These legal requirements will be discussed alongside other legislation dealing with more specific situations. As such, this chapter will make reference to the Public Order Act 1986, the Criminal Justice and Public Order Act 1994 and the Public Order Act 2023 in the context of ensuring that the exercise of power is compatible with the rights of those living in the state. More specifically, the powers will be considered in relation to the Right to Liberty and Security of the Person, protected by Article 5 of the ECHR, and the Right to a Fair Trial under Article 6.

Events such as the Brixton Riots and miners' strikes in the 1980s, the riots of 2011, disruption caused by more recent protests involving protestors such as Just Stop Oil or those relating to the Israel-Hamas war, and the 2024 riots starting in Stockport, demonstrate the fragile and often fragmented relationship between the police and members of society. The aim of this chapter is to ensure that aspiring and serving police officers and police community support officers understand their legal obligation to act proportionately when exercising powers so as not to interfere unnecessarily with the rights of the citizens involved, thus helping to promote a harmonious and reciprocated relationship ensuring public faith in the criminal justice system.

Historical context

The exercise of power in the United Kingdom (UK) differs from that in most democratic states. The UK lacks a written constitution, so there is no single codified document listing the powers of each state branch. Power is divided among three main branches, each holding the others to account (Baron de Montesquieu, 1748). The Executive (government), led by the Prime Minister, manages the state, implements policies, and maintains national security. This branch includes those elected by the people via general election (governed by the Dissolution and Calling of Parliament Act 2022). The police, whose powers are of a public nature, also fall under this category.

Parliament, responsible for making laws, comprises the House of Commons, the House of Lords, and the Monarch. Through legislation (statutes/ Acts of Parliament), it holds supreme law-making power, rarely questioned (*Pickin v British Railways Board* (1974); *Jackson v Attorney General* (2005)). Recently, courts have considered the Parliament/government relationship concerning issues like Brexit (*R (Miller and another) v Secretary of State for Exiting the European Union* (1997)).

The Judiciary, the body of courts and judges, interprets and applies the law, resolves disputes, and upholds Parliament's wishes. This power distribution is crucial for discussing modern police power. All three branches must ensure the protection of people's rights (Goldsmith, 2006). For effective police-society relations, police powers and the mechanism for challenging abuses must be open and accessible. Thomas Hobbes (1651) suggested a social contract where citizens give up some rights to the state for better protection. For this to work, the exercise of power over citizens must be regulated, and accountability mechanisms must exist. This legitimacy is facilitated by the way that power is distributed between the three branches; however, it could also be argued that the introduction of PACE and the HRA represent more contemporary examples of this which are relevant to police officers in practice.

Prior to the enactment of PACE, there was less regulation of police powers leading, it was felt, to the abuse and disruption of the social contract. As a result of the Brixton Riots in 1981, the Home Office ordered a review of the exercise of police powers, amid allegations of bias and institutional racism. The findings of the investigation concluded that the stop and search powers adopted by the police during Operation Swamp 81 were prejudicial towards, in particular, the Afro-Caribbean members of the community, and that they had been exercised without any reasonable grounds for suspicion (Scarman, 1982). The Scarman Report led to the statutory codification of police powers (some of which will be discussed in more detail later in this chapter) and a more rigid process for exercising them, without prejudice or discrimination based on subjective criteria such as stereotyping, age, race, gender or previous criminal convictions (Code A, para. 2.2).

The requirement for 'reasonable suspicion' is an important and essential component for maintaining public confidence in the police. This requirement extends beyond powers of stop and search into entry and search of property and, perhaps most importantly, the powers of arrest. This protection has been further enforced through the Codes of Practice (Code A, para. 2.2B) which prohibit the exercise of stop and search powers based on reasonable suspicion founded on facts which would in any way violate the relevant protected characteristics under the Equality Act 2010.

The Human Rights Act 1998 has provided an additional mechanism for challenging police action in the exercise of duty. Prior to the Act coming into force in October 2000, human rights were not guaranteed under UK law but were merely residual. This meant that people were entitled to do anything that had not been expressly prohibited by Parliament or the courts. For example, the right to peaceful protest was assumed provided that none of the offences under the Public Order Act 1986 such as riot (s.1), violent disorder (s.2) or affray (s.3) were committed. However, under the HRA, the positive protection of Freedom of Expression (Article 10) and Freedom of Assembly and Association (Article 11) can be seen. These rights should not be interfered with or restricted by the state or any of its representatives, such as the police, unless necessary for the maintenance of public order or the prevention of crime. Therefore, in addition to acting within the legal limits prescribed under PACE and other statutes, the police must also ensure that their actions are compatible with the rights of the people.

More recently, the introduction of evidence-based policing (EBP) as a core theme across the police service has arguably helped to ensure greater consistency between the police forces in England and Wales in an effort to determine the most cost-effective way of tackling crime (Lumsden, 2017).

Current professional practice

In the aftermath of the Second World War, the Council of Europe drafted a revolutionary rights-based document with the aim of all people living in signatory states with universal protection for each of the rights and freedoms contained within it. Council of Europe membership currently stands at 46 (Council of Europe, 2024). The European Convention on Human Rights and Fundamental Freedoms 1950 (ECHR) and the more recently adopted additional protocols provide the basis for the rights of citizens living in the UK. Of particular relevance are the following rights:

Table 4.1 Human Rights Act 1998, Schedule 1.

Article 2	Right to life
Article 3	Prohibition of torture
Article 4	Prohibition of slavery and forced labour
Article 5	Right to liberty and security
Article 6	Right to a fair trial
Article 7	No punishment without law
Article 8	Right to respect for private and family life
Article 10	Freedom of expression
Article 11	Freedom of assembly and association
Article 14	Prohibition of discrimination

The rights within the Convention can be classified as absolute, limited, or qualified (Costigan and Stone, 2017). Absolute rights, such as those prohibiting torture and slavery (Articles 3 and 4), cannot be interfered with and allow no justification for violations (*Ireland v The United Kingdom* (1978)). Limited rights are those seemed essential to the functioning of a democratic society and can only be interfered with under specific conditions. For instance, Article 2, the right to life, can be restricted by the use of reasonable, strictly necessary force (*McCann v The United Kingdom* (1995)). Article 5, the right to liberty, is limited in the context of the investigation of crime, allowing arrest (Article 5(1)(b)) under reasonable suspicion and (Article 5(1)(c)). These rights will be explored further in this chapter.

Qualified rights are subject to a broader range of limitations. The Council of Europe accepts that these will differ from state to state depending on the cultural, social and religious requirements of an individual state's society. Examples of qualified rights include the Freedom of Expression (Article 10) and Freedom of Assembly and Association (Article 11) where rights can be interfered with for a number of prescribed reasons such as the prevention of crime and the interests of national security or the protection of rights of another. Accordingly, issues such as terrorism, media reporting of active criminal proceedings and the disruption of public order are often cited as valid justifications for interfering with these rights (*Attorney-General v MGN Limited and News Group Newspapers Ltd* (2011); *I v DPP* (2001)).

The ECHR is an international treaty. In order for the rights contained within it to be directly effective in our own courts, thus enabling citizens to rely on them without having to go to the European Court of Human Rights, the rights need to be incorporated into an Act of Parliament. Despite the fact that the UK was one of the founder states to the Convention and one of its first signatories, it was not until the HRA 1998 was enacted that these rights became enforceable in the domestic courts. The delay between the Act being passed and it coming into force in October 2000 was deliberate, the rationale behind this being that the judiciary needed to familiarise itself with the wealth of Strasbourg caselaw that it would have a duty to take into account when considering human rights issues (s.2) and interpreting legislation (s.3). In addition, the courts, police and other public authorities needed time to understand their new found obligations to act in accordance with the rights contained within the ECHR. By virtue of s.6 HRA, there is a legal obligation on all public authorities to act in a way that is compatible with the Convention.

S.6 provides (in part) that:

1. It is unlawful for a public authority to act in a way which is incompatible with a Convention right.
2. Subsection (1) does not apply to an act if –

a   as the result of one or more provisions of primary legislation, the authority could not have acted differently ...

3   In this section 'public authority' includes –

a   a court or tribunal, and
b   any person certain of whose functions are functions of a public nature but does not include either House of Parliament or a person exercising functions in connection with proceedings in Parliament.

(Human Rights Act 1998, s.6)

The exclusion of both Houses of Parliament from the definition of 'public authority' under s.6(3)(b) is significant. Parliament could, should it wish to, legislate in a manner that is incompatible with the rights that the HRA seeks to protect. This is because, as already mentioned, Parliament is the supreme law-making body in the UK and can therefore 'make or unmake any law whatever' (Dicey, 1885). In practice, Parliament has chosen to do this only once since the HRA came into force. This was in respect of the Anti-Terrorism, Crime and Security Act 2001 which allowed the Home Secretary to detain non-British terrorism suspects indefinitely without charge or trial (s.23). This provision was later amended and replaced by the Prevention of Terrorism Act 2005 as a result of the House of Lords decision in *A (FC) and Others (FC) v Secretary of State for the Home Department* (2004) where the court stated that the use of powers by the government were disproportionate to the threat being posed.

The House of Lords' decision illustrates that citizens can challenge a public authority's action as incompatible with a Convention right in domestic courts within a year (HRA, s.7). For such actions, the court must confirm the decision was made by a 'public authority' as defined in s.6(3). Determining this has sometimes been complex (*Parochial Church Council of the Parish of Aston Cantlow and Wilmcote with Billesley, Warwickshire v Wallbank and Another* (2003)). However, the police service clearly falls under s.6(3)(b) as a body with public functions, requiring officers to act consistently with Convention rights.

S.6 HRA therefore requires the striking of a careful balance between the exercise of police powers under PACE and other relevant legislation and the need to ensure that there is no unnecessary interference with the individual rights of the suspect(s) or citizens involved when doing so. This will be considered in more detail in the context of a number of different powers allowing the police to investigate crime and maintain public order.

Proportionality and evidence-based policing

The police powers discussed in this chapter must be considered in the context of the rights that they have the potential to breach. The European Court of Human Rights (ECtHR) is the Council of Europe's judicial organ. It sits in Strasbourg and can hear allegations of breaches, where all domestic remedies have been exhausted, under Article 34 ECHR. The ECtHR has recognised, using the doctrine of proportionality, that limited and qualified rights can be subject to interference provided that the aims in doing so are legitimate and necessary.

Proportionality is a concept that must be considered on a daily basis in the context of police officers exercising their powers. It will often be necessary for an officer to act quickly, using their judgement, to deal with a situation. However, as a result of s.6 HRA, the officer must also ensure that any interference with the rights of a suspect is absolutely necessary. For example, when a police officer exercises their powers of arrest under s.24 PACE, the right to liberty and security is interfered with. The police must not only satisfy the statutory requirements under ss.24 and 28 of PACE for the arrest to be lawful but must also be certain that the investigation requires an interference with the suspect's fundamental rights. If it is possible to investigate an offence effectively without making an arrest, Article 5 and Code G make this a requirement. A decision or action deemed to be disproportionate could result in the police, as a public authority, being subject to a challenge under s.7 HRA or Article 34 ECHR with compensation being awarded to the victim.

The adoption of the EBP model arguably makes it easier to ensure that the exercise of police powers is consistent. Officers are now encouraged to incorporate research, evidence and analytics when making on the job decisions. This continuous tracking of daily delivery should, in turn, improve the public's perception of police legitimacy (Lumsden, 2017).

It could be argued that the doctrine of proportionality offers some stability to the relationship between the citizen and the state. The fact that rights can only be interfered with when strictly necessary satisfies the social contract theory in ensuring that the rights are protected unless interference is in the best interests of society. The deprivation of liberty, for example, may be justified for the purposes of preventing crime and ensuring state security.

The right to liberty and security under Article 5 of ECHR

The right to liberty is one of the hallmarks of a free society. Citizens should be able move and act freely without the need to explain their actions to anyone in authority and without the fear that they might be subject to arbitrary arrest or challenge. On this basis, interference with Article 5 should only be permitted if absolutely necessary.

Article 5 sets out the right to liberty and security and the standards to be applied in relation to interference of personal freedom. As already established, Article 5 is a limited right and, as such, any interference with it should be minimal and interpreted in as narrow a way as possible (*Secretary of State for the Home Department v JJ and Others (FC) (2007)*).

Article 5 is as follows:

1. Everyone has the right to liberty and security of person. No one shall be deprived of his liberty save in the following cases and in accordance with a procedure prescribed by law:

a the lawful detention of a person after conviction by a competent court
b the lawful arrest or detention of a person for non-compliance with the lawful order of a court or in order to secure the fulfilment of any obligation prescribed by law
c the lawful arrest or detention of a person effected for the purpose of bringing him before the competent legal authority on reasonable suspicion of having committed an offence or when it is reasonably considered necessary to prevent his committing an offence or fleeing after having done so
d the detention of a minor by lawful order for the purpose of educational supervision or his lawful detention for the purpose of bringing him before the competent legal authority
e the lawful detention of persons for the prevention of the spreading of infectious diseases, of persons of unsound mind, alcoholics or drug addicts or vagrants
f the lawful arrest or detention of a person to prevent his effecting an unauthorised entry into the country or of a person against whom action is being taken with a view to deportation or extradition.

2 Everyone who is arrested shall be informed promptly, in a language which he understands, of the reasons for his arrest and of any charge against him.
3 Everyone arrested or detained in accordance with the provisions of paragraph c of this Article shall be brought promptly before a judge or other officer authorised by law to exercise judicial power and shall be entitled to trial within a reasonable time or to release pending trial. Release may be conditioned by guarantees to appear for trial.
4 Everyone who is deprived of his liberty by arrest or detention shall be entitled to take proceedings by which the lawfulness of his detention shall be decided speedily by a court and his release ordered if the detention is not lawful.
5 Everyone who has been the victim of arrest or detention in contravention of the provisions of this Article shall have an enforceable right to compensation.(Article 5, ECHR)

Article 5(1) provides detail of the situations in which the right to liberty can be interfered with, allowing the deprivation of liberty in accordance with a procedure prescribed by law such as the provisions of PACE or the Criminal Justice and Public Order Act 1994, some of which will now be discussed in more detail.

Stop and search of the person and the right to liberty

The stop and search powers under PACE were introduced as a direct result of the Scarman Report (Scarman, 1982) and took into account the need for a more consistent approach. Evidence suggests that everyday policing activity, including stop and search, has an impact on the reduction of crime (McNeill & Wheller, 2019). In exercising these powers, the police also have a duty under s.6 to act in accordance with Convention rights. For example, they need to ensure that they do not subject a suspect to torture, inhuman or degrading treatment (Article 3) and that they do not act in a way that interferes with a suspect's right to liberty (Article 5), their right to a fair trial (Article 6) or their right to a private and family life (Article 8). In essence, the HRA has not changed the powers that the police possess but have required them to consider their exercise in a new light.

Under s.1 of PACE, a police officer has the power to stop and search a person in a public place (s.1(1)(a)), for the purposes of looking for stolen or prohibited articles (s.1(2)(a)) if they have reasonable grounds to suspect they will find said stolen or prohibited articles (s.1(3)). Prohibited articles are defined under ss.1 (7), 1(8) and 1(9) of the Act. S.1 has recently been amended by s.10 of the Public Order Act 2023 to extend stop and search powers in protest related circumstances. The Public Order Act 2023 is discussed further in the next section.

Most stop and search powers require reasonable grounds for suspicion, and these must exist before a person is stopped. There is no power available to police officers for stopping a person in order to find reasonable grounds for suspicion. The objective test provides that appearance cannot be enough to satisfy the requirement that reasonable grounds for suspicion exists and previous convictions cannot be used in isolation or in combination with each other as the sole basis for the suspicion. However, it is possible that these factors could be taken alongside other issues (such as a description, or suspicious behaviour).

The exercise of these powers unquestionably has the potential to restrict or interfere with some of the rights contained within the ECHR, although it has generally been accepted that provided the length of time of the search is kept only to what is necessary to obtain the relevant information, it will not constitute an interference with the right to liberty under Article 5 (*Gillan and Quinton v The United Kingdom* (2010); *Austin v Metropolitan Police Commissioner* (2009); *Austin v The United Kingdom* (2012)).

S.2 of PACE offers some additional guidance on how the stop and search powers should be exercised. S.2(3) provides that if a search is to be carried out without an arrest, the following information must be provided prior to the search:

- the constable's name and the name of the police station to which he is attached.
- the object of the proposed search.
- the constable's grounds for proposing to make it.(PACE, s.2)

The provisions under s.2(3) are important as they require the police to inform the suspect of the reasons for the search which helps to ensure the right to liberty is protected. It also provides the suspect with the opportunity to question the legitimacy of the search. This is further supported by s.2(9) which limits the scope of the search and provides that the conferment of stop and search powers should not be construed as authorising a police officer to require a suspect to remove any of his clothing in public other than an outer coat, jacket or gloves.

These provisions clearly act as a mechanism for maintaining a balance between the police, acting as a public authority, and the need to protect the rights of society, in accordance with the social contract theory. Furthermore, Code A ensures that the police should carry out all stops and searches with consideration and, wherever possible, the cooperation of the person to be searched, in order to protect public confidence in the police and to minimise embarrassment (Code A, paras. 3.1 and 3.2).

Stop and search under the Criminal Justice and Public Order Act

More specific stop and search powers also exist under s.60 of the Criminal Justice and Public Order Act 1994 (CJPOA). The provisions under the CJPOA can be used when a senior police officer reasonably believes that:

- incidents of serious violence may take place within his area (s.60(1)(a)); or
- people may be carrying dangerous instruments or offensive weapons (s.60(1)(aa)(ii)).

Under s.60(4)(a), once an order has been authorised, a police officer in uniform has the power to stop any pedestrian and search him or anything carried by him for offensive weapons or dangerous instruments.

Offensive weapons have the same definition as under s.1(9) PACE and dangerous instruments are defined as anything with a blade or sharply pointed (CJPOA s.60(11)).

The officer can issue written authorisation which will bring into force certain stop and search powers in that area for up to 24 hours. These powers are intended to be used relatively restrictively and really only in situations where there is the potential for some public disorder which it may be necessary to control.

Random searching is permitted under the CJPOA meaning the officer does not need to have reasonable grounds for actually stopping the person, only that incidents of serious violence may take place or that people may be carrying dangerous instruments or offensive weapons.

Failure to stop when asked by an officer exercising their power under the CJPOA is a criminal offence under s.60(8) provided the powers have not been used oppressively (*R (Roberts) v Commissioner for the Metropolitan Police* (2012)).

Additional stop and search powers under the Public Order Act 2023

New stop and search powers were introduced in response to concerns for public safety following an increase in disruption during public protests. The new public order legislation, which came into force on 20 December 2023, provide additional powers specifically in relation to the protest related offences established in s.1 of the 2023 Act. S.10(b) amends s.1(8) of PACE to expand search on reasonable suspicion to cover wilful disruption, public nuisance, locking on, tunnelling, obstruction of major transport works and interference with key national infrastructure.

S.11 provides for stop and search without suspicion, similar to those under s.60 CJPOA. Under these powers, police can stop and search people without needing reasonable suspicion in designated areas (no bigger than necessary) for a set period (maximum 24 hours with a possible 24-hour extension) in connection to protest related activity (s.11(1)(a)(i)–(vii)). This must be authorised by a senior (inspector or higher) officer if they reasonably believe that offences such as public nuisance or obstructing traffic are likely. The legislation also introduced the offence of intentionally obstructing a protest-related stop and search (s.14). The rationale behind these new provisions is that they will help the police to stop people from carrying items that could be used to cause disruption such as equipment for 'locking on' to infrastructure or tunnelling. Critics however have argued that these powers could disproportionately target peaceful protestors and interfere with the right to freedom of assembly (see, for example, Office of the High Commissioner for Human Rights, 2024).

Safeguarding against misuse of stop and search powers

The provisions within PACE and its Codes of Practice provide safeguards against the misuse of stop and search powers. In addition, Community Scrutiny Panels (CSPs), made up of representatives from the local authorities, police, fire service etc. can review anonymised stop and search data, including body-cam footage to ensure procedures are followed. The Inclusive Britain paper's focus on tackling discrimination aligns with concerns about the disproportionate use of stop and search (Department for Levelling Up, Housing and Communities, 2022). With PACE setting the legal framework, CSPs providing independent scrutiny and the Inclusive Britain paper promoting fair police practices, these elements together aim to create a system where stop and search is used effectively and fairly.

Powers of arrest

The power of arrest without a warrant are covered by s.24 PACE. These powers represent an obvious interference with the right to liberty under Article 5. In order for an arrest to be lawful, a suspect must be informed of the details of their arrest:

S.28(1)…where a person is arrested, otherwise than being informed that he is under arrest, the arrest is not lawful unless the person arrested is informed that he is under arrest as soon as is practicable after his arrest; …
S.29(b)he shall be informed at once that he is under arrest if a decision is taken by a constable to prevent him from leaving at will.(PACE 1984)
The ECtHR has determined that the requirement to inform the suspect of the interference with their liberty and the reasons for it is it allow the suspect to challenge the legitimacy of it. (*Fox, Campbell and Hartley v United Kingdom* (1990)). Code C also states that it is important for the purposes of

confession evidence that the suspect knows the offence about which they are being questioned. It also links closely to the right to silence contained within the police caution.

S.24 PACE allows for the arrest, without a warrant, of anyone who is:

- about to commit an offence;
- in the act of committing an offence;
- whom an officer has reasonable grounds for suspecting is about to commit an offence;
- whom an officer has reasonable grounds for suspecting is committing an offence.

In order for these powers to be exercised legitimately, the arrest must be justified under one of the reasons set out in s.24(5). These include:

- to establish the name and/or address of the person;
- to prevent the person injuring himself or another, suffering physical injury, causing loss of or damage to property, committing an offence against public decency or unlawfully obstructing the highway;
- to protect a child or other vulnerable person;
- to allow the prompt and effective investigation of the offence or the person in question;
- to prevent prosecution being hindered by the disappearance of the suspect.

The test for reasonable grounds for suspicion is the same as that under s.1(3) and Code A in relation to stop and search. It must be based on objective criteria (*Alanov v Chief Constable of Sussex* (2012)). S.24 was amended by the Serious Organised Crime and Police Act 2005. This has helped to ensure that its application is compatible with Article 5 provided that the arresting officer uses their powers within their legal limits. S.25(5), read in accordance with Code G (paras 2.4–2.9), provides that an arrest will only be lawful where reasonable suspicion exists, and the arresting officer believes that an arrest is necessary. If reasonable suspicion exists but the officer does not believe that an arrest is necessary, they should instead take the suspect's details and issue a summons, thus preventing a disproportionate interference with the right to liberty.

Code G provides further guidance on how the power of arrest should be exercised, acknowledging that the exercise of the power 'represents an obvious and significant interference with the right to liberty and security' (para 1.2). It goes on to state:

> The use of the power must be fully justified and officers exercising the power should consider if the necessary objectives can be met by other, less intrusive means. Absence of justification for exercising the power of arrest may lead to challenges should the case proceed to court. It could also lead to civil claims against police for unlawful arrest and false imprisonment.

When the power of arrest is exercised, it is essential that it is exercised in a non-discriminatory and proportionate manner which is compatible with the Right to Liberty under Article 5.

(para 1.3)

Ensuring that the arrest is 'reasonable' is one of the ways of ensuring that it is compatible with Article 5(1)(c). It is however important to note that the arresting officer does not have to prove that they had sufficient evidence to bring charges at the time of the arrest but only that they had reasonable grounds for believing it to be necessary (*O'Hara v United Kingdom* (2002)).

The right to a fair trial

It is also necessary to consider the right to a fair trial under Article 6 when exploring the exercise of police powers. In order for evidence obtained by the police to be admissible in court, it is important to ensure that it has been obtained correctly. Article 6 contains a number of provisions to assist in guaranteeing this. These include the requirement that all cases be heard by an independent and impartial tribunal (Article 6(1)), that a suspect is informed of any charges in a language that he understands (Article 6(3)(a)) and that the suspect has the right to cross-examine witnesses (Article 6(3)(d)). The principle most relevant to the discussion in this chapter can be found in Article 6(2) which provides that: '[e]veryone charged with a criminal offence shall be presumed innocent until proved guilty according to law'. Article 6(2) therefore ensures that there is a presumption of innocence which, although not an absolute provision, is a longstanding established rule within the English legal system (*Woolmington v DPP* (1935); *R v Lambert* (2001)). The Council of Europe, ECtHR and other international organisations have determined that this presumption links directly to the right to silence which, in the UK, relates to the police caution.

The right to silence and the police caution

The right to remain silent is not expressly stated in Article 6 but has been accepted as falling within the general scope of the presumption of innocence under Article 6(2) in that '...the right to silence and the right not to incriminate oneself, are generally recognised international standards which lie at the heart of the notion of fair procedure under Article 6' (*Funke v France* (1993) at para. 297; see also *Saunders v The United Kingdom* (1997), *Murray v The United Kingdom* (1996)). The purpose of the right to silence is to prevent the admission of evidence obtained through oppression or compulsion. However, the right is not absolute, and it is generally accepted that it cannot be used to protect a suspect from answering questions which it is reasonable to expect an answer to. This is in contrast to other jurisdictions- in the USA for example, the right to silence is absolutely guaranteed as a constitutional right (Constitution of the United States, Amendment V, 1791).

In England and Wales, the police caution must be given to all suspects during questioning. The caution states, '[y]ou do not have to say anything. But it may harm your defence if you do not mention when questioned something which you later rely on in court. Anything you do say may be given in evidence'. (Code C, para. 10). The rules relating to silence when being questioned by the police can be found in s.34 Criminal Justice and Public Order Act 1994:

S.34(1) Where in any proceedings against a person for an offence, evidence is given that the accused –

- a at any time before he was charged with the offence, on being questioned under caution by a constable trying to discover whether or by whom the offence had been committed, failed to mention any fact relied on in his defence in those proceedings; or
- b on being charged with the offence or officially informed that he might be prosecuted for it, failed to mention any such fact ...

being a fact which in the circumstances existing at the time the accused could reasonably have been expected to mention when so questioned, charged or informed as the case may be, subsection (2) below applies.
(2) Where this subsection applies ...

- a the court, in determining whether there is a case to answer; and
- b the court or jury, in determining whether the accused is guilty of the offence charged,
- c may draw such inferences from the failure as appear proper.

Similar inferences can be drawn in relation to an accused's silence at trial (s.35), failure to account for objects, substances or marks (s.36) or failure to account for presence at a particular place (s.37).

Future developments

The powers available to police officers in England and Wales are in a continuous state review. The efficiency and relevance of provisions under PACE, the CJPOA and more recent legislation are often at the fore of political and legislative debate. Following a Ministry of Justice report in 2019, there were calls to allow more suspicion-less searches under s.60 CJPOA following the finding that convictions for knife and offensive weapons offences were at a ten year high. Serious Violence Reduction Orders (SVROs), civil orders introduced under the Police, Crime, Sentencing and Courts Act 2022 and piloted by Thames Valley, West Midlands, Merseyside and Sussex police forces, aim to reduce knife crime and serious violence. SVROs can be issued when someone is convicted of such an offence; these grant the police enhanced stop and search powers if they have reasonable suspicion that someone is carrying a knife or offensive weapon in a public place. As already discussed, the Public Order Act 2023 expanded stop and search powers for protest related situations which have raised concerns about disproportionate interference with the rights of peaceful protesters.

Conclusion

While the right to liberty continues to be of fundamental importance in a democratic society, the need to balance it against the broader needs of public policy cannot be ignored. The enactment of the HRA in 1998, making Article 5 ECHR directly effective across the UK, has provided a legal safeguard for the right, which must now be considered alongside the limited nature of its protection. The restrictions embedded within Article 5 itself allow our courts and public authorities (including the police) a margin of discretion in the exercise of the right. The responsibility for ensuring this balance is proportionate must, inevitably, be the responsibility of all three arms of the state but is particularly relevant to the police exercising their powers as a public authority, in accordance with s.6 HRA.

The continued use of the EBP approach will arguably help to ensure that a more consistent and cost-effective approach to policing practice is maintained. However, the approach is not without criticism and its efficiency challenged. Research has shown that it is the view of many serving personnel that the EBP approach of targeting, testing and tracking should be used as a guide rather than a hard and fast rule for the exercise of police powers. The EBP philosophy has also been criticised for failing to take into account the different ideological battles and the inevitable conflicting interests both within and across forces. As such, it is expected that while EBP will continue to be present, when police on the street need to act quickly, they may rely more on their experience rather than evidence (Lumsden, 2017).

The issues discussed throughout this chapter demonstrate only a small proportion of instances where interference with the right to liberty may be necessary. However, the jurisprudence of both the domestic courts and the ECtHR would seem to suggest that the legislation, enacted by Parliament, providing powers to stop and search, arrest and question suspects, satisfies the proportionality test, as long as the provisions are exercised legitimately and within the scope of the power provided.

Evidence-based case study illustrating professional practice

PC Grove and PC Shepherd receive reports of a fight taking place on the street near the local pub. They set off to the scene in their police van and see three adults, two male and one female, punching and kicking one another. PC Grove recognises Sid, who used to live next door to him. He knows Sid was arrested on numerous occasions when he was younger. When they see the police arrive, the three individuals stop fighting and the woman, Tracy, is seen to be putting something up her sleeve. The second man, Keith, is bleeding from his arm.

PC Grove goes up to Sid and says, 'Still beating people up, then, are you, Sid?' Sid replies, 'I am asserting my right to remain silent', and tries to walk away. PC Grove grabs him and puts him in a headlock, handcuffs him and throws him in the back of the police van.

PC Shepherd introduces himself to Tracy and asks her to show him what she has hidden under her sleeve as he suspects she has something to do with Keith's injury. She refuses. He pushes her up the side of the police van and searches under her coat. He finds nothing, so he then pulls her by her arm into the police van and forcibly removes her top. He finds a metal nail file under her watch strap.

Reflective question

Discuss the legal issues arising from the scenario in the case study.

References

A (FC) and Others (FC) v Secretary of State for the Home Department. (2004). UKHL 56.
Alanov v Chief Constable of Sussex. (2012). EWCA Civ 234.
Anti-Terrorism, Crime and Security Act. (2001). [online] www.legislation.gov.uk/ukpga/2001/24/contents (accessed 19 November 2024).
Attorney-General v MGN Limited & News Group Newspapers Ltd. (2011). EWHC 2074 (Admin).
Austin v Metropolitan Police Commissioner. (2009). UKHL 5.
Austin v The United Kingdom. (2012). 55 EHRR 14.
Baron de Montesquieu, C. D. S. (1748). *Of the Laws Which Establish Political Liberty with Regard to Constitution. In The Spirit of Laws.* Translated 2001 edition (Book XI, Chapter 6, pp.171–205). Ontario: Batoche Books. [online]. https://socialsciences.mcmaster.ca/econ/ugcm/3ll3/montesquieu/spiritoflaws.pdf (accessed 27 June 2024).
Constitution of the United States, Amendment V. (1791). [online]. www.senate.gov/about/origins-foundations/senate-and-constitution/constitution.htm#amdt_5_1791 (accessed 27 June 2024).
Costigan, R. & Stone, R. (2017). *Civil Liberties and Human Rights*, 11th edition. Oxford: Oxford University Press.
Council of Europe. (2024). Our Member States. [online]. www.coe.int/en/web/about-us/our-member-states (accessed 27 June 2024).
Criminal Justice and Public Order Act. (1994). [online] www.legislation.gov.uk/ukpga/1994/33/contents (accessed 19 November 2024).
Department for Levelling Up, Housing and Communities. (2022). Policy Paper. Inclusive Britain: Government Response to the Commission on Race and Ethic Disparities. [online]. www.gov.uk/government/publications/inclusive-britain-action-plan-government-response-to-the-commission-on-race-and-ethnic-disparities/inclusive-britain-government-response-to-the-commission-on-race-and-ethnic-disparities (accessed 27 June 2024).
Dicey, A. V. (1885). *Lectures Introductory to the Study of the Law of the Constitution.* No. 43445–43449. London: Macmillan.

Dissolution and Calling of Parliament Act. (2022). [online] www.legislation.gov.uk/ukpga/2022/11/contents (accessed 19 November 2024).

Equality Act. (2010). [online] www.legislation.gov.uk/ukpga/2010/15/contents (accessed 19 November 2024).

European Convention on Human Rights and Fundamental Freedoms (as amended by Protocols Nos. 11 and 14, supplemented by Protocol Nos. 1, 4, 6, 7, 12, 13 and 16). [online]. www.echr.coe.int/documents/d/echr/Convention_ENG (accessed 27 June 2024).

Fox, Campbell and Hartley v United Kingdom. (1990). 13 EHRR 157.

Funke v France. (1993). 16 EHRR.

Gillan and Quinton v The United Kingdom. (2010). ECHR 28.

Goldsmith, P. H. (2006). Government and the Rule of Law in the Modern Age. [online]. www.cpl.law.cam.ac.uk/sites/www.law.cam.ac.uk/files/images/www.cpl.law.cam.ac.uk/legacy/Media/THE%20RULE%20OF%20LAW%202006.pdf (accessed 27 June 2024).

Hobbes, T. (1651). *Leviathan.* London: Penguin Books.

Human Rights Act. (1998). [online] www.legislation.gov.uk/ukpga/1998/42/contents (accessed 19 November 2024).

I v DPP. [2001] 2 WLR 765.

Ireland v The United Kingdom. (1978). App No 5310/71, A/25. ECHR 1.

Jackson v Attorney-General. (2005). UKHL 56.

Lumsden, K. (2017). 'Police Officer and Civilian Staff Receptivity to Research and Evidence-Based Policing in the UK: Providing a Contextual Understanding through Qualitative Interviews'. *Policing: A Journal of Policy and Practice*, 11 (2), 157–167. DOI:10.1093/police/paw036..

Ministry of Justice. (2019). Knife and Offensive Weapon Sentencing Statistics, England and Wales – 2018. [online]. https://assets.publishing.service.gov.uk/government/uploads/system/uploads/attachment_data/file/785745/Knife_and_Offensive_Weapon_Sentencing_Pub_Q4_2018.pdf. (accessed 27 June 2024).

McCann v The United Kingdom. (1995). 21 EHRR 97.

McNeill, A. & Wheller, L. (2019). Knife Crime Evidence Briefing. Ryton: College of Policing. [online]. https://assets.college.police.uk/s3fs-public/2022-03/Knife_Crime_Evidence_Briefing.pdf (accessed 27 June 2024).

Murray v The United Kingdom. (1996). ECHR 3.

Office of the High Commissioner for Human Rights. (2024). The Public Order Act will have a Chilling Effect on Your Civic Freedoms – it Must Be Repealed. 28 May. [online]. www.ohchr.org/en/opinion-editorial/2023/05/public-order-act-will-have-chilling-effect-your-civic-freedoms-it-must-be. (accessed 27 June 2024).

O'Hara v United Kingdom. (2002). 34 EHRR 34.

Parochial Church Council of the Parish of Aston Cantlow and Wilmcote with Billesley, Warwickshire v Wallbank and another. (2003). UKHL 37.

Pickin v British Railways Board. (1974). UKHL 1.

Police and Criminal Evidence Act. (1984). [online] www.legislation.gov.uk/ukpga/1984/60/contents (accessed 19 November 2024).

Police, Crime, Sentencing and Courts Act. (2022). [online] www.legislation.gov.uk/ukpga/2022/32/contents (accessed 19 November 2024).

Prevention of Terrorism Act. (2005). [online] www.legislation.gov.uk/ukpga/2005/2/enacted (19 November 2024).

Public Order Act. (1986). [online] www.legislation.gov.uk/ukpga/1986/64 (19 November 2024).

Public Order Act. (2023). [online] www.legislation.gov.uk/ukpga/2023/15 (19 November 2023).

R (Miller and another) v Secretary of State for Exiting the European *Union.* [2017] UKSC 5.

R (Roberts) v Commissioner for the Metropolitan Police. (2012). EWHC 1977.
R v Lambert. (2001). UKHL 37.
Saunders v The United Kingdom. (1997). 23 EHRR 313.
Scarman, L. G. (1982). *The Scarman Report: The Brixton Disorders 10–12 April 1981: Report of an Inquiry by the Rt Hon The Lord Scarman.* Harmondsworth: Penguin.
Secretary of State for the Home Department v JJ and others (FC). (2007). UKHL 45.
Serious Organised Crime and Police Act. (2005). [online] www.legislation.gov.uk/ukpga/2005/15/contents (accessed 10 November 2025).
Woolmington v DPP. (1935). AC 462.

5 Evidence-based policing

Helen Selby-Fell and Ian Pepper

Introduction

The links between 'research', 'evidence' and 'knowledge' are complex and difficult to disentangle (Nutley et al., 2007). It can be argued that research, evidence and knowledge are terms that reflect the perceptions, priorities and power of those who use them (Foucault, 1977; Giddens, 1987).

The three are, however, commonly perceived to be in a hierarchical relationship, with research as one form of evidence and evidence as one source of knowledge (Nutley et al., 2007). Whether and how different ways of 'knowing' can be combined and integrated is a source of considerable debate (Nutley et al., 2007; Wood et al., 2017; Fleming & Rhodes, 2016).

A review of the literature relating to evidence-based policing (EBP) reveals that the terms 'research', 'evidence' and 'knowledge' are frequently used interchangeably and 'evidence' is sometimes used to refer simply to 'information'. Goldstein (1979), in his work on problem orientated policing (POP) referred to 'knowledge' rather than 'evidence', using the term similarly to apply to the use of research and intelligence to inform policing (Chapter 7). In the broader arena of evidence-based practice and evidence-based management, the terms are also used interchangeably. For example, Barends et al. (2014) use the terms 'evidence' and 'information' interchangeably. Similarly, Langer et al. (2016), in their review of interventions applied to increase the use of research evidence in decision making across different sectors, use the terms 'evidence' and 'research' interchangeably.

The term evidence-based policing (EBP) was coined by Sherman (1998), albeit the idea that police should utilise research evidence when conducting their business has a long history (Knutsson & Tompson, 2017). However, there is a continuing debate among scholars regarding what should constitute 'evidence' in the policing context, and how evidence should be created and disseminated to practitioners (Sherman, 2015; Sparrow, 2016; Fleming et al., 2016; Lumsden, 2017; Wood et al., 2017; Pepper et al., 2020).

Nevertheless, there is a consensus that a strong case can be made for systematically utilising research within policing (Tilley & Laycock, 2017) and EBP is a key driver of contemporary reform of policing in the UK (College of Policing, 2014). This approach is part of a broader agenda to recognise the

DOI: 10.4324/9781003492948-6

profession of policing that seeks to facilitate a process of organisational change and improve the quality of its individual professionals (Fleming et al., 2016). The College of Policing continues to promote the adoption of EBP within the police service, the strategy being in line with the National Police Chiefs' Council (2024) Vision for policing in 2030, aiming to develop a learning and evidence informed culture as an approach to everyday professional practice.

Defining evidence-based policing

Policing scholars have generated a number of definitions to describe EBP, and there is ongoing debate regarding how it should be conceptualised and defined.

Sherman (1998) explained that 'evidence' in this context referred to scientific research findings, rather than case evidence commonly used in policing (Bullock & Tilley, 2009). Central to Sherman's (2013) conceptualisation of EBP was the importance of testing and retesting hypotheses with findings from new good quality research.

However, a number of scholars define EBP in much broader terms than Sherman's original definition to include evaluative research and analysis along with wider scientific processes, which could assist in informing operational policing decisions (Lum & Koper, 2017; Knutsson and Tompson, 2017). Across many of the definitions that have been offered, several common themes emerge, including the importance of utilising research evidence, the need to conduct evaluations and the value of crime analysis focused on specific problems (Telep & Somers, 2017; Selby-Fell, 2018; Selby-Fell & Newton, 2022). There is a consensus that the process is in contrast with making decisions based solely upon tradition, convention or assumption (Sherman, 2013).

However, debate remains regarding what constitutes 'evidence', as well as how it should be disseminated to, or with, practitioners, and ultimately, how it should be incorporated into regular police problem solving and decision making.

The College of Policing definition of evidence-based policing

The original conceptualisation of EBP offered by the College of Policing (2014) appeared to be strongly influenced by Sherman's (1998) definition of EBP, positing 'the best available evidence' as synonymous with experimentation and meeting explicit standards.

However, the College of Policing have continued to refine their formal definition of EBP. The College of Policing (2017) definition re-positioned the 'best available evidence' as methods or sources that are 'most appropriate for the research question being asked'. In the absence of 'formal' research, the College asserted that 'informal' research may be utilised, subject to 'careful and transparent collection and documentation'. Further, this definition alluded to police officers' involvement in the creation and review of evidence and also included 'professional consensus' as 'other evidence', again, indicating a shift in tone from the original conceptualisation (College of Policing, 2017). The latest definition is far broader defining EBP as being 'the best available evidence' which is to be used to 'inform and challenge policies, practices and decisions' (College of Policing, 2024a). The description of EBP continues to explain how it can be used by the whole workforce and benefits from collaborations such as those with academia (College of Policing, 2024a). Despite the move towards a broader conceptualisation of EBP, implicit in many definitions of EBP is the notion that some evidence is better than others and that decisions should be informed by the 'best' available evidence (Bowers et al., 2017).

Historical context

There is nothing new about the idea that policy and practice should be informed by the best available evidence (Nutley et al., 2002). Although the term EBP was coined in the late 1990s, the idea that police should utilise research evidence has a long history (Knutsson & Tompson, 2017).

Evidence-based practice has been implemented in other fields and policy areas, including health care, social care and educational professions. Such evidence-based practice originated in medicine in the 1980s, with the goal of promoting the more systematic use of robust scientific evidence in physician education and clinical practice (Barends et al., 2014). It arose out of recognition that physicians had tended to prioritise tradition and personal experience, giving rise to variation in treatment quality. Underlying this issue was the tendency for medical schools to teach their own specific approaches to clinical problems, without clear or explicit links to scientific evidence (Rousseau & Gunia, 2015).

In coining the term EBP, Sherman (1998) drew heavily upon experience in the medical sciences and argued that the research designs commonly used in medicine should be used as the quality standard for policing research. Central to this is the notion that randomised controlled trials (RCTs) generate the strongest evidence for forming a robust evidence-base for policing. This idea has later been championed by other proponents of EBP such as Weisburd and Neyroud (2011).

Building upon Sherman's approach, Weisburd and Neyroud (2011) promoted the development of the 'science of policing' based on the premise that there is a disconnect between science and the practice of policing. Police innovations are, they contend, rarely science based. Sherman (2013) in turn strongly endorsed the arguments of Weisburd and Neyroud (2011), arguing that EBP is needed in order to improve the effectiveness of the police and to enhance police legitimacy.

The contribution by Sherman (1998), and other proponents of embedding research as a formalised approach for informing policing practice (Braga & Weisburd, 2010; Neyroud, 2011), appears to have been influential within the College of Policing's original conceptualisation of EBP and their adoption of a 'hierarchy of evidence' based upon the Maryland Scientific Methods Scale (SMS).

Measurement scales and a hierarchy of evidence

In their review of what works in crime prevention, Sherman et al. (1997) proposed the five-point Maryland Scientific Methods Scale. This formal scale rated the research design and its internal validity on a 5-point scale from 1, being weakest, to 5, the strongest, thus enabling a user to formally assess the evidence from different studies (Sherman et al., 1997). A range of approaches exist to assist a user in measuring and/or valuing research evidence from studies. It must always be kept in mind that the reliability of research (the ability to reproduce the findings under the same conditions) is different to the validity of the research (has the research accurately measured what it set out to measure).

Systematic reviews and randomised controlled trials (RCTs) are usually at the top of such scales measuring the quality and rigour of research. Systematic reviews are championed by proponents of EBP as a means of pooling data from a range of primary evaluation studies, in order to provide conclusions regarding the effectiveness of specific interventions. As Tilley and Laycock (2017) assert, single pieces of evidence are rarely sufficient to warrant the drawing of conclusions on patterns, however, if several types of evidence point in the same direction then the evidence is much stronger, this being preferable to single sources of evidence. The process of conducting a review is characterised by explicit objectives and a rigorous searching and screening process, whereby primary studies are accepted or rejected on the basis of explicit eligibility criteria, with exclusions justified and documented (Bowers et al., 2017). Systematic reviews are considered to be an important means of distilling research evidence to decision-makers within policing (Bowers et al., 2017).

Systematic reviews can assist practitioners with the task of making sense of sometimes contradictory evidence from different research studies. Systematic reviews have been widely employed within the College of Policing and in particular the establishment of the 'What Works Centre for Crime Reduction' (WWCCR) (College of Policing, 2024b). One of the main aims of the WWCCR is to identify whether the evidence suggests that specific interventions lead to an increase, decrease, or have no impact at all, on the commission of crime (College of Policing, 2017). The WWCCR has sought to systematically identify, rate and rank existing systematic reviews of crime prevention interventions, with the aim of providing accessible information to those in policing. In addition, the College of Policing have committed to conducting new systematic reviews to fill knowledge gaps (Bowers et al., 2017). It should be noted, however, that there are challenges and limitations associated with systematic reviews, for example high-quality primary evaluations are rare and for some topics virtually absent (e.g. organised crime, terrorism, modern slavery; Bowers et al., 2017).

Even though there are gaps in the available evidence-base and there is an ongoing need to evolve the evidence base, there are numerous policing topics where there is a well-developed existing evidence base (contained within the

WWCCR Toolkit and available elsewhere). For example, the WWCCR Toolkit summarises the findings of systematic reviews in relation to hot spot policing, street lighting, health care screening for domestic abuse etc. Systematic reviews are published elsewhere, for example Dau et al. (2023) reports on the evidence of effectiveness of a policing presence, and Petersen et al. (2023) discusses the evidence relating to effects of the police stopping pedestrians.

RCTs attempt to mimic the methods used in clinical trials to test the effectiveness of drug treatments, by comparing the outcome of intervention(s) in a treatment area with a closely matched control area. Such approaches using RCTs can be transposed to some areas of policing research such as that by Ariel et al. (2017) exploring the use of body-worn cameras and their effect on reducing complaints against the police.

At the other lower end of the scale are the more simplistic comparative before and after research studies, often with no matched comparison group, and descriptive studies with no comparison group at all (Tilley & Laycock, 2017). Beneath these are expert opinions and/or reports written by committees. However these sources of evidence at the lower end of the scale should not be written off, as they can still be used to inform decisions and practice, but their limitations in research design and subsequent transferability of findings must be acknowledged.

Such rigid scales range from statements about 'what works' at the top (based on systematic reviews and RCTs), followed by 'what's promising', to what might have a 'possible impact' – each based upon the research methods employed and the quality of the evidence provided.

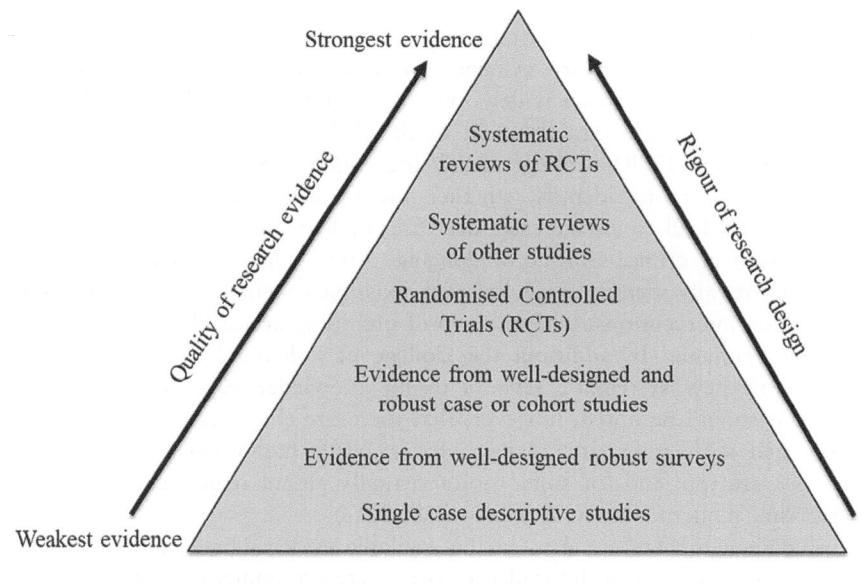

Figure 5.1 A hierarchy of research evidence.

The 'EMMIE' Scale

Bowers et al. (2017) present and discuss the introduction of EMMIE, which is used in the WWCCR Toolkit. The EMMIE framework is designed to gather evidence on five key dimensions of specific interventions – encapsulated by the acronym 'EMMIE':

- Effect of the intervention, what was its impact in practice,
- Mechanism(s) through which interventions are intended to work,
- Moderate intervention factors affecting effectiveness and the context within which the approach works,
- Implementation issues for use in practice,
- Economic costs of intervention.

Bowers et al. (2017) explain that the five elements of EMMIE were selected to ensure that reviews do not focus solely on the quantitative outcomes of an intervention (the Effect). Rather, the inclusion of the other elements of EMMIE allows the practitioners to consider the different contexts in which an intervention may be applied, the challenges they may face in implementing, such as the gathering and mobilising of agencies, individuals and equipment, along with both the direct and indirect costs which need to be funded (Bowers et al., 2017; College of Policing, 2024b).

The evidence-based policing debate

The evidence-based approach, championed by Sherman (1998, 2013, 2015), continues to grow in popularity within policing internationally and has been described as the 'EBP Movement' by those who discuss and challenge a number of the assumptions associated with the approach (Knutsson & Tompson, 2017). An important debate has followed regarding the nature of evidence, the relationship between research and policing practice, and the need to extend the remit of what constitutes evidence to inform practice (Fleming, 2015; Brown et al., 2018; Brown, 2019).

Sparrow (2016) argues that the fundamental problem with the original EBP conceptualisation is that it has become synonymous with experimental research designs to the exclusion of all other designs. Sparrow (2016) continues to suggest that the social–scientific research methods embraced under the traditional conceptualisation of EBP represent a fraction of the scientific methods relevant and available to grow the evidence-base in support of policing. This view of EBP has increasingly been supported by a number of authors (Moore, 2006; Knutsson & Tompson, 2017; Tilley & Laycock, 2017; Wood et al., 2017). Fyfe and Wilson (2012) contend that in order to effectively inform policing, there is a requirement to utilise a range of methods and frameworks to assist in informing the service. Veltri et al. (2014) argue that the potential of qualitative research to help decision and policymaking remains largely unexplored.

It can be argued that the traditional EBP approach risks dominating the research approach and ignoring other forms of valuable research and knowledge generation (Lumsden, 2017). Lumsden (2017) also suggests that police officers and staff might find other aspects of social scientific research (in addition to experimental designs such as RCTs) useful in informing practice. In particular, qualitative research is necessary to better understand some areas of policing business, for example to provide greater insight into community engagement (Lumsden, 2017). Koehle and Hanrahan (2010) suggest that those in policing may be more receptive to qualitative research rather than quantitative data alone. The triangulation of research findings using alternate methods is always valuable and assists in testing the validity of findings. It can therefore be argued that it would be counterproductive to confine sources of evidence to any one specific form or to that collected using any specific method (Tilley & Laycock, 2017).

The use of research evidence in contemporary professional policing practice

Nutley et al. (2012) consider how research evidence might be used in practice, and the need to differentiate between the various uses of research in practice. Much of the debate around standards of evidence has focused on an instrumentalist view of evidence use, which involves the direct application of research to both practice and policy decisions. However, Nutley et al. (2012) argue that research can often be utilised in much more subtle and indirect ways. Writing from an evidence-based practice perspective, Nutley et al. (2012) report that in many instances, the use of research may be about shaping decision making in a broad sense, rather than indicating which particular tactics are 'effective'. Pepper et al. (2021) add that there are a number of challenges with sharing research findings to influence practice including translating the academic language used and the need for timely research along with the ability to disseminate the findings.

Sparrow (2016) argues that EBP rests on an underlying assumption that the only way for those in policing to know what works is for them to allow social scientists to make determinations for them, as researchers are trained in statistical and empirical methods, whereas police officers generally are not. Sparrow (2016) goes on to argue that academics have elevated expectations in relation to police officers' interest in the outcomes of research.

Nutley et al. (2012) argue that research only really has the power to change views when it attracts advocates for the messages it contains. The role of advocates (or champions) aiding the adoption of EBP within professional practice is no more evident than the need for first line leaders to both understand and embrace such an evidence-based approach (Pepper et al., 2024). Thus, endorsements of research as evidence reflect judgements that are socially and politically situated in the organisation (Nutley et al., 2012). Similarly, Fleming and Rhodes (2016) argue that all sources of knowledge have their limits and all are constructed in an organisational and political context that selects the facts and their believed relevance.

The role of professional experience

It is clear from numerous studies that professional experience is heavily utilised and valued in policing practice (Lum et al., 2012; Stanko & Dawson, 2016; Hunter et al., 2017). Accordingly, some such definitions of EBP now include 'professional experience' as a potential source of evidence. Certainly the College of Policing (2024b) WWCCR now includes a 'practice bank' sharing interventions from practitioners and a 'research map' of ongoing research based within higher education external to the college.

Much broader conceptualisations of EBP have been proposed, with an increasing consensus that the original conceptualisation of EBP was too narrow. For example, Fleming and Rhodes (2016) suggest that preference should not be given to any one approach to knowledge generation and that the experiences of professionals add significantly to such a process. Fleming and Rhodes (2016) suggest that varying types of knowledge generation are of value, especially when collated together into a coherent piece of work. This conceptualisation of EBP can be seen to be more in line with the broader conceptualisations of evidence-based practice (Nutley et al., 2014) and evidence-based management (Barends et al., 2014) in which evidence-based practice is conceptualised of consisting of four component sources which are: research evidence, experiential knowledge, organisational data and stakeholder views.

It is important to note that professional experience differs from intuition and personal opinion. Professional experience reflects the specialised knowledge acquired by repeated experiences and activities (Barends et al., 2014). This is in contrast with intuition, which by definition does not involve conscious reasoning. Barends et al. (2014) argue that many practitioners take seriously the need to reflect critically on their experiences and distil practical lessons, the benefits of reflective practice being embedded within the initial routes of entry for policing.

In addition to their own professional experience, a number of commentators have argued that police officers also favour the experience of other officers as opposed to other sources of information such as research evidence (Pease & Roach, 2017; Selby-Fell, 2018). Pease and Roach (2017) discuss how this is linked to a collegiate approach among officers as an enduring feature of policing culture. Fleming (2015) reports, from her experience of working with police officers in a variety of contexts, that learning from colleagues, peers and leaders is a preferred method of learning for police officers. Similarly, Hunter et al. (2017) and Stanko and Dawson (2016) report that police officers and staff regularly drew upon the experiences of their colleagues to inform their own decision making.

Fleming et al. (2016) discusses how the credibility of an idea is enhanced if a policing colleague has endorsed it, which can be linked to the telling of unwritten stories in which officers recount their various experiences and challenges. Pease and Roach (2017) argue that policing experience (rather than the research conducted by social scientists), is so embedded in operational decision making that it has to be the point at which any research is commenced and a result should be built upon using a variety of research methodological approaches.

Challenges associated with embedding evidence-based policing

Williams and Stanko (2016) argue that there is a fundamental challenge of EBP that gets overshadowed, how to embed EBP within policing in order to drive change in policing practice. This alludes to the added consideration of what might be needed within the police organisation to facilitate an EBP approach being operationalised (Bullock and Tilley, 2009). Although HM Government (2021) highlight the importance of an evidence-based approach to policing and a range of initiatives to grow the evidence-base to inform practice, the wholesale adoption of such an evidence-based approach is still slow.

There are a number of recognised challenges associated with the implementation of EBP in practice. Some of the challenges relate to interpreting the research evidence itself, while others relate to organisational constraints within the policing organisation, including leadership and culture (Hunter et al., 2017; Lumsden, 2017; Selby-Fell, 2018; Selby-Fell & Newton, 2022; Pepper et al., 2024). In research conducted by Selby-Fell and Newton (2022) less than one fifth of respondents reported having received either formal training or support in the use of research to aid their policing practices

Hunter et al. (2017) discusses how nearly half of respondents in their survey of policing practitioners reported that research findings were unclear and full of jargon, and a third believed research lacked clear enough messages to make it usable. Pepper et al. (2021) agrees that the language used should be accessible and usable by policing practitioners. Unsurprisingly, Hunter et al. (2017) reports that the accessibility and relevancy of research was a huge barrier in determining whether those in policing utilised such work. However, Hunter et al. (2017) raises a more fundamental issue, the importance of practitioners' involvement in, and co-production of, research. The researchers' understanding of the realities of policing practice had a significant impact upon how receptive practitioners were to utilising research evidence. Fleming et al. (2016) discuss the necessity for research to be relevant to the roles of operational officers. As many new police officers complete evidence-based projects as an elements of their entry routes as new recruits, this in part may be overcome. Rogers et al. (2022) identifies in their research how well over half of police recruit respondents improved their knowledge of EBP through their studies and almost two thirds reported using an evidence-based approach in some way during their working day. The role of first line leadership in understanding, championing and maintaining this momentum in the use of EBP is paramount (Pepper et al., 2024), with the 'buy-in' from those in senior leadership positions essential (Selby-Fell & Newton, 2022).

The perceived status of the researcher can present challenges in terms of how research is received within policing organisations, as well as the extent to which police officers or staff might be willing to engage with the research process. Brown (1996) suggests that there are a number of different types of researchers within policing which can be broadly distinguished across two dimensions, those on the inside and those on the outside. Drawing upon the work of Sheptycki

(1994), Brown (1996) describes the academic community as being outside and outlines some of the difficulties such researchers may face when conducting research on the police, such as gaining access to participants. Conversely, Brown (1996) describes researchers employed by police organisations as those on the inside. These researchers on the inside have additional knowledge and can improve the analysis of information using their academic skills to provide interesting observations relating to the culture and practice of policing (Brown, 1996).

However, various commentators have also discussed the potential challenges and biases associated with being on the inside; often based upon their own experiences of the dilemmas they faced between being a employee within policing and a researcher (Holdaway, 1983; Young, 1991). However, Stockdale (2017) argues that it is important to acknowledge that researchers' positions are not always stable, nor are they easily categorised purely by being on the inside or outside, rather, the researcher's identity needs to be fluid.

Pease and Roach (2017) also discuss the lack of evaluation across the police service in their work on how police experiences themselves may be more systematically evaluated. They argue that for most policing services, such as large-scale events (football matches, public disorder etc.), are followed by either ad hoc or formal evaluation; however, in contrast, routine evaluation of everyday working practices and initiatives are unusual. This lack of evaluation in policing practice is now widely recognised and acknowledged by policing practitioners and academics (Selby-Fell & Newton, 2022).

Research frameworks and evidence-based policing

Increasingly, there has been recognition that all types of research evidence have strengths and weaknesses, and that evidence always needs to be carefully interpreted and critically appraised. A number of frameworks have been suggested by scholars to assist practitioners to evaluate and utilise evidence generated by research. Many of the frameworks revert to grading research in a hierarchical format in a similar way to the Maryland SMS.

However, a criticism of hierarchical frameworks is that they do not take sufficient account of the methodological suitability of the selected research design in relation to the research question (Guyatt et al., 2008). Barends et al. (2014) argue that different types of research questions require different types of research methodologies and approaches to answer them. For example, the strongest evidence regarding cause-and-effect questions is likely to be derived from RCTs, however, the strongest evidence regarding questions about side effects and risk factors may be more likely to be derived from observational case study research. In addition, the strongest evidence regarding questions about the way in which an effect has occurred frequently comes from qualitative research (Petticrew & Roberts, 2003).

A number of scholars have highlighted the importance of research methodologies being matched appropriately to the question to be addressed (Bowers et al., 2017). For example, Barends et al. (2014) discuss a model for identifying the appropriate methodology for the research question to be considered.

Wood et al. (2017) argue that everyone in policing needs to develop the ability to critically assess research evidence, for example, in terms of methodologies adopted, data collection and internal and external validity. A number of scholars have reported that the intellectual development of officers and staff of all ranks and grades in terms of their critical thinking skills is necessary to embed an EBP approach across the whole of policing (Wood et al., 2017; Selby-Fell, 2018).

Barends et al. (2014) assert that all decision-making sources should be critically appraised by carefully and systematically assessing trustworthiness and relevance, added to which is the transferability of findings to the current situation. Critical appraisal also encourages policing practitioners to question their colleagues' experiences with a particular problem, for example, how many times he or she has experienced that particular issue and whether previous situations were comparable. Barends et al. (2014) continue to argue that similar questions need to be asked about organisational information, such as how data and figures were collected, recorded and calculated, enabling a discussion as to how accurate the data is likely to be.

Conclusion

There is a broad consensus that EBP represents an acknowledgment of the importance of knowledge through research within policing that is arguably well overdue (Weisburd & Neyroud, 2011; Sherman, 2011; Fyfe & Wilson, 2012). The introduction of EBP has been credited with assisting to undermine the more traditional scepticism towards the application of research in practice (Wood et al., 2017). Indeed, the increasing support for EBP has been partly shaped by policing practitioners, who should be involved with the generation of such knowledge. There are also EBP champions employed within some forces. Since 2010, dedicated professional societies have also been established to promote EBP across policing, largely by police officers in the UK, USA, New Zealand, Canada and Australia (Knutsson & Tompson, 2017), an example is the UK-based Society for Evidence Based Policing (2019).

The choice of which evidence to use in EBP is complex and controversial (Tilley & Laycock, 2017), not only for those new to policing but also to existing practitioners. At one end of the spectrum are those who argue that there is a definitive hierarchy of evidence and that which falls below a minimum standard should not be used (Sherman et al., 1997). At the other end of the spectrum, others suggest that various forms of research are acceptable, provided it is of use in effecting improvements (Tilley & Laycock, 2017), importantly evidence should be used to inform decisions not direct them (Pepper et al., 2024). Scholars are increasingly conceding that there is no simple answer to the question of what counts as good evidence (Nutley et al., 2012).

As Tilley and Laycock (2017) assert, it is important to remember that all types of evidence are fallible, and that there are risks of biases that can lead to the selective collection and use of evidence, regardless of the type of evidence. No single approach to conducting policing focused research will always be the

Evidence-based policing 93

most appropriate; rather, research methodologies should be matched appropriately to the questions to be addressed.

> **Evidence-based case study illustrating professional practice**
>
> While working as a neighbourhood officer, you have been tasked by your sergeant to access and read the research on hotspot policing and report back your findings. Hotspot policing is a strategy that involves the targeting of resources and activities to those places where crime is most concentrated. The strategy is based on the premise that crime and disorder is unevenly spread within neighbourhoods, being clustered in small locations (Braga et al., 2012). Your findings will be used to help inform a local policing initiative aimed at targeting a 'high crime' neighbourhood.
>
> You begin by searching on the College of Policing's 'What Works Centre for Crime Reduction' Toolkit (College of Policing, 2024b). The Toolkit reports the findings of a systematic review of 19 studies, the authors calculated the overall effect of all 19 studies on crime. A small, statistically significant effect was found, suggesting that hotspot policing led to reductions in crime. The Toolkit also explained that the findings of the review revealed different levels of effectiveness for different crime types, it was more effective for drug offences, violent crime and disorder than it was for property crime.
>
> The review reported that when the authors compared the effect of taking a problem-oriented policing (POP) (Chapter 7) approach within hotspots to traditional policing tactics (e.g. directed patrols, increased enforcement) they found that POP was twice as effective (Braga et al., 2012). The Toolkit reported that taking a POP approach increased the effectiveness of hotspot policing for all crime types but was notably more effective for property crime and disorder offences.
>
> However, the EMMIE assessment contained in the Toolkit reported that little was known from the review about how hotspot policing was implemented. The specific activities undertaken as part of a hotspot policing strategy varied between studies, dependent upon the nature of the intervention.
>
> In terms of challenges to a successful implementation, the review reported that on occasions, interventions were not implemented as intended due to staffing issues in three of the studies. In particular, assigning officers to too many crime hotspots and shortage of officers (due to peaks in service demand, operational requirements or redeployment) undermined the effectiveness of the interventions. In addition, officer resistance to the programme was found to threaten the integrity of the intervention in two studies.
>
> You note that the authors of the review also emphasise the importance of considering how different activities undertaken in hotspots may be perceived by the community to avoid adverse effects of concentrated police

> activity, particularly enforcement activity, but the effect of hotspot policing on community perceptions was not explored in detail.
>
> You therefore conclude (and report back to your sergeant) that 'hotspot policing' is likely to reduce crime in the chosen area, however, it is more effective for certain crime types, should be based around POP techniques and is dependent upon careful implementation (including officer 'buy in'). However, you also conclude that some qualitative research with community members should also be conducted to explore how different activities undertaken in hotspot neighbourhoods may be perceived by the local community.

Reflective question

Consider how different research methods might be employed to better understand the following:

1 The effectiveness of a policing operation designed to reduce crime in a location repeatedly targeted.
2 The experiences of repeat burglary victims and their perceptions of the police response to their victimisation.
3 Levels of unreported burglary in a particular basic command unit.

References

Ariel, B., Sutherland, A., Henstock, D., Young, J., Drover, P., Sykes, J., Megicks, S. & Henderson, R. (2017). 'Contagious Accountability': A Global Multisite Randomized Controlled Trial on the Effect of Police Body-Worn Cameras on Citizens' Complaints against the Police. *Criminal Justice and Behavior*, 44(2), 293–316. https://doi.org/10.1177/0093854816668218.

Barends, E., Rousseau, D. & Briner, R. (2014). *Evidence-Based Management: The Basic Principles*. Amsterdam: Centre for Evidence-Based Management. https://cebma.org/assets/Uploads/Evidence-Based-Practice-The-Basic-Principles.pdf.

Bowers, K., Tompson, L., Sidebottom, A., Bullock, K. & Johnson, S. D. (2017). Reviewing evidence for evidence-based policing. In J. Knutsson & L. Tompson (eds), *Advances in Evidence-Based Policing*. Abingdon: Routledge.

Braga, A., & Weisburd, D. (2010). *Policing Problem Places: Crime Hot Spots and Effective Prevention*. Oxford: Oxford University Press.

Braga, A., Papachristos, A. & Hureau, D. (2012). Hot Spots Policing Effects on Crime. *Campbell Systematic Reviews*, 8. https://doi.org/10.4073/csr.2012.8.

Brown, J. (1996). Police Research: Some Critical Issues. In F. Leishman, B. Loveday & S. P. Savage (eds), *Core Issues in Policing*. London: Longman.

Brown, J., Belur, J., Tompson, L., McDowall, A., Hunter, G., & May, T. (2018). Extending the remit of evidence-based policing. *International Journal of Police Science & Management*, 20(1), 38–51. https://doi.org/10.1177/1461355717750173.

Brown, J. (2019). Evidence-Based Policing: Competing or Complementary Models. In N. Fielding, K. Bullock & S. Holdaway (eds), *Critical Reflections on Evidence Based Policing* (pp. 95–114). Abingdon: Routledge.

Bullock, K. & Tilley, N. (2009). Evidence-Based Policing and Crime Reduction. *Policing*, 3(4), 381–387. https://doi.org/10.1093/police/pap032.

College of Policing. (2014). Five-Year Strategy. [online]. www.college.police.uk/About/Documents/Five-Year_Strategy.pdf (accessed 3 August 2017).

College of Policing. (2017). What Works: Crime Reduction Toolkit. [Online]. http://whatworks.college.police.uk/toolkit/Pages/Toolkit.aspx (accessed 9 December 2018).

College of Policing. (2024a). Evidence-Based Policing. [online]. www.college.police.uk/research/evidence-based-policing-EBP (accessed 5 August 2024).

College of Policing. (2024b). What Works Centre for Crime Reduction. [online]. www.college.police.uk/research/what-works-centre-crime-reduction (accessed 10 August 2024).

Dau, P., Vandeviver, C., Dewinter, M., Witlox, F. & Vander Beken, T. (2023). Policing Directions: a Systematic Review on the Effectiveness of Police Presence. *European Journal on Criminal Policy and Research*, 29, 191–225. https://doi.org/10.1007/s10610-021-09500-8.

Fleming, J. (2015). *Police Leadership*. Oxford: Oxford University Press.

Fleming, J., Fyfe, N. & Wingrove, J. (2016). *Evidence-Informed Policing: An Introduction to EMMIE and the Crime Reduction Toolkit: A Pilot Training Evaluation*. Sunningdale: College of Policing.

Fleming, J. & Rhodes, R. (2016). Can Experience Be Evidence? Paper to the Public Policy and Administration Specialist Group, Panel 2: Policy Design and Learning, PSA 66th Annual International Conference, Brighton, 21–23 March.

Foucault, M. (1977). *Discipline and Punish: The Birth of the Prison*. New York: Vintage Books.

Fyfe, N. & Wilson, P. (2012). Knowledge Exchange and Police Practice: Broadening and Deepening the Debate Around Researcher–Practitioner Collaborations. *Police Practice and Research*, 13(4), 306–314. https://doi.org/10.1080/15614263.2012.671596.

Giddens, A. (1987). *Social Theory and Modern Sociology*. Stanford: Stanford University Press.

Goldstein, H. (1979). Improving Policing: A Problem-Oriented Approach. *Crime & Delinquency*, 25(2), 236–258. https://popcenter.asu.edu/sites/default/files/improving_policing_a_problem-oriented_approach_goldstein_crime_delinquency.pdf.

Guyatt, G., Oxman, A., Kunz, R., Vist, G., Falk-Ytter, Y. & Schunemann, H. (2008). Rating Quality of Evidence and Strength of Recommendations: GRADE: An Emerging Consensus on Rating Quality of Evidence and Strength of Recommendations. *British Medical Journal*, 336(7650), 924.

Holdaway, S. (1983). *Inside the British Police*. Oxford: Basil Blackwell.

HM Government. (2021). Beating Crime Plan: Fewer Victims, Peaceful Neighbourhoods, Safe Country. [online]. https://assets.publishing.service.gov.uk/government/uploads/system/uploads/attachment_data/file/1015382/Crime-plan-v10.pdf (accessed 10 August 2024).

Hunter, G., May, T. & Hough, M. (2017). *An Evaluation of 'What Works Centre for Crime Reduction'*. Final Report. Institute for Criminal Policy Research.

Knutsson, J. & Tompson, L. (eds). (2017). *Advances in Evidence-Based Policing*. Abingdon: Routledge.

Koehle, G. & Hanrahan, K. (2010). Citizen Concerns and Approval of Police Performance. *Professional Issues in Criminal Justice*, 5, 9–24.

Langer, L., Tripney, J. & Gough, D. (2016). *The Science of Using Science: Researching the Use of Research Evidence in Decision-Making*. London: EPPI-Centre, Social Science Research Unit, UCL Institute of Education, University College London.

Lum, C. & Koper, C. (2017). *Evidence-Based Policing: Translating Research into Practice*. Oxford: Oxford University Press.

Lum, C., Telep, C., Koper, C. & Grieco, J. (2012). Receptivity to Research in Policing. *Justice, Research and Policy*, 14(1), 1–35. http://cebcp.org/wp-content/evidence-based-policing/matrix-demonstration-project/Lum-etal-2012.pdf.

Lumsden, K. (2017). Police Officer and Civilian Staff Receptivity to Research and Evidence-Based Policing in the UK: Providing a Contextual Understanding through Qualitative Interviews. *Policing: A Journal of Policy and Practice*, 11(2), 157–167. https://doi.org/10.1093/police/paw036.

Moore, M. (2006). Improving Policing Through Expertise, Experience, and Experiments. [online]. https://scholar.harvard.edu/markmoore/publications/improving-police-through-expertise-experience-and-experiments.

National Police Chiefs' Council. (2024). Policing Vision 2030. [online]. www.npcc.police.uk/publications/policing-vision-2030/ (accessed 6 August 2024).

Neyroud, P. (2011). Review of Police Leadership and Training: Volume 1. [online]. https://assets.publishing.service.gov.uk/media/5a7ae186ed915d71db8b3247/report.pdf (accessed 8 August 2024).

Nutley, S., Davies, H. & Walter, I. (2002). *Evidence Based Policy and Practice: Cross Sector Lessons from the UK*. London: ESRC UK Centre for Evidence Based Policy and Practice.

Nutley, S., Davies, H. & Walter, I. (2014). *Using Evidence*. Bristol: Policy Press.

Nutley, S., Powell, A. & Davies, H. (2012) *What Counts as Good Evidence?* London: Alliance for Useful Evidence.

Nutley, S., Walter, I. & Davies, H. (2007). *Using Evidence*. Bristol: Policy Press.

Pease, K. & Roach, J. (2017). How to Morph Experience into Evidence in Advances in Evidence-Based Policing. In J. Knutsson & L. Tompson (eds), *Advances in Evidence-Based Policing*. Abingdon: Routledge.

Pepper, I., Rogers, C. & Martin, H. (2020). Evidence Based Policing: A View on its development within the police service. *Journal of Work-Applied Management*, 12(1), 91–96. https://doi.org/10.1108/JWAM-01-2020-0001.

Pepper, I., Brown, I. & Stubbs, P. (2021). A Degree of Recognition across Policing: Embedding a Degree Apprenticeship Encompassing Work-Based Research. *Journal of Work Applied Management*, 14(1), 34–45. https://doi.org/10.1108/JWAM-12-2020-0056.

Pepper, I., Rogers, C. & Turner, J. (2024). The Adoption of Evidence-Based Policing: The Pivotal Role of First-Line Police Leaders across England and Wales. *International Journal of Emergency Services*, 13(1), 111–122. https://doi.org/10.1108/IJES-05-2023-0020.

Petersen, K., Weisburd, D., Fay, S., Eggins, E. & Mazerolle, L. (2023). Police Stops to Reduce Crime: A Systematic Review and Meta-analysis. *Campbell Systematic Reviews*, 19, e1302. https://doi.org/10.1002/cl2.1302.

Petticrew, M. & Roberts, H. (2003). Evidence, Hierarchies and Typologies: Horses for Courses. *Journal of Epidemiology and Community Healthcare*, 57, 527–529. https://doi.org/10.1136/jech.57.7.527.

Rogers, C., Pepper, I., & Skilling, L. (2022). Evidence-Based Policing for Crime Prevention in England and Wales: Perception and Use by New Police Recruits. *Crime Prevention and Community Safety*. https://doi.org/10.1057/s41300-022-00158-w.

Rousseau, D. & Gunia, B. (2015). Evidence-Based Practice: The Psychology of EBP Implementation. *Annual Review of Psychology*, 67(1), 667–692. https://doi.org/10.1146/annurev-psych-122414-033336.

Selby-Fell, H. (2018). *Embedding Evidence Based Policing (EBP): A Case Study Exploring Challenges & Opportunities*. PhD thesis, University of Huddersfield.

Selby-Fell, H. & Newton, A. (2022). Embedding Evidence-Based Policing (EBP): A UK Case Study Exploring Organisational Challenges. *The Police Journal*, 97(1), 73–91. https://doi.org/10.1177/0032258X221128404.

Sheptycki, J. W. E. (1994). *A Case Study of the European Liaison Unit at Dover in Kent*. London: Nuffield Foundation.

Sherman, L. (1998). *Evidence-Based Policing: Ideas in American Policing*. Washington, DC: Police Foundation. www.policinginstitute.org/wp-content/uploads/2015/06/Sherman-1998-Evidence-Based-Policing.pdf.

Sherman, L. (2011). *Professional Policing and Liberal Democracy. The 2011 Benjamin Franklin Medal Lecture*. London: Royal Society for the Encouragement of Arts, Manufactures and Commerce London.

Sherman, L. (2013). The Rise of Evidence-Based Policing: Targeting, Testing, and Tracking. *Crime and Justice*, 42(1), 377–451. https://doi.org/10.1086/670819.

Sherman, L. (2015). A Tipping Point for 'Totally Evidenced Policing': Ten Ideas for Building an Evidence Based Police Agency. *International Criminal Justice Review*, 25(1), 11–29. https://doi.org/10.1177/1057567715574372.

Sherman, L., Gottfredson, D., MacKenzie, D., Eck, J., Reuter, P. & Bushway, S. (1997). *Preventing Crime: What Works, What Doesn't, What's Promising*. Report to the U.S. Congress. Washington, DC.

Society for Evidence Based Policing. (2019). About Us. [online]. www.sebp.police.uk/about (accessed 4 August 2024).

Sparrow, M. (2016). *Handcuffed: What Holds Policing Back*. Washington, DC: Brookings Institution Press.

Stanko, E. & Dawson, P. (2016). *Police Use of Research Evidence*. Cham: Springer International Publishing.

Stockdale, K. (2017). Insider? Outsider? Reflections on Navigating Positionality When Researching Restorative Justice Policing. In S. Armstrong, J. Blaustein & A. Henry (eds), *Reflexivity and Criminal Justice: Intersections of Policy, Practice & Research*. London: Macmillan Publishing.

Telep, C. & Somers, L. (2017). Examining Police Officer Definitions of Evidence-Based Policing: Are We Speaking the Same Language? *Policing and Society*, 29(2), 1–17. https://doi.org/10.1080/10439463.2017.1373775.

Tilley, N. & Laycock, G. (2017). The Why, What, When and How of Evidence-Based Policing. In J. Knutsson & L. Tompson (eds), *Advances in Evidence-Based Policing*. Abingdon: Routledge.

Veltri, G. A., Lim, J. & Miller, R. (2014). More than Meets the Eye: The Contribution of Qualitative Research to Evidence-Based Policy-Making. *Innovation: The European Journal of Social Science Research*, 27(1), 1–4. https://doi.org/10.1080/13511610.2013.806211.

Weisburd, D. & Neyroud, P. (2011). *Police Science: Toward a New Paradigm*. Washington, DC: National Institute of Justice.

Williams, E. & Stanko, B. (2016). Researching Sexual Violence. In M. Brunger, S. Tong & D. Martin (eds), *Policing Research: Taking Lessons from Practice*. London: Routledge.

Wood, D., Cockcroft, T., Tong, S. & Bryant, R. (2017). The Importance of Context and Cognitive Agency in Developing Police Knowledge: Going Beyond the Police Science Discourse. *The Police Journal*, 91(2), 173–187https://doi.org/10.1177/0032258X176961.

Young, M. (1991). *An Inside Job: Policing and Police Culture in Britain*. Oxford: Oxford University Press.

6 Communication skills, decision-making and managing conflict

Ruth McGrath, Ian Pepper and Mark Thornton

Introduction

When canvassing members of the public about their experiences of policing, key factors affecting satisfaction often relate to individual communication skills and decision-making (FitzGerald et al., 2002). Comments refer to perceived fairness, the manner of speaking experienced (including politeness and use of appropriate, unbiased language) and ability or effectiveness in completing the task related to their encounter. HM Inspectorate of Constabulary and Fire & Rescue Services (HMICFRS) assess the effectiveness, efficiency and legitimacy of police forces and continue to measure this aspect of police service activity. This can be seen in the 2023/25 PEEL assessments of forces, questions used continue to measure and examine how good forces are at treating the public fairly, appropriately, and respectfully (HMICFRS, 2023). There is no doubt that a high level of importance is placed on the skills of communication, but what are these communication skills and what part do they have in decision-making, managing conflict and being a good police officer?

Historical context

Communication was a critical element of early law enforcement, even prior to the development of the police service as we know it today. During the Middle Ages, the 'hue and cry' was an effective method of peacekeeping and control of crime (e.g. to communicate the presence and identify of a thief). Onlookers were required to 'raise the hue' in such circumstances, to alert others equally obliged to assist with the detention of the offender. Failure to participate could result in a fine (Rawlings, 2002; Sagui, 2014). This was an effective method of drawing attention to a criminal matter, which relied on accurate and timely communication.

In the 1700s communication between the authorities enforcing the law and 'unlawful' gatherings was to have the Riot Act (1715) read out loud by a magistrate which was then accompanied by an order to disperse, which if not complied with, could result in the problem being dealt with by violent enforcement of the law by the military (Morgan & Rushton, 1998).

DOI: 10.4324/9781003492948-7

The possibilities of misunderstandings through the way this dispersal order was communicated to a gathered crowd of people with high tension are many and numerous, likely to raise the possibilities of escalation of conflict with potentially deadly outcomes (Chapter 14) rather than de-escalation, which is common practice today. Although it must be noted that others, such as Westley (1953), suggested from their research with US municipal police, that officers believed their use of sometimes-excessive violence was acceptable, forming part of their occupational culture and a required part of their job to be utilised as required and at their discretion.

In the late eighteenth century, the common method of communicating more widely to inform the public of unsavoury characters active in an area of the northeast of England was to use both newspapers and flyers (Morgan & Rushton, 1998). Today this has inevitably been superseded with multiple social media, online and broadcast forums. Effective communication continues to be a key tool in the armoury of those in policing. The College of Policing (2023a) highlighting in professional practice how vital effective working relationships are with the media, and the impact when relationships with the media are not effectively co-ordinated and managed, such as during the search for Nicola Bulley in 2023 (College of Policing, 2023b).

One to one communication needs to be a two-way process, with communication between individuals commencing with a police officer, staff member or volunteer planning and 'coding' a fact, idea or concept into a message ready for sending. Important in this stage is the selection of the many and varied mediums through which the message is to be communicated. This message is then communicated (or transmitted) verbally, non-verbally or in writing, for it to be then received.

On its reception by an individual, the communication is then decoded, interpreted and understood by the other person. In face-to-face communication, the person receiving the message will then hopefully send some kind of feedback, which will evidence their reception and understanding of the message along with the possibility of the requirement for further clarification. This will then continue to become a cyclical process, which then spirals into effective two-way communication. However, with larger groups, telephone, or online communication the opportunities for feedback and the checking of understanding are much more limited.

Regardless of whether the communication takes place in the eighteenth or twenty-first century, there are of course many factors which may interfere with this coding, transmission, reception, and interpretation of the message. Such interferences may include the choice of language, jargon, accents, different viewpoints on a subject, cultural differences, external noises etc.

Communication between two parties takes place using various mediums, however a more subtle, harder to control method is that of non-verbal communication, which includes 'reading' clues expressed by an individual's posture, orientation, gestures, touch, personal space, eye contact, vocal cues, and facial expressions. Although the research has been questioned, it is suggested that approximately 93% of our interpretation of communication comes from both vocal and facial cues (Hall & Knapp, 2013).

Within policing, the context for interference can be even broader, for example, there may be a heightened sense of tension when called to deal with some individuals, or the need to communicate urgent messages via a radio or mobile system in relation to the preservation of life.

The incorporation of the topic of communication skills into initial police education and training is not a new concept. Examples of late twentieth century recruit training courses indicate an emphasis on the development of personal communication skills, giving close attention to the significance of non-verbal communication during interviewing processes (Central Planning Unit, 1989).

Wilson (1968) details how easy it is for a police officer to reveal sub-consciously their apprehension in relation to individuals with whom they are communicating on the street. As a result, it is important that police officers take great care in how they judge others and are very conscious of how their own words and actions are perceived by others. With the decision making on the streets being devolved to the lower ranks of police officers (Bayley & Bittner, 1984), the simplest of communications and actions can lead to misinterpretation and mistrust. For example, Krameddine and Silverstone (2015) describe how the single action of handcuffing a homeless person has much longer-term impacts on the individuals respect for and willingness to cooperate with the police, although the police officer may have used the handcuffs to ensure their own safety from potential violence.

Naturally, methods emphasised during initial police training will vary in accordance with developments in technology and in keeping with current day issues.

Current professional practice

Communication skills

Today there continues to be recognition of the need for police officers to have well-developed communication skills, and these are established at an early stage of initial police learning, irrespective of the entry route used to enter the police service (Gander, 2023).

Police officers around the world are required to 'work' with people. In the UK, training, both in the classroom and in the workplace strives to ensure these skills are developed if not already well-established in the individual officer, staff member or volunteer. Research indicates that police officers themselves consider communications skills to be among the most important skills for their role (Charman, 2017). Officers communicate either at the business level within the organisation, perhaps negotiating over meeting divisional objectives, at a social level on a daily basis with colleagues, and the public, where it is an essential element for interacting with community members (Oxholm & Glaser, 2023; see also Chapter 8). Often officer's interactions with members of the public are at the point of crisis; but this may involve communicating with the wider community; linking with partner agencies and interacting with perpetrators of crime and anti-social behaviour. More than often though, communication is through face-to-face contact, where both verbal and non-verbal skills come to the fore. Willis and Mastrofski (2018) suggest that police officers should be skilled at using language to both control and inspire others, often in challenging situations; this should be coupled with their ability to listen and accurately interpret various forms of feedback and communication. Officers also reported the difficulties often faced communicating with irrational people with whom they regularly dealt with, this included those addicted to drugs, alcohol and with a mental illness (Willis & Mastrofski, 2018).

Therefore, the skill for police officers is not in coding and getting the message across first; but first assessing with whom they are communicating. The significance of this is recognised by the College of Policing in developing guidance for training of police offers responding to situations involving vulnerable persons who might be at risk of harm (College of Policing, 2024a, 2024b).

It is imperative that police officers *stop* (if possible), *look* (assess) and *listen* (effectively) to those they want or need to communicate with.

The extremes of either empathy or controlled aggression may actually be the message that officers need or want to convey. However, unless they have first assessed the recipients of that message, the required response may be failing before it even starts.

Willis and Mastrofski (2018) supports Bayley and Bittner (1984) in describing how domestic incidents can be among the most challenging incidents for officers to utilise their discretion and make decisions as to how to proceed. One may assume that officers find domestic incidents challenging due to the context (e.g. the emotions of those involved and multitude of communication received at such an event). For example, the victim of domestic violence who repeatedly apologises for 'their' own actions, which may have led them to having been beaten on several occasions; may well not yet be ready to listen to the importance to the officer of providing a statement. They need the police officer to listen, observe and provide support for them until realising they have gained, or re-gained control.

Similarly, a young person standing on a bridge over a major arterial road, the wrong side of the barrier on a Christmas Day afternoon, needs to hear and truly believe the message from the first police officer attending that life on the safe side of the barrier makes it worth climbing back over. Although specialist negotiators will have been called, the first officer attending needs to communicate both verbally and non-verbally in such a way as to influence the person before them. There is the need for the police officer to respect the decisions that have gone before, but then call upon the officers' empathetic tone of the voice, truly listening to them, filling the void of silence with words that mean something, while also conveying the suggested direction of coming back onto the safe side of the bridge barrier. It is imperative throughout this that the police officer through all their actions never makes a promise they cannot keep, they must remain truthful and honest.

Of course, there are many different approaches to communication in an operational policing role. Some examples include:

- Dealing with situations in an assertive manner where appropriate e.g. calming someone angry in the street or in a domestic-related situation (conflict resolution).
- Investigative interviewing skills with witnesses, victims, suspects, being aware of any specific vulnerabilities.
- Responding to a range of situations involving individuals who are vulnerable, either by age or capacity, e.g. application of the Right Care, Right Person initiative (College of Policing, 2024c).
- Bearing bad news, e.g. dealing with a sudden, unexpected death or informing loved ones of their loss.
- Briefing others to pass on information and debriefing others following a specific operation or task.
- The need to express impact of dealing with some incidents upon the officer themselves, e.g. via wellbeing support services (National Police Wellbeing Service, 2024).

Although by no means conclusive, the above examples demonstrate the requirement of a range of personal approaches adapted to the specific experience. Graef's (1989) research undertaken with serving police officers of all ranks recognised the necessity for active listening and the use of good communication skills at all times. More recently Charman (2017) refers to changes in society's requirements of the police service, yet effective communication skills are still considered a priority by police officers. The publication of the updated Code of Ethics (College of Policing, 2023c; see also Chapter 1) reinforces this, emphasising the need to listen effectively to others to develop an effective and appropriate response irrespective of the situation. Maintaining this awareness will enable an approach to be tailored and will reinforce steps taken towards building or maintaining trust in the police.

Decision-making

Daily police officers, staff members or volunteers on the frontline of policing encounter situations which require them to use their decision-making skills. Some situations are relatively straight-forward, others are much more complex, and an officer can find themselves making decisions which have a major impact on the lives of others, with limited, or contradictory information to assist in supporting those decisions.

To support decision-making the police service adopted the National Decision Model (NDM) (College of Policing, 2024d) which was aligned to the Code of Ethics. The Code of Ethics was updated in 2023, leading to some amendments to the NDM to ensure a continued affiliation to the Code of Ethics (College of Policing, 2023d). Commonly represented as a cyclical model, this has not been reproduced here as it is anticipated at the time of writing this model may shortly be updated. Thus, references here relate to the six-element model introduced in 2013 and encouraged for use across the police service, in all

Communication skills, decision-making and managing conflict 103

decision-making whether operational or not, and in relation to spontaneous or planned operations.

At the heart of the NDM, the Code of Ethics, its Ethical policing principles and Guidance for ethical and professional behaviour in policing provide a constant focus (College of Policing 2023c, 2023d, 2024e; see also Chapter 1).

The user is also required to consider the following elements:

- Gather information and intelligence.
- Analyse the situation to assess any threats and the risks of harm in order to develop a working strategy.
- Consider police powers, policies and legislation which may be relevant in this situation.
- Identify different options available when making the decision, ensuring you can say the final decision was both reasonable in the specific circumstances and proportionate, legitimate, necessary, and ethical.
- Once the action has been taken, outcomes should be reviewed.

(College of Policing, 2024d)

It can be important, and helpful to record the decision-making process, either during that decision-making (in the event of an ongoing operation) or following the actions undertaken (in the event of a more spontaneous incident, or one which is a little more routine). Doing so can help demonstrate impartiality, reducing later claims of bias in decision-making. A record can also assist in demonstrating ongoing thought processes, helping to demonstrate that even if a course of action is later considered to have negative outcomes, based on the information available at that time the decision-making process was sound. One recommendation arising from the Independent Police Complaints Commission (IPCC) investigation following the Stockwell shooting of Jean Charles de Menezes referred to the failure to make notes or keep logs of their decision-making processes by senior police officers. This called into question decision-making at the time (IPCC, 2007, recommendation 6, p. 108; Henriques, 2020).

The significance of use of body-worn video (BWV) should not be overlooked in recording of situations leading to spontaneous decision-making (Richards et al., 2018).

Managing conflict

It is almost assured that a police officer will have to use force (through controlled aggression) at some point during their career. This will likely involve the officer putting themselves between the public and someone intent on causing harm to either the officer, colleagues or the public. In an extreme example, during the summer of 2011, some 16,000 police officers from across the UK were deployed in London to quell rioters (Bridges, 2012). In August 2024, following a serious incident in Southport, once again there was a requirement for a widespread police response to the outbreaks of riots around England and Wales (Downs, 2024).

Police Officers, and those in frontline operational policing roles, complete and regularly renew nationally developed public and personal safety training (PPST). The content of the training can differ between roles, such as police officer or community support officer, but typically involves learning and practicing use of the NDM, tactical communications, medical implications, personal protection, and in the case of police officers and special constable, baton use, restraints, etc. (Kent Police, 2024).

When faced with a situation which may require the use of controlled force, the officer should initially pause (if only for a second) to assess the situation, including considering the threat posed by the potential opponent, the environment, personal skill level enabling the officer to deal with the situation and the options available for resolution. When questioned, Police officers felt that they were best placed to resolve any problem they faced with non-compliance of individuals, as by using a decision-making model, they could decide what the most appropriate level of force was to be used in a given situation (Independent Police Complaints Commission, 2015).

When police officers were questioned with regards to their views of the severity of the choice of force to be used by them when dealing with non-compliant persons, the IPCC (2015) found that officers perceived that verbal orders and the physical restraint of a person was at the lower end of a response, with the use of a taser (a less lethal weapon), a police baton and finally firearms the most severe responses.

Models for conflict management have now largely been superseded by use of the NDM. However, there are many and numerous factors which should be taken into consideration by the officer when working through a decision-

Table 6.1 Level of resistance, likelihood of harm and person's behaviour.

Risk of harm to officer or public	Level of resistance by an individual	Witnessed behaviour of an individual
↑	Serious aggression	Violence by person which could result in the grievous bodily harm or death of others
	Aggression	Person intentionally fights officer
	Active	Person pulls away or pushes officer away without any hitting
	Passive	Person stands still, digs heels in and will not move
	Verbal and gestures	Person refuses to comply with orders and/or aggressive body language witnessed
	Complies	No resistance offered and person complies

Source: adapted from West Yorkshire Police (2011)

making model and deciding the action to take. These factors include the environment where the incident is occurring, presence of others or crowds, weapons present, other dangers present such as vehicles or rivers, the person's believed use of alcohol and/or drugs, the physical ability and mental capacity of the individual, etc.

All these factors should be considered by the police officer before acting to ensure the safety of all parties. If the decision by the police officer is to use force, the options available to an officer range from primary responses, which include the use of restraints and handcuffs to secondary responses, which include use of less lethal weapons which include incapacitant sprays and Taser. Whatever models, factors and decisions are considered and made; it is imperative that the principles of the Code of Ethics are maintained throughout (College of Policing, 2024f).

As an example, the decision by armed officers performing a vehicle stop in London during 2011, to use force, where they believed firearms were present, led to the fatal shooting of Mark Duggan and subsequently escalated to riots involving an estimated 15,000 people across numerous locations (Bridges, 2012).

The use of force continuum captured in the subsequent review (HMIC, 2011) indicated the mere presence of the police officer to be a starting point of any model managing conflict. This is far more subtle than just verbal/non-verbal communication as a professional. As the mere physical presence and position of an officer in uniform, perhaps supported by colleagues or a blue light may be enough of a message to get a person to desist their actions.

Verbal communication must continue throughout the continuum and must never cease. Initially calmly asking for information or action, although the volume and tone may change to commands to ensure compliance, for example this could be instructing an individual to put a baseball bat on the ground. As this would be the key message an officer wants the aggravated person to receive. The response may have to be escalated through the continuum to become primary such as the use of hand techniques to restrain an individual, if this fails to meet the desired outcome then secondary techniques may be deployed such as the baton. However throughout, the officer should be telling the person to put the bat down.

Aftercare is also extremely important for both the person on whom force has been used and the officer using that force. For example, following deployment of an incapacitant spray – the detained person should be instructed to stand up, face into the breeze and let the incapacitant dry with reassurance from the police officer. When performing physical restraints, officers should be very aware of the potential for positional asphyxia during and afterwards, this is usually as a result of some kind of constriction of the airway. Fernanado and Byard (2013) detail how an individual died because of positional asphyxia following an assault where he was then wedged into a car.

Evidence-based case study illustrating professional practice

During a hot summer's night, two police officers in a patrol car were asked to attend the report of a disturbance at sheltered accommodation bungalows occupied by elderly people.

As the police officers arrived, they heard music blaring from the bungalows and saw many angry residents in the street, pointing to a specific address. While gathering information and assessing the risk, the officers clearly heard a loud, repetitive tune coming from a fully- illuminated bungalow with all its windows open. Hoping to resolve the issue and calm the residents, the officers knocked at the door. It was opened by an elderly female; she was polite, sober, appeared well and happy, and invited both officers in. Considering the impact of both police powers and policy, the officers decided to explain to the elderly resident why they were there and how she was inconveniencing her neighbours. Immediately she apologised, turned off her music and shut the windows, turning off most of the lights, telling the officers she would also apologies to her neighbours the following day.

As the officers walked away, residents thanked them and returned to their own homes. The situation seemed calm. The police officers communicated the sequence of events to their control room while reflecting on their response, as they walked. However, as they reached their police vehicle, they again heard music bellowing out into the night from the same bungalow. The officers returned to the address, once again well-lit and with windows open, and were again greeted by the same polite occupant. They repeated their previous actions, the noise abated and officers walked away only to re-visit again and again, each time considering additional options to resolve the disturbance.

Using effective communication over a two-hour period, the police officers gathered information and established the elderly woman had dementia, discovering also this date was the first anniversary of the death of her husband. It became evident that what she wanted was some company.

To resolve the problem that night, the police officers decided they were not best equipped to deal with the elderly woman and instead followed their force procedures, mindful of the woman's vulnerability, requesting the on-call emergency duty team from social services be called by the police control room. Once they arrived the police officers could be released from dealing with the incident and at least the immediate problem was solved for that night. In the longer term the woman's specific needs would be handled by a more appropriate supporting agency.

Duane, Brasher and Koch (2011) identified from their research how those with dementia value continued interactions with neighbours, carers and health professionals to deal with their feelings of loneliness. The use of communication, and eventual identification of the root problem enabled the police officers in the case study above, to take a decision which facilitated the resolution of the disturbance described and helped to provide continued daily interaction for the elderly woman to support needs associated with her dementia.

Future developments

Initial police training is regularly reviewed, and approaches updated, with the National Police Curriculum being updated at least on an annual basis, or more frequently in the event of changes to practice, policies and guidance. At the time of writing the Communication Skills element of the National Policing Curriculum (NPC) in respect of Professional Policing graduates, includes, in addition to standards in respect of protocols of radio communication and briefings, communication models; ethical and moral implications of use of force; and managing conflict (College of Policing, 2024e) once again placing emphasis on the importance of well-developed communication, decision-making and conflict resolution skills.

Such skills underpin the majority of interactions between members of the police service, the public in general, and local communities in particular. It can be confidently stated that in the fact of rapid changes in technology communication methods will evolve to provide what may be considered to be the best methods to meet the requirements of the public, and there is evidence of a growth in use of social media both to convey messages to, and to gain information from, local communities. This is not without its difficulties and leads to the introduction of further training and guidance in its use (NPCC, 2022). However, evidence suggests that appropriate strategies can lead to enhanced engagement of citizens with positive outcomes for the investigative process (Dekker, van den Brink & Meijer, 2020).

The publication of the revised Code of Ethics (College of Policing, 2023c) naturally has implications on other guidance, the National Decision Model being one such example. At the time of writing, some interim updating has been undertaken (College of Policing, 2023d) however, it is anticipated that in the near future this too may be subject of a deeper level of review.

As technology develops ever-more rapidly, the use of the telephone (mobile) continues to be used for the verbal reporting of crime and other ongoing incidents, but increasingly the use of mobile phone applications takes over some of these functions. While some of these are still relatively basic, recognition grows as to their value in providing reassurance and in supporting personal safety (Ford, Bellis, Judd, Griffith & Hughes, 2022). New technology also includes the adoption of artificial intelligence (AI) by police forces, and it is recognised early use will continue to grow both in respect of combatting and preventing crime, but also as a means of communication between the community and local police forces (Ezzeddine, Bayerl & Gibson, 2023). Such use enables the police service to continue to function despite reduced resources and is increasingly accepted by a more IT-literate society. This will not, however, remove the need for the human element of policing.

Conclusion

The skills of communication, the ability to engage in decision-making and resolving conflict remain key skills required of the police service as part of daily functions and duties.

The need to communicate effectively in a range of situations is essential to the role of the police officer. Link this to having the knowledge of relevant legislation and guidance, the ability to assess a situation, take decisions and manage conflict to assist in protecting those present and the complexity of the role becomes apparent. Awareness of the varied needs of differing situations, individuals, groups and communities is also essential to a successful outcome.

Being a police officer is not easy. It requires recognition and continuous analysis of demanding situations faced daily. It can be both rewarding and challenging, requiring focus and determination, and the continuous use of communication skills to support decision-making often in situations which draw on conflict management skills, to balance the needs of the public with officer safety. It requires individuals to continually be aware of and follow the Code of Ethics – to do the right thing for everyone.

> **Evidence-based case study illustrating professional practice**
>
> While on foot patrol as a neighbourhood officer you come across a group of young people on a usually quiet street who are shouting obscenities at each other, playing loud music and disturbing the peace.
>
> The force has a published priority of dealing with anti-sociable behaviour. On this occasion it could of course be dealt with by engaging with the group and issuing anti-social behaviour orders. This could result in the young person or their parents paying a fine or a community sentence/detention order along with the young person being 'labelled' as being anti-social and/or deviant.
>
> However, when considering the appropriate level of response, the evidence base suggests that police practitioners benefit from initially using their softer skills (Crawford, Lewis & Traynor, 2012). This includes communicating respectfully as professionals with the group and if necessary, advising them of the nature of their behaviour, its impact on others and what is and is not acceptable, this is often communicated both verbally and followed up with a warning letter (Crawford et al., 2012).
>
> Indeed, when considering the 'Use of Force Continuum,' the presence of a police officer and the use of good verbal and non-verbal communication skills are the correct position to start any such interaction (Wolf et al., 2009). A proportionate response with the young people will yield many results, both in the form of their personal identities, and other information and intelligence-gathering that can be useful to the officer and the police service.
>
> As a result, the young people will not be labelled as anti-social, which may reduce the likelihood of them being further engaged within the criminal

justice system. Instead, it enables the development of the police officers' reputation within the wider community and force, along with being seen in a positive light by the young people, their peers and parents, showing it is possible to deal with a situation of this nature using effective communication skills, enabling an appropriate decision to be taken, while observing the principles of the Code of Ethics.

Reflective question

If one of the actors in the case study described decided to become verbally aggressive towards you and strikes out, reflect upon the National Decision Model (NDM) to consider possible proportionate tactical responses.

References

Bayley, D. H. & Bittner, E. (1984). Learning the Skills of Policing. *Law and Contemporary Problems*, 47(4), 35–59.

Bridges, L. (2012). Four Days in August: the UK Riots. *Race and Class*, 54(1), 1–12.

Central Planning Unit. (1989) *Trainer Notes on Social Issues: Non-verbal Communication*. Harrogate: Central Planning Unit.

Charman, S. (2017) *Police Socialisation, Identity and Culture: Becoming Blue*. London: Palgrave Macmillan.

College of Policing. (2023a). Media Relations: Authorised Professional Practice. [online]. www.college.police.uk/app/engagement-and-communication/media-relations (accessed 18 November 2024).

College of Policing. (2023b). Independent External Review of Lancashire Constabulary's Operational Response to Reported Missing Person Nicola Bulley. [online]. https://assets.college.police.uk/s3fs-public/2023-11/Nicola-Bulley-independent-external-review.pdf (accessed 19 November 2024).

College of Policing. (2023c). Code of Practice for Ethical Policing. [online]. www.college.police.uk/ethics/code-of-practice (accessed 8 August 2024).

College of Policing. (2023d). Latest Changes – National Decision Model. [online] www.college.police.uk/app/national-decision-model/national-decision-model/changes (accessed 2 November 2024).

College of Policing. (2024a). Vulnerability-Related Risks: Clues. [online] www.college.police.uk/guidance/vulnerability-related-risks/clues#e2573960-e0c3-4ed0-b19b-720380ebb620 (accessed 3 November 2024).

College of Policing. (2024b). Professional Development: Developing the Right Skills and Knowledge to Respond Effectively to Vulnerable Individuals. [online]. www.college.police.uk/guidance/vulnerability-related-risks/professional-development#a215e2bb-8ba5-49b3-b1ad-8fcad735ee92 (accessed 2 November 2024).

College of Policing. (2024c). Right Care Right Person Toolkit. [online] www.college.police.uk/guidance/right-care-right-person-toolkit (accessed 3 November, 2024).

College of Policing. (2024d). National Decision Model. [online] www.college.police.uk/app/national-decision-model (accessed 2 November, 2024).

College of Policing. (2024e). Professional Policing Degree (PPD) 'Bridging': National Policing Curriculum. Coventry: College of Policing.

College of Policing. (2024f). Ethical Policing Principles. [online]. www.college.police.uk/ethics/code-of-ethics/principles (accessed 8 August 2024).

Crawford, A., Lewis, S. & Traynor, P. (2012). *Research Findings: Anti-social Behaviour Interventions with Young People.* University of Leeds.

Dekker, R., van den Brink, P. & Meijer, A. (2020). Social Media Adoption in the Police: Barriers and Strategies. *Government Information Quarterly*, 37(4). https://doi.org/10.1016/j.giq.2019.

Downs, W. (2024). Policing Response to the 2024 Summer Riots. [online]. https://commonslibrary.parliament.uk/policing-response-to-the-2024-summer-riots/ (accessed 2 November 2024).

Duane, F., Brasher, K. & Koch, S. (2011). Living Alone with Dementia. *Dementia*, 12(1), 123–136https://doi.org/10.1177/1471301211420331.

Ezzeddine, Y., Bayerl, P. S. & Gibson, H. (2023). Safety, Privacy, or Both: Evaluating Citizens' Perspectives around Artificial Intelligence Use by Police Forces. *Policing and Society*, 33 (7), 861–876. https://doi.org/10.1080/10439463.2023.2211813.

Fernanado, T. & Byard, R. (2013). Case Report: Positional Asphyxia without Active Restraint Following an Assault. *Journal of Forensic Sciences*, 58(6), 1633–1635.

FitzGerald, M., Hough, M., Joseph, I. & Qureshi, T. (2002). *Policing for London: Report of an Independent Study Funded by the Nuffield Foundation, the Esmée Fairbairn Foundation and the Paul Hamlyn Foundation.* Cullompton: Willan.

Ford, K., Bellis, M. A., Judd, N., Griffith, N. & Hughes, K. (2022). The Use of Mobile Phone Applications to Enhance Personal Safety from Interpersonal Violence – an Overview of Available Smartphone Applications in the United Kingdom. *BMC Public Health*, 22, 1158. https://doi.org/10.11186/s12889-022-13551-9.

Gander, S (2023) *The Essential Police Constable Degree Apprenticeship EPA Handbook.* St Albans: Critical Publishing.

Graef, R (1989) *Talking Blues.* London: Collins Harvill.

HMIC. (2011) *The Rules of Engagement: A Review of the August 2011 Disorders.* London: HMIC.

Hall, J. & Knapp, M. (2013). *Nonverbal Communication.* Berlin: Gruyter.

Henriques, R. (2020) *From Crime to Crime.* London: Hodder & Stoughton.

HMICFRS. (2023) PEEL Assessments 2023–2025. [online]. https://hmicfrs.justiceinspectorates.gov.uk/peel-assessments/what-is-peel/peel-assessments-2023-2025/ (accessed 1 November 2024).

IPCC. (2007) Stockwell Two: An Investigation into Complaints about the Metropolitan Police Service's Handling of Public Statements Following the Shooting of Jean Charles de Menezes on 22 July 2005. [online] www.jesip.org.uk/wp-content/uploads/2022/03/Stockwell-Shooting-Report-Jean-Charles-De-Menzes-Part-2.pdf (accessed 2 November 2024).

IPCC. (2015). *Police Use of Force.* Sale: TNS/Independent Police Complaints Commission.

Kent Police. (2024). Operational Partnerships - Public and Personal Safety Training SOP (O43a). [online]. www.kent.police.uk/foi-ai/kent-police/Policy/operational-partnerships/personal-safety-training-sop-o43a/ (accessed 18 November 2024).

Krameddine, Y. & Silverstone, P. (2015). Police Use of Handcuffs in the Homeless Population Leads to Long-Term Negative Attitudes within this Group. *International Journal of Law and Psychiatry*, 44, 81–90. https://doi.org/10.1016/j.ijlp.2015.08.034.

Morgan, G. & Rushton, P. (1998). *Rogues, Thieves and the Rule of Law: The Problem of Law Enforcement in North East England, 1718–1820.* London: UCL Press.

National Police Wellbeing Service. (2024). The National Police Wellbeing Service. [online]. www.oscarkilo.org.uk/ (accessed 3 November 2024).

NPCC. (2022). NPCC Strategy 2022: Misuse of Instant Messaging and Social Media. [online]. www.npcc.police.uk/SysSiteAssets/media/downloads/publications/disclosure-logs/workforce-coordination-committee/2023/139-2023-1.-30.11.2022iuimsm-wg-minutes-embedded-doc-02-c.pdf (accessed 5 November 2024).

Oxholm, P. D. & Glaser, J. (2023). Goals and Outcomes of Police Officer Communication: Evidence from in-depth Interviews. *Group Processes & Intergroup Relations*, 26 (4), 875–890https://doi.org/10.1177/13684302221121585.

Rawlings, P. (2002). *Policing: A Short History*. Cullompton: Willan.

Richards, P. (2018). The Exploration of Body-Worn Video to Accelerate the Decision-Making Skills of Police Officers within an Experiential Learning Environment. *Policing: A Journal of Policy and Practice*, 12(1), 43–49https://doi.org/10.1093/police/pax017.

Sagui, S. (2014). The Hue and Cry in Medieval English Towns. *Historical Research*, 87 (236), 179–193. https://doi.org/10.1111/1468-2281.12030.

Westley, W. (1953). Violence and the Police. *The American Journal of Sociology*, 59(1), 34–41.

West Yorkshire Police. (2011). Use of Force – Force Policy. [online]. www.westyorkshire.police.uk/about-us/policies-and-procedures/policies/operational-policing/use-of-force (accessed 27 October 2024).

Willis, J. & Mastrofski, S. (2018). Improving Policing by Integrating Craft and Science: What Can Patrol Officers Teach Us about Good Police Work?, *Policing and Society*, 28(1), 27–44. https://doi.org/10.1080/10439463.2015.1135921.

Wilson, J. Q. (1968). *Varieties of Police Behavior: The Management of Law and Order in Eight Communities*. Cambridge, MA: Cambridge University Press.

Wolf, R., Mesloh, C., Henych, M. & Frank-Thompson, L. (2009). Police Use of Force and the Cumulative Force Factor. *Policing: An International Journal of Police Strategies & Management*, 32(4), 739–757. https://doi.org/10.1108/13639510911000795.

7 Problem solving and problem-oriented policing

Jane Baxendale

Introduction

In many industries the notion of problem solving is often seen as both a skill and behaviour. Problem solving in policing can be defined as identifying the root causes of reoccurring problems in a community and using strategies that are long term and preventative to solve core issues (Lewis, 2011). Problem solving has been developed from a skill that is used in practice into multiple models, theories and methodologies. These range from use with the National Health Services as an approach to clinical trials (NHS Health Research Authority, 2022), to being used by private businesses to resolve perennial issues, the use of CCTV as a deterrent to crime and anti-social behaviour (POP Center, 2024a). In policing it has been embraced in many forms and embedded into the policing of neighbourhoods, communities and crime prevention. The development of a problem-oriented approach by those in policing therefore underpins the integration of problem solving into professional practice as a key methodology to preventing and reducing crime.

Historical context

Underpinning the development of a problem-oriented approach in policing, are a range of methods, models and theories that need to be considered.

Problem-oriented policing (POP) focuses on understanding reoccurring problems, adapting responses to a workable solution, has an emphasis on prevention and involvement from those impacted by the problem (Goldstein, 2018). The approach is underpinned by the scanning, analysis, response and assessment (SARA) framework. This is used nationally across policing and law enforcement agencies, enabling an approach to be followed that is both cyclical and systematic, rather than linear (Eck, 2010). There should be a logical sequence throughout its use but as each part of SARA is intrinsically linked to decision making, this may result in modification of the process. Therefore ongoing assessment may redefine the problem and lead to the model becoming cyclical or aspects of the SARA process being revisited out of its logical initial sequence.

DOI: 10.4324/9781003492948-8

Sidebottom et al. (2020) defines scanning as looking for patterns, analysis as the identification of the cause or problem, response as the development of an intervention to reduce or eliminate the problem, and assessment as the component that makes the links to the response or intervention and if it has been successful or not.

SARA is a framework which supports, identifies and addresses a key and underlying problem. Movement between all stages should be considered and each stage revisited as the problem may change or be redefined. Using SARA as a working model should be about constantly reviewing and refining knowledge at each stage of the process. Accurate monitoring of each stage will support the assessment of overall effectiveness.

SARA also aligns to the requirements for entry into the Tilley Awards (POP Center, 2024b). These awards recognise good problem-solving practice in police forces and their partners across the UK. This also provides the opportunity for great projects to be recognised by the Goldstein awards (POP Center, 2024a), submissions for which must follow the four broad stages of the SARA approach: scanning, analysis, response and assessment.

In conclusion the SARA framework can provide an effective method in the creation of a problem-solving plan for both everyday policing activity and to support deeper analysis of long-term perennial issues to pursue a prevention approach.

Following on from the use of SARA, several theories, models and methods can be associated with a problem solving and problem-oriented approach to professional practice in the policing and law enforcement.

Routine activity theory (RAT) stems from a criminological perspective. Routine activity was developed by Felson and Clarke (1998) who produced this crime prevention theory.

RAT examines crime from an offender's perspective. A crime will only be committed if a likely offender thinks that a target is suitable and a capable guardian is absent. It is their evaluation of a situation that determines if the crime is undertaken.

RAT is based on the concept that for a criminal activity to occur, three elements must be present:

1   A suitable target is available.
2   There is a lack of a suitable guardian to prevent the crime from happening.
3   A likely and motivated offender is present.

The first requirement for a crime to take place, the availability of a suitable target, can be categorised as a person, object or place.

The second requirement, the presence of a suitable guardian to discourage a crime from taking place, can be a person (such as security guard) or an object (such as CCTV), which acts as a deterrence to a crime being committed. Such guardians can be formal and deliberate, such as security alarms, or informal, such as neighbours.

It is also possible for a guardian to be present, but ineffective such as CCTV not being in the appropriate place or security staff who do not have sufficient training and awareness to be an effective deterrent. Modern technology such as 'video' doorbells and home security technology with built in cameras are often cited as 'guardians' of the home but their appropriate usage and accuracy can lead to issues linked to lack of accurate information and data sharing (Gee, 2022).

The final element of the RAT theory is a likely offender. If a target is unprotected by a capable guardian there is the opportunity for a crime to take place.

RAT argues that a crime can only exist when a motivated offender comes together, at the same time and place, as a vulnerable victim, in the absence of a capable guardian (Clarke & Eck, 2003).

The problem analysis triangle (PAT) assists such an analytical process by considering what is it about the location or individuals that enables the opportunity for the crime to take place. When the issues are established and defined, then the model can be used to create possible responses to deter opportunities for crime to be committed in an effort to resolve ongoing problems.

The PAT model can also help identify partnerships and collaborations to assist the police (the council or charities), such as looking at potential managers of the place where crime may be committed, a handler for the offender and a guardian for the victim.

The utilisation of theories, such as RAT and the complementary model of PAT, can support the development of a preventative approach to policing practice.

Furthermore, additional theories can be explored that support critical ways of thinking about crime prevention with an underpinning problem-solving stance. One example is rational choice theory (RCT), which operates on the premise that a potential offender weighs up the possible risk of committing an offence as opposed to the benefits before deciding whether to commit or otherwise, although Thomas et al. (2020) also highlight additional influencing factors such as the excitement associated with the crime need to be considered, to 'Hotspot' policing where areas of high crime in proportion to population are identified and data analysed to put in place measures to deter such crime (Ariel, 2023). For example, targeted foot patrols in hot spots seem to be effective and to improve public confidence and perceptions of safety Tuffin et al. (2006), at least for the duration of the presence of the guardian.

The concepts of broken windows and target hardening are also linked to the previously discussed theories and models of hotspot policing and routine activity theory. The broken windows concept was initially developed in New York to support creation of urban environments where there is an 'atmosphere of order'. This is rather than disorder where minor violations, such as broken windows and graffiti, lead to community decline and crime (Gau et al., 2014). The theory and its value to policing, although regularly referred too, is also regularly revisited and debated by both practitioners and academics. The notion that targeting neighbourhood disorder improves conditions and reduces crime must also be tempered with the impact of social processes (Gau et al., 2014). With O'Brien et al. (2019) questioning the effectiveness of broken windows as a theory at all. Whatever stance is taken, the idea of broken windows needs further thought and research on its impact as an approach to practice.

Target hardening is a measure that complements hot spot policing and broken windows methods in placing extra preventative means in place to deter crime. The College of Policing (2022) guidance for effective interventions for addressing neighbourhood crime includes various target hardening measures linked to physical security such as window locks, alley gating, lighting and property marking.

Many of the theories, methods and models associated with problem solving or a problem-oriented approach interconnect in their utilisation.

Current professional practice

Problem solving is embedded into the policing professional profiles (College of Policing, 2024a) which underpin the requirements for roles within policing. Within policing the term problem solving has been incorporated into a methodology using the term problem-oriented policing (POP) and is acknowledged as an effective evidence-based policing strategy (Weisburd et al., 2010).

The key differences between problem solving and problem-oriented policing is that the term 'problem-oriented policing' describes a comprehensive structure which, in an overarching way, helps the police to achieve their overall goals (Scott & Kirby, 2012). In contrast, the term 'problem-solving' describes a cognitive process that is used to work through a problem.

There are numerous reasons for using a POP approach as a core method to counterbalance reactive policing. Sidebottom et al. (2020) discuss an evidence-base from an evidence review conducted by the Campbell Collaboration which suggests the POP approach as being effective, efficient, reduces demand, fosters innovation, promotes public satisfaction and is good for morale. This list encompasses some of the core values of policing within the competency and values framework (CVF) that puts the public at the heart of its service (College of Policing, 2023).

Dahl et al. (2022) suggest that a performance culture can be linked to a reactive approach to policing in an age where cost cutting measures have meant a workforce where greater efficiency is needed and individuals are expected to deliver more. This can lead to allocation of resources on more high-profile areas where the merge of a proactive prevention and a reactive approach is not always clear. The concept of moving policing from a reactive to more proactive preventative approach was examined by HMIC (2012), who explored opportunities to further this move in response to challenges faced at the time by austerity. The suggestion is that a preventative approach not only reduces crime but also demands on policing.

As the evidence-base increases and police learning has evolved to encompass POP, the barriers that have prevented a problem-oriented approach being more widely adopted are reducing, as these issues are explored and brought to the forefront, there are opportunities for prevention to be used more consistently across contemporary policing.

Neighbourhoods and communities: adopting POP

The nature of problem solving and using problem-oriented policing as a method is often aligned to some key areas of policing, namely those involved in crime prevention, communities and neighbourhoods. Tilley (2009) explores the notion of crime prevention using terms such as crime reduction, public and community safety and explored how crime prevention encompasses a range of tools and methods with a goal to reducing crime. Many of these aspects are linked to the underpinning skill of problem solving and using the POP approach. This important role of problem solving for officers, staff and volunteers to utilise when engaging in neighbourhood policing as a tool to resolve perennial issues of crime and disorder is identified by HMICFRS (2024). Tilley (2009) also notes how no one tool or method supports crime prevention but it is a range of approaches tailored to an issue that may be identified using the SARA framework that would support effective crime prevention. The use of the term crime prevention is alternated with crime reduction as the association is that in preventing crime it would also be reduced. It is also significant that crime prevention is seen as core strategy in policing alongside other more proactive approaches to form a more holistic response.

The use of crime prevention or reduction strategies as a default policing method can be challenging, one barrier can be the lack of data, information and timely research on the impact of such approaches. Policing often uses data and cost benefit to ascertain effectiveness and if the nature of prevention is to avoid crime, then the data on how many crimes it deters can be challenging to measure. Cherney (2006) considers how problem solving is a core component of crime prevention and that data can be both generated and analysed from crime prevention activity. Historical data can be analysed before the use of a particular prevention method to ascertain if a reduction a crime has occurred, however if the nature of the reduction is to prevent a crime type before it has occurred this could prove far more challenging.

The College of Policing What Works Centre for Crime Prevention developed a Manning cost-benefit tool (MCBT) (College of Policing, 2024b). This tool seeks to address the issue of generating evidence and applying a measure to evaluate the impact of a prevention programme in terms of cost, therefore adding credence to the use of crime prevention methods linked to problem solving as a core approach to policing. Such tools support increasing both the impact and use of crime prevention as the first response for policing, this then gives executives insight into the impact of measures from both a financial and data perspective. Other models have also been developed to enhance information on cost benefits of crime reduction initiatives in other jurisdictions, such as in Australia (Manning et al., 2016), the aim throughout to make better evidence-informed decisions as to where best invest in crime reduction for the highest return on investment. The challenge of course is that such measures do not necessarily take into account wider social benefits of initiatives.

In addition, the College of Policing (2024b) supports a crime reduction toolkit via the What Works Centre that utilises the EMMIE framework (effect, mechanism, moderators, implementation and economic cost) to present evidence from systematic reviews. This toolkit allows forces and individuals to assess the impact of different interventions on reducing crime and the strength of the evidence that then allows the sharing of good practice on crime prevention initiatives across the country.

Egbert and Esposito (2024) explore how digitalisation and the use of algorithms may also offer support for a preventative approach in policing. They examine how digitalisation of crime prevention can support precision through a 'predicative policing' approach, which is a methodology that is often associated with supporting POP. Such 'predicative policing' approaches are not without their challenges, with Mugari and Obioha (2021) highlighting how questions are still to be answered as to the effectiveness of predictive policing software, the scope for crime type predictions, the quality of the data utilised, how such data is stored and for what purposes. This method of predicative policing is explored by Egbert and Esposito (2024) with the use of algorithms focusing patrols on areas that could be termed as hotspots. Braga (2017) defines such hotspots as not just applying problem solving to a specific geographical area but instead 'micro units' such as buildings, addresses or core segments of streets so that such hot spot policing can be seen as not just the focus of one division of policing but more on a locality. The notion of using crime prevention, problem solving and POP as the remit of only those in communities and neighbourhoods is integral to reinforcing these as a core approach in policing in all areas.

The common association of a problem-solving approach to the functions of those in the neighbourhood and community facing teams is one that is embedded across policing. Problem solving is often perceived as the remit of those in operational neighbourhood and community roles and therefore police initial education and training approaches this as a core aspect of the initial learning curriculum. O'Reilly (2024) acknowledges the resurgence of problem solving as part of reestablishing the Neighbourhoods function and a move away from a reactive model that may not meet long term demand. The use of a problem-solving approach as one aligned to working with the community stems from the perception that this approach works best when used collaboratively with communities, so enforcing a model of policing that puts the public first and embracing the values of public service.

This is an aspect of police learning that is a cornerstone of operational practice and aligns to the values of the competency and values framework. On review of learning for initial entry in to policing in England and Wales both the curriculum and assessment components continue to embed community learning in recognition of this key aspect of policing, with content coverage on problem solving and use of the SARA approach.

The benefits of community policing are recognised across the United Kingdom and many other nations globally, firmly establishing it as a key aspect of the policing model with problem solving linked as the main role of those in this area. Donnelly (2013) explores community policing in Europe and makes links to the level of involvement police have in core community issues. As such the problem-solving approach can lead to wider involvement in policy discussion in certain European settings and therefore the establishment of the importance of a problem-solving approach more widely.

Operational policing: embedding POP

Problem-solving approaches are often linked with those working in operational roles within community and neighbourhood teams. If problem solving is to be viewed as a competitive model for preventative measures in policing whether used as a skill, method or model, the concept can and should be applied to all aspects of policing.

For example, in an investigative setting the nature of problem solving can underpin the investigative process. Eck and Rossmo (2019) offer a cyclical process, where if problem solving is embedded into the investigative cycle it can assist in defining an issue in the investigation.

Similarly, problem solving can be applied in the digital arena where widespread use of social media, access to police data and links to crime can be explored. Elphick et al. (2021) discuss the use of digital apps as a way of engaging with communities to support building trust and confidence. The use of apps and digital capability to engage the community can lead to increased communications, information sharing on crimes or perceived crime concerns in local areas, which can lead to shared ownership and collaboration. Elphick et al. (2021) caution however that the use of digital apps are best used and monitored by skilled officers (staff and volunteers) to ensure digital accountability and avoid negative outcomes impacting on public perceptions. Egbert and Esposito (2024) continue to debate digital policing and its potential in predictive policing by using data collated via algorithms to 'predict' areas of crime or likely crime, which endorses a problem-solving approach. The potential of such digital capability in policing to assist in crime reduction and problem-solving is limitless if the skills and technology are acquired, developed and utilised in professional policing practice, however financial implications and lack of resource can be a significant limitation in its application.

The increasing development of artificial intelligence (AI) continues to pose both challenges and opportunities for new problem-solving capacity in policing as the automated and predictive nature of AI can be used to inform and assess issues while using the intelligence to create solutions. Singh and Nambiar (2024) examined the use of AI to tackle online child sexual abuse (OCSA), a crime that can be challenging to both identify and report due to dark web activities and increased online crime that can evade security measures and therefore detection (Chapter 11). When AI is controlled and utilised cautiously it can be effective in the detection and prediction of OCSA, as well as affording tools that recognise patterns such as chatbots, mobile computing, machine learning and pattern recognition that aid in the identification and therefore the prevention of such crimes (Singh & Nambiar, 2024). By harnessing digital and AI as problem-solving tools, policing can add credence to using POP as an effective operational method.

Indeed in other areas of policing such as public protection, tool kits, strategies and policy aligned to key national initiatives such as combatting violence against women and girls (VAWG) and domestic violence with updated risks assessment tools of domestic abuse risk assessments (DARA) can all be said to derive from a problem-solving approach. Their development stems initially from a problem or issue that those in the policing arena review and then develop such tools in response to the problem. True (2020) identifies issues linked to violence against women, utilising the term problem in defining such a core subject. This in turn links to the principle that a problem-solving approach is needed from such an identification of a key societal issue such as VAWG. However to embed a valid problem-solving approach the development of tools, strategies, policies or approaches should be assessed and refined, with further exploration into the root cause of the problem to analyse and assess to put prevention methods in place from the outset.

Response and roads policing are operational roles that are public facing, involving community interactions that are usually associated with the neighbourhood and community teams. These areas involve policing in some complex and critical situations, where quick problem solving as well as longer term prevention methods can be applied. Problem-solving methods and tools can be seen clearly in many aspects of roads and driving today such as the use of road calming measures linked to signage designed by children in areas where there are schools, speed bumps and traps, cameras and even some much-debated tools such as smart motorways. All stem from problem-solving activity and solutions that link due to enforcement to both roads and response activity. The varying use of police discretion and involvement of the community can lead to a more adaptable use of problem solving linking into a more iterative approach (Lumsden, 2013). Rather than one method suiting all situations, public perception and comparison in response can be a factor in how the crime is perceived and therefore effect the solution to the problem.

Problem solving and using a POP approach can and should be a core aspect of professional policing practice. The embedding of this approach is intrinsic to changing the culture and nature of predominantly a reactive approach and one that aligns to those in the neighbourhoods and community policing functions to a core component that informs and drives all areas of policing.

The importance of partnerships in POP

For many public sector areas such as health and education the nature of partnership working is a basis for success in most projects and initiatives. Key examples where this can be seen is when working with vulnerable people where agencies need to work in partnership to provide the correct support. One of the highest use of police resources can be associated with missing persons, domestic situations and mental health support. By collaborating with key partners to problem solve, resources can be shared and the appropriate support provided. Such a collaborative approach can be seen through the Right Care Right Person

(RCRP) national partnership agreement and toolkit (Gov.uk, 2024). This agreement and toolkit endorse partnership work through identifying the correct agency or partner to support those in mental health crisis and identify practice and process that improves partnership working and the care for those who are at their most vulnerable. A further initiative that supports vulnerable people through partnership working is the 'Herbert Protocol' (Age UK, 2024) that supports the sharing of information across partners and the police to provide a more effective response if a person goes missing. This is facilitated by collecting key facts about that person linked to their patterns and key places of interest which may support locating them using local businesses, settings and charities (Age UK, 2024).

Both examples demonstrate problem-solving initiatives that have led to long-term preventative approaches that are being used nationally to assist in reducing police response in these areas and utilise partners effectively in supporting vulnerable people. This also highlights that problem solving and an initial response does not always have to be led primarily by the police and that in some cases the correct identification of a problem is the remit of the partner organisation.

Leadership and POP

As intrinsic as embedding a problem-oriented approach is to different areas of policing, a key factor to embedding such a method successfully is effective leadership and leaders who choose to advocate a problem-oriented approach as equal to that as a reactive model. Scott and Kirby (2012) also highlight the importance of leaders supporting the implementation of such change, continuing to identify how supportive champions can easily change roles and be replaced by less supportive leaders. Many leadership styles such as transactional, situational, transformational leadership have been explored and considered as to their effectiveness in a policing organisation (Chapter 14).

However it is important to focus on a whole organisational approach to change the perspective and priority away from reactive approaches to ones that are preventative. The context of problem-oriented policing includes features that the police organisation can either facilitate or deter when considering the adoption of problem-oriented ways of working (Bullock et al., 2022) such factors include leadership. The presence of committed leaders champion this approach and allow capacity, access to data, analysis and learning in this area is a main component in its success as a primary approach in a force. There is compelling evidence (Bullock et al., 2022) in support of the effectiveness of problem-oriented policing, with an increasing evidence base it is important to ensure the key markers of data, evidence and cost are continually assessed for effectiveness and as key indicators that leaders use to ascertain success and therefore continued use. This evidence base linked to crime prevention is further restated by Rogers et al. (2022) who explore the high compatibility of evidence-based approaches to crime prevention.

In order to engage with and inform leaders, the national Problem Solving and Demand Reduction Programme (PSDRP) was established (College of Policing,

2021). The PSDRP highlights the requirement for senior leaders to be committed to problem solving, with a focus on embedding POP learning and research within practice.

Diversity, equality and inclusion: an opportunity through problem-solving

When considering wider policing issues, diversity, equality and inclusion (DEI) is a significant aspect to address. Thought needs to be given to cultural change and how problem solving can assist this. The Baroness Casey Review (2023) highlights core perennial problems of short-term solutions and initiatives making officers, staff and force culture weary of implementing change as the next 'new thing'. Scott and Kirby (2012) also identify how cynicism towards change by those on the frontline can lead to failure of reform. Therefore consideration of longer-term problem-solving approaches linked to cultural change should be reflected on and methods adopted associated with problem solving over a longer term. This could counter a cultural reactionary approach to short term projects and initiatives as defined by the Baroness Casey Review (2023).

Future developments

Problem-oriented approaches can be applied to all areas of policing, partnership working and cultural issues, demonstrating that a problem-oriented approach is one that is already intrinsic to the service. However the question remains; why is POP not the core approach in the current policing environment? If evidence suggests that this approach is both successful and has a cost benefit, how can we balance proactive and reactive policing in professional policing practice?

Bullock (2012) discusses the perception of community policing as being the alternative to a reactive approach, with problem-oriented approaches being linked intrinsically to this area. However, the notion of moving other areas of policing to use this as a primary approach is more challenging. This may stem from cultural expectations of police 'reacting' to a crime in a prompt and visible manner or from the nature of crimes evolving, policing technology and methods being out of sync with societal shifts.

Regardless of the reasons, as the evidence base increases and practice evolves to highlight the benefits of the prevention approach, this will assist in raising the profile of POP. Key initiatives such as the revitalisation of the Tilley Awards that filter into the international Goldstein awards (POP Center, 2024b) will increase the visibility and share the benefits of problem-solving. Embedding a problem-solving approach culturally within policing at all levels, sharing successes and increasing participation will, in the longer term, lead to the approach becoming adopted in everyday policing. This will ensure that POP is not a relatively short-term initiative but an approach that is embedded and intrinsic in policing.

The topics of problem solving and evidence-based practice can often be intrinsically linked as an evidence-base can provide research and practice that supports problem-solving activity (Chapter 5). Linking problem solving and evidence-based policing within police learning seems to be a natural evolution, as connections can be sought in both terminology used and approaches. Moreover evidence-based policing may set the basis or become the methodology behind a problem-solving approach.

Intrinsic links between evidence-based policing and POP are seen in current professional practice. For example, Gibbons (2024) reports on research which recognises that the use of evidence-based policing is needed to identify a problem-solving approach to tackling VAWG hotspots.

A future where the concepts of evidence-based and POP are interconnected, could lead to both an increase in evidence of what does and what does not work in policing and the embedding of a problem-solving approach as the core policing model.

Conclusion

Embedding a problem-oriented approach throughout policing is multi-faceted and as the originator of the term Goldstein (2015) recognised this approach is as relevant today as its first conception. The policing role is complex but needs to continue to be efficient and effective, these are attributes that can be addressed through adopting a POP approach.

The POP approach is gaining an evidence-base that is changing its status and leading to a shift in how policing addresses and responds to protecting the public it serves. As new information and data challenge the cost effectiveness, learning is enhanced to embed the concept and leaders champion expected standards, a longer-term commitment to the practice of POP is being instilled across the service. Through community and partnership working, celebrating and sharing successes regularly, the POP approach is being firmly established in professional policing practice today.

The collaboration of these factors is giving way to a change in policing focus and affording credibility to the methods, theories, models and evidence, that support a problem-solving way of working, and a shift to a problem-oriented approach that applies to all areas, functions, ranks and roles in contemporary professional policing practice.

Evidence-based case study illustrating professional practice

As a new graduate officer working in neighbourhoods and with communities, you have been asked by your first line leader to review how the team develop, use and review their POP plans and how problem-solving approaches can be further embedded both in force and with partners. You use evidence from force developed POP plans as well as the forces previous Tilley Award submissions.

On reviewing the Tilley Award submissions, the SARA method is seen to be embedded in developing both POP plans and problem-solving submissions. Through the use of this method the force can review its approach to both engaging with partners and employing the SARA methodology in the teams' ways of working as well as sharing the approach across the force.

The findings and review of using SARA could assist in the redevelopment of the POP plans in force and the updating of initiatives linked to partners as well as encouragement of the force members to enter good practice for Tilley awards.

To further gain evidence into other problem-solving approaches, you search the College of Policing's 'Practice Bank' and 'What Works Centre' (College of Policing, 2024c) to complement findings from the Tilley submissions.

Your review leads to qualitative findings that most successful POP not only uses SARA but incorporates an element of partnership with, for example, stakeholders, communities, charities or other public and private sector areas. Therefore the successful embedding of a POP approach is intrinsic on involving partners.

You present your findings to your leader, who requests you initiate a review of the teams POP plans, wider policies and initiatives to embed a problem-solving approach.

Reflective questions

Reflect on why the use of partners may be a contributing factor to successful problem solving. Consider:

- How can a methodology such as SARA be utilised in a force to influence POP plans?
- How can partners be involved in a POP approach?
- Which policies, procedures or processes could be reviewed to further support a POP approach?

References

Age UK. (2024). The Herbert Protocol. [online]. www.ageuk.org.uk/calderdaleandkirklees/about-us/latest-news/articles/2018/the-herbert-protocol/ (accessed 21 May 2024).

Ariel, B. (2023). Implementation Issues with Hot Spot Policing. *International Journal of Law, Crime and Justice*, 75. https://doi.org/10.1016/j.ijlcj.2023.100629.

Baroness Casey Review. (2023). Final Report: An Independent Review into the Standards of Behaviour and Internal Culture of the Metropolitan Police Service. [online]. www.met.police.uk/SysSiteAssets/media/downloads/met/about-us/baroness-casey-review/update-march-2023/baroness-casey-review-march-2023a.pdf (accessed 20 July 2024)

Braga, A. (2017). Hot Spots Policing: Theoretical Perspectives, Scientific Evidence, and Proper Implementation. In B. Teasdale & M. Bradley (eds), *Preventing Crime and Violence. Advances in Prevention Science.* Cham: Springer. https://doi.org/10.1007/978-3-319-44124-5_23.

Bullock, K. (2012). Community, Intelligence-Led Policing and Crime Control. *Policing and Society*, 23(2), 125–144. https://doi.org/10.1080/10439463.2012.671822.

Bullock, K., Sidebottom, A., Armitage, R., Ashby, M. P. J., Clemmow, C., Kirby, S., Laycock, G. & Tilley, N. (2022). Problem-Oriented Policing in England and Wales: Barriers and Facilitators. *Policing and Society*, 32(9), 1087–1102. https://doi.org/10.1080/10439463.2021.2003361.

Cherney, A. (2006). Problem Solving for Crime Prevention. *Trends & Issues in Crime and Criminal Justice*, (314), 1–6. www.aic.gov.au/sites/default/files/2020-05/tandi314.pdf.

Clarke, R. V. & Eck, J. (2003). *Become a Problem-Solving Crime Analyst in 55 Steps.* London: Jill Dando Institute of Crime Science, University College London. https://popcenter.asu.edu/sites/default/files/55stepsuk_0_0.pdf.

College of Policing. (2021). Problem-Oriented Policing: Effective Implementation of Problem Solving. [online]. https://assets.college.police.uk/s3fs-public/2021-05/problem-solving-scope-of-practice-guidelines-250521.pdf (accessed 19 July 2024).

College of Policing. (2022). Effective Interventions for Tackling Neighbourhood Crime. [online]. www.college.police.uk/guidance/neighbourhood-crime/interventions-situational-crime-prevention (accessed 16 July 2024).

College of Policing. (2023). Competency and Values Framework (CVF). [online]. www.college.police.uk/career-learning/competency-and-values-framework (accessed 22 April 2024).

College of Policing. (2024a). Professional Profiles. [online]. https://profdev.college.police.uk/professional-profiles/ (accessed 30 May 2024).

College of Policing. (2024b). Practical Evaluation Tools. [online]. www.college.police.uk/research/practical-evaluation-tools (accessed 15 July 2024).

College of Policing. (2024c). What Works Centre for Crime Reduction. [online]. www.college.police.uk/research/what-works-centre-crime-reduction (accessed 20 May 2024).

Dahl, J., Fyfe, N., Gundhus, H., Larsson, P., Skjevrak, P., Runhovde, S. & Vestby, A. (2022). Old, New, Borrowed and Blue – Shifts in Modern Policing. *The British Journal of Criminology*, 62(4), 931–947. https://doi.org/10.1093/bjc/azab085.

Donnelly, D. (2013). *Community Policing in the EU.* London: Palgrave Macmillan. https://doi.org/10.1057/9781137290618_4.

Eck, J. (2010). Assessing Responses to Problems: An Introductory Guide for Police Problem-Solvers. [online]. https://live-cpop.ws.asu.edu/sites/default/files/tools/pdfs/AssessingResponsesToProblems-2.pdf.

Eck, J. & Rossmo, D. (2019). The New Detective: Rethinking Criminal Investigations. *Criminology & Public Policy*, 18(3), 601–622. https://doi.org/10.1111/1745-9133.12450.

Egbert, S. & Esposito, E. (2024). Algorithmic Crime Prevention: From Abstract Police to Precision Policing. *Policing and Society* [Preprint]. https://doi.org/10.1080/10439463.2024.2326516.

Elphick, C., Philpot, R., Zhang, M., Stuart, A., Walkington, Z., Frumkin, L., Pike, G., Garner, K., Lacey, M., Levine, M., Price, B., Bandara, A, & Nuseibeh, B. (2021). Building Trust in Digital Policing: A Scoping Review of Community Policing Apps. *Police Practice and Research*, 22 (5), 1469–1491. https://doi.org/10.1080/15614263.2020.1861449.

Felson, M. & Clarke, R. (1998). *Opportunity Makes the Thief: Home Office Police Research Series Paper 98.* London: Policing and Reducing Crime Unit. http://webarchive.nationalarchives.gov.uk/20110218135832/rds.homeoffice.gov.uk/rds/prgpdfs/fprs98.pdf.

Gau, J., Corsaro, N. & Brunson, R. (2014). Revisiting Broken Windows Theory: A Test of the Mediation Impact of Social Mechanisms on the Disorder–Fear Relationship. *Journal of Criminal Justice*, 42(6), 579–588. https://doi.org/10.1016/j.jcrimjus.2014.10.002.

Gee, J. (2022). Surveillance Cameras, Facial Recognition Software and False Arrests. *Journal of Offender Monitoring*, 35(1), 17–26. https://civicresearchinstitute.com/online/PDF/JOM-3501-04-Gee-Surveillance.pdf.

Gibbons, S. (2024). Research Calls for Evidence-Based Policing Approach to Tackle Public Space VAWG Hotspots. 21 May. [online]. https://policinginsight.com/feature/analysis/research-calls-for-evidence-based-policing-approach-to-tackle-public-space-vawg-hotspots/ (accessed 22 May 2024).

Goldstein, H. (2015) *Problem-Oriented Policing*. New York: McGraw-Hill.

Goldstein, H. (2018). On Problem-Oriented Policing: The Stockholm Lecture. *Crime Science*, 7(13), 1–9. https://doi.org/10.1186/s40163-018-0087-3.

Gov.uk. (2024). National Partnership Agreement: Right Care, Right Person (RCRP). [online]. www.gov.uk/government/publications/national-partnership-agreement-right-care-right-person/national-partnership-agreement-right-care-right-person-rcrp (accessed 21 May 2024).

HMIC. (2012). Taking Time for Crime: A Study of How Police Officers Prevent Crime in the Field. [online]. https://assets-hmicfrs.justiceinspectorates.gov.uk/uploads/taking-time-for-crime.pdf (accessed 30 June 2024).

HMICFRS. (2024). State of Policing: The Annual Assessment of Policing in England and Wales 2023. [online]. https://hmicfrs.justiceinspectorates.gov.uk/publication-html/state-of-policing-the-annual-assessment-of-policing-in-england-and-wales-2023/ (accessed 20 July 2024).

Lewis, A. (2011). Implementing A Problem Solving Approach to Neighbourhood Policing: The Camden Experience. *Police Journal*, 84(1), 35–46. https://doi.org/10.1350/pojo.2011.84.1.509.

Lumsden, K. (2013). Policing the Roads: Traffic Cops, 'Boy Racers' and Anti-Social Behaviour. *Policing and Society*, 23(2), 204–221. https://doi.org/10.1080/10439463.2012.696642.

Manning, M., Wong, T. & Vorsina, M. (2016). *Manning Cost-Benefit Tool*. Canberra: ANU Centre for Social Research and Methods. [online]. https://csrm.cass.anu.edu.au/research/projects/manning-cost-benefit-tool (accessed 20 July 2024).

Mugari, I. & Obioha, E. (2021). Predictive Policing and Crime Control in The United States of America and Europe: Trends in a Decade of Research and the Future of Predictive Policing. *Social Sciences*, 10(6), 234. https://doi.org/10.3390/socsci10060234.

NHS Health Research Authority. (2022). Our Full Response to WHO Consultation on improving clinical Trials. [Online]. www.Hra.Nhs.Uk/About-Us/News-Updates/Our-Response-Who-Consultation-improving-clinical-trials/ (accessed 19 September 2023).

O'Brien, D., Farrell, C. & Welsh, B. (2019). Looking Through Broken Windows: The Impact of Neighborhood Disorder on Aggression and Fear of Crime Is an Artifact of Research Design. *Annual Review of Criminology*, 2, 53–71. https://doi.org/10.1146/annurev-criminol-011518-024638.

O'Reilly, C. (2024). *Neighbourhood Policing: Context, Practices and Challenges*. Bristol: Policy Press.

POP Center. (2024a). Goldstein Awards. [online]. https://popcenter.asu.edu/content/goldstein-awards (accessed 16 July 2024).

POP Center. (2024b). Tilley Awards and Submissions. [online]. https://popcenter.asu.edu/content/tilley-award-submissions (accessed 17 July 2024).

Rogers, C., Pepper, I. & Skilling, L. (2022). Evidence-Based Policing for Crime Prevention in England and Wales: Perception and Use by New Police Recruits. *Crime Prevention & Community Safety*, 24(4), 328–341. https://doi.org/10.1057/s41300-022-00158-.

Scott, M. & Kirby, S. (2012). *Implementing POP: Leading, Structuring, and Managing a Problem-Oriented Police Agency*. Washington, DC: Office of Community Oriented Policing Services, US Dept. of Justice. [online]. https://popcenter.asu.edu/sites/default/files/implementing_pop.pdf.

Sidebottom, A., Bullock, K., Ashby, M., Kirby, S., Armitage, R., Laycock, G. & Tilley, N. (2020). Successful Police Problem-Solving: A Practice Guide. [online]. https://popcenter.asu.edu/sites/default/files/successful_police_problem_solving_a_guide.pdf.

Singh, S. & Nambiar, V. (2024). Role of Artificial Intelligence in the Prevention of Online Child Sexual Abuse: A Systematic Review of Literature. *Journal of Applied Security Research*, online ahead of print. https://doi.org/10.1080/19361610.2024.2331885.

Thomas K., Loughran, T, & Hamilton, B. (2020). Perceived Arrest Risk, Psychic Rewards and Offense Specialisation: A Partial Check on Rational Choice Theory. *Criminology*, 58(3), 485–509. https://doi.org/10.1111/1745-9125.12243.

Tilley, N. (2009). *Crime Prevention*. Cullompton: Willan Publishing.

Tuffin, R., Morris, J. & Poole, A. (2006). *An Evaluation of the Impact of the National Reassurance Policing Programme*. Home Office Research Study 296. London: Home Officehttps://doc.ukdataservice.ac.uk/doc/7450/mrdoc/pdf/7450_hors296.pdf.

True, J. (2020) *Violence against Women: What Everyone Needs to Know*. Oxford: Oxford University Press.

Weisburd, D., Telep, C., Hinkle, J. & Eck, J. (2010). Is Problem-Oriented Policing Effective in Reducing Crime and Disorder? Findings from a Campbell Systematic Review. *Criminology and Public Policy*, 9, 139–172. https://doi.org/10.1111/j.1745-9133.2010.00617.x.

8 Community and neighbourhood policing
The shifting sands

Mollie Rennoldson

Introduction

The interpretation of what constitutes community policing varies. Defining 'community policing' is, as famously described by Williamson (2005), a slippery process, aligning the definition to catching wet soap. It has been described slightly differently, depending on time, place, author and context. However, scholars and police professionals can somewhat agree that community policing should aim to improve day-to-day life for communities, solve locally identified problems and focus on working with local groups to achieve this (Tilley, 2008).

Historical context

The development of community policing can be pinpointed to various key milestones. While these milestones offer some context to the contemporary state of community policing within England and Wales, such as the medieval practice of 'hue and cry' or discussions of the 1829 Peelian Principles, a much more relevant place to begin is the introduction of the 1967 Unit Beat Policing scheme.

The Unit Beat Policing scheme addressed concerns raised by the 1962 Association of Chief Police Officers (ACPO). Detrimental impacts of the Second World War on crime and policing, led to changing crime patterns and a shortage of police officers meaning a more efficient model was required to address such developments (Rawlings, 2002). The Unit Beat Policing scheme strove to tackle growing urban crime and improve contact between the police and the public. The force areas were split into specific beats, with these beats being designed to have a combination of police officers on foot patrol and motor patrol, supported by radio communication and detectives (Rawlings, 2002). Some local police stations were closed, and the remaining stations reduced their opening hours (Longstaff et al., 2015). While the unit beat model did catalyse the use of the then new technology within policing to increase efficiency, a core purpose of the model was to increase contact between the public and police, however this was not achieved. As such changes were leading to a more reactive police force, which left less time for building community relationships.

DOI: 10.4324/9781003492948-9

As the socio-economic and political landscape of the United Kingdom evolved, a number of factors have been identified as responsible for the lack of social harmony in the 1960s and 1970s including conflict and class war in industry, a sharp downturn in the economy, extremism in politics and the rise of violence (Morgan, 2017). Crimes Recorded crime within the United Kingdom rose drastically during the 1960s, 1970s and 1980s (UK Parliament, n.d.). This led to a rise in the political, organisational and public fear of crime. In response, and heavily influenced by Alderson's (1979) *Policing Freedom*, the growing narrative of 'community policing' promoted the strength of enforcing community values and utilising multiagency approaches. Alderson (1979) put forward a set of objectives and argued a shift was needed to a more proactive, consensual model of policing, rather than the reactive, authoritarian model that emerged since the Unit Beat Policing scheme. Police forces, both nationally and internationally, started to adopt problem-oriented policing (POP) introduced by Goldstein (1979). Goldstein (1979) rejected reactive policing, arguing that it did little to prevent reoffending and did not provide communities with a good quality service. Goldstein (1979) introduced the 'SARA' model, standing for scanning, analysis, response and assessment (Chapter 7). This model, constructed through research, was supposed to aid police in identifying problems and creating strategies that would attract long-term results.

The events of the late 70s and early 80s, caused further damage to police and minority ethnic community relationships, which solidified the need for a new policing model. The Brixton Riots in 1981 resulted in two days of violence towards police and the uprising of predominantly young black males, in response to the perceived over-policing and discriminatory treatment of such communities. An inquiry by Scarman (1981) into the riots found that the police had disproportionately stopped and searched black males, finding that the riots were caused by frustration and resentment set within a context of deprivation on multiple fronts and that reform was irrefutably required, particularly in relation to community policing. The frail relationship between the black and minority ethnic groups and the police, triggered by alleged police abuse of power, has been viewed as a causal link to several examples of rioting and disorder during the late twentieth and early twenty-first centuries (Newburn, 2015).

After the report by Scarman (1981), there became a noticeable shift towards adopting community policing within most forces in England and Wales (Kavgaci Ma, 1995). Despite positive changes, the urgent narrative put forward by Lord Scarman (1981) was still somewhat ineffective in raising public confidence. A supplementary report of the 1988 British Crime Survey (BCS) showed a decline in such areas (Skogan, 1990; Kavgaci Ma, 1995). Rebuilding the relationship that had begun to deteriorate decades earlier proved, both then and now, difficult to repair.

The influence on community policing was further catalysed by similar challenges faced by police departments in the USA with regards to racial tensions, urban crime rates and community relations. The 1993 Chicago Alternative Policing Strategy (CAPS) provided a range of research and practices to work from concerning community policing (O'Reilly, 2024). CAPS promoted problem-solving initiatives, proactive strategies, the analysis of recorded crime and the engagement of the community in the prevention of crime. Bullock (2014) describes that such programmes are exemplars of how policing can become increasingly democratic, through the engagement of communities.

Intelligence-led policing (ILP) models grew in importance around the mid-1990s to promote synergy within the organisation, which were arguably working in silos and failing to share information (James, 2013). It also strived to address weaknesses in the existing reactive policing model (Cope et al., 1997). The idea of the timely and quality use of intelligence was viewed as pivotal in crime prevention. However, such methods were hard to implement due to existing cultural practices (James, 2013). The embedding of the National Intelligence Model (NIM) followed (Chapter 5), requiring all basic command units (BCUs) to adopt its outlined practices (John & Maguire, 2007). The NIM is therefore closely entwined with the enforcement of ILP. While the practice around problem orientated and intelligence led policing have differences, they are both indicators of the move towards problem-solving and proactive policing (John & Maguire, 2003).

As crime rates began to fall, public perceptions of crime did not. This phenomenon was named the 'reassurance gap'. The public appeared to be disproportionately fearful of crime, indicating a lack of confidence in policing services (Longstaff et al., 2015). Based on the concept of Innes (2004a) 'signal crimes', whereby the criminal activity important to the public behaves as a signal for the police to act, 'reassurance policing' was developed. Combatting the fear of crime and reassuring communities became key priorities, alongside further reducing crime and disorder (Tuffin et al., 2006).

The National Reassurance Policing Programme (NRPP) was developed. This implemented test sites within communities to tackle local problems, like anti-social behaviour (ASB). NRPP was influenced by existing models of community policing, such as those presented by CAPS. The trial sites adopted the use of visible foot patrols, problem-solving and community engagement as a part of their strategies. The programme was successful, with noticeable decreases over twelve months in crime, ASB and increases in public confidence (Tuffin et al., 2006).

This period saw a shift in terminology; 'community policing', became more commonly referred to as 'neighbourhood policing'. After the success of the NRPP, the Home Office Strategy Plan 2004–2008 introduced a new neighbourhood approach (Home Office, 2004a). The approach endeavoured to allow communities to be more involved in tackling local problems. The 2004 Police Reform White Paper, 'Building Communities, Beating Crime' presented three main objectives relating to this, these were predominantly based on supporting the embedding of neighbourhood policing nationally and involving citizens in how their own communities were policed (Home Office, 2004b).

By 2005, the NRPP was scaled up, with broader intentions, and was newly named the 'Neighbourhood Policing Programme'. It had ten key principles for successful neighbourhood policing such as conducting intelligence-led deployment, community engagement and communication, and being locally dependent (Quinton & Morris, 2008). Neighbourhood policing teams (NPTs) are staffed with police community support officers (PCSOs), police officers and sergeants (College of Policing, n.d.), PCSOs being introduced through the Police Reform Act 2002. Neighbourhood policing teams are also often supported by various forms of volunteers, such as special constables (SC) and police support volunteers (PSV). Citizens within policing continue to make up an integral part of the police family (National Police Chiefs' Council, 2018) (Chapter 12).

A thematic inspection by Her Majesty's Inspectorate of Constabulary (HMIC, 2008) found that the Neighbourhood Policing programme had successfully implemented 3600 teams nationally, alongside offering recommendations for improvement. Additional areas for improvement came from Flannigan's (2008) Independent Review of Policing, stating that neighbourhood teams were not a 'one size fits all' and flexibility was needed in their approach depending on the varying culture and demographic of the community. Ultimately, Flannigan's review strove for a citizen-focused approach to policing (Longstaff et al., 2015).

The 2008 financial crisis saw government policy emerging that justified a decrease in police investment (Greig-Midlane, 2019). From 2010, radical changes to policing were implemented, such as the reversal of the 'Policing Pledge'; a promise to better serve communities and closely meet their needs. The conservative party also reduced the role of the police to focus on fighting crime (Home Office, 2010). The funding cuts directly impacted neighbourhood policing, with individual forces on average having to absorb 18% reductions. Most forces made cuts to staffing, resulting in the loss of over 2,0000 police officers from 2010–2016 (Laub, 2023). Efforts were made to improve practice through legislation, such as the Police Reform and Social Responsibility Act 2011 and the introduction of police and crime commissioners (PCCs) who were tasked with working with chief constables to deliver flexibility relating to the needs of differing communities (Longstaff et al., 2015). However, concerns were continually raised across policing and communities about the ability of neighbourhood policing teams to effectively police their areas.

Current professional practice

Policing has been affected by cuts to public services and austerity has created an imbalance between demand and available resources (Elliot-Davies et al., 2016). An increase in the pressures and volume of work has encouraged a policing environment where forces are performance-driven, with targets to meet (Ratcliffe, 2016), this leaves little room for more time-consuming approaches, success in which is often hard to measure, such as neighbourhood policing and community engagement.

Community policing and the effective implementation of engagement have been historically undervalued, even after respective professionals, such as Alderson (1979) and Scarman (1981), stressed its importance. What is often criticised for not being 'real' police work (Lloyd & Foster, 2009) is now being described by academics, policing professionals and government organisations as a key factor in preventative policing and keeping communities safe. Numerous police failings and ongoing tension between the community and the police, alongside the push towards evidence-informed policing and the implementation of the 'what works' initiatives by the College of Policing, indicate that the value of community engagement is positively shifting.

The HMIC (2017) PEEL report revealed recommendations in three main areas. One of these was directly related to neighbourhood policing and crime prevention. The PEEL report stated that their inspection strongly indicated an erosion of skilled investigators and effective local policing. It is noteworthy that at this point, the officer numbers lost during this period had not been supplemented, leaving small margins for forces to effectively make the expected adjustments, alongside the rising requirements to deal with vulnerability-related issues. The reasoning for such recommendations include a lack of investment, failure to redefine local policing models in response to budget restrictions, societal changes and a lack of national guidance in comparison to alternative areas of policing. Due to this, HMIC (2017) strongly recommended that the College of Policing (2018a) developed a set of clearly structured guidelines for neighbourhood policing. These guidelines being embedded into all forces to ensure policing is evidence-informed, proactive and preventative to regain public confidence within communities.

To alleviate HMIC's concerns, subject matter experts and academics were employed to analyse two rapid evidence assessments (REAs): REA1 was titled 'What constitutes effective neighbourhood policing?' and REA2 was 'What acts as a facilitator or barrier to successful implementation of neighbourhood policing?'. After completing their research, the findings were presented to the College of Policing Guideline Committee in order to inform future policing practice and determine the most appropriate language for the new neighbourhood policing guidelines (Colover & Quinton, 2018).

The 'Neighbourhood Policing Guidelines', published by the College of Policing (2018a), are the current basis for professional practice in England and Wales. Six dominant areas, all derived from the findings of the rapid evidence assessments, have been implemented. The guidelines are focused on delivering neighbourhood policing through 'engaging communities, solving problems and targeting activity' and supporting it by 'promoting the right culture, building analytical capability and developing officers, staff and volunteers'. Additionally, the guidelines are split into three different versions, depending on the individual's role. The most relevant to those beginning their policing careers is for frontline officers, staff and volunteers. The others refer to guidance for first line and senior leaders.

It must the stressed that neighbourhood policing needs to cater for the shifting demographics and circumstances of any community, thus, professional practice may look slightly different depending on the time frame in which it is conducted and any socioeconomic and political developments. The approach to neighbourhood policing must be adaptable to local circumstances (Longstaff et al., 2015). Neighbourhood policing has many functions, including problem-solving, visibility, community engagement and so forth. However, these all revolve around a higher priority, building public confidence and policing by consent (HMIC, 2017).

The below will identify the dominant characteristics of neighbourhood policing.

Multi-agency and partnership working

The governmental change with New Labour in 1997 saw the importance of partnerships for crime prevention not only being encouraged but also a legal requirement. The Crime and Disorder Act 1998 enforced this by introducing community safety partnerships (CSPs), where local authorities, the probation service and clinical commissioning groups had to join efforts. Having such partnerships, in theory, allowed local communities to express their priorities with these concerns being heard by a multitude of services (O'Reilly, 2024). Despite this, there was little guidance as to how to effectively enact such relationships. Agencies often operated as silos and working harmoniously proved difficult. Issues arose around communication tactics, information sharing and clashes with alternative policies and agendas (Davies, 2022).

While these criticisms are lasting, effective multiagency and partnership collaboration is still seen as a pivotal aspect in delivering impactful neighbourhood policing. Thus, strategies have been developed to facilitate these relationships. It has become well-recognised that the police cannot solve complex community issues alone and that the role of crime prevention is not solely the responsibility of the police (Home Office, 1984). Partnership collaboration is now well embedded within current policing professional practice. Such relationships allow for the sharing of expertise, resources, cultural learning and assist in advocating for evidence-based preventative solutions, those which are essential to preventing crime and disorder. Successful multi-agency policing strategies require significant effort and commitment to alleviate the potential organisational and cultural barriers between parties (Crawford and L'Hoiry, 2015). Neighbourhood policing teams work with a plethora of organisations to manage important local issues such as anti-social behaviour, dangerous offenders, safeguarding vulnerable communities and gathering essential intelligence to facilitate evidence-based practice. Participation is demonstrated in strategic arrangements, some of which include local safeguarding boards, multi-agency public protection (MAPPA) strategies and local criminal justice boards (LCJBs) (O'Reilly, 2024).

Successful partnerships, between organisations and the communities they serve, are built on trust, confidence and clear communication. Such relationships can only be built over time, by those who have extensive knowledge and understanding of the context in the areas they serve. Signori et al. (2023) argue that issues around retention and staff turnovers threaten this system, and that 'relational continuity' is essential in ensuring community-based policing is successful. Continuity promotes familiarity with locals, accessibility to the public, facilitates partnerships and develops personalised trust. The current climate and retention issues observed within policing threaten to remove longstanding knowledge and dampen relationships that have been fostered over time. The Home Office (2023) presented records stating that 6.6% of police officers had left the force, for various reasons. This is the highest leaver rate since comparable records began and as such, may threaten the quality of partnerships within policing moving forward.

Police culture has been long theorised as possessing an innate conservative culture in the sense that traditional practices and values are particularly difficult to change (Gundhus, 2013). Neighbourhood policing relies on positive partner relationships to succeed in community engagement and improving public confidence, partners which will require a degree of flexibility and compromise. For multi-agency collaborations to thrive, priorities between the organisations involved must be managed. Working in silos creates a state where each party sees their values and priorities as more important than the other, creating more hostility, rather than encouraging working relationships. Partnership working should understand the priorities and values of the other organisations, while having an inclusive approach to decision-making (Department for Education, 2021).

Community engagement

The College of Policing (2018a) highlight vital elements of community engagement such as officers having a visible presence, being transparent with activities, having regular and varied contact with communities and working with partners to increase the effectiveness of strategies. The police cannot however tackle complex issues alone. Alongside building partnerships with external organisations, building a successful partnership with communities is just as, if not more, pivotal. A visible policing presence and the community having access to related resources can have a strong impact on their ability to take responsibility for local issues, act upon and work collectively to prevent crime. Lister et al. (2015) argue that successful engagement allows partners, police and citizens to tackle local issues together.

Yesberg et al., (2021) argue collective efficacy within communities, i.e., achieving desired results, is dependent on several factors relating to police activity, such as trust in the police, police legitimacy and effective policing strategies. Their findings presented that police visibility was a strong predictor of trust in police fairness and effectiveness and therefore, of collective efficacy. However, it must be considered that the literature also indicates the more effective the public believes the police to be, the less they will intervene or act upon local problems (Kochel, 2016; Yesberg et al., 2021). Therefore, empowering the community to work as a collective, alongside the police and relevant parties, is essential. Overreliance on the police may create a disconnect with personal responsibility around tackling crime and disorder within the area.

The implementation of section 34 of the Police Reform and Social Responsibility Act 2011 means that chief officers have a legal requirement to consult with members of the public within their neighbourhoods. Meetings should be held whereby the chief officer, or their nominated representative, can provide information regarding local crime and policing issues. Policing professionals must be active in policing local areas to improve the level of communication between the public and the police and to ensure the police have a high understanding of the needs, risks and threats of the communities they serve (College of Policing, 2018a). Successful neighbourhood policing teams, in their strategic endeavours, should strive to increase visibility, open purposeful lines of communication and be transparent regarding the impact of police activity on issues important to the community (College of Policing, 2018a). In turn, if the community does act collectively to combat crime and disorder, they can be reassured that their neighbourhood policing team will support their efforts and have the authority to make meaningful changes, without negative consequences on those involved.

There are various methods used in current practice to encourage this collaborative approach and engage communities in crime prevention. Some of the most used methods are discussed below.

Public meetings

Police and Community Together (PACT) meetings are derived from the early introduction of neighbourhood policing. PACT is a purposeful method of community collaboration, where members of such communities can express and share concerns around issues that are most important to them. The police, alongside other partners, will engage in discussion about how best to tackle the raised concerns (Mangan et al., 2017). This allows the police, alongside attending partners, to set priorities in line with the issues most important to the public, then action and offer updates at subsequent meetings (College of Policing, 2013). PACT is one, and arguably the most popular, example of public meetings, however, these do vary in name and strategy.

The College of Policing (2013) developed a method for best practice in 'beat meeting'. This included 8 steps revolving around engaging Community Safety Partnerships (CSP), identifying and tracking short- and long-term goals in conjunction with relevant partners, considering any impactful community triggers and making information accessible to those who require it. Despite this, public meetings, have come under scrutiny, with socio-political and cultural elements impacting effective community collaboration. While public meetings attempt to empower those attending, such individuals can often have asymmetrical views of what is most prevalent, risking increased conflict between sub-groups and cultures. Power imbalances during meetings can further impact efficacy. As aforementioned, police culture can often view their priorities as superior to those of others. Since PACT meetings were traditionally constructed by the police, this creates an element of 'tokenism', and a hierarchy of decision-making can occur (Mangan et al., 2017). In essence, this does not contribute to empowering citizens. Public meetings are also difficult to manage, interactions are unpredictable, and those conducting such meetings need to provide members of the public with meaningful answers, while maintaining control (Mangan et al., 2017). Due to other related issues, attendance at public meetings is noticeably scarce (College of Policing, 2018b).

Despite their negative reputation, public meetings can be useful for neighbourhood policing in relation to building intelligence and gaining some perception of local priorities. Those who attend such meetings are not always representative of the local community. Therefore, public meetings should not be relied upon solely for community engagement and other methods should be utilised for hard-to-reach groups, such as the use of social media.

Foot patrols

The fast-paced nature of counterpart policing units means that achieving a consistent and visible policing presence within communities is predominantly facilitated by neighbourhood policing teams. The ability for the public to see police officers out on foot patrol is symbolic. A high police presence is associated with what Innes (2004b) discussed as 'control signals', where concerns raised by the public appear to be acted upon and validated, in turn, building a relationship of trust and confidence over time (Innes, 2004b). Employing such methods can promote more meaningful interactions with the community, informal conversations, network development and the ability to gather intelligence through alternative means (College of Policing, 2018a) to public meetings and therefore engaging with harder-to-reach community members. Acknowledging differing perceptions within communities, generally police visibility impacts positively on the trust of residents in policing (Yesberg et al., 2021). Hanway and Hambly (2023) argue that confidence is built through public interactions with the police, particularly if individuals feel they have some power over decisions made. Having such informal interactions is particularly useful for engaging with younger groups. While research suggests young people often view increased police visibility as threatening (HMICS, 2002), having positive and indirect exposure to police early in life can combat future anti-police narratives (Sindall et al., 2017).

In relation to crime prevention, visibility and foot patrols have more than just a symbolic importance. Such methods are associated with reduced rates of violent crime, anti-social behaviour and burglaries; however, is this a temporary reduction? Basford et al. (2021) argues that the key to success in such operations is a dedicated and consistent team of officers, those who do not have concerns about additional duties or being extracted to deal with alternative problems.

Foot patrols are one of the dominant methods of delivering hotspot policing tactics. Hotspot policing deals with micro-units of geography and uses evidence-based practice to identify areas where crime presents in small clusters (Chapter 5). Utilising such intelligence means that policing can utilise their resources and attempt to target problem areas effectively (Basford et al., 2021). Increasing guardianship in hotspot areas, according to Cohen and Felson's

(1979) routine activity theory (RAT) will reduce the likelihood of a motivated offender committing a crime against a suitable target. As such, preventing crime using situational methods, with teams that are dedicated to tackling such localised issues. Preventative strategies such as these may also have a profound impact on policing demand in other areas.

Targeting hotspot areas with foot patrols can have an impactful effect initially on reducing crime, but there are common concerns around both spatial and temporal displacement of such activity. However, conflicting studies conducted by Braga et al. (2019) suggest that hotspot policing diffuses crimes in surrounding areas rather than displacing them. Other studies suggest crime rates can rise after increased foot patrols; however, this could be due to the increase in reporting because of accessibility to police, rather than the increase in crime. As with most policing models, foot patrols are not always effective in reducing crime on their own. Neighbourhood teams should use foot patrols as a means of crime prevention, alongside longer-term solutions constructed through problem-solving approaches (College of Policing, 2018a).

Use of intelligence

When initially introduced, neighbourhood policing teams were not only to be proactive and solve problems, while also adopting an intelligence-led approach (Home Office, 2004b), It became increasingly apparent that some crimes could not be dealt with in a reactive manner, this was particularly notable after the 9/11 attacks in the US (Ratcliffe, 2016). While intelligence has been used in policing for much longer than this, the use of such intelligence and the methods involved were criticised. Its efficiency would be an essential tool in future preventative tactics. To provide a standardised, minimum level of practice in relation to the collation and use of intelligence, the National Intelligence Model (NIM) was released. All police forces nationally were to adopt its code of practice (NCIS, 2000). The NIM codes of practice were released in 2005 and chief officers are responsible for ensuring their force complies with these codes. The NIM codes of practice specifically state that the framework should allow for problem-solving, an increase in public reassurance and confidence and improved community safety. Thus, aligning with the intentions of contemporary neighbourhood policing (NCPE, 2005).

The NIM, while it stems from the organisation of criminal intelligence, is a business process model. It seeks to hold community safety as one of its core intentions. To achieve this, the model identifies the management of policing taking place on three levels. The first, local policing, the second, is force or regional issues and the third, is national and international threats (John & Maguire, 2003). Tasking and co-ordinating groups (TCGs) are responsible for allocating sufficient resources on each level, alongside the outcomes produced from such demands. They are usually of a managerial status. The model outlines four key intelligence products of strategic and tactical assessments, alongside target and problem profiles (John & Maguire, 2007). Information gathered at each level must be graded as to determine its status and worth, with a grading system allowing for the consideration of the reliability of the information and how it became known to the source (College of Policing, 2022).

The efficient use of intelligence in neighbourhood policing is essential in its crime prevention tactics and employment of POP strategies. Frameworks like the NIM allow for intelligence to be collated, stored and analysed in an actionable manner (Maguire, 2008). In a community policing setting, intelligence can be used for both individual policing tactics and those that involve partner agencies. Involving partner agencies facilitates the sharing of wider intelligence and uses powers to tackle crime and disorder that may not be available to the police (Maguire, 2008), such as those retained by local councils, social services and the healthcare profession.

It is important to understand the relationship between neighbourhood policing and intelligence-led policing (ILP). Conceptual issues have arisen in defining the role of intelligence in neighbourhood policing. The concepts became popular within a similar timeframe but are separate. Neighbourhood policing engages in elements of ILP, and efforts have been made to see that the models interact with one another (Bullock, 2012). Differences between the two have made this a challenge, community, or neighbourhood, policing can focus much more on the fear of crime, disorder and managing the perceptions of the public (Bullock, 2012), whereas ILP is based on objectivity and data analysis, for efficient use of resources (Ratcliffe, 2008). This is not to suggest there are no similarities between the two, i.e. the use of data analysis and problem-solving in POP and that they both heavily rely on the NIM. Therefore, in current practice, there will be a noticeable crossover between neighbourhood policing and ILP.

Community intelligence was highlighted as particularly important by HMIC (2001). This is local information that provides intelligence on community quality of life, arguing it is essential to both strategic and operational policing strategies (HMIC, 2001). With the development of neighbourhood policing and its guidelines, community intelligence is useful when carrying out hotspots and POP-related policing.

Unfortunately, the introduction of the NIM is viewed as having little operational value in practice (James, 2013). Specifically relating to neighbourhood policing, POP tactics, such as the SARA model, have experienced confusion as to how the NIM and POP can be integrated fluidly (Kirby & McPherson, 2004). James (2017) argues that the success of integrating such models is mostly reliant on the people handling the intelligence. Collier (2006) argues that although information is primarily collected, there is a lack of utilisation when it comes to using this knowledge productively as intelligence. Thus, intelligence models within neighbourhood policing settings must be used cautiously and precisely.

The historical context and current professional practice highlight the shifting nature of community policing. The enactment of successful community policing has been relentlessly restricted and adjusted by socioeconomic and political circumstances, often outside of the control of individual forces themselves. The shifting nature of such a model has caused confusion in practice, particularly while utilised alongside alternative policing models. Nevertheless, evidence-based initiatives heavily indicate that community engagement, problem-solving, and intelligence-led tactics are an essential part of reducing crime and increasing public confidence. Policing cannot keep up with the complexities of modernity through reactive and rigid strategies. Consistency, building partnerships and open communication are necessary, regardless of the seemingly never-ending changes that political agendas present.

Future developments

Neighbourhood policing adapts to its ever-changing environment. Considering the noticeable shift in strategies throughout the late 1990s and early 2000s, such environments are often difficult to predict. Unsurprisingly, the predictions of future developments in community policing are synonymous with some uncertain themes for the future.

The Strategic Review of Policing in England and Wales (Police Foundation, 2022) aims to make neighbourhood policing central to policing and discusses the positive impacts that the 20,000 police officer uplift would bring. Now that the results of the uplift are becoming apparent, and conclusions suggest that the 20,000 uplifts have not replaced the numbers and experience of those who have left policing in recent years, it is difficult to see how staffing will be made available for neighbourhood policing strategies. Particularly considering that building relationships is key to community engagement; such prevalent staff turnover will be detrimental to making neighbourhood policing central. Although HM Government (2024) has pledged many more police officers, community support officers and special constables to support neighbourhood policing, it is difficult though to see how significant additional numbers will be achieved. In addition new training is being piloted to improve and standardise approaches to the policing of neighbourhoods (HM Government, 2024).

Artificial intelligence (AI) will be increasingly used for preventative and proactive policing. Trials of the use of AI in policing have been ongoing, with the National Police Chiefs' Council (2024) stating that their use of such technology will be responsible and transparent. The College of Policing (2020) states that AI neighbourhood teams specifically could utilise it to better understand their community dynamics. The introduction of new technology, technology as advanced as AI, needs to be managed carefully and provisions should be in place to maintain existing forms of community engagement. However, a balance must be struck between the use of such technology and protecting human rights (Police Foundation, 2022).

The College of Policing (2020) identifies potential future trends for policing strategy up to 2040. Although it rejects the idea that the concepts are predictions, it identifies some trends in relation to community policing. One identified is rising inequality and social fragmentation. Poverty, crime and health issues such as ill mental health and drug and alcohol dependency have causal links. Potentially meaning that organisations dealing with such issues will be in even more demand. Healthy partnerships are important for community policing to be successful, increased demand for services threatens these relationships. Fragmentation within communities leads to difficulties in knowing what issues are most important to the public. Valuing one group's priorities over another can lead to crime and disorder. This has been demonstrated in scenes of violent disorder across England in the late summer of 2024. The premise for such crimes was arguably aligned with an inability of far right-wing groups to tolerate those of alternative backgrounds and cultures and the view that authorities were placing their needs above those of white British descent. This placed a relentless demand on police, with resources having to be pulled from various units to address the disorder. Such demands may make slower-paced policing units unmanageable, as resources are being pulled elsewhere.

Pillars within the Policing Vision 2030 (National Police Chiefs' Council, 2023) appear to be based on aspects of community policing such as keeping communities safe, focusing on partnerships and crime prevention. Yet traditional models of community policing may not be sufficient to tackle future societal challenges. However, the core of community policing must stay the same to retain public confidence: visibility, community engagement and problem-solving (O'Reilly, 2024).

Conclusion

As an entity community, or neighbourhood, policing has shifted forms over decades, with its routes embedded pre the Peelian principles, and has continued to increase in its importance, although the complexities of policing neighbourhoods should not be overlooked.

Changes in approaches to policing communities have predominantly been dictated by political climates, levels of social fragmentation and austerity. While the model's and structures of neighbourhood policing have developed, its increasing perceived importance to policing has also grown with the focus of neighbourhood policing relying on effective multi-agency and partnership working, community engagement and effective use of intelligence.

The Government has championed the use of neighbourhood policing, but note should be taken of where lessons have been learned, positive professional practice should be championed and characterised with direction imparted through evidence-informed strategies.

Evidence-based case study illustrating professional practice

The community covered by the neighbourhood policing team is urban, deprived and has a multicultural population. The residents of this area have been known to mistrust the police and some have also accused the police of favouritism.

There has been a number of burglaries in the area. The neighbourhood team suspect more incidents have gone unreported due to the limited police–community relations. An anonymous tip informs the police that the criminality is

> focused on the Jewish community and most of the incidents are occurring near the local synagogue and the surrounding residential properties.
>
> Attendees at PACT meetings raise concerns about the lack of police presence in the community; this makes them feel unsafe and some are considering relocating. Response policing teams have also responded to the few incidents that have been reported, but on arrival, suspects have gone and any witnesses are not willing to support further police action. There is no CCTV in the area.
>
> The neighbourhood policing team need to make meaningful, proactive progress in building a relationship with the community to gather information and take control of the continuing criminal activity.
>
> Checking the existing information and intelligence on the location of reported offences, confirms that the reported offences are occurring near the synagogue. As a result police officers partner with special constables to conduct additional foot patrols in the immediate areas affected, using intelligence to inform the timing and locations of patrols. Additional regular community meetings are arranged in a 'neutral' building near the synagogue, held at different times of the day to encourage open and honest two-way engagement between the police and the whole community, these meetings being advertised through face-to-face conversations with residents at any opportunity, the police and community Facebook pages. Leaflet drops across the whole community advising of increased police patrols in the area and additional community meetings. The team also engage with the local council to improve lighting and the installation of CCTV.
>
> However, great care must be taken not to disenfranchise the rest of the community by focusing patrols in one area, so with limited resources in the team, the PCSO is tasked with continuing to focus patrols, either on foot or in a vehicle, in the other areas of the community.
>
> What additional actions can the neighbourhood policing team take?

Reflective question

As a new police officer attached to a neighbourhood policing team, consider how you can approach and engage in conversation with a small group of teenagers stood on a residential street corner who are playing loud music on their phones and blocking the pavement.

References

Alderson, J. (1979). *Policing Freedom: A Commentary of Dilemmas of Policing in Western Democracies*. Estover: MacDonald and Evans.

Basford, L., Sims, C., Agar, I., Harinam, V. & Strang, H. (2021). Effects of One-a-Day Foot Patrols on Hot Spots of Serious Violence and Crime Harm: A Randomised Crossover Trial. *Cambridge Journal of Evidence Based Policy*, 5(3–4), 119–133. https://doi.org/10.1007/s41887-021-00067-2.

Braga, A., Turchan, B. & Papachristos, A. (2019). Hot Spots Policing and Crime Reduction: An Update of an Ongoing Systematic Review and Meta-analysis. *Journal of Experimental Criminology*, 15, 289–311. https://doi.org/10.1007/s11292-019-09372-3.

Bullock, K. (2012). Community, Intelligence-Led Policing and Crime Control. *Policing and Society*, 23(2), 125–144. https://doi.org/10.1080/10439463.2012.671822.

Bullock, K. (2014). Community Policing. Citizens. In K. Bullock (ed.), *Community and Crime Control. Crime Prevention and Security Management*. Palgrave Macmillan, London. https://doi.org/10.1057/9781137269331_5.

Cohen, L. & Felson, M. (1979). Social Change and Crime Rate Trends: A Routine Activity Approach. *American Sociological Review*, 44(4), 588–608.

College of Policing. (2013). Communication. [Online]. www.college.police.uk/app/engagement-and-communication/communication#:~:text=Beat%20meetings%20are%20intended%20to,is%20left%20to%20force%20discretion (accessed 20 September 2024).

College of Policing. (2018a). Neighbourhood Policing Guidelines. [online]. www.college.police.uk/guidance/neighbourhood-policing (accessed 20 August 2024).

College of Policing. (2018b). Effects of Police Community Support Officer Hotspot Foot Patrol on Crime and Incidents in a Small City Centre Setting. [online]. www.college.police.uk/research/projects/effects-police-community-support-officer-hot-spot-foot-patrol-crime-and-incidents-small-city-centre-setting (accessed 20 September 2024).

College of Policing. (2020). Policing in England and Wales: Future Operating Environments 2040. [online]. www.college.police.uk/article/preparing-policing-future-challenges-and-demands (accessed 30 September 2024).

College of Policing. (2022). Intelligence Report. www.college.police.uk/app/intelligence-management/intelligence-report (accessed 27 September 2024).

College of Policing. (n.d.). Neighbourhood Policing Career Pathway. [online]. www.college.police.uk/career-learning/career-development/career-pathways/neighbourhood-policing#:~:text=Generally%2C%20neighbourhood%20policing%20teams%20are,be%20a%20higher%2Dranking%20officer (accessed 29 September 2024).

Collier, P. (2006). Policing and the Intelligent Application of Knowledge. *Public Money & Management*, 26(2), 109–116. https://doi.org/10.1111/j.1467-9302.2006.00509.x.

Colover, S. & Quinton, P. (2018). *Neighbourhood Policing: Impact and Implementation. Summary Findings from a Rapid Evidence Assessment*. Coventry: College of Policing.

Cope S., Leishman, F. & Starie P. (1997). Globalization, New Public Management and the Enabling State: Futures of Police Management. *International Journal of Public Sector Management*, 10(6), 444–460. https://doi.org/10.1108/09513559710190816.

Crawford, A. & L'Hoiry, X. (2015). Partnerships in the Delivery of Policing and Safeguarding Children. An Exploratory Knowledge Platform for Policing: Exploiting Knowledge Assets, Utilising Data and Piloting Research Co-production. [online]. www.law.leeds.ac.uk/research/projects/an-exploratory-knowledge-platform-for-policing/ (accessed 17 September 2024).

Crime and Disorder Act1998, c.1. [online]. www.legislation.gov.uk/ukpga/1998/37/section/5 (accessed 12 September 2024).

Davies, P. (2022). How Far Has Multi-Agency Policing Travelled in 30 Years? Reflecting on Progress in the Context of 'Policing' Domestic Abuse in England and Wales. *Crime Prevention and Community Safety*, 24, 1–17. https://doi.org/10.1057/s41300-022-00161-1.

Department for Education. (2021). Multiagency Reform: Key Behavioural Drivers and Barriers. Summary Report. [online]. https://assets.publishing.service.gov.uk/media/61b9c9d6e90e070441bcf9b8/MultiAgencyReform_Kantar_Report.pdf (accessed 28 September 2024).

Elliott-Davies, M., Donnelly, J., Boag-Munroe, F. & Van Mechelen, D. (2016). 'Getting a Battering': The Perceived Impact of Demand and Capacity Imbalance within the Police Service of England and Wales: A Qualitative Review. *Police Journal: Theory, Practice and Principles*, 89(2), 93–116. https://doi.org/10.1177/0032258X16642234.

Flannigan, R. (2008). *The Review of Policing: Final Report*. London: Home Office. https://assets-hmicfrs.justiceinspectorates.gov.uk/uploads/flanagan-review-of-policing-20080201.pdf.

Goldstein, H. (1979). Improving Policing: A Problem-Oriented Approach. *Crime and Delinquency*, 25(2), 236–258.

Greig-Midlane, J. (2019). An Institutional Perspective of Neighbourhood Policing Reform in Austerity Era England and Wales. *International Journal of Police Science & Management*, 21(4), 230–243. https://doi.org/10.1177/1461355719889464.

Gundhus, H. (2013). Experience or Knowledge? Perspectives on New Knowledge Regimes and Control of Police Professionalism. *Policing: A Journal of Police and Practice*, 7(2), 178–194. https://doi.org/10.1093/police/pas039

Hanway, P. & Hambley, O. (2023). Home Office: Public Perceptions of Policing: A Review of Research and Literature. [online]. www.gov.uk/government/publications/public-perceptions-of-policing-a-review-of-research-and-literature/public-perceptions-of-policing-a-review-of-research-and-literature (accessed 12 September 2024).

HM Government. (2024). News Story: Government Kick-Starts Plan to Restore Neighbourhood Policing. [online]. www.gov.uk/government/news/government-kick-starts-plan-to-restore-neighbourhood-policing (accessed 5 October 2024).

HMIC. (2001). Winning the Race: Embracing Diversity. Consolidation Inspection of Police and Community Race Relations 2000. [online]. https://assets-hmicfrs.justiceinspectorates.gov.uk/uploads/winning-the-race-embracing-diversity-20010114.pdf (accessed 4 October 2024).

HMIC. (2008). Serving Neighbourhoods and Individuals: A Thematic Report on Neighbourhood Policing and Developing Citizen Focus Policing. [online]. https://assets-hmicfrs.justiceinspectorates.gov.uk/uploads/durham-phase2-neighbourhood-policing-citizen-focus-20080830.pdf (accessed 20 September 2024).

HMIC. (2017). PEEL: Police Effectiveness 2016. A National Overview. [online]. https://hmicfrs.justiceinspectorates.gov.uk/publications/peel-police-effectiveness-2016/#:~:text=This%20report%20presents%20a%20national,and%20data%20provided%20by%20forces (accessed 5 October 2024).

HMICS. (2002). *Narrowing the Gap: Police Visibility and Public Reassurance*. Edinburgh: The Stationery Office.

Home Office. (1984). *Crime Prevention*. HOC 8/1984. London: Home Office.

Home Office. (2004a). *Confident Communities in a Secure Britain: The Home Office Strategic Plan 2004–2008*. London: HMSO.

Home Office. (2004b). *Building Communities, Beating Crime*. London: HMSO.

Home Office. (2010). Police Reform: Theresa May's Speech to the National Policing Conference. [online]. www.gov.uk/government/speeches/police-reform-theresa-mays-speech-to-the-national-policing-conference (accessed 12 September 2024).

Home Office. (2023). Police Workforce, England & Wales: 31 March 2023 (second edition). [online]. www.gov.uk/government/statistics/police-workforce-england-and-wales-31-march-2023/police-workforce-england-and-wales-31-march-2023 (accessed 15 September 2024).

Innes, M. (2004a). Signal Crimes and Signal Disorders: Notes on Deviance as 'Communicative Action. *British Journal of Sociology*, 55(3), 335–355. https://doi.org/10.1111/j.1468-4446.2004.00023.x.

Innes, M. (2004b). Reinventing Tradition? Reassurance, Neighbourhood Security and Policing. *Criminology and Criminal Justice*, 4(2), 151–171. https://doi.org/10.1177/1466802504044914.

James, A. (2013). Forward to the Past: Reinventing Intelligence-Led Policing in Britain. *Police Practice and Research*, 15(1), 75–88. https://doi.org/10.1080/15614263.2012.754126.

James, A. (2017). The Path to Enlightenment: Limiting Costs and Maximizing Returns from Intelligence-Led Policy and Practice in Public Policing. *Policing*, 11(4), 410–420. https://doi.org/10.1093/police/paw050.

John, T. & Maguire, M. (2003). Rolling out the National Intelligence Model: key challenges. In K. Bullock & N. Tilley (eds), *Crime Reduction and Problem-Oriented Policing* (pp. 38–66). Cullompton: Willan.

John, T. & Maguire, M. (2007). Criminal Intelligence and National Intelligence Model. In T. Newburn, T. Williamson & A. Wright (eds), *Handbook of Criminal Investigation* (pp. 199–225). Cullompton: Willan.

Kavgaci Ma, H. (1995). The Development of Police/Community Relations Initiatives in England and Wales Post Scarman and Their Relevance to Policing Policy in Turkey. Thesis, University of Leicester. https://hdl.handle.net/2381/35276.

Kirby, S. & McPherson, I. (2004). Integrating the National Intelligence Model with a 'Problem Solving' Approach. [online]. http://eprints.lancs.ac.uk/31778/1/nim.pdf (accessed 30 September 2024).

Kochel, T. (2016). Police Legitimacy and Resident Cooperation in Crime Hotspots: Effects of Victimisation Risk and Collective Efficacy. *Policing and Society*, 28(3), 251–270. https://doi.org/10.1080/10439463.2016.1174235.

Laub, M. (2023). Austerity-Driven Policification: Neoliberalisation, Schools and the Police in Britain. *The Sociological Review*, 72(3), 651–672. https://doi.org/10.1177/00380261231202649.

Lister, S., Adams, B. & Phillips, S. (2015). Evaluation of Police-Community Engagement Practices. An Exploratory Knowledge Platform for Policing: Exploiting Knowledge Assets, Utilising Data and Piloting Research Co-production. [online] www.law.leeds.ac.uk/research/projects/an-exploratory-knowledge-platform-for-policing/ (accessed 5 October 2024).

Lloyd, K. & Foster, J. (2009). Citizen Focus and Community Engagement: A Review of the Literature. [online]. www.police-foundation.org.uk/publication/citizen-focus-and-community-engagement-a-review-of-the-literature/ (accessed 16 September 2024).

Longstaff, A., Willer, J., Chapman, J., Czarnomski, S. & Graham, J. (2015). Neighbourhood Policing: Past, Present and Future – A Review of the Literature. [online]. www.police-foundation.org.uk/wp-content/uploads/2017/06/neighbourhood_policing_past_present_future.pdf (accessed 15 September 2024).

Maguire, M. (2008). POP, ILP and Partnership. *Criminal Justice Matters*, 32, 21–22. https://doi.org/10.1080/09627259808552749.

Mangan, A., Thomas, R., Davies, A., & Gasper, R. (2017). The Challenges of Police-Community Collaboration: Identity Manoeuvres and Power Struggles in a Neighbourhood-Based Meeting. *Public Management Review*, 20, 1–21. https://doi.org/10.1080/14719037.2017.1383718.

Morgan, K. (2017). Britain in the Seventies – Our Unfinest Hour? *French Journal of British Studies*, XXII. https://doi.org/10.4000/rfcb.1662.

National Police Chiefs' Council. (2018). Police Support Volunteer National Strategy 2019–2023. [online]. www.npcc.police.uk/SysSiteAssets/media/downloads/publications/publications-log/2019/npcc-national-police-support-volunteers.pdf (accessed 12 September 2024).

National Police Chiefs' Council. (2023). Policing Vision 2030. [online]. www.npcc.police.uk/publications/policing-vision-2030/ (accessed 1 October 2024).

National Police Chiefs' Council. (2024). Police Will Always Use Artificial Intelligence Responsibly. [online]. https://news.npcc.police.uk/releases/policing-will-always-use-artificia

l-intelligence-responsibly#:~:text=%E2%80%9CAI%20offers%20huge%20opportunities%20for,patterns%20and%20trends%20in%20evidence (accessed 30 September 2024).

NCIS. (2000). *The National Intelligence Model*. London: National Criminal Intelligence Service.

NCPE. (2005). *National Intelligence Model: Minimum Standards*. London: National Centre for Policing Excellence.

Newburn, T. (2015). The 2011 Riots from a Historical Perspective. *British Journal of Criminology*, 55(1), 39–64. https://doi.org/10.1093/bjc/azu074.

O'Reilly, C. (2024). *Neighbourhood Policing: Context, Practices & Challenges*. Bristol: Bristol University Press.

Police Foundation. (2022). A New Mode of Protection: Final Report of the Strategic Review of Policing in England and Wales. [online]. https://police-foundation.org.uk/policingreview2022/ (accessed 5 October 2024).

Police Reform Act (2002), c 30. [online]. www.legislation.gov.uk/ukpga/2002/30/schedule/4 (accessed 15 September 2024).

Police Reform and Social Responsibility Act (2011), c. 5. [online]. www.legislation.gov.uk/ukpga/2011/13/section/34 (accessed 12 September 2024).

Quinton, P. & Morris, J. (2008). *Neighbourhood Policing: The Impact of Piloting and Early National Implementation*. London: Home Office.

Ratcliffe, J. (2008). *Intelligence-Led Policing*. Cullompton: Willan Publishing.

Ratcliffe, J. (2016). *Intelligence-Led Policing*, 2nd edition. London: Routledge.

Rawlings, P. (2002). *Policing: A Short History*. Cullompton: Willan Publishing.

Scarman, L. (1981). *Scarman Report: The Brixton Disorders, 10–12 April, 1981*. London: HMSO.

Signori, R., Heinrich, D., Wootton, A. & Davey, C. (2023). Relational Continuity in Community Policing: Insights from a Human-Centred Design Perspective. *Policing: A Journal of Policy and Practice*, 17, paad038. https://doi.org/10.1093/police/paad038.

Sindall, K., McCarthy, D.J. & Brunton-Smith, I. (2017). Young People and the Formation of Attitudes towards the Police. *European Journal of Criminology*, 14(3), 344–364. https://doi.org/10.1177/1477370816661739.

Skogan, W. (1990). *Disorder and Decline: Crime and the Spiral of Decay in American Cities*. New York: The Free Press.

Tilley, N. (2008). Modern Approaches to Policing: Community, Problem-Orientated and Intelligence-Led. In T. Newburn (ed.), *Handbook of Policing*, 2nd edition. Cullompton: Willan.

Tuffin, R., Morris, J. & Poole, A. (2006). *An Evaluation of the Impact of the National Reassurance Policing Programme* (Vol 296). London: Home Office Research, Development and Statistics Directorate.

UK Parliament. (n.d.). Crimes of the Century: Recorded Crimes. [online]. www.parliament.uk/business/publications/research/olympic-britain/crime-and-defence/crimes-of-the-century/#:~:text=Crime%20continued%20to%20rise%20according,3.5m%20in%20the%201980s (accessed 18 May 2024).

Williamson, T. (2005). Community Policing. *Journal of Community and Applied Social Psychology*, 15(3), 153–155.

Yesberg, J., Brunton-Smith, I. & Bradford, B. (2021). Police Visibility, Trust in Police Fairness, and Collective Efficacy: A Multilevel Structural Equation Model. *European Journal of Criminology*, 20(2), 712–737. https://doi.org/10.1177/14773708211035306.

9 Policing vulnerability attrition, rape and domestic abuse

Emma Williams, Jennifer Norman and Katy Barrow-Grint

Introduction

Violence against women and girls (VAWG) remains a core priority for the police and policy makers. Significant government reviews and academic research highlights the ongoing and historical issues with attrition and the disparities in accessing justice for among victims of VAWG (Charman & Williams, 2022). Over recent years high profile incidents such as Sarah Everard have impacted on public confidence and perceptions of trustworthiness and legitimacy in the police in relation to how they approach these crimes (Hohl & Stanko, 2015).

Since the last iteration of this chapter there have been significant moves to improve the way the police deal with vulnerability which is a core feature in reports of domestic abuse (DA) and rape and serious sexual offending (RASSO). In 2018, the Home Office launched the Vulnerability Knowledge and Practice Programme (VKPP). The programme was a collaborative effort with the National Chief Police Council (NPCC) to enhance policing responses to VAWG, to improve criminal justice outcomes, and to reduce the risk of harm for vulnerable victims. Research consistently highlights the need to further understand intersectionality and different forms of vulnerability in VAWG and this is a key priority for the VKPP.

The VAWG delivery framework was developed in 2021 that aimed to influence the development of consistently high standards to the police response to VAWG. This was followed by a government announcement in February 2023, when the Home Secretary included VAWG within the Strategic Policing Requirement. This recognised VAWG as a national threat, alongside terrorism and serious and organised crime. The first VAWG Strategic Threat and Risk Assessment (STRA) was published in December 2023. The STRA aimed to assist police forces to optimise resources and protect women from sexual and violent crimes, with sexual crimes and DA identified as top priorities. Concurrently, legislative changes have also been introduced to address the complexities and nature of DA. The Domestic Abuse Act 2022 has expanded the scope of offences, including new crimes such as non-fatal strangulation, and extending the definition of DA to include emotional abuse, coercive behaviour, and economic abuse, alongside physical abuse. These recent initiatives and

DOI: 10.4324/9781003492948-10

legislative changes acknowledge different forms of abuse from suspects, aiming to provide better protection and justice for victims of VAWG.

As a result of the publication of the Home Office Rape Review, in 2022 and a small pilot study reviewing rape investigation in Avon and Somerset Police, extensive research was commissioned to explore the investigation of RASSO through a government funded initiative called Operation Soteria Bluestone. Operation Soteria Bluestone was a collaborative project involving six academic institutions and five police forces across England and Wales. The findings highlighted the vital need for investigations of this nature to shift from being victim-centric, with an overfocus on victim credibility to a more suspect focused, context led and victim centred approach. The research also highlighted the organisational challenges to support investigating officers and staff to effectively manage the complexities present in cases of RASSO (Stanko, 2022). As a result of the research, the National Operating Model (NOM) for RASSO was introduced in 2023, offering a completely new way for investigating rape and sexual crime.

This chapter reflects on two examples of crimes under the VAWG umbrella – RASSO and DA. The discussion explores the recent research and reconsiders meanings of vulnerability. Furthermore, the authors demonstrate the complexities involved for officers dealing with VAWG investigations and the need for specialist knowledge, attitudes, and skills to equip them to provide a more professional service to victims. The chapter offers a refreshed understanding of how investigations can be strengthened with specialist learning and development offers and effective support for vulnerable victims to improve justice outcomes and their experiences of the criminal justice system (CJS). The authors consider the organisational context in which policing is operating, highlighting the impact of sustained cuts to resources, reduced time for learning and professional development, increased demand and recognises impact of having an organisational profile that is comprised of younger officers with less experiential knowledge and a different experience of initial recruit training and tutoring.

Research example 1: rape and serious sexual offences

Vulnerability and attrition in rape and sexual violence: what do we know?

The first VAWG example the authors draw on is in relation to research on rape and serious sexual offences (RASSO). Rape has been the focus of academic research since the 1970s, with studies consistently posing significant challenges for policing (Stanko, 1985; Edwards, 1989; Kelly, 1999). The complexities involved in rape investigations are multifaceted, particularly concerning issues of consent and the subsequent prosecution processes, which impact on responses from the CJS. The implications of these issues have consistently resulted in high attrition rates at various stages of the CJS process and is often driven by a police assessment of the victim in terms of their credibility and believability, the difficulty in ascertaining consent at the time of the alleged rape, and presence of vulnerable characteristics of the victims (Munro & Kelly, 2009; Williams et al., 2009; Jordan, 2011; Hohl & Stanko, 2015; Stanko, 2022).

Understanding victimisation and victim typologies is crucial in the context of rape investigation. The London Rape Review carried out in the Metropolitan Police Service (MPS) during 2005 (Stanko, 2007) tracked the journey of 677 rape cases reported in April and May 2005, from initial allegation to outcome. The data was overlayed with victim characteristics forming an evidence-base to understanding rape victimology. The research provided recommendations about victim vulnerabilities to strategic decision-makers and operational officers who worked in sexual violence to encourage more proactive approaches to minimising the risk of attrition for victims of rape. The research evidence in this rape review highlighted four points of attrition:

- When the police decide to classify the allegation as a crime.
- When the police arrest the suspect.
- When the police decide whether to charge the suspect of rape.
- At the outcome of the prosecution at court.

The most critical point of attrition was at the police investigation stage (with 75% of cases falling out of the system at this point), highlighting the importance for the police to understand the wider context around the issues that rape victims face, and the provision of support required to ensure the victim remains on board. The research found that most of the victims who alleged rape were female and described as vulnerable (Williams et al., 2009). The typical outcome of those allegations reported by a victim classified as vulnerable, was attrition. The four common vulnerable victim typologies were identified:

- Being young (32%) – allegations that involved victims under the age of 18.
- Knowing the suspect (39%) – allegations that involved victims who were or had been in a relationship with the perpetrator.
- Consuming alcohol (35%) – allegations that involved victims who had consumed alcohol before the offence.
- Having a mental health issue (18%) – allegations that noted the victim as having a mental health issue.

From the overall sample drawn in 2005, 87% of cases involved victims with one or more of these vulnerable factors. This initial MPS London Rape Review was repeated year on year between 2005 and 2012 and was reported to be the world's largest study of rape (Hohl and Stanko, 2015). Insights from this longitudinal study in London demonstrated the consistent theme around high attrition rates and victim vulnerabilities being a significant predictor of their case exiting the CJS. Two subsequent reviews conducted by the Mayor's Office for Policing and Crime built on the MPS London Rape Review and further examined rape cases alleged in April 2016 and over three timeframes in 2017, 2018 and 2019 (Wunsch et al., 2021). In the most recent review similar dominant themes continued to present in the data alongside high attrition rates. 65% of cases ended in victim withdrawal, 25% ended in police 'No Further Action'. Just 6% of cases were committed by a stranger, 35% were committed by a current/former partner and 29% by an acquaintance/friend. The strongest predictors of victim withdrawal and no further action from the police were procedural characteristics but variables relating to an assessment of the victim's account and victim credibility also impacted on outcomes. This further supports the evidence concerning a consistent investigative focus on victim behaviour rather than the focus being on the suspect (Wunsch et al., 2021).

The key issues raised from the in-depth and longitudinal studies conducted over the past twenty years in London show that nothing has changed. Attrition of rape cases remain high, conviction rates remain low, and victim vulnerabilities remain a consistent theme.

What does this tell us about vulnerability and attrition in rape and sexual violence?

Rape cases are complex, and accurate assessments of vulnerability are required to ensure that victims are referred to the correct support agencies for help and that the context of these factors are considered as part of the investigation strategy. However, previous studies indicate that the police find the identification of vulnerability challenging (Williams et al., 2009). They highlight the importance of getting this identification correct from the onset to ensure needs are properly met both at the police stage and further into the CJS (Burton, Evans & Saunders, 2006; Stanko & Williams, 2009). Having access to information and advice from expert partners such as health agencies, independent sexual violence advisors (ISVAs) is key to this being effective (Topping, 2022).

The MPS Rape Reviews undertaken in London (Stanko, 2007; Hohl & Stanko, 2015; Wunsch et al., 2021) provide robust examples of how research findings can provide an evidence base to assist officers to think differently about rape investigations and the victims involved. Research continues to illustrate that supporting victims who present complexities when reporting RASSO is challenging for the police (Charman & Williams, 2022; Tidmarsh, 2021). From both a strategic and operational perspective, the evidence derived from research should be used and applied through continuous professional development and training to help officer better understand these complexities, how they impact on victims and their experience of the police and provide ways of identifying new solutions for police officers who manage victims of rape and investigate sexual violence. The findings reaffirm the consistent messages found historically by researchers about attrition and should offer operational officers applied and practical guidance through processes of getting this knowledge into their working practice. Vulnerabilities such as mental health, language barriers, neurodiversity and drug/alcohol use need to be properly identified at the start of the police investigation. Considering such factors in problem solving around how best to support and engage with victims via partner agencies and safeguarding options is critical to reduce risk and exposure to future harm.

However, while these studies provide an in-depth analysis of victim vulnerabilities and attrition the authors argue that the understanding of vulnerability and what these findings mean in practice still requires much attention.

Reconsidering vulnerability and intersectionality

There has been recent debate about how common blanket definitions of vulnerability can negate the importance of individual positionalities and contexts and how certain characteristics intersect with each other and impact on the way in which people experience both risk and an assault itself, and their relationship with the police (Kessel, 2022; Hohl & Stanko, 2024). A person is deemed vulnerable, according to the College of Policing (2017) if, 'as a result of their situation or circumstances, they are unable to take care of or protect themselves or others from harm and exploitation'. Other authors use broader definitions to explore the term. As Brown et al. (2019) argue vulnerability is a complex and highly heterogeneous concept with different meanings. Enang et al. (2021, p. 542) suggest definitions need to encompass other 'situational and contextual' and 'person specific aspects' which introduces the notion of intersectionality. We will consider vulnerability further using the ideas from Enang et al. (2021) around intersectionality in the context of victims of rape and sexual violence and consider how contextual factors in the working practices of the police organisation itself can further problematise and compound the issues surrounding effectively understanding these complicated factors.

Person-specific aspects of vulnerability

Person specific aspects of vulnerability can be understood in the previous research outlined in the sections above and in our chapter in the first edition of this book. The rape victim typologies established from research identify person-specific aspects of vulnerability pertained to the victim and it is these characteristics that are associated with attrition. During investigations, the characteristics present in the victims can become the focus of officers' attention, making the investigation focused on the victim's credibility, rather than the suspects' behaviour (Hohl & Stanko, 2024). A fuller understanding of the person-specific aspects of vulnerability and how these factors interact with both each other is central to understanding the ongoing problem with attrition in allegations of rape. Victims need to be treated with dignity and fairness despite the challenges that some of these complex issues present to the police. Indeed, procedural fairness consists of four key components: voice, dignity and respect, neutrality, and trustworthy motives (Bradford & Jackson, 2024). As Hohl et al. (2022) claim, officers need to act in ways that demonstrate fairness, dignity and respect regardless of any specific characteristics.

Contextual and situational aspects of vulnerability

When considering the importance of fair treatment and transparent decision making from the police and how this can enhance the victim experience, it is important to consider how the operational environment within which the police work may compound how victims are perceived and dealt with. Officer decision-making and the organisational context within which those decisions are made is a key issue in this debate and can paradoxically exacerbate the problems presented by certain vulnerabilities when victims report rape or sexual violence.

Contextual aspects in policing are characterised by the sustained resource cuts to policing alongside a rise demand. These factors contribute to the vulnerability of investigating RASSO. While in 2019 the government introduced the Policing Uplift Programme that recruited 20,000 new officers over three years, rape and sexual investigative teams remain under resourced with the retention of detectives being a national crisis. The national issue of retaining officers across a range of roles is a critical area of concern (Charman & Williams, 2022). The implications of officers leaving has impacted on the broader age profile of officers in England and Wales with 40% of policing comprising of officers with less than 5 years' service. Reduced experience within investigation teams to both conduct investigations and mentor new investigators and, the dissolution of specialist units to investigate RASSO (Rumney et al., 2020) all contribute to the ongoing challenge of attrition in this area.

Situational aspects within policing relates to the vulnerability of investigations themselves due to the limited experience many investigating officers and first responders have in this area in policing. This questions the quality of the initial education and training provision for new recruits, given the increased likelihood in them being a first responder in a case of rape or sexual violence. A core justification for the Policing Education Qualifications Framework (PEQF) introduced in 2016, was to provide officers with the wider knowledge required to assist them in thinking more critically and with reflection about such complex issues (Norman & Williams, 2017; Williams & Cockcroft, 2018). The National Policing Curriculum (NPC) underpinned the PEQF programmes to improve the breadth and depth of knowledge for police officers in relation to the changing nature and complexity of contemporary society. A core aspect of the NPC is focused on contextual vulnerability and aims to improve the ability of officers to respond to the needs of these individuals and communities as they experience crime. While it is encouraging that vulnerability is prioritised within the curriculum, it is presented as a siloed issue and not as an intrinsic part of much that the police do. Arguably, the curriculum does not capture some of the recent debates around how common definitions of vulnerability can negate the importance of more complex understandings of the term (Kessel, 2022). As the police education and training landscape for new recruits has continued to change, the Police Constable Entry Programmes (PCEP) now includes a non-accredited training programme which dilutes the importance of these core skills and knowledge from the outset of a police career. Operation Soteria has developed a first responders programme for officers in conjunction with the College of Policing. This course was rolled out early in 2024 however its' impact is yet to be evaluated.

The lack of learning and development for existing officers across areas of VAWG provides a further layer to *situational aspects* of vulnerability in terms of equipping officers with the specialised knowledge they require to deal with RASSO confidently and competently. This has been a key focus of government initiatives and academic research over recent years (Casey, 2023; Williams et al., 2022; Hohl & Stanko, 2024). Much research has found that limited specialist knowledge is a core factor in inhibiting an effective response to VAWG, particularly for victims with vulnerabilities (Rumney et al., 2020).

Given the complexity of demand particularly in relation to person-specific aspects of vulnerabilities, the police service needs to ensure that they deal with encounters in a consistent, ethical, and effective manner. It remains clear that defining and addressing vulnerability is problematic.

New insights from Operation Soteria Bluestone

The framework of Operation Soteria Bluestone was organised into six pillars. Pillar one explored suspect focused investigations to address the current over-focus on victim credibility. Pillar two considered the opportunities to disrupt repeat offenders of RASSO to prevent the risks of further sexual harm. Pillar three applied procedural justice theory in the context of victim engagement. The further three pillars related to the important organisational enablers for police corporate change and the organisational responsibility for facilitating this. These were focused on officer well-being, learning and development (pillar four): the use of data and analytics (pillar five); and digital forensics (pillar six) (Hohl & Stanko, 2024). This section of the chapter will focus on pillar 4 and the exploration of learning and development opportunities for officers who investigate RASSO.

Learning and development: a focus on specialist knowledge for RASSO

Valuing and cultivating learning and knowledge are critical for organisational development and improving service delivery in policing. Facilitating access to learning resources and continuing professional development (CPD) is central to both individual professional identity and organisational commitment (Williams et al., 2022). However, research has shown that access to learning and CPD in policing is sporadic and challenging for many officers (Norman & Williams, 2017). The crucial need for this learning to better understand the described *person-specific aspects* – complex victim needs and vulnerabilities can be undermined by internal *contextual and situational aspects* such as austerity measures, increasing demand, and a shortage of experienced investigators (outlined in the section above) as these factors further restrict officers' ability to access available learning opportunities.

Pillar four aimed to explore the current situation in policing regarding the training, learning and development available for officers who investigate RASSO. The work aimed to:

- Assess the extent to which officers possess the necessary specialist knowledge to investigate and respond to RASSO and their ability to apply this knowledge in practice.

152   Introduction to Professional Policing

- Explore the support for the welfare needs of RASSO investigators.
- Understand the drivers of welfare issues for RASSO investigators.
- Identify the limitations to learning in the field of RASSO.
- Review the content and delivery style of the current learning offer for RASSO investigators.

Methodology

Pillar four researchers utilised a mixed-method approach, combining qualitative and quantitative data collection methods to address several research questions regarding the learning materials, delivery styles, barriers, and enablers to learning and wellbeing support for RASSO officers. The study also examined the availability of resources and the relationship between learning opportunities and officers' wellbeing.

Qualitative research

The qualitative component involved 28 interviews and 23 focus groups with 119 participants across four deep dive sites. Participants included senior leaders (Chapter 14), learning and development leads, wellbeing coordinators, first response officers, RASSO investigators, and supervisors. Interviews and focus groups were recorded, transcribed, and thematically analysed using NVivo15. An open coding framework was used to identify top-level themes, ensuring independent inter-rater reliability by two researchers. Additionally, force learning materials and local wellbeing resources were reviewed, and training sessions observed. Materials reviewed included lesson plans, course materials, and supporting references, focusing on RASSO-specific content. The College of Policing curriculum for the Serious Sexual Assault Investigators Development Programme (SSAIDP) was also reviewed.

Quantitative research

Quantitative analysis was carried out via a learning and wellbeing survey administered across the four Operation Soteria Bluestone areas and a fifth pilot site. The survey, co-produced with ex and serving police officers, included validated tools from organisational behaviour domains, the NHS Staff Survey, and a licensed schedule measuring symptoms of burnout. The survey received 538 responses (37% response rate), though operational reconfigurations made it challenging to determine the exact number of eligible officers. The quantitative data, analysed alongside qualitative evidence, provided insights into the relationship between work demands, learning environments, and burnout, using multivariate analyses to explore the correlates of burnout components.

Findings

The research conducted under pillar four revealed three core strategic themes central to understanding the challenges to investigating RASSO and understanding issues with vulnerability. Despite some variations across the four forces, these themes are consistent and highlight systemic issues affecting officers' professional development, structural barriers, and individual resilience.

1. THE DE-PROFESSIONALISATION OF THE RASSO OFFICER ROLE

Capacity building vs. capability building: Due to high demand and a shortage of detectives, forces focused on increasing team capacity rather than enhancing officers' competencies. This trend is exacerbated by the Uplift and direct entry detective programmes, which introduced inexperienced officers to complex cases without adequate training to fill capacity gaps. Many officers lacked specialised training for RASSO investigations despite completing basic detective certification courses. Over 80% of surveyed officers expressed a need for more training, though operational demands often prevented them from participating in such programs which were considered an 'abstraction' rather than an 'investment'. Insufficient training leads to a reliance on 'omnicompetence,' where officers act as investigative generalists without the necessary expertise in sexual offence cases, impacting victim support and case outcomes. The inconsistent, didactically presented and superficial training materials further hinder officers' development, affecting their confidence, professionalism and effectiveness.

2. STRUCTURAL AND SYSTEMIC BARRIERS TO LEARNING AND ORGANISATIONAL HEALTH

Transactional decision-making: Decisions about training and resource allocation were often made quickly and without strategic foresight, hindering long-term improvements. Structural changes in investigative teams, driven by various reviews and inspections, led to confusion and fatigue among officers. A performance-driven culture added to this stress, with officers feeling pressured to meet targets at the expense of thorough investigations and victim care. This further impacted on the way that officers over focused on the victim's behaviours and credibility as they made decisions about how to manage demand alongside the targets they were given (Harding et al., 2024). The use of local data to understand and manage demand and victim 'types' is limited, resulting in ineffective allocation of resources and prioritisation of cases. High workload and insufficient supervisory time further exacerbated these issues, leading to poor case management and officer welfare.

3. INDIVIDUAL RESILIENCE TO COPE WITH ORGANISATIONAL SHORTCOMINGS

Toxic coping strategies: officers resort to unhealthy coping mechanisms due to overwhelming demand and lack of support, severely impacting their well-being and home life. The survey revealed high levels of stress and burnout among RASSO officers, with many working while ill and experiencing compassion fatigue towards victims. The organisational culture did little to address these issues, with a significant portion of officers feeling unsupported in terms of health and welfare offers and effective supervision to identify and prevent stress build up. This environment not only affects officers' personal health but also their professional performance, leading to diminished quality in handling cases and supporting victims.

Further insights

The need for more effective training has been a recurring theme in government, third sector, and academic reviews exploring the ongoing issues with attrition and unequal distribution of justice at the police stage of the CJS. The longevity of the problem clearly illustrates the need to upskill officers and ensure access to specialist knowledge and to foster a professional approach to this complex crime.

Pillar 4 researchers explored their findings through the lens of organisational justice theory, emphasising the importance of inclusive participation and the role of the workplace in empowering individuals to perform their roles effectively and professionally (Nilsson & Townsend, 2010). Research indicates that fair and just organisations are associated with feelings of being valued, loyalty, commitment to organisational goals, and emotional attachment to the police force (Williams et al., 2022). Accessing and applying specialist knowledge and CPD improves officers' confidence, professionalism, and capacity to handle the complexities RASSO cases present. This is what is required to provide a procedurally just service to victims of all types. The Pillar four research acknowledges the positive outcomes of critically reflective working practices at each stage of the investigative process to check on assumptions about victims and victim – suspect relationships for example.

Resulting from the work of Operation Soteria Bluestone there has been a complete redesign of the SSAIDP in collaboration with the College of Policing. Based on the core findings of the Operation Soteria Bluestone research there is much hope to change the current application of specialist knowledge about sexual offending among RASSO investigators.

Research example 2: domestic abuse

Vulnerability and domestic abuse: what do we know?

The second example the authors draw on in this chapter in relation to VAWG is the current knowledge around domestic abuse (DA). Approximately one in four women and one in ten men have been victims of DA in their lifetime, with 100,000 victims subjected to severe DA in the UK every year (Howarth et al., 2009). Figures from the Crime Survey of England and Wales published by the Office for National Statistics (ONS, 2023) suggest that 2.1 million people aged 16 years and over (1.4 million women and 751,000 men) experienced domestic abuse in the year ending March 2023. During the 12 months ending March 2023, police recorded 889,918 domestic abuse-related crimes (excluding Devon and Cornwall), a similar number to the previous year, and there were 51,288 domestic abuse-related prosecutions in England and Wales, a reduction on the year ending March 2022 which saw 53,207 prosecutions. There may be a number of reasons for this reduction, but delays in the CJS will no doubt have an impact on victim attrition rates in particular. Indeed, from February 2022 to February 2023 there was a 6% increase in the Crown Court backlog of outstanding cases according to the Law Society (2024). The Domestic Abuse Commissioner is explicit in her findings that victims and survivors have for too long borne the brunt of a 'postcode lottery' in the response to domestic abuse, in all parts of the CJS (Domestic Abuse Commissioner, 2023) which no doubt impacts vulnerability and attrition.

DA is a serious human rights abuse and because of the vulnerable nature of its victims has been termed a public health issue (Garcia-Moreno et al., 2006; Williams et al., 2018). DA is not a new concept, indeed there may never have been a time when it did not exist (Hague et al., 2005) but historically it has been seen as private family issue rather than an issue for policing or the CJS. DA has been on the rise however for several years, perhaps in part because victims are more confident in reporting to the police, but also as society reimagines the acceptability of inter-familial violence. The impact of the VAWG agenda for policing since the horrific murder of Sarah Everard in 2021 has brought it rightly to the forefront of policing activity and resulted in all forces in England and Wales focusing on improving responses to domestic abuse as part of this wider VAWG agenda through the VAWG framework (NPCC & College of Policing, 2021).

In conjunction with other key players in the CJS, the new Joint DA Action Plan is also of paramount importance ensuring agencies work better together with a joint commitment to transform domestic abuse victims' experiences of the CJS. It is hoped that this will increase confidence to report, as well as reduce victim attrition (NPCC, 2023). This is particularly important given that it is estimated that only 24% of domestic violence crime is actually reported to the Police (HMIC, 2014; Walby & Allen 2004). DA affects people of all ages, genders, classes, ethnicities, and vulnerabilities. Barrow-Grint et al. (2023) set out the limits of research on protected characteristics, with more to do in this space, particularly in relation to adolescent domestic abuse, elderly abuse, and abuse involving those from different ethnic backgrounds.

The police in the UK have utilised the domestic abuse, stalking and harassment and honour-based violence (DASH) tool since 2009 as a way of identifying evidence-based risk in DA victims (Richards, 2009). This multi-agency assessment tool is utilised to identify those at high risk of domestic violence by any agency working with victims or perpetrators. The DASH question set is based on a review of 30 domestic homicide investigations and nearly 400 domestic and sexual abuse crimes, as well as specialist knowledge from victims and DA charities (Richards, 2004; Robinson, 2006).

There is significant scrutiny of police action at domestic abuse incidents, with safeguarding activity a priority both for local forces and Her Majesty's Inspectorate of Constabulary and Fire & Rescue Services (HMICFRS). Domestic abuse-related crimes represent 16.2% of all offences recorded by the police, with Violence against the person being the highest proportion of offences identified as domestic abuse-related (34.0%) (ONS, 2023). DA related crimes recorded by the police do not always result in arrest and a large proportion have evidential issues in proceeding with prosecution. In some cases, the police and Crown Prosecution Service (CPS) will take forward a case to trial without the support of the victim if there is sufficient evidence to do so, conducting what is termed an evidence led or 'absent-victim' prosecution (Barrow-Grint et al., 2023). The increase in the use of body worn video has undoubtedly had an impact on the increasing number of such prosecutions (Lister, Burn & Pina-Sanchez, 2018).

A large amount of work has been undertaken by the police, CPS and the courts to introduce fast-track domestic violence courts within the Magistrates Courts, as a significant body of academic work explores the benefits of swift processes for all concerned (Cook et al., 2004). Indeed, this can impact on decisions about victims withdrawing their case from the process (Williams et al., 2009). A pilot to fast-track DA cases into the Crown Court in the Thames Valley Police and Thames & Chiltern CPS region has also drawn similar conclusions (Synnott & Ioannou, 2019). There is less clarity, however, on the reasons why many victims who decide to withdraw their complaint do so even before the court process is initiated.

Domestic abuse attrition

The high attrition rate in cases of DA, which in this context means the number of cases initially reported to the police which do not proceed, is an area of concern and one which all police practitioners should understand in order to improve outcomes. Barrow-Grint (2016) conducted research in Thames Valley Police demonstrating that most domestic violence victims who have been subject to a criminal offence withdraw their support in the initial ten days after the incident, with days five to eight most crucial for attrition. This is normally while police are still investigating the crime and is definitely before a standard case would be heard at the Magistrate's Court under the fast-track system within specialist domestic violence courts. The question that arises, therefore, is what the police service can do to prevent such withdrawals for vulnerable victims, and whether the CJS should further focus on providing victims with better support in the initial stages of investigation, after first disclosure of DA. This is important for all police officers to recognise when faced with difficult investigations featuring vulnerable individuals who are likely to have suffered abuse previously and are often subject to features of coercive control (Stark, 2007).

While there is a body of work on DA attrition, it is limited and generally focuses on cases that have reached the court stage of the criminal justice process rather than those victims who withdraw in the immediate aftermath of the abusive event. There appears to be no theoretical links between DA attrition and time theories or temporal sequencing. Going forward discussing vulnerability and attrition in the context of temporal sequencing may allow the problem to be reframed.

The CJS has developed considerably in relation to dealing with DA, with a plethora of policy initiatives aimed at increasing prosecutions and convictions. Reducing attrition in domestic violence is a key goal of government (Hester, 2006). Similarly, there is a large body of academic work seeking to research and address the societal problem of DA, but there are few studies into victim withdrawal or retraction from the process (Robinson & Cook, 2006; Hester, 2006). Of concern, recent work by Brewster (2023) found that whether deliberate or otherwise, officers' attitudes towards domestic abuse and its victims, could be negatively impacting on victim decision-making towards engaging with the judicial system, possibly exposing them to increased risk.

DA could be described as a wicked problem (Grint, 2005). Its extent is not truly known, there is no easy way to solve it and it is not the responsibility for any one agency to do so (Williams et al., 2018). Indeed, it is a complex and 'cross cutting' phenomena (McGarry, Hussain & Watts, 2019). Victim retraction is almost universally viewed as a problematic outcome of domestic violence, and Robinson and Cook (2006) suggest that academic understanding of the causes and consequences of retraction are limited. Some qualitative explorations have explored notions of misperceptions and frustrations with the CJS, fear of keeping themselves and family safe while awaiting court or believing that rehabilitation is required rather than criminal punishment (Bennett, Goodman & Dutton, 1999).

Hester (2006) considers the perspectives of women experiencing domestic violence and their reasons for attrition. The requirement for immediate violence to stop and the need for longer-term protection were the two key factors that affected attrition. Moreover, for some women, the fact that police attended and stopped the immediate violence was all that they wanted. Following that they wanted no further engagement in the CJS. This is also an outcome found by Ford (1991) in the USA. For other victims, a longer-term solution was required, but frustrations at the length of time and the lack of impact a criminal justice solution might lead to, increased attrition.

Evaluations of specialist domestic violence courts (SDVCs) have reported positive benefits in a number of key areas such as victim participation and satisfaction, ensuring effective victim support services, and effective information sharing within the CJS. Despite the pilot of these courts experiencing victim retraction (Cook et al., 2004), since their introduction in 2005 they have achieved better outcomes than normal courts in relation to guilty verdicts (CAADA, 2012). The SDVC is a system that needs continual review and support to ensure it works. Dame Vera Baird's report 'Specialist Domestic Violence Courts – How Special Are They?' (Baird et al., 2018) articulates this well, noting that there are significant gaps in the system and that, if funding were to be improved, SDVCs would work as was originally intended.

This is important given the Centre for Justice Innovation (2014) found that SDVCs increased successful prosecutions, ensured justice for victims was faster and kept them safer. Indeed, a pilot study at Aylesbury Crown Court between Thames Valley Police, Thames & Chiltern CPS and the Judiciary found similar findings, where offences are more serious and investigations more complicated (Synnott & Ioannou, 2019). While the evidence base around victim attrition is relatively limited, Synnott and Ioannou's (2019) important research is both compelling and persuasive that the impact of vulnerability on the investigative and criminal justice process is significant, and speed of inquiry and prosecution are both fundamental to the victim's psychological well-being and reducing the cost to the public purse of domestic abuse. This is estimated at costing £66 billion a year (Synnott & Ioannou, 2019). It seems clear that increasing the speed of cases being dealt with makes a considerable difference in engaging the victim.

CAADA (2012) research reviewed 526 cases where a charge was laid in relation to DA. In 28 of these cases the victim withdrew their statement and support for court proceedings. Of these 28, 50% continued to remain in a relationship with the perpetrator compared to 29% of those that continued to support a prosecution. This indicates that those victims in continuing relationships are less likely to support a prosecution and provide evidence.

Interestingly, Hester's (2006) research showed that while the police and other criminal justice agencies viewed the victim as the main reason for disengagement, victims themselves suggested that cases were not effectively pursued, and support was not provided. These were reasons for not proceeding.

Temporal sequencing

Theories of time are important to acknowledge for practitioners and temporal sequencing may provide a different explanation for why victims of domestic violence withdraw their complaints. Time is a social construct which, suggests Bluedorn and Denhardt (1988), has an impact on an individual's decision making and motivation.

Dawson (2014) reviews time within the construct of organisational change as either a recurrent cyclical sequence or a linear sequential process. Metaphorical analyses of time as cyclic (Eliade, 1959) or linear (de Grazia, 1972) are interesting concepts. For Eliade (1959), life develops in an ever-recurring rhythm or cycle, while de Grazia (1972) believes that time should be considered as a straight line, which is irreversible. Both these theories could be applied to DA victims: for example, victims that withdraw their complaints within a certain timescale and remain within an abusive relationship may be viewing time as cyclical. Therefore, the relationship reoccurs, as does the abuse, as does their desire to involve the CJS then retract from it.

Victims who view time in a linear manner may consider a start and end to the process of making a criminal complaint. They may follow through the stages without retracting as they see time as irreversible. Bluedorn and Denhardt (1988) discuss the linear concept of time in modern society, arguing that it is difficult to recognise differing views on time when we generally view it as steadily moving forward. Anyone who digresses from this approach is seen as anomalous. This might offer explanation as to why the police often find it difficult to understand those that call for help, then retract rather than progress down the assumed pathway of criminal justice proceedings.

Gurvitch (1964) suggests that differing societies have divergent and often contradictory time perspectives. This leads to separate cultures having different rhythms and seeing problems with a contrary temporal perspective. In relation to

DA, a victim may alternate their decision to make a formal police complaint, they may be deceptive and withhold facts, some will see themselves as in a cyclical process where after a certain timescale the process of a relationship followed by DA is normalised. Applying this theory of time can explore why an individual assesses the temporal sequence of their everyday lives and how this impacts on their decision making. In Gurvitch's (1964) view this can develop understanding about why the characteristics of individuals and communities can often be so very different to institutions. The fact of the matter is that DA is complicated, as are individuals that are victims of it. Therefore, different people will use different variations of time to make sense of their own predicament.

If victims are more likely to withdraw their criminal complaints at a particular point in time, to try and change or stop this may be futile. A victim may 'give it a week', to see if the suspect apologises or their bruises fade, at which point they wish to forget about what happened and withdraw their support for a police investigation and prosecution. Hassard (2000) suggests that participation in society and culture ensures that an individual follows a normative route and subscribes to times that are rational. If, as discussed earlier, a victim's rational thought process is that timescales for withdrawal are culturally or socially embedded, it is this cultural barrier that the authorities will be required to overcome in order to persuade a victim to continue. Understanding temporal sequencing is key to the police improving outcomes for vulnerable victims of DA.

Barrow-Grint's (2016) research into DA attrition exposed a correlation between attrition and time, namely that victims tended to withdraw their support for criminal action between days one and ten after the violent act, but mostly around five days. Barrow-Grint (2016) randomly reviewed 50 cases of DA where a victim had withdrawn their complaint. She analysed the cases to ascertain at what point in time the attrition had occurred. In all of the cases but one, an arrest was made, with 76% of cases having the arrest of the offender occurring on the same day the offence was reported to the police. In 22% of cases, the arrest was made after this, with the longest delay being just 11 days. In the case where no arrest was made, the suspect was summonsed to court.

Of the 50 cases, a significant number (21 cases) withdrew before five days had passed, with a further nine cases withdrawing before ten days had passed (slightly under an additional 20%). This data is shown in Table 9.1.

Table 9.1 Withdrawal of complaints.

Total number of withdrawals	Days since incident occurred	Overall % of incidents withdrawn
21	5	42%
30	10	60%
37	20	74%
41	30	82%

Source: adapted from Barrow-Grint (2016)

Further qualitative work by Barrow-Grint (2016) examined the impact of temporal sequencing on victims of high-risk DA and draws conclusions about perpetrator persuasiveness, relationships, time and withdrawal being linked to attrition. These are important considerations to examine in order to reduce the loss of victims from the CJS going forward. This is similar to the work conducted by Williams et al. (2009).

DA is a key concern for the police, more so because the rate of victim attrition is so significant, and the vulnerability of those involved so substantial. Similar to the work reported on rape earlier, a victims vulnerability impacts on both their victimisation and the likelihood of them receiving justice in court. DA is a wicked problem (Grint, 2005) and taming it is complex and multi-faceted. Practitioners and policy/strategy developers need to consider how we can hold perpetrators to account more firmly by ensuring prosecutions are viable and attrition is mitigated wherever possible. There are obvious practical matters which can help address this, but by using temporal sequencing theory, the problem can be reframed to understand how a victim's propensity to adopt a linear or cyclical model of time may impact their situation and what the police can do to address this.

Conclusion

Considering these two specific areas of VAWG, where vulnerabilities are central to understanding the complexities of both harm and the investigation process, using an evidence-based approach (Chapter 5) to practice is vital to drive an effective approach to investigating these examples of interpersonal criminality. The chapter has focused on the longevity of the problem and the problematic nature of applying the evidence available into a practical context. The most recent research into rape and sexual violence provides new insights into the context of vulnerabilities and highlights how the personal aspects of victims and the context of offending needs to be considered alongside organisational contexts within which these cases are investigated that may in fact compound issues. The lack of resources for policing and the reduction in training and learning and development have been to the detriment of officers investigating rape and sexual violence and its' victims. While the Soteria Bluestone research has focused on RASSO, the provision and acquisition of learning and specialist knowledge across DA and other areas of VAWG is clear as the issues are analogous. A commitment to CPD and learning is essential. As Raaijmakers et al. (2024) report the lack of conceptual clarity and robust identification of vulnerability and the influence it can have on cases puts justice outcomes at risk. Indeed, those who characteristics are ignored can be at risk of re-victimisation (Enang et al., 2021). Training police officers on the importance of prior crime experiences, experiences with the police, individual characteristics, and transient and chaotic lifestyles as indicators of vulnerability is key (Williams et al., 2022; Tidmarsh, 2021).

Further understanding of the complexities involved for women who have experienced domestic and/or sexual violence is crucial in developing a co-ordinated response to the problem (Williams et al., 2018). Reflecting on where

Policing vulnerability attrition, rape and domestic abuse 161

issues might arise in cases involving such factors is necessary in both the short and longer term. Reporting an event is often assumed to be the difficult part of the process, however, feeling fearful, lonely, apprehensive, and confused after the report is made can be when victims need the most support (Williams et al., 2009).

The findings outlined earlier provide a more nuanced approach to the consideration of vulnerability, suggesting that vulnerability in the context of policing is not simply about what is encapsulated in the characteristics of the victim and their subsequent chances of being further victimised. This knowledge is applicable at a more practical level. Indeed, by understanding how these complexities interact with time and the differing points of the policing process, the knowledge offers an opportunity for officers to consider the effect such factors have on the investigation of cases of DA and RASSO being successful. By understanding these nuances and the relationship vulnerable factors have with both attrition and the victims' decisions to stay on board with the process, appropriate support strategies might impact on the delivery of justice in these complex areas of police work.

> **Evidence-based case study illustrating professional practice**
>
> The following case study details a victim who reported her allegation of rape to the police. She subsequently withdrew her allegation. Consider how learning from the research outlined earlier might facilitate the delivery of a more effective police response to support the victim.
>
> When reviewing the case study, consider the following points:
>
> - What vulnerable characteristics does this victim present to the police on reporting her allegation?
> - What might this mean for the investigation?
> - What assumptions might be made about this case?
> - What are the potential longer-term implications?
>
> The victim in this case is noted (on the police record) as not being vulnerable. However, she has a long history of mental health issues and a transient lifestyle. She has been reported as missing in the past. She reported being raped by a man she met in a club while she was out with some friends. She claims he took her back to his flat and raped her, but she has very little memory of the event. She woke up in his bed and left immediately. She reported the case to the police but subsequently withdrew her allegation.
>
> The learning from the Soteria research suggests that victim vulnerabilities are not effectively identified by the police. In this case study the victim had made previous related allegations, yet her crime report was not flagged accordingly. The repeat nature of this offending pattern supports the findings undertaken by Barrow-Grint (2016) and illustrates the cyclical offending models that occur. The lack of identification of this victim's vulnerability

> compounds her risk of future victimisation and, therefore, the potential longer-term implications for future exposure to assault. Not identifying this risk meant that the victim withdrew her complaint and could not access the support she may have needed to help prevent future assaults.

Reflective question

By focusing on the needs of the victim what could have been done to support this individual in order to facilitate engagement with the police?

Acknowledgements

The authors would like to acknowledge both the lead, Betsy Stanko and the research team in the Strategic Research and Analysis Unit who worked on the MPS Rape Review for over a decade.

References

Asquith, N. (2012). Vulnerability and the Art of Complaint Making. In I. Bartkowiak-Theron & N. Asquith (eds), *Policing Vulnerability*. Sydney: The Federation Press.

Baird, V., Lord, A., Lawson, R., Durham, R. & Soroptimists of Northern England. (2018) Specialist Domestic Violence Courts: How Special Are They? Office of the Northumbria Police & Crime Commissioner. [online] https://sigbi.org/lichfield/files/2020/05/OPCC_037_Specialist-domestic-violence-courts-Court-Observers-Panel-A4-booklet-2018-V2.pdf (accessed 11 May 2024).

Barrow-Grint, K. (2016). Attrition Rates in Domestic Abuse: Time for a Change? An Application of Temporal Sequencing Theory. *Policing: A Journal of Policy and Practice*, 10(3), 250–263.

Barrow-Grint, K., Sebire, J., Turton, J. & Weir, R. (2023). *Policing Domestic Abuse: Risk Policy and Practice*. London: Routledge.

Bartkowiak-Théron, I. & Asquith, N. L. (2012). The Extraordinary Intricacies of Policing Vulnerability. *Australasian Policing: A Journal of Professional Practice and Research*, 4(2), 43–49.

Bennett, L., Goodman, L. & Dutton, M. A. (1999). Systemic Obstacles to the Criminal Prosecution a Battering Partner: A Victim's Perspective. *Journal of Interpersonal Violence*, 14(7), 761–772. https://doi.org/10.1177/088626099014007006.

Bluedorn, A. C. & Denhardt, R. B. (1988). Time and Organizations. *Journal of Management*, 14(2), 299–320. https://doi.org/10.1177/014920638801400209.

Bradford, B. & Jackson, J. (2024). Trust in the Police: What is to be Done? *The Political quarterly (London. 1930)*, 95(3), 442–449. https://doi.org/10.1111/1467-923X.13274.

Brewster, N. (2023). Exploring Officer-Influence on Disengagement Among Domestic Abuse Victims in Lincolnshire. a Mixed Methods Study. BA thesis, University of Sunderland.

Brown, J. (2011). We Mind and We Care but Have Things Changed? Assessment of Progress in the Reporting, Investigating and Prosecution of Allegations of Rape. *Journal of Sexual Aggression*, 17(3), 263–272. https://doi.org/10.1080/13552600.2011.613280.

Brown, R. L. & Moloney, M. E. (2019). Intersectionality, Work and Wellbeing: The Effects of Gender and Disability. *Gender & Society*, 33(1), 94–122. https://doi.org/10.1177/0891243218800636.

Burton, M., Evans, R. & Saunders, A. (2006). *An Evaluation of the Use of Special Measures for Vulnerable and Intimidated Witnesses*. London: Home Office.

CAADA. (2012). IDVA Insights into Domestic Violence Prosecutions. [online]. www.cps.gov.uk/publications/docs/idva_dv_prosecutions_insights_executive_summary.pdf (accessed 20 July 2018).

Casey, L. (2023). Baroness Casey Review Final Report: March 2023. [online] www.met.police.uk/SysSiteAssets/media/downloads/met/about-us/baronesscasey-review/update-march-2023/baroness-casey-review-march-2023a.pd (accessed 10 November 2024).

Centre for Justice Innovation. (2014). A Snapshot of Specialist Domestic Violence Courts. [online]. https://justiceinnovation.org/publications/snapshot-specialist-domestic-violence-courts (accessed 5 May 2024).

Charman, S. & Williams, E. (2022). Accessing Justice: The Impact of Discretion, 'Deservedness' and Distributive Justice on the Equitable Allocation of Policing Resources, *Criminology & Criminal Justice*, 22 (3), 404–422. https://doi.org/10.1177/17488958211013075.

College of Policing. (2015). College of Policing Analysis: Estimating Demand on the Police Service. [online]. www.college.police.uk/News/College-news/Documents/Demand%20Report%2023_1_15_noBleed.pdf (accessed 20 July 2018).

College of Policing. (2017). Vulnerability. [online]. www.college.police.uk/What-we-do/Development/Vulnerability/Pages/Vulnerability.aspx (accessed 12 August 2019).

College of Policing. (2024) Vulnerability-Related Risks. [online] www.college.police.uk/guidance/vulnerability-related-risks (accessed 23 March 2024).

Cook, D., Burton, M., Robinson, A. & Vallely, C. (2004). *Evaluation of Specialist Domestic Violence Courts/Fast Track Systems*. London: Crown Prosecution Service and Department of Constitutional Affairs. [online]. www.cps.gov.uk/publications/docs/specialistdvcourts.pdf (28 February 2019).

Cummins, I. (2016). *Mental Health and the Criminal Justice System*. London: Critical Publishing.

Dawson, P. (2014). Reflections: On Time, Temporality and Change in Organizations. *Journal of Change Management*, 14(3), 285–308. https://doi.org/10.1080/14697017.2014.886870.

de Grazia, S. (1972). Time and Work. In H. Yaker, H. Osmond & F. Cheek (eds), *The Future of Time*. New York: Anchor Books.

Domestic Abuse Act (2021). [online] www.legislation.gov.uk/ukpga/2021/17/contents (accessed 15 November 2024).

Domestic Abuse Commissioner. (2023) *'A Patchwork of Provision': How to Meet the Needs of Victims and Survivors Across England and Wales*. London: The Domestic Abuse Commissioner for England and Wales.

Edwards, S. (1989). *Policing 'Domestic' Violence: Women, the Law and the State*. London: Sage.

Eliade, M. (1959). *Cosmos and History: The Myth of the Eternal Return*. New York: Harper & Row.

Enang, I., Murray, J., Dougall, N., Aston, E., Wooff, A., Heyman, I. & Grandison, G. (2021). Vulnerability Assessment across the Frontline of Law Enforcement and Public Health: A Systematic Review, *Policing & Society*, 32(4), 540–559. https://doi.org/10.1080/10439463.2021.1927025.

Ford, D. A. (1991). Prosecution as a Victim Power Source: A Note on Empowering Women in their Violent Conjugal Relationships. *Law & Society Review*, 25(2), 313–334. https://doi.org/10.2307/3053801.

Garcia-Moreno, C., Jansen, H., Ellsberg, M., Heise, L. & Watts, C. (2006). Prevalence of Intimate Partner Violence: Findings from the WHO Multi-Country Study on Women's Health and Domestic Violence. *The Lancet*, 368(9551), 19–37.

Grint, K. (2005). *Leadership: Limits and Possibilities*. Basingstoke: Palgrave Macmillan.

Grint, K. (2010). Wicked Problems and Clumsy Solutions: The Role of Leadership. In S. Brookes & K. Grint (eds), *The New Public Leadership Challenge* (pp. 169–186). Basingstoke: Palgrave Macmillan.

Gurvitch, G. (1964). *The Spectrum of Social Time*. Dordrecht: D Reidel.

Hague, G. M., Malos, E. M. & Wilton, T. (2005). *Domestic Violence: Action for Change*. New Clarion.

Harding, R., Maguire, L. & Williams, E. (2024). Competing Concepts of Public Value and Legitimacy in the Police: Organisational Challenges in the Investigation of Rape and Serious Sexual Offences, *International Journal of Law, Crime and Justice*, 76, 100646. https://doi.org/10.1016/j.ijlcj.2023.100646.

Hassard, J. (2000). Images of Time in Work and Organization. In K. Grint (ed.), *Work and Society: A Reader*. Cambridge: Polity.

Hester, M. (2006). Making It Through the Criminal Justice System: Attrition and Domestic Violence. *Social Policy and Society*, 5(1), 79–90. https://doi.org/10.1017/S1474746405002769.

HMIC. (2014). *Everyone's Business: Improving the Police Response to Domestic Abuse*. London: Her Majesty's Inspectorate of Constabulary.

HMIC. (2015). Increasingly Everyone's Business: A Progress Report on the Police Response to Domestic Abuse. [online]. www.justiceinspectorates.gov.uk/hmic/wp-content/uploads/increasingly-everyones-business-domestic-abuse-progress-report.pdf (accessed 20 January 2019).

Hohl, K., Johnson, K. & Molisso, S. (2022). A Procedural Justice Theory Approach to Police Engagement with Victim-Survivors of Rape and Sexual Assault: Initial Findings of the 'Project Bluestone' Pilot Study. *International Criminology*, 2(3), 253–261.

Hohl, K. & Stanko, E. (2015). Complaints of Rape and the Criminal Justice System: Fresh Evidence on the Attrition Problem in England and Wales. *European Journal of Criminology*, 12(3), 324–341. https://doi.org/10.1177/1477370815571949.

Hohl, K. & Stanko, E. (2024). *Policing Rape: The Way Forward*, 1st edition. Abingdon: Routledge.

Howarth, E., Stimpson, L., Barran, D. & Robinson, A. (2009). Safety in Numbers: Summary of Findings and Recommendations from a Multi-site Evaluations of Independent Domestic Violence Advisors. [online]. www.henrysmithcharity.org.uk/documents/SafetyinNumbers16ppSummaryNov09.pdf (accessed 28 February 2019).

Jordan, J. (2011). Here We Go Round the Review-Go-Round: Rape Investigation and Prosecution – Are Things Getting Worse Not Better? *Journal of Sexual Aggression*, 17(3), 234–249. https://doi.org/10.1080/13552600.2011.613278.

Kelly, L. (1999). *Domestic Violence Matters: An Evaluation of a Development Project*. Home Office Research Study, 193. London: Home Office.

Kessel, A. (2022). Rethinking Rape Culture: Revelations of Intersectional Analysis. *The American Political Science Review*, 116(1), 131–143. https://doi.org/10.1017/S0003055421000733.

Khalifeh, H., Moran, P., Borschmann, R., Dean, K., Hart, C., Hogg, K., Osborn, D., Johnson, S. & Howard, L. (2014). Domestic and Sexual Violence Against Patients with Severe Mental Illness. *Psychological Medicine*, 45(4), 875–886. https://doi.org/10.1017/S0033291714001962.

Law Society. (2024). Government Set to Miss Target to Reduce Court Backlogs. [online] www.lawsociety.org.uk/contact-or-visit-us/press-office/press-releases/government-set-to-miss-target-to-reduce-courts-backlog (accessed 5 May 2024).

Lister, S., Burn, D. & Pina-Sanchez, J. (2018). *Innovation and the Application of Knowledge for More Effective Policing*. N8 Policing Research Partnership Catalyst Project.

Loftus, B. (2009). *Police Culture in a Changing World*. Oxford: Oxford University.

McGarry, J., Hussain, B., & Watts, K. (2019). Exploring Primary Care Responses to Domestic Violence and Abuse (DVA): Operationalisation of a National Initiative. *Journal of Adult Protection*, 21(2), 144–154. https://doi.org/10.1108/JAP-10–2018–0025.

MPS. (2005). Review of Rape Investigations. [online]. http://content.met.police.uk/News/Review-of-Rape-Investigations/1260267633108/1257246745756 (accessed 15 February 2018).

Munro, V. & Kelly, L. (2009). A Vicious Cycle? Attrition and Conviction Patterns in Contemporary Rape Cases in England and Wales. In M. Horvarth & J. Brown (eds), *Rape: Challenging Contemporary Thinking* (pp. 99–123). Cullompton: Willan.

Myhill, A. & Johnson, K. (2016). Police Use of Discretion in Response to Domestic Violence. *Criminology & Criminal Justice*, 16(1), 3–20. https:///doi.org/10.1177/1748895815590202.

Nilsson, I. & Townsend, E. (2010). Occupational Justice—Bridging theory and practice. *Scandinavian Journal of Occupational Therapy*, 17(1), 57–63. https://doi.org/10.3109/11038120903287182.

Norman, J. & Williams, E. (2017). Putting Learning into Practice: Self Reflections from Cops. *European Law Enforcement Research Bulletin*, (3), 197–203.

NPCC & College of Policing. (2021). Policing Violence Against Women and Girls – National Framework for Delivery. [online] www.npcc.police.uk/SysSiteAssets/media/downloads/our-work/vawg/vawg-framework-for-delivery.pdf (accessed 5 May 2024).

NPCC. (2023). Transforming Investigation and Prosecution of Domestic Abuse. [online]. https://news.npcc.police.uk/releases/transforming-investigation-and-prosecution-of-domestic-abuse (accessed 5 May 2024).

Office for Policing and Crime. (2017). Sexual Violence. [online]. www.london.gov.uk/sites/default/files/mopac_lcpf_co-commissioning_workshop_sv_july_2017.pdf (accessed 15 March 2018).

ONS. (2023). Domestic Abuse Prevalence and Trends. [online]. www.ons.gov.uk/peoplepopulationandcommunity/crimeandjustice/articles/domesticabuseprevalenceandtrendsenglandandwales/yearendingmarch2023 (accessed 6 May 2024).

Pearce, C. (2004). The Future of Leadership: Combining Vertical and Shared Leadership to Transform Knowledge Work. *Academy of Management Executive*, 18(1), 47–57.

Raaijmakers, N., Bosma, A. & Scholte, R. (2024). Better Safe than Sorry? Police Officers' Identification of and Responses to Vulnerable Crime Victims. *Policing and Society*, online ahead of print. https://doi.org/10.1080/10439463.2024.2347660.

Richards, L. (2004) *Getting Away with it: A Strategic Overview of Domestic Violence, Sexual Assault and 'Serious' Incident Analysis*. London: Metropolitan Police Service.

Richards, L. (2009). Domestic Abuse, Stalking and Harassment and Honour Based Violence (DASH, 2009) Risk Identification and Assessment and Management Model. [online]. www.dashriskchecklist.co.uk/wp-content/uploads/2016/09/DASH-2009.pdf (accessed 15 December 2019).

Robinson, A. (2006) Reducing Repeat Victimization among High-Risk Victims of Domestic Violence: The Benefits of a Co-ordinated Community Response in Cardiff, Wales. *Violence Against Women*, 12, 761–788. https://doi.org/10.1177/1077801206291477.

Robinson, A. & Cook, D. (2006). Understanding Victim Retraction in Cases of Domestic Violence: Specialist Courts, Government Policy, and Victim Centred Justice. *Contemporary Justice Review*, 9(2), 189–213. https://doi.org/10.1080/10282580600785017.

Robinson, A. L., & Stroshine, M. S. (2005). The Importance of Expectation Fulfilment on Domestic Violence Victims' Satisfaction with the Police in the UK. *Policing: An International Journal of Police Strategies & Management*, 28(2), 301–320. https://doi.org/10.1108/13639510510597924.

Rumney, P. N. S., McPhee, D., Fenton. R. A. & Williams, A. (2020). A Police Specialist Rape Investigation Unit: A Comparative Analysis of Performance and Victim Care. *Policing and Society*, 30 (5): 548–568. https://doi.org/10.1080/10439463.2019.1566329.

Stanko, E. (1985). *Intimate Intrusions*. London: Pandora.

Stanko, E. (2007). *MPS Rape Review: The Attrition of Rape in London: Strategic Research and Analysis Unit*. London: Metropolitan Police Service.

Stanko, B. (2022). Operation Soteria Bluestone year 1 Report 2021–2022. www.gov.uk/government/publications/operation-soteria-year-one-report (accessed 18 November 2024)

Stanko, E., & Williams, E. (2009). Reviewing Rape and Rape Allegations in London: What Are the Vulnerabilities of the Victims Who Report to the Police? In M. Horvarth & J. Brown (eds), *Rape: Challenging Contemporary Thinking*. Cullompton: Willan.

Stark, E. (2007). *Coercive Control: The Entrapment of Women in Personal Life*. Oxford: Oxford University.

Synnott, J. & Ioannou, M. (2019). *An Evaluation of the 'Protocol for the Handling of Domestic Abuse Cases at Aylesbury Crown Court'*. Thames Valley Police.

Tidmarsh, P. (2021). *The Whole Story: Investigating Sexual Crime – Truth, Lies and the Path to Justice*. London: Jonathan Cape.

Topping, A. (2022). 'Everyone Wants to Get Involved': Inside a New Police Approach to Tackling Rape. *The Guardian*, 24 October. [online]. www.theguardian.com/society/2022/oct/24/operation-bluestone-inside-new-police-approach-to-tackling-rape (accessed 18 November 2024).

Walby, S. & Allen, J. (2004) *Domestic Violence, Sexual Assault and Stalking: Findings from the British Crime Survey*. Home Office.

Williams, E. & Cockcroft, T. (2018). Knowledge Wars: Professionalisation, Organisational Justice and Competing Knowledge Paradigms in British Policing. In L. Huey & R. Mitchell (eds), *Evidence-Based Policing: An Introduction*. Bristol: Policy Press.

Williams, E., Norman, J. & Nixon, K. (2018). Violence Against Women: Public Health or Law Enforcement Problem or Both? *International Journal of Police Science & Management*, 20(3), 196–206. https://doi.org/10.1177/1461355718793666.

Williams, E., Norman, J. & Rowe, M. (2019). The Police Education Qualification Framework: A Professional Agenda or Building Professionals? *Police Practice and Research: An International Journal*, 20(3), 259–272. https://doi.org/10.1080/15614263.2019.1598070.

Williams, E., Norman, J. & Wunsch, D. (2009). Too Little Too Late: Assessing Vulnerability. *Policing: A Journal of Policy and Practice*, 3(4), 373–380. https://doi.org/10.1093/police/pap042.

Williams, E. & Stanko, B. (2009). Reviewing Rape and Rape Allegations in London: What are the Vulnerabilities of the Victims who Report to the Police. In M. Horvath & J. Brown (eds), *Rape: Challenging Contemporary Thinking* (pp. 207–227). Cullompton: Willan.

Williams, E., Miller, N., Harding, R., Sondhi, A., Maguire, L., Norman, J., Abinashi, D. & Ward, R. (2022). Appendix 10 – Pillar four: Officer Learning, Development and Wellbeing. [online]. https://assets.publishing.service.gov.uk/government/uploads/system/uploads/attachme nt_data/file/1128688/E02836356_Operation_Soteria_Y1_report_Accessible.pdf (accessed 5 May, 2024).

Wunsch, D., Davies, T. & Charleton, B. (2021). The London Rape Review 2021. [online]. www.london.gov.uk/sites/default/files/final_rr_victimtech_61221.pdf (accessed 23 October 2023).

Willis, J. & Mastrofski, S. (2016). Improving Policing by Integrating Craft and Science: What Can Patrol Officers Teach Us About Good Police Work? *Policing and Society*, 28(*1*), 27–44. https://doi.org/10.1080/10439463.2015.1135921.

Wood, D. & Williams, E. (2016). The Politics of Establishing Reflexivity as a Core Component of Good Policing. In S. Armstrong, J. Blaustein & A. Henry (eds), *Reflexivity and Criminal Justice: Intersections of Policy, Practice and Research*. London: Palgrave.

10 Counter-terrorism
The front line

Peter Williams

Introduction

The world changed on 11 September 2001 with attacks by Al-Qaeda-inspired insurgents against the World Trade Center in New York City, the Pentagon in Virginia, and Pennsylvania. Over 3000 people, including the insurgents, died during the commission of these attacks. This signalled another mode of terrorism; what we now call the new terrorism (Martin, 2017).

This development in respect of political violence, now known as the 'religious wave', was first witnessed in the late 1970s (Rapoport, 2001). In order for individual states and countries to keep their citizens safe, the present approaches to the commission of terrorist acts require different responses than those applied hitherto. This is known as counter terrorism and refers to proactive policies that are structured to track and remove terrorist environments and groups (Martin, 2017). This is not to be confused with anti-terrorism, which is designed to deter or prevent terrorist attacks (Martin, 2017).

Countries formulated their counter-terrorism policies and strategies, led by the USA who had declared the 'War on Terror'. The United Kingdom (UK) was no exception and by 2003, the first formal UK counter-terrorism strategy was published known as CONTEST, an acronym for Counter-Terrorism Strategy.

Historical context

While the launch of the Counter-Terrorism Strategy in 2003 was the first for the United Kingdom, the UK has considerable longevity in this area, which has involved both the police and intelligence services. Both organisations, which also includes the Government Communications Headquarters (GCHQ), are those at the forefront of the fight against terrorism. The longevity of the British state in responding to terrorism is somewhat reflected by internal developments within the police service, that still have resonance today. Such developments pre-dates the inception of the Secret Service Bureau in 1909, which was an attempt to counter the perceived threat of German spies being active across the UK. At the conclusion of the First World War, a new threat was considered a genuine and real threat, Bolshevism. As a consequence, the Bureau was split into two functions and became MI5 and MI6 (Gill & Phythian, 2009). However, for the police service such threats had started well before this period and for varied reasons.

In 1867, 12 people were killed and dozens injured around Clerkenwell Prison, when Irish dissidents, in an attempt to free a prisoner, planted a large bomb, which was powerful enough to blow a whole wall away and destroy some nearby buildings (Hewitt, 2008). This was not an isolated incident and during the 1880s Irish dissidents, in what became known as the 'Fenian Campaign', conducted a series of bombings on the British mainland. A number of attacks were committed, including one against Scotland Yard and as a result in 1883 the Metropolitan Police created, from the ranks of the Criminal Investigation Department, the Special Irish Branch (Innes & Thiel, 2008), who were responsible for investigating and responding to this insurgency of politically motivated violence. In 1888, the word 'Irish' in the title was dropped and Special Branch was fully instituted. Special Branch departments were eventually established in all constabularies throughout the UK (Newburn & Matassa, 2003).

The 'Branch' has always worked closely with the Security Service, and their primary role has always been associated with threats to the state/public order. Their remit today is to access and develop intelligence, necessary to provide protection for the public from terrorist and other threats (Blake et al., 2012). However, their significance and contribution to the ever-evolving response in respect of counterterrorism and their pivotal role in relation to that contemporary threat will be developed later in the chapter.

Another politically motivated group that deployed a bombing campaign was the often-forgotten Angry Brigade. Over the two-year period commencing in December 1970, the Metropolitan Police was forced to deploy resources against their first attack, a machine-gun attack on the Spanish Embassy, and during December 1972, the group claimed responsibility for ten attacks across London (Taylor, 2015). During this time, the group issued communiqués which were sent to the underground press, providing details of the attacks and, in fact, the communiqués, produced on a 'John Bull' printing kit (a model most associated with home printing), referred to other attacks, which had not been reported. The Angry Brigade was very much of the 'New Left' wave (Rapoport, 2001) and its activities presented problems for the Metropolitan Police in terms of their response.

Consequently, following an attack on the computer room at New Scotland Yard, a 'Bomb Squad' was formed comprising of CID and Special Branch officers, together with Explosives experts (Taylor, 2015). The 'Bomb Squad' was later renamed the 'Anti-Terrorism Branch' (Newburn & Matassa, 2003) and although most associated with the Irish Republican Army attacks on the British mainland in the 1970s and 1980s, the reason for the creation of this specialist unit was due to the activities of the Angry Brigade.

The Metropolitan Police Special Branch did retain lead responsibility for intelligence matters in relation to Irish dissident terrorism on the UK mainland until 1992, when the role was re-allocated to MI5 (Gregory, 2008). This decision reflected what was happening in the wider world at that time; the Berlin Wall came down in 1989 and the 'Cold War' was effectively over. It was felt that the Security Service had greater capacity in the light of these events, as their role was about to change away from the counterespionage and counter-intelligence, symbolic of the Cold War. At the time, little was known of events that were about to unfold in relation to Islamic-based terrorism.

The Good Friday Agreement in 1998, ended 30 years of counterinsurgency for the UK in Northern Ireland, which had been led by the Provisional IRA. Their tactics and targets included bombing campaigns on the British mainland, to which the police service, led by the Metropolitan Police Anti-Terrorism Branch or Specialist Operations (SO13) at New Scotland Yard, had to respond. The events in London on 7 July 2005 (7/7) brought further changes and saw the amalgamation of the Special Branch and the Anti-Terrorism Branch (Blair, 2009), the merger creating Counter Terrorism Command (SO15) (Hayman, 2009), which is what it is currently.

Two issues are worthy of further explanation in respect of SO15: firstly, the Metropolitan Police retains primacy in respect of counterterrorism nationally, including Scotland and Northern Ireland (Holford, 2023) and the Assistant Commissioner Specialist Operations is the ex-officio chair of the National Police Chiefs' Council (NPCC) Terrorism Committee (Blair, 2009).

Attacks by Irish dissident groups on the UK mainland led to the passing of the Prevention of Terrorism (Temporary Provisions) Act, 1974 and terrorism was defined as using violence for political means while placing any section of the public in fear (Hewitt, 2008). This legislation would remain on the statute book until replaced by the Terrorism Act, 2000, eventually enacted in February 2001 (Hewitt, 2008). This followed a two-volume report published in 1996 by Lord Lloyd of Berwick, entitled the 'Inquiry into Legislation against Terrorism' which drew the conclusions that terrorism in relation to 'The Troubles' was likely to recede and rather presciently, other forms of global terrorism were likely to increase (Hewitt, 2008).

The Terrorism Act (2000) defines 'Terrorism' as:

'Terrorism' means the use or threat of action if:

- the action falls within subsection (2)
- the use or threat is designed to influence the government or to intimidate the public or a section of the public, and
- the use or threat is made for the purpose of advancing a political, religious or ideological cause.

(2) Action falls within this subsection if it:

- involves serious violence against a person,
- involves serious damage to property,
- endangers a person's life, other than that of the person committing the action,

- creates a serious risk to the health or safety of the public or a section of the public, or
- is designed seriously to interfere with or seriously to disrupt an electronic system.

(3) The use or threat of action falling within subsection (2) which involves the use of firearms or explosives is terrorism whether or not subsection (1)(b) is satisfied.

(Terrorism Act, 2000)

Definitions of terrorism vary across jurisdictions and therefore it lacks precision and transferability globally; this imbues reflection as to what terrorism actually is and promotes critical consideration as to who the terrorist is. Stereotyping, reinforced by media coverage, may lead us to conclude that the contemporary threat is associated exclusively to the 'religious wave' (Rapoport, 2001) and is connected to Islamic extremism. However, as the UK definition can be succinctly summarised as politically motivated violence, further critical analysis is justified.

For example, in June 2019 two males, Michal Szewzuk and Oskar Dunn-Koczorowski, pleaded guilty and received custodial sentences at the Old Bailey for terrorist offences, including encouraging terrorism and possession of terrorist material. The offences were committed on-line, and the targets of the posts included members of the Jewish community, non-white people and anyone 'perceived to be complicit in the perpetuation of multiculturalism'.

In this case, the offences were committed entirely on-line by targeting, or encouraging others to target, minority groups who are so often victims of hate crime, it is worthy noting that this is a traditionally an under-reported area of crime. If the definition is returned too, it can be seen that in this case, two people have been convicted of terrorist offences, which were committed remotely by means of the internet, and their motive was not related to Islamic extremism. This is far-right ideology, which broadly seeks to preserve the social order, or return it to what they perceive it to have been previously, not change it.

Far-right groups are also of interest to the police, if only in their role of maintaining public order at public meetings and marches. However, as the previous example illustrates, there is much more to far-right ideology that does impinge and transgress terrorist legislation and there are now several far-right groups that have been proscribed (Home Office, 2024a). The decision being taken following the conviction in 2016 of Thomas Mair for the murder of the MP Jo Cox during the General Election campaign, the murder of whom had been motivated by far-right ideology. As indicated, hate crime is under-reported and in 2016 the government launched a 'Hate Crime Action Plan', reviewed and updated (HM Government, 2018). However, the events in Gaza that occurred on the 7 October 2023 and subsequent to that action by the Hamas group, have witnessed an unwelcome rise in antisemitic attacks in the UK, motivated by the apparent unjustified response by Israel to the actions of Hamas and its supporters in the Gaza area. When reflecting on the definitions of terrorism, it is clear there is a need to consider the actions of the far right and what it actually means, vis-a-vis hate crime legislation.

Following the events in Gaza, which have attracted global interest, the UK and London in particular has seen an unprecedented number of large public demonstrations and protests, many in support of Palestinian action, by inference therefore Hamas, or to give its full title, Harakat al-Muqawamah al-Islamiyyah, which is a proscribed terrorist group in the UK (Home Office, 2024a).

There is also another proscribed group, who so far have been on the periphery of the military action in Gaza, Hizballah, which translates to the 'Party of God' (Home Office, 2024a). However, while the demonstrations that are pro-Palestine are overtly at least just that, it has been made clear that some of the demonstrators may support the actions of Hamas and therefore potentially commit one or more of the following offences contrary to the Terrorism Act 2000:

Proscription makes it a criminal offence to:

- belong, or profess to belong, to a proscribed organisation in the UK or overseas (section 11 of the act)
- invite support for a proscribed organisation (the support invited need not be material support, such as the provision of money or other property, and can also include moral support or approval) (section 12(1))
- express an opinion or belief that is supportive of a proscribed organisation, reckless as to whether a person to whom the expression is directed will be encouraged to support a proscribed organisation (section 12(1A))
- arrange, manage or assist in arranging or managing a meeting in the knowledge that the meeting is to support or further the activities of a proscribed organisation, or is to be addressed by a person who belongs or professes to belong to a proscribed organisation (section 12(2)); or to address a meeting if the purpose of the address is to encourage support for, or further the activities of, a proscribed organisation (section 12(3))
- wear clothing or carry or display articles in public in such a way or in such circumstances as to arouse reasonable suspicion that the individual is a member or supporter of a proscribed organisation (section 13)
- publish an image of an item of clothing or other article, such as a flag or logo, in the same circumstances (section 13(1A))(Home Office, 2024a)

Such massive protests have created challenges for the police, not just from a public order perspective and maintaining order due to the sheer weight of numbers, but also enforcing this legislation. Where the legislation has been enforced, the police have been accused of suppressing democracy and political bias, by appearing to side with the Israel against the Palestinians. However, it does not end there as far-right groups, those that are not proscribed organisations, have staged anti-protests and when the police have attempted to impose conditions on their protests and marches, they have in turn accused the police of favouring the Palestinians and therefore Hamas. This is not a desirable position for the police service to find itself; particularly where terrorist legislation is involved, as their legitimacy is being called into question and in a wider perspective, the police need to be seen to be acting both impartially, ethically

Counter-terrorism 173

and need the support of all sides of the community, in countering acts of preparation for terrorism, or indeed committing politically motivated violence itself.

Post 9/11

All the acquired skills of the security services, the re-structuring and clarification responsibilities, implemented during the period of the 'The Troubles', would prove invaluable when the 'religious wave' arrived in 1979 (Rapoport, 2001). This became centre stage in a global sense in New York in September 2001, as this heralded the onset of the 'War on Terror' and what happens globally affects us all, locally.

The world changed on 11 September 2001 when global events, spread almost instantaneously by the media, became local issues. This prompted significant change in the realm of counter terrorism by the UK Government. The primary feature in the array of changes implemented by the British authorities was the introduction of CONTEST; the provisions of which we will look at in some more detail shortly, but prior to that, other measures implemented with a view to enhancing the counter-terrorism response of the UK will be explored.

Joint Terrorism Analysis Centre

The Joint Terrorism Analysis Centre (JTAC) was established in June 2003 and based in Thames House, the then headquarters of MI5 (Hewitt, 2008). JTAC is staffed by intelligence analysts from 16 government agencies and departments, which include the police (Hayman, 2009). The first national Security and Intelligence Coordinator appointed by Tony Blair, Sir David Omand, previously of the Government Communications Headquarters (GCHQ) (Hewitt, 2008), implemented JTAC. It operates under the authority of the Director General of the Security Service, although it has its own Director and reports to an inter-agency management board (Gregory, 2008).

The overall idea is to bring together all the key agencies, thereby avoiding silos and providing a clearer picture of the terrorist threat to the UK. The task of JTAC is to consider international terrorism via a longer-term lens as well as providing up-to-date reports on current threats. This breaks down into three key functions: the analysis of terrorist groups and associates; terrorist trends analysis; and country-based threat analysis for the UK, from which the threat level is formulated (Gregory, 2008).

The threat level is not set by a meeting at COBRA (Cabinet Office Briefing Room 'A') as is commonly perceived, or by the Prime Minister or Home Office, but by JTAC. The current threat levels are as follows:

> Low means an attack is highly unlikely.
> Moderate means an attack is possible, but not likely.
> Substantial means an attack is likely.
> Severe means an attack is highly likely.
> Critical means an attack is highly likely in the near future.
>
> (Security Service MI5, 2024)

JTAC sets two threat levels, one is for 'international terrorism' and the second is the threat to both the British mainland and Northern Ireland in respect of Irish nationalism and other domestic terrorism, such as far-right groups. Occasionally they are at various levels, for example in the last few years, the threat level from international terrorism has been set at 'Severe', while the Irish and other domestic terrorism threat to the British mainland has been at 'Substantial'. Following the attacks in 2017 in London and Manchester, the threat level for international terrorism did rise to 'Critical' for several days on two occasions and this was accompanied by the sight of armed British military personnel on the streets of the UK. This reflects a contingency plan implemented when the threat level is at the highest point and an attack is imminent. Currently at the time of publication, both threat levels are set at 'Substantial'.

Regional counter-terrorism units

These Units were established in 2006 following a decision by the then ACPO-TAM (Association of Chief Police Officers, Terrorism and Allied Matters) (Gregory, 2008) while developing a regional structure that had previously been implemented in relation to individual police forces and Special Branch departments. MI5 followed suit with a regional structure to mirror those of Special Branch (Gregory, 2008), the first time on the mainland that MI5 operatives had re-located outside of London (excluding wartime, when MI5 re-located to Oxford). There had been a more robust recommendation from the HM Inspector of Constabulary in 2003 along the lines of a national Special Branch structure, so the Special Branch Regional Intelligence Centres (SB RIC) was something of a compromise (Gregory, 2008) and provided a footprint for ACPO-TAM to build upon following the 2005 attacks in London and the announce the formation of the Regional Counter-Terrorism Units.

The Regional Counter-Terrorism Units (RCTU), now known as Counter-Terrorism Policing (CPT), of which there are four outside of London, are co-located within police forces covering the Northwest (CPTNW), Northeast (CTPNE), Southeast (CTPSE) and West Midlands (CTPWM) areas. There is also Counter Terrorism Command (SO15) based in New Scotland Yard, which also retains primacy in counter terrorism operations throughout the UK, including Scotland and Northern Ireland (Holford, 2023). These are supported by Regional Counter-Terrorism Intelligence Units (CTIU) in the Southwest, Wales, East of England, East Midlands, Scotland and Northern Ireland. In November 2020 the government announced plans for a Counter Terrorism Operations Centre to open in London to co-ordinate operations throughout the UK (Counter Terrorism Policing, n.d.). This was reflecting the recommendations in the Anderson Report (Anderson, 2017, paragraph 5.4.b) and the Intelligence and Security Committee (n.d.) Report, *What Needs to Change?* (section 9, paragraph 139).

As these CPT Units are multi-agency, this can create potential strains for agency working practices, as identified by Brodeur (1983; 2007) and the concept of 'high' and 'low' policing.

In the original paper Brodeur (1983), asserts that 'high policing' is the paradigm for political policing, which is that more associated with the security and intelligence services. High policing is characterised by features, all of which are relevant to this concept of high policing. Low policing, however, traditionally associates with criminal policing, although in his paper he does take this further to include conspicuous signs of public disorder, criminal or not. With low policing, police forces collect intelligence to gather evidence for the purpose of criminal prosecutions (Brodeur, 1983).

Firstly, Brodeur, (1983), discusses high policing describing it as 'absorbent policing' in that it aims to control by storing information. Secondly, the intelligence is comprehensive in that it extends to any function of the state, in other words the furtherance of state power. High policing is not solely mandated to enforce the law as formulated by an independent legislator. Thirdly, crime control can be utilised as a tool to engender information which can be implemented to exploit state coercion against any individual or group that threaten the established social order. Fourthly, it employs undercover agents and paid informers, and, in this regard, it is widely acknowledged that this is an accepted practice (Brodeur, 1983). To take this latter point further, the cultivation of and the relationship with a secret but highly sensitive source, has often been later publicly acclaimed by state intelligence services, for example the defection to Moscow in January 1963 of the British spy Kim Philby, who for decades had been actively passing state secrets to the Soviet Union, highly sensitive material to which from his position within the Secret Intelligence Service (MI6) he had privileged access (Macintyre, 2014). Additionally, the Soviet spy Oleg Gordievsky, who eventually became head of the KGB station in London, had been an MI6 asset for some years prior to this, had passed vital information to the West, especially during heightened tensions in the Cold War. In 1983 his information was seen as vital to both Prime Minister Margaret Thatcher and US President Ronald Reagan in their negotiations with the then Soviet leader Mikhail Gorbachev over arms reduction and control.

Gordievsky was clandestinely smuggled out of the Soviet Union, via Finland by MI6 in 1985, having been recalled to Moscow, by a suspicious KGB hierarchy. Gordievsky then officially defected to the United Kingdom. In the Queen's birthday honours in 2007, appointed Companion of the Most Distinguished Order of St Michael and St George, for 'services to the security of the United Kingdom' (Macintyre, 2018). It is difficult to envisage an undercover source within low policing commended in a similar fashion.

However, between the period of the fall of the Berlin Wall in 1989 and 9/11 in September 2001, there were clear moves to merge the two approaches together. For example, intelligence agencies became involved in investigating organised crime. Law enforcement became involved in the fight against transnational crime and established intelligence units to facilitate that. In the aftermath of 9/11, it emerged that a division still existed and 'cops' cannot do the work of 'spies' (Brodeur, 2007). This is often described as 'intelligence versus evidence' and intelligence agencies remain reticent in sharing their intelligence with the police, in an attempt to avoid their methods and sources being disclosed in a criminal trial (Brodeur, 2007).

To highlight this schism between high and low policing in an operational setting, the Saunders Enquiry into the 2017 Manchester Arena Bombing, Volume Three 'Radicalisation and Preventability' (Home Office, 2023), perhaps acts as an example.

Paragraphs 24.59 to 24.81 under Section 24, 'Preventing the Attack' refer to the 'Sharing of Intelligence' (Home Office, 2023). The Report refers to two pieces of intelligence that were not shared with Counter Terrorism Policing (NW). While it is unclear what this intelligence actually was due to national security issues, it is know that on the day the Report was published, the Director of MI5 issued an unprecedented public apology and that he was 'profoundly sorry' for not preventing the attack (BBC, 2023). In his introduction to the report, Sir John Saunders refers to a 'missed opportunity for actionable intelligence to have been taken' (Home Office, 2023). The issue of 'actionable intelligence' is defined by Brodeur (2007), as being 'intelligence that will spur an agency to undertake public proceedings beyond covert or overt surveillance. By applying the evidence, Brodeur (2007), together with the Report's findings and the public apology by the Director, it can be deduced that this intelligence was not shared between MI5 and CTPNW and therefore the inference is clear; it is Brodeur's concept of 'high and low' policing highlighted in practice.

Another key agency that is a core member of the UK counter-terrorism plan is the Government Communications Headquarters (GCHQ) that is based in Cheltenham. Due to the design of the building it is housed in, it is known colloquially as 'The Doughnut'. The Director of GCHQ is accountable to the Foreign Secretary. GCHQ deals with what is known as 'SIGINT' which is an acronym for signals intelligence and given the known reliance of terrorist groups who are operating globally on mobile telephones, social media and the internet, the pivotal role of GCHQ within intelligence gathering cannot be over-stated. However, GCHQ has a long and successfully legacy in this regard as a member of the Second World War alliance, when it was known as the Government Code and Cypher School (GC & CS) based at Bletchley Park, Buckinghamshire. This arrangement eventually became known as the 'Five Eyes' partnership, between the five wartime allies (Australia, Canada, New Zealand, UK and the USA). The Cold War hastened the working practices further, with the initial 1946 UK/USA Communication Intelligence Agreement, where the wartime allies collaborated by sharing signals intelligence (Walsh, 2011; Kerbaj, 2022).

CONTEST

'CONTEST' is the acronym for 'Counter-Terrorism Strategy' first introduced by the Government in 2003. It was initially intended to be a five-year strategy to counter the terrorist threat from the *new terrorism* (Martin, 2017) of the religious wave (Rapoport, 2001) and was initially described as a 'slender document' by the House of Commons Home Affairs Committee (2009). The strategy was intended to co-ordinate the response of government to the 9/11 attacks in the USA, with updates in 2008 and 2009. CONTEST is still regularly reviewed, with the HM Government (2023a) updates incorporating the recommendations in to Prevent by Shawcross (2023).

The CONTEST strategy is split into four areas:

- Pursue
- Protect
- Prepare
- Prevent

Despite the regular updating, the four areas remain as they were initially published in the original 'slender document' in 2003 and at that time were described by the Security and Intelligence Co-Ordinator, Sir David Omand, appointed to formulate the UK response by commencing the work in November 2002, as a strategic campaign (Omand, 2014).

Their individual purposes are as follows:

- Pursue (near term) and Prevent (longer term) to reduce the likelihood of a terrorist attack,
- Protect to reduce the vulnerability of the public and the national infrastructure to attack,
- Prepare to reduce the impact and duration from attacks, should they occur.

(Omand, 2014)

Protect and Prepare would fall into the category of anti-terrorism in which the overall objective is to deter or prevent terrorist attacks; with the hardening of possible targets being a key strategic approach (Martin, 2017).

However, the overall objective of the CONTEST is referred to as 'ALARP' a principle derived from risk management, which means 'as low as reasonably practicable'. This is based on the premise that there is no complete defence against a terrorist attack, so the aim therefore is to reduce the risk to the public, by employing measures which are workable (Omand, 2014). Furthermore, it aims to uphold human rights, the rule of law, legitimate and accountable government and the core values of justice and freedom. In respect of Pursue in particular, it seeks to uncover, interrupt and prosecute those involved in or aiding terrorist activity (Omand, 2014). This justifies further development in that from those original purposes, it can be deduced that the UK Counter Terrorism Strategy is effectively criminal justice led, as opposed to the original US Strategy, which was military led, with the then President, George W Bush, announcing the 'War on Terror'. Also, it seeks to adhere to the rule of law, for example in practical terms, a terrorist suspect held in police custody would be subject to the same rights and treatment as any other suspect being held and processed as per the Police and Criminal Evidence Act, 1984. Contrast that with US policy in relation to Guantánamo Bay in Cuba, an offshore detention facility which is specifically designed to hold 'enemy combatants', is outside the scope of the US criminal justice system and where terrorist suspects have been held indefinitely and without charge.

Pursue

Pursue is the element of the counter-terrorism strategy that is mostly referred to in this chapter, as it is primarily focused on targeting suspected terrorists at home and abroad, through military, policing, intelligence and judicial measures (Sabir, 2017).

The absence of mass casualty attacks can be taken as some measure of success in keeping the public safe, but the terrorist attacks of 2017 in London and Manchester require further scrutiny. As a result, a previous reviewer of terrorist legislation, David Anderson QC, conducted a retrospective analysis and the findings were published later on that year in a report by Anderson (2017). Some of the recommendations from Anderson (2017) have now been incorporated in CONTEST including the change in the abilities of the security services and policing to investigate domestic terrorism.

This is a result of evidence-based practice identified by Anderson (2017) and included in the report as a way of sharing best practice. Where all operations are intelligence-led and therefore conducted covertly, it is a rare insight and therefore worthy of exploration through the following case study.

> **Evidence-based case study illustrating professional practice**
>
> Given the subject matter of this chapter, it is not as apparent as other areas of policing where the preferred practice, based on an evidence-base, actually lies. Nor should it be, the police and security services are not going to make public their most successful working practices, often covert and undertaken in secret. When cases are processed via the criminal justice system, evidence from the security services is given in camera. However, conclusions can be drawn from the material that is in the public domain.
>
> Access the report by Anderson (2017) on the attacks in London and Manchester. Read paragraph 3.41 on page 33 and having done so, reflect upon the following question: The sharing of intelligence is crucial to the success of intelligence-led operations, but given the recent reductions in Neighbourhood Policing Teams, how could this impact on counter-terrorism operations and CONTEST in general?

Protect and Prepare

Protect and Prepare are complimentary to each other, so it is entirely appropriate to discuss their areas of responsibility together, but it is prudent to mention that while they rarely receive the publicity that Pursue and Prevent receive, they are indispensable to the critical infrastructure of the UK. Protect is concerned with improving physical security precautions, while Prepare is designed to mitigate the effects of a terrorist attack, if it cannot be stopped before it occurs (Sabir, 2017).

In relation to the physical security precautions, a major strand of Protect is the safeguarding of the national infrastructure such as chemical, water and electrical sites, accordingly, The Centre for the Protection of the National Infrastructure (CPNI) was a government agency, accountable to the Director General of MI5. This has now been replaced by the National Protective Security Authority (NPSA; www.npsa.gov.uk). The NPSA works closely with the National Counter Terrorism Security Office (NaCTSO) which is a police unit that supports the 'Protect and Prepare' strands of the Government's counter-terrorism strategy. There are also Counter Terrorism Advisory Officers, who provide liaison and advice to businesses and other organisations, based in each police force area (Protect UK, 2024).

Prevent

This element of CONTEST has hitherto attracted the most criticism, not without good reason, and has been the area that has witnessed the most amendments in the CONTEST updates. As a result of the Shawcross (2023) report in to Prevent, further updates are in the HM Government (2023a) CONTEST strategy document.

The original implementation of Prevent targeted radicalisation, challenged radical ideologies that promote terrorism, but also gave a commitment to address inequality and discrimination (Hewitt, 2008). While at first glance that may seem reasonable, the downside is that Muslim communities perceive they are subject to unjustifiable surveillance. For example, when CONTEST was introduced, the Home and Foreign Offices embarked on a joint study into Muslim extremism in the UK and this culminated in the drafting of a report on 'Young Muslims and Extremism' (Hewitt, 2008). Concurrently, MI5 and the police began their own research into the same broad issue, and this was under the MI5 codename of 'Project Rich Picture' and all officers from the newest recruits upwards received 'Rich Picture' briefings. The idea was to appraise themselves of Muslim communities and individuals sympathetic to radicalisation and therefore potential terrorists (Hewitt, 2008). It was an intelligence-gathering exercise and the stigma connected to that and other forms of surveillance that have been made public totally impinge on the credibility of the Prevent strategy.

In respect of individuals believed to be at risk of radicalisation, the strategy has long operated a programme called Channel, aimed at de-radicalisation. The over-riding idea is that this is a multi-agency approach to persons believed to be at risk and operates in that regard, similar to a case conference convened under Safeguarding policies when a child at-risk has been identified. However, this is a balancing act, and it needs to be operated ethically and professionally by implementing evidence-based practices, otherwise sections of the community can feel subject to unwarranted surveillance. The Counterterrorism and

Security Act, 2015 has now placed statutory responsibilities on schools and other child-care providers in relation to persons being subject to influences of radicalisation (Dryden, 2017).

In January 2021 William Shawcross CVO, was requested by the then Home Secretary to carry out a review of Prevent. There clearly was some concern within government that Prevent, and the associated Channel programme were not working as effectively as they should and the decision to implement the review was no doubt hastened by a series of attacks in the preceding years leading up to January 2021. For example, 2017 was the first year since 2005 that Britain witnessed mass casualty attacks, five in total and thirty-six lives were lost. Of the six known offenders, 3 were known to both the police and MI5 and of those three, one had direct links to a proscribed Islamic terrorist organisation (Anderson, 2017). As Shawcross highlights: 'Since then, Britain has continued to suffer terrorist attacks, in Parliament Square (2018), Fishmongers Hall (2019), HMP Whitemoor (2020), Streatham (2020), Reading (2020), Southend (2021), and Liverpool (2021). All these attacks were associated with Islamist terrorism' (Shawcross, 2023, paragraph 2.11).

The cases of Fishmongers Hall (2019) and Streatham (2020) illustrate why the Home Office took the decision to instigate a review of Prevent. In the former incident, the offender Usman Khan had been released on licence for terrorist offences and while in prison had written to authorities on several occasions claiming that he had become de-radicalised, claiming to no longer hold the views held before his arrest and demonstrating he had undertaken the requisite courses while in prison. Following release, he was placed under surveillance by MI5 and assessed as being a 'low to medium' risk to the public (Walker and Cawley, 2021). In the Streatham case, Sudesh Amman refused to enrol on de-radicalisation programmes while serving a sentence at HMP Belmarsh for terrorist-related offences and was placed under active armed surveillance by the police. These cases also question the efficacy and difficulty of delivering de-radicalisation programmes in prison.

Shawcross (2023) made thirty-four recommendations which the government accepted in their entirety. This signals a fresh new approach to the operation of Prevent, however a review of some of the major points is justified.

Shawcross refers robustly to the first objective of Prevent – 'to tackle the causes of radicalisation and respond to the ideological challenge of terrorism' – is not being sufficiently met (Shawcross, 2023, paragraph 1.5), further explaining:

'Prevent is not doing enough to counter non-violent Islamist extremism. Challenging extremist ideology should not be limited to proscribed organisations but should also cover domestic extremists operating below the terrorism threshold who can create an environment conducive to terrorism' (Shawcross, 2023). This point is also made in relation to Extreme Right Wing (XRW) and Islamic extremism.

Prevent has a double standard when dealing with the Extreme Right-Wing and Islamism. Prevent takes an expansive approach to the Extreme Right-Wing, capturing a variety of influences that, at times, has been so broad it has included mildly controversial or provocative forms of mainstream, right-wing leaning commentary that have no meaningful connection to terrorism or radicalisation (Shawcross, 2023). However, with Islamism, Prevent tends to take a much narrower approach centred around proscribed organisations, ignoring the contribution of non-violent Islamist narratives and networks to terrorism (Shawcross, 2023). Prevent must ensure a consistent and evidence-based approach to setting its threshold and criteria and ensure it does not overlook key non-violent radicalising influences (Shawcross, 2023). Shawcross (2023) reflects on Prevent and its place within Contest alongside the on-going threat of terrorist violence, concluding that Prevent is out of alignment with the counter terrorism system and the picture of threat, highlighting how although the majority of the counter terrorism networks investigations are Islamist and a small minority extreme right wing focused, yet only slightly over a fifth of Prevent referrals for 2020–2021 concerned Islamism, suggesting a loss of focus and ability to identify warning signs. This may be due to a sharp change in the reasons and types of referrals, for example Shawcross (2023) highlights how vulnerable people, who may not pose a risk of terrorist related activity, are being referred to Prevent in order to access the support they need.

Shawcross (2023) provides a comprehensive and evidence-based examination of Prevent and has made recommendations across all the functions of Prevent, including training of personnel and the effectiveness of Prevent panels in the community. It is not feasible to discuss all the key issues here and therefore it is necessary to read Shawcross in its entirety to fully understand the content and context. However, twelve months after the publication of Shawcross the government released a paper detailing the progress made in implementing the recommendations of Shawcross and a look at that here, will assist in fully understanding the impact of the Report and how Prevent will operate in the future.

The Home Office (2024b) issued their review of Prevent, twelve months after the publication of Shawcross. The reading of this in its entirety is worthwhile and will enable a fuller understanding as to progress on all the thirty-four recommendations made by Shawcross (2023).

Future developments

There are those who would argue that there is currently a religious wave of terrorism (Rapoport, 2001) and Shawcross (2023) reinforces that to some extent, but it will end eventually. As leaders of the police and security services constantly remind us, attacks will continue and some will, unfortunately, be successful. However, as Ken McCallum (the director of MI5) outlined in his public address (Security Service MI5, 2022), the threat of state terrorism is specifically from Russia, China and Iran.

In the case of Russia, there have been attacks in Salisbury in 2018 and in London against Alexandra Litvinenko in 2006. To counter this threat the government enacted the National Security Act (HM Government, 2023b). An additional reason was to update outdated espionage offences by repealing offences in the Official Secrets Acts, of 1911, 1920 and 1939, add new laws to reflect the threats faced by the UK in the twenty-first century and facilitate new powers available to the police and other partners.

The counter-terrorism strategies, legislation, policy and guiding principles will continue to evolve accordingly and be informed by ever-increasing evidence-based practices.

One issue that may impinge on the future is the UK relationship and arrangements for the sharing of counter-terrorism information with other nation states. For example, Europol has been one the successes of the European Union (EU), and British influence has played a major part in some of the developments in professional practice, based squarely on evidence-based policing, but the UK has now left the EU and takes on a different relationship with Europol (Europol, 2023).

Conclusion

Counter terrorism policing has evolved in recent years, with major events such as the 9/11 attacks in the USA and 7/7 bombings in London, impact both globally and locally; obviously the UK has been no exception to that and in some regard can be considered to have responded to the challenge. The response has been modelled on evidence-based practices and clear that the police and the intelligence services now enjoy a far closer relationship than hitherto, but this remains a work-in-progress (Home Office, 2023).

Counter-terrorism policing has and is, evolving newer skills and abilities which are now required to meet the constantly changing roles, necessary to meet the threats, many based on evidence-based policing and identified preferred practice.

It is clear that such evolutionary trends will continue and all personnel in policing irrespective of rank or role, not just specialists in counterterrorism, will need to acquire fresh knowledge and develop the necessary skills required to ensure the successful delivery of the counter-terrorism strategy within the policing environment.

> **Evidence-based case study illustrating professional practice**
>
> During March 2018 in Salisbury, Wiltshire, an attack using poison targeted two Russian citizens, Sergei and Yulia Skripal, and although they thankfully survived, it necessitated a long period of hospitalisation.
>
> Unfortunately, an innocent member of the public, Dawn Sturgess, was fatally affected by the contamination. The UK Government publicly blamed Russia for the attack, and this promulgation is reiterated in the Intelligence and Security Committee of Parliament (2017–2018), therefore this is a case of state-sponsored terrorism.
>
> Accordingly, the investigation was led by Counter-Terrorism Command from New Scotland Yard, supported by Wiltshire Police, and clearly involved both the Security Service MI5 and MI6 (Secret Intelligence Service) in what is

potentially a sensitive and complex criminal investigation and one with heightened public interest and the most poignant political implications, globally.

A key feature of this investigation was the forensic examination, which involved several agencies working together in unique circumstances, including the military. However, the overall direction of the enquiry needed to be intelligence-led, which involved several agencies that adhered to recognised evidence-based practice in this pivotal area of the investigation; just one public statement from the counter-terrorism team that was not based on gathered intelligence or evidence could potentially provoke a diplomatic incident.

After several weeks of evidence gathering, the Crown Prosecution Service announced that there was sufficient evidence to charge two individuals, later identified as Russian nationals, with serious criminal matters directly linked to the attack.

Reflective question

Consider the number and types of both police and civil agencies that were involved in both the initial response to the March 2018 attacks in Salisbury and subsequently those agencies dealing with the aftermath.

References

Anderson, D. (2017). Attacks in London and Manchester Between March and June 2017. [online]. www.gov.uk/government/publications/attacks-in-london-and-manchester-between-march-and-june-2017 (accessed 14 July 2024).

BBC. (2023). Manchester Arena Inquiry: MI5 'Profoundly Sorry' for Not Stopping Attack, 02 March. [online]. www.bbc.co.uk/news/uk-england-manchester-64815723 (accessed 26 July 2024).

Blair, I. (2009). *Policing Controversy*. London: Profile.

Blake, C., Sheldon, B., Strzelecki, R. & Williams, P. (2012). *Policing Terrorism*. London: Learning Matters/Sage.

Brodeur, J. P. (1983). High Policing and Low Policing: Remarks about the Policing of Political Activities. *Social Problems*, 30(5), 507–520. https://doi.org/10.2307/800268.

Brodeur, J. P. (2007). High and Low Policing in Post-9/11 Times. *Policing*, 1(1), 25–37. https://doi.org/10.1093/police/pam002.

Counter Terrorism Policing. (n.d.). Our Network. [online]. www.counterterrorism.police.uk/our-network/ (accessed 16 July 2024).

Counter terrorism and Security Act (2015). [online]. www.legislation.gov.uk/ukpga/2015/6/contents (accessed 30 October 2018).

Dryden, M. (2017). Radicalisation: The Last Taboo in Safeguarding and Child Protection? Assessing Practitioner Preparedness in Preventing the Radicalisation of Looked-After Children. *Journal for Deradicalisation*, 13, 101–135. https://journals.sfu.ca/jd/index.php/jd/article/view/125.

Europol. (2023). Working and Administrative Arrangement Establishing Co-Operative Relations Between the Competent Authorities of the UK and Europol. [online]. www.europol.europa.eu/partners-collaboration/agreements/working-and-administrative-arrangement-establishing-cooperative-relations-between-competent-authorities-of-uk-and-europol (accessed 17 July 2024).

Gill, P. & Phythian, M. (2009). *Intelligence in an Insecure World*. Cambridge: Polity Press.

Gregory, F. (2008). The Police and the Intelligence Services: With Special Reference to the Relationship with MI5. In C. Harfield, A. MacVean, L. Grieve & D. Phillips (eds), *The Handbook of Intelligent Policing: Consilience, Crime Control and Community Safety*. Oxford: Oxford University Press.

Hayman, A. (2009). *The Terrorist Hunters*. London: Bantam Press.

Hewitt, S. (2008). *The British War on Terror*. London: Continuum Books.

HM Government. (2018). Action Against Hate. The UK Government's Plan for Tackling Hate Crime 'Two Years On'. [online]. www.gov.uk/government/news/hate-crime-plan-refreshed-to-protect-victims-and-promote-shared-values (accessed 28 June 2019).

HM Government. (2023a). CONTEST, The United Kingdom's Strategy for Countering Terrorism 2023. [online]. https://assets.publishing.service.gov.uk/media/650b1b8d52e73c000d54dc82/CONTEST_2023_English_updated.pdf (accessed 15 July 2024).

HM Government. (2023b). National Security Act: New Security Laws Come into Force. [online]. www.gov.uk/government/news/new-national-security-laws-come-into-force (accessed 16 July 2024).

Holford E. (2023). A scoping analysis of the counter terrorism command policing structure and its impact on intelligence sharing between the police and the security services. *Journal of Policing, Intelligence and Counter Terrorism*, 18(3), 353–374. https://doi.org/10.1080/18335330.2023.2171309.

Home Office. (2023). Manchester Arena Inquiry Volume 3: Radicalisation and Preventability. [online]. www.gov.uk/government/publications/manchester-arena-inquiry-volume-3-radicalisation-and-preventability (accessed 25 July 2024).

Home Office. (2024a). Policy Paper: Proscribed Terrorist Groups or Organisations. [online]. www.gov.uk/government/publications/proscribed-terror-groups-or-organisations–2/proscribed-terrorist-groups-or-organisations-accessible-version (accessed 11 July 2024).

Home Office. (2024b). Independent Review of Prevent: One Year on Progress Report. [online]. www.gov.uk/government/publications/independent-review-of-prevents-report-and-government-response/independent-review-of-prevent-one-year-on-progress-report-accessible (accessed 15 July 2024).

House of Commons Home Affairs Committee. (2009). Project CONTEST: The Government's Counter Terrorism Strategy. [online]. https://publications.parliament.uk/pa/cm200809/cmselect/cmhaff/212/212.pdf (accessed 5 November 2018).

Innes, M. & Thiel, D. (2008). Policing Terror. In T. Newburn (ed.), *The Handbook of Policing*, 2nd edition. Cullompton: Willan Publishing.

Intelligence and Security Committee. (n.d.). What Needs to Change? [online]. http://isc.independent.gov.uk/ (accessed 18 July 2024).

Kerbaj, R. (2022). *The Secret History of Five Eyes: The Untold Story of the International Spy Network*. London: Blink Publishing.

Macintyre, B. (2014). *A Spy Among Friends: Kim Philby and the Great Betrayal*. London: Bloomsbury.

Macintyre, B. (2018). *The Spy and the Traitor: The Greatest Espionage Story of the Cold War*. London: Viking.

Martin, G. (2017). *Essentials of Terrorism Concepts and Controversies*, 4th edition. London: Sage Publications.
Newburn, T. & Matassa, M. (2003). Policing and Terrorism. In T. Newburn (ed.), *The Handbook of Policing*, 2nd edition. Cullompton: Willan Publishing.
Omand, D. (2014). *Securing the State*. Oxford: Oxford University Press.
Prevention of Terrorism (Temporary Provisions) Act, 1974. [online]. www.legislation.gov.uk/ukpga/1974/56/contents/enacted (accessed 30 October 2018).
Protect UK. (2024). Protect your business, Protect the public. [online]. www.protectuk.police.uk/ (accessed 12 July 2024).
Rapoport, D. (2001). The Four Waves of Terrorism. In J. Horgan & K. Braddock (eds), *Terrorism Studies: A Reader*. New York: Routledge.
Sabir, R. (2017). Blurred Lines and False Dichotomies: Integrating Counterinsurgency into the UK's Domestic 'War on Terror'. *Critical Social Policy*, 37 (2), 202–224. https://doi.org/10.1177/0261018316683471.
Security Service MI5. (2022). Director General's Annual Threat Update, 16th November. [online] www.mi5.gov.uk/news/director-general-ken-mccallum-gives-annual-threat-update (accessed 16 July 2024).
Security Service MI5. (2024). Threat Levels. [online]. www.mi5.gov.uk/threats-and-advice/terrorism-threat-levels (accessed 12 June 2024).
Shawcross, W. (2023). Independent Review of Prevent: Home Office. [online]. www.gov.uk/government/publications/independent-review-of-prevents-report-and-government-response (accessed 12 July 2024).
Taylor, J. (2015). The Party's Over? The Angry Brigade, the Counterculture and the British New Left. *The Historical Journal*, 58(3), 877–900. https://doi.org/10.1017/S0018246X14000612.
Terrorism Act (2000). [online]. www.legislation.gov.uk/ukpga/2000/11/contents (accessed 17 June 2019).
Walker, C, & Cawley, O. (2021). De-Risking the Release of Terrorist Prisoners. *Criminal Law Review*, 4, 252–268. https://papers.ssrn.com/sol3/papers.cfm?abstract_id=3800473.
Walsh, P. (2011). *Intelligence and Intelligence Analysis*. Abingdon: Routledge.

11 Digital policing

Benjamin Findlay, Shawn Robertson and Harry Stewart

Introduction

While many might imagine crimes involving computers (such as hacking) to be exciting, the reality of digital evidence is far different from what we typically see on streaming services, television or in film.

Over the past few decades, there has been an explosion in consumer technology and growth of the Internet. In recent years, the growth in the prevalence and capabilities of mobile technology has been extreme. Technology is now a pervasive part of society, putting it at the core of what we do and how we live. Similarly, the Internet has grown and changed how we interact with the world. We can now reach people in other countries easily and inexpensively. With this comes new opportunities and capabilities for how crimes can be committed, along with new challenges with regards how to tackle them.

Technology is a great leveller. It is increasingly accessible to all; prices continue to decrease and capabilities are increasing. This means that more and more people are in possession of a digital device. What was once luxury, afforded only by the few; is now routine, and is increasingly involved in a diverse number of crimes. As a result, offenders and victims come from all walks of life.

It is vital that policing keeps pace with the rapidly changing world of technology. Formal digital policing curricula are now part of internal and induction training, professional policing qualifications and degrees such as the Police Constable Degree Apprenticeship (PCDA) and Degree Holder Entry Programme (DHEP). As such, police officers, staff and volunteers need to understand not only the rapidly evolving world of digital devices and their capabilities, but also the role that enforcement agencies can play in the prevention of digital crime, how technology can be used as a force for good (as well as bad!), and what is required of a policing professional to keep both themselves and others safe from potential threats and risks of digital and online harm. It is not sufficient to simply understand the types of digital and Internet-facilitated crimes, or to expect that specialist teams and units will exclusively handle cases of digital crime anymore.

The Cabinet Office (2022) National Cyber Strategy defines two types of cybercrime: cyber-enabled and cyber-dependent crimes. Cyber-enabled crimes

DOI: 10.4324/9781003492948-12

are traditional crimes, which can be facilitated by the use of a digital device. Examples of cyber-enabled crimes include fraud and theft of data. Cyber-dependent crimes are crimes that can only be committed by using technology. Examples of cyber-dependent crimes include hacking, and the use of ransomware for financial gain. From a typical domestic burglary, in which the offender happens to have taken their GPS-enabled smartphone with them, to the paedophile who has distributed illegal imagery via a file-sharing medium such as BitTorrent; the potential for digital evidence to be involved in any investigation is very much real.

Digital investigation and digital forensics has historically been heavily focused on the investigation of child abuse. However it is important to recognise that a wide variety of different crimes and offences exist, all of which may have some form of digital component. These include, but are not limited to, exploitation offences, extortion, hate crimes, abuse and cyberbullying, fraud and financial crimes, radicalisation and human trafficking.

This chapter explores current issues, challenges and policing priorities which are key to the current digital investigation, crime, and forensic landscape, and is written based on perspectives drawn from both academic literature and the authors' first-hand experiences of working in a digital forensic unit and within the wider digital policing landscape.

Historical context

The opportunity for a digital device to be involved in any type of crime is, and has been, steadily increasing for years. Digital crime is clearly growing; as is our need to react to, and account for, an increasing number of digital crimes. Sachowski (2018) highlights this fact well, providing a potted summary of the evolution of digital forensics as a discipline.

Mobile technology in particular has developed significantly in recent years. The first generation (1G) of mobile networks were created in the late 1970s, the second generation (2G) networks appearing in the early 1990s. With the advent of the third generation (3G) of mobile network technology in the late 1990s, the world gained access to 'mobile broadband'. Subsequent generations have come along, with fifth generation (5G) now becoming increasingly and widely available. Both fourth generation (4G) and 5G have significant speed advantages over 3G and therefore bring new capabilities with them; especially relating to the consumption of media-based content, such as video.

The mobile handset itself has also evolved significantly over the course of mobile history as highlighted by Sachowski (2018), from the early days of batteries only enabling the mobile user to make a few minutes' of calls before needing to recharge for hours, to the current modern smartphone with numerous advanced features including photography, video and sound, GPS, Wi-Fi, Bluetooth, games, augmented reality, and wireless charging. It is almost bizarre to think that the earliest mobile phones could not even send text messages (SMS); yet now have communication apps such as Snapchat, WhatsApp,

Facebook messenger etc., which support not only text-based messaging, but also picture and video transmission. Indeed, criminals are finding new and innovative ways to use technology in an attempt to evade detection and capture. Recent press coverage of *EncroPhone* and the European policing operation to infiltrate and bring down *EncroChat* highlights the criminal use of such technologies (Europol, 2023). With *EncroPhone* seemingly no longer an option for criminals, a number of alternative solutions have appeared to fill the void; such as *Omerta*. It is safe to consider that the immediate future of digital investigation is most definitely a focus on mobiles.

In the UK, digital forensic investigations are conducted according to the principles and guidelines outlined in the Association of Chief Police Officers (2012) Good Practice Guide for Digital Evidence. This guidance was most recently updated in 2012 and, as a result, does not account for the more recent developments in technology. For instance, in providing guidance regarding mobile communication records between two parties, the guidance only really addresses telephone calls and 'traditional' text based messaging such as SMS. While it is clear that the guidance needs a significant update, it should be recognised that the 4 key principles are still generally sound. As such, anyone working with digital devices and evidence should have an awareness of these principles. They are:

1. No action taken by law enforcement agencies, persons employed within those agencies or their agents should change data which may subsequently be relied upon in court.
2. In circumstances where a person finds it necessary to access original data, that person must be competent to do so and be able to give evidence explaining the relevance and the implications of their actions.
3. An audit trail or other record of all processes applied to digital evidence should be created and preserved. An independent third party should be able to examine those processes and achieve the same result.
4. The person in charge of the investigation has overall responsibility for ensuring that the law and these principles are adhered too.(Association of Chief Police Officers, 2012)

In recent years, the Forensic Science Regulator has introduced ISO 17025 accreditation into the digital forensic arena, which has led to the development of formalised policies and procedures for the handling, processing and analysis of digital evidence. As each police force or organisation obtains their own individual accreditation, based on their own internally chosen and developed methods, it is not feasible to discuss specific details here, and therefore the reader is advised to contact the relevant team within their organisation for specific advice on such matters.

Data from the Office for National Statistics (2022) shows that, of the 4.5 million incidents of fraud in the year ending March 2022, approximately 2.7 million of these (61%) were cyber-related. The report also highlights significant year-on-year rises of such cases. The report highlights that only an estimated one in seven fraud cases are reported, indicating that the real figures are in fact considerably higher (Office for National Statistics, 2024).

Such growth in the number of crimes reported which involve at least one digital device is compounded by the fact that technology is getting more and more powerful and accessible. In 1995 a typical new consumer-grade computer had a hard drive with storage capacity in the region of 1 gigabyte. As of writing, a new iPhone comes with a minimum of 64 gigabytes of storage. The 1995 computer would have taken up most of a moderately sized desk; the new iPhone will fit in a pocket. The iPhone can do much more, and costs less than what the 1995 computer would have cost (around a third of the cost). As technology advances and storage capability goes up, and digital devices are used more, the amount of data stored increases. Therefore investigative workloads increase due to the existence of more data to sift through and review. While it is true that the corresponding increase in computing power can also be put to use to process the data more quickly, a fundamental bottleneck still exists: eventually a person needs to look at key data and determine its relevance to an investigation. This isn't to say that all of the data shouldn't be checked. There are risks in not considering all of the available evidence, including of course missing something which later becomes relevant to an investigation.

A report by the Internet Watch Foundation (2023) highlights the prevalence of child sexual abuse, and in particular the impact which the COVID pandemic has had upon the number of cases. The Internet Watch Foundation (IWF) provides some rather sobering figures, for example in 2022 they received 63,050 reports of websites containing imagery of children aged 7–10. These figures represent an increase of 129% from the previous year; and a staggering increase of 1058% since 2019.

With such an increasing number of digital crimes comes an increased demand for staffing and resources to tackle it. Historically, outsourcing has been a solution to this problem. However, with a significant number of recent changes to the landscape within digital forensics, and not least the advent and enforcement of ISO 17025 accreditation by the Forensic Science Regulator, there has been a much greater emphasis placed on having enough, suitably trained, specialist staff within forces (Forensic Science Regulator, 2023). Consequently, the staffing of Digital Forensic Units (DFU) has increased significantly. By way of example, in 2010 North Yorkshire Police employed 5 people in what was then called the Hi-Tech Crime Unit. By August 2016, the (now) DFU had grown to approximately 20 staff and an additional, specialist Cybercrime Unit had been created. The DFU has subsequently grown further, to around 35 staff and police officers. This example is by no means an isolated situation; Greater Manchester Police's DFU grew from approximately 15 to 75 staff, in the period between 2018 and 2024. Police forces now routinely have dedicated digital forensic units, cybercrime units, online child protection and investigation teams, and staff who are specially trained in areas such as digital media investigation.

Offences (in particular sexual offences) can be reported historically such as in the case of Operation Yewtree (Home Office, 2015), but they can also be reported contemporaneously. Either way, with society's growing reliance on technology, it is highly likely that digital evidence will be seized and examined during all types of investigations.

Protection of children is a concern which is not unique to a specific country, unfortunately it is a global challenge. With the Internet allowing access to information anywhere in the world, the sharing of indecent images and images of child abuse is not restricted to geographical borders. As such, intelligence and evidence of this may often be stored online in the Cloud. Individual countries may form strategies to fight child sexual exploitation; however, jurisdictional challenges can arise meaning that only through international co-operation can they succeed. Organisations such as INTERPOL and the WePROTECT Global Alliance are spearheading and co-ordinating international co-operation (INTERPOL, 2018; WePROTECT Global Alliance, 2016). In recent years, there have been several high-profile operations focussing on child abuse in addition to Yewtree e.g. Operations Ore, Spade, Clover, Delego, Notarise, and Midland, but sadly these represent only a few. Many of these have or have had an international component to them.

Because of the sheer scale and challenge of tackling child abuse, in 2015 the Home Office launched the Child Abuse Image Database (CAID) in the UK. This database allows law enforcement agencies to work together, share intelligence and to work more efficiently, by storing and automatically recognising and categorising any previously encountered imagery in subsequent cases. CAID has a number of additional, intelligence led functions which can be put to use to help identify, locate, and ultimately safeguard victims more expeditiously (Home Office, 2015).

Over the past few years, a number of support organisation and agencies have emerged, who offer advice on good practice, digital safety and various other related topics. Organisations such as the Get Safe Online, IWF and WePROTECT, along with agencies such as the Child Exploitation and Online Protection (CEOP) and National Cyber Security Centre (NCSC), all provide a valuable resource and wealth of advice, both for the police and the public.

Current professional practice

It is vitally important that those involved in the investigation of digital crime keep pace with the ever changing nature of technology. Gone are the days of digital forensics being just about investigating computer towers or laptops. As technology advances, the police are faced with an increasing number of new devices with new capabilities, and/or existing devices gaining new capabilities. As a result, investigators now have to consider a myriad array of different digital devices and digital evidence sources including, but not limited to:

- Computers including desktops, laptops and servers
- Mobile phones and tablets
- Portable and removable storage devices, such as USB memory sticks
- Games consoles (either static or handheld)
- Drones
- Networking equipment
- Wearable technology such as smart watches, medical technologies, virtual reality headsets, and action cameras
- Remote storage, such as network or cloud storage
- CCTV systems
- Increasingly 'smart' vehicles, which may contain onboard infotainment systems, inbuilt GPS, etc.
- Portable GPS, such as a TomTom or Garmin satellite navigation system
- *Internet of Things* and Smart home devices, such as doorbell cameras, smart washing machines, and smart fridges.

While it may seem far-fetched that certain devices in the list above might be relevant in a criminal investigation, it is important to consider that the technology used every day is increasingly capable, and is storing an increasing amount of data, as records and logs, images and videos, communication records and Internet use history. For example, it is not beyond the realms of possibility that the logs from a smart fridge, perhaps showing that the door was opened and closed at a specific time, could help support or refute the account of a person of interest in an investigation. Put simply, an investigator must have a good overall awareness of digital technologies otherwise, when encountering such devices during the course of an investigation, evidence risks being missed.

Data from digital devices can provide a range of intelligence and evidence. The first and most obvious evidence that data from a digital device may provide is factual that an illegal act has occurred, for example, the presence of imagery depicting child sexual abuse material (CSAM), which may attribute physical activities to a specific individual, recordings by such digital devices can be highly valuable to an investigation (Servida & Casey, 2019). Other evidential opportunities include an incriminating email, a Google search, or visit to a specific website, all might show that an illegal or notable act has been performed. However, it is important to recognise that, in isolation, some evidence may not show who was directly responsible for an act. The second, and less intuitive, source of evidence is that provided by ancillary data present on the device. In particular, artefacts such as those that demonstrate user activity or interaction with specific files can be invaluable. Most modern computer operating systems keep track of all sorts of pieces of information. From a record of when the computer was powered on or when a user logged in and out, to a list of the recently accessed files, to an application such as a web browser which keeps track of the websites visited using it; there is a wealth of activity oriented and time-stamped information potentially available. Combining all of this information together with other information, such as a suspect's account of their computer usage (likely obtained from interview under caution), is what ultimately leads to offences being proven and cases being concluded.

It is for these reasons that everyone involved in the investigation of crime should be aware of and capable of dealing with digital evidence. However, owing to the still rather specialist and important nature of such evidence, specialist units typically exist, made up of specially trained police officers, staff (or some combination of both), whose job it is to specifically tackle this digital evidence.

Anecdotal evidence very much suggests that each individual force implements this in their own way. As a result, the precise nature of how digital evidence is investigated, and digital crime is tackled, might appear somewhat inconsistent. What is common to most, if not all, UK-based police forces, is the existence of the DFU and a Cyber Crime Unit (CCU). Other units, such as a Hi-Tech Crime Unit (HTCU), may still exist, although this is now largely an obsolete name.

In addition to DFUs and CCUs, other departments and units exist that may have some form in in-house digital investigative capability or remit. Examples of these units and teams might include the Financial Investigation Unit, Open Source Intelligence (OSINT) Team, the Covert Standards team, and the Digital Media Investigator (DMI) Team. In some forces, DMIs are a dedicated, specialist resource; in other forces they are an area, divisional or regionally allocated one, and may be seconded or attached to other investigative teams, such as CID

There are also typically teams responsible for investigation of CSAM, although historically (and still currently in certain forces) this was often done within the DFU itself. These specialist teams are typically known by several different terms, for example the Paedophile Online Investigation Team (POLIT), Online Child Abuse (Investigation) Team (OCAT/OCAIT), the Online Child Sexual Exploitation Team (OCSE), and the Online Abuse Team (OAT). There is also typically a team responsible for the management of violent offenders and/or registered sex offenders, again known somewhat inconsistently by various different names, such as Multi-Agency Public Protection Arrangements (MAPPA), the Sex Offender Management Unit (SOMU), Violent and Sex Offender Register (ViSOR), or Management of Sexual or Violent Offenders (MOSOVO) teams.

What is almost certainly universally common to units that investigate digital evidence is that they face significant challenges; ranging from large case backlogs due to an ever-increasing number of cases with some element of digital evidence within them, to the challenging and distressing nature of the cases they have to investigate, and of course the constant reality of a rapidly changing and evolving technological world.

Each individual police force has its own unique priorities and individual methods of working; however, what is common to all police forces is a focus on tackling child abuse. The Association of Police and Crime Commissioners & National Police Chiefs' Council (2016) Policing Vision 2025 discussed the challenges faced in combatting child abuse and grooming, and the role technology can play in these areas. The Policing Vision 2030 builds on the earlier ten-year plan ensuring that both technology and data enable the evolution of a police service that safeguards the vulnerable and supports victims (National Police Chiefs' Council, 2024). The type of material encountered in child abuse investigations is often distressing in nature, the wellbeing of those serving in this area must be considered. It is vital when examining such material that this is completed in an ethical and professional manner, lest bias can cloud judgement. If this were to happen, then the investigation could ultimately be compromised. This is discussed further in Sachowski (2018).

Cloud computing, a technology by which data is stored remotely and accessed over an Internet or network connection, represents a very significant and current challenge for investigators. In simple terms; with cloud storage, the data is stored elsewhere, on someone else's computer. In a typical digital investigation, the Cloud may therefore represent a remote store of data which may or may not be relevant to the enquiries at hand. This remote data may or may not be located within the geographical jurisdiction of the investigating agency. There are several well-known providers of cloud services which users of technology interact with on a daily basis (perhaps without even realising it), such as Google Drive, Apple iCloud, Microsoft OneDrive, Mega, and Drop Box. It is important to also realise that cloud computing is not just about storage of people's personal or work files. Indeed, users of social media platforms, such as Facebook, YouTube, Instagram, and Discord, who post messages, pictures and videos for the world to see, are using cloud computing.

Cloud computing is an ever-expanding area of the Internet as we are posting an ever-increasing amount of information to such platforms. Once something is posted online, it is often very difficult to get it completely removed. Cloud computing is also slowly but surely becoming increasingly relied upon by normal everyday users for an increasing number of tasks, for example the integration of smart home technologies such as Amazon's Alexa and range of smart home speakers. The cloud technologies allow for near instant sharing of files and data streaming between local networks and internet-enabled devices quite possibly on the other side of the world. Personal privacy and security are absolute paramount importance to the public and the providers themselves often don't know what data is being shared. Yet with in excess of 6 million echo dots worldwide, criminal activity is bound to be captured in some way by such devices (Pawlaszczyk et al., 2019).

Cloud storage such as Google Drive and Apple iCloud in particular can be extremely beneficial to an investigation for two key reasons. Firstly, with Android devices typically integrating with Google Drive services, and with Apple devices being connected to iCloud, it is likely that backups of devices will be present, which can potentially be retrieved. This can be especially useful in situations where the original device is no longer available, for example if accidentally damaged or intentionally destroyed to hamper an investigation. Secondly, and particularly in the case of historic crimes; older backups may be present that still contain data that might otherwise have been lost to time. It should also be noted that sometimes data is simply not held locally and is instead streamed 'on the fly' to an app, upon demand.

Social media accounts can therefore be considered cloud computing as the services they provide are held remotely and accessed either via a website or dedicated app. The data from such platforms and accounts can be great sources of evidence due to the presence of messages, calls and other interactions a user may have engaged with while on the platform.

Smart home devices, such as Amazon's Alexa and smart speakers, Blink and Ring cameras, and Google Home devices; can be used to provide households with a range of services, such as smart home automation, safety and security, and comfort and convenience. Such devices and platforms typically store a variety of different types of data and, if it can be recovered, this data can be useful in a variety of different ways. Most simply, the logs of device usage can potentially provide valuable information about a person's pattern of life, behaviours, and routines. Sometimes this data is retrievable from the user's mobile device, as such technologies usually have a mobile 'app' associated with them to allow for configuration and management of the devices, however this is not always the case. There may also be some form of smart hub that can be used in conjunction with the devices themselves. Ultimately, this data will most likely be present somewhere in the Cloud and therefore should be considered where appropriate.

The legal means to access data held in the cloud typically varies depending on which police force is investigating. There are two approaches that are typically taken; the first to consider is use of section 49 of the Regulation of Investigatory Powers Act (RIPA), 2000, and the second is to use section 19 of the Police and Criminal Evidence Act (PACE), 1984. If in doubt, when dealing with cloud-based data of potential or apparent relevance to an investigation, seek advice rather than running the risk of contravening legislation. Contact either or both the DFU and Covert Standards Unit, prior to doing anything.

As a professional working in a policing or government-based role, it is important to be aware of the risks and sensitivities associated with such employment. As a result, employees should be cautious of their use of personal devices in the workplace and should practice good digital hygiene.

Of foremost concern is the security risk to police officers and staff, and of course their families. This is especially important in terms of the use of social media and their online presence; you are likely findable on such networks if the correct privacy settings are not used, and so could potentially be located and tracked down by criminals and those who might wish you harm. It is therefore advised to lock down privacy settings as much as possible, so that only friends and family are able to view any material that you post online or choose to share. There are other methods which you can take to obfuscate your online presence further. An example of such as action might be changing your surname on Facebook to a middle name or your mother's maiden name, so that you are less likely to be found.

As a matter of good practice, it is recommended that police officers and staff test the privacy settings of any of their social media accounts This can be done a number of different ways, such as attempting to view your account and details while not logged in, by using an account that is not connected to you (for instance by enlisting the assistance of a colleague or departmental test account), and by simply googling yourself. The amount of information you can access using these methods should help inform you as to whether it is time for a privacy update. If the role you do is sensitive enough, then it is worth considering whether having a social media account is appropriate at all. Indeed, some law enforcement agencies with specific vetting and employment requirements do not permit their employees to have such accounts for this very reason.

It is also important that you be mindful of how your personal devices are used when investigating cases, attending crime scenes etc. There are ways and means for you to inadvertently interact with devices at a crime scene, and for you to be tracked, even by accident. One such example of this is that anyone who is a BT broadband customer is able to connect to other BT routers through means of BT's shared Wi-Fi functionality. There is a risk that anything you do while connected to such a hotspot might be viewable on that individual router. Being aware of the digital footprints your devices can inadvertently leave is incredibly important; with the ever-changing technology around us, we don't know what impact such actions might necessarily have, and also we don't necessarily know what capabilities and expertise a suspect or person of interest might have, and therefore whether they might use any such information.

This also applies to the use of personal devices for official policing purposes; employees could leave themselves open to the potential of having their personal devices seized, for example if they have been used to capture or preserve a video of something evidential, or alternatively if they have been used for the purposes of capturing crime scene photographs. Most important to consider is the fact that, if personal devices have been used for policing purposes and they are seized for presentation in evidence, this does introduce the possibility of personal data having to be disclosed as part of court proceedings.

Finally on digital hygiene, keeping personal devices separate to work devices is good practice as it prevents the risk of accidental data leakage during normal device usage. Examples of this might be the uploading of the wrong images, sending the wrong file or answering personal video calls in sensitive locations. This is trivially mitigated by simply keeping these devices and their usage completely separate.

As a potential first responder or as the first point of contact in a case with digital evidence, there is much to be mindful of, and you must be conscious to conduct actions to ensure best evidence is obtained and that the quality of the investigation can be maximised. A first responder needs to be mindful to preserve potentially volatile evidence. Screenshots (or indeed video recording of information on a screen, using an organisation-approved device) can be used to capture information that is highly likely to be imminently lost. If the evidence is web-based and can be accessed by others, then also consider contacting the DFU (or appropriate department) to ask them to capture the website/data with any specialist software that they may possess. The College of Policing (2024) CyberDigiTools app is also available to assist officers identifying sources of digital evidence at a scene.

While first responders should be aware that specialist evidential formats exist for the preservation of important files and data, the software to carry out such actions is not typically present on everyday user's computers, and is not typically user friendly, Therefore the use of this is best left to specialists in the DFU.

In the event that files or data does need to be preserved and the device cannot be seized, then a first responder might consider a more targeted or selective collection of date or files. Making use of department-issued storage media (such as a USB stick) for the collection of files is an option, however it would be better if files could be collected together into some form of container, such as a ZIP file. Such containers can subsequently be converted into an evidential format by the DFU with relative ease. It is of course generally considered best practice to seize a pertinent digital device, wherever possible.

Where device seizure is an option, the first responder may find themselves with the responsibility of packaging an exhibit for transport and storage. You should therefore consult your organisation's guidance on seizure and packaging to ascertain what is considered good practice for the device you are dealing with. When seizing devices, thought must also be given to obtaining relevant details relating to passwords, PINs or other methods to unlock the device. Encryption poses significant challenges to the digital forensic processes which will follow, and so gathering such information at the point of seizure will help the subsequent investigation move forward more quickly. Refusal to provide such information is often significant and telling, and at this point further steps can be taken. Specialist equipment exists which is capable of brute-forcing PINs and passwords (although this typically takes quite some time), and legislation exists which can be used to encourage a device owner to disclose their PIN or password. If this situation occurs, it is recommended to seek advice from the DFU.

Another crucial role of the first responder is that of providing support to victims and those involved. As with the investigation of any crime, expectations must be managed, and victims should be made aware of the potential impact that the investigation will have on them. For example, if they hand over their mobile phone for examination, they should be told how long they might expect to wait before it is returned, and the nature of the data that will be extracted from their device. They may have concerns over invasion of privacy (and the potential impact of disclosure) that should be addressed at the earliest possible opportunity.

The UK Government has published the Code of Practice for Victims of Crime in England and Wales, known better as the Victim's Code (Ministry of Justice, 2020). This provides an invaluable resource and reference to assist with such issues.

Future developments

The immediate future of the majority of digital evidence is certainly mobile. Devices are becoming increasingly powerful and portable. The capabilities of mobile devices are improving at a tremendous pace. Therefore it should be anticipated and expected that offenders in many different crimes will move their behaviour towards mobile devices, which will of course include child protection cases. With mobiles' increasing integration of Cloud based services for storage of photographs, videos and backup of data, a knock-on effect is likely to occur in which Cloud evidence becomes more and more relevant.

Getting timely information out of a mobile handset may be achievable while a suspect is in custody. For this reason, and because a mobile device contains lots of valuable information and intelligence which can be used to demonstrate a person's movements. Police forces are increasingly utilising 'kiosk' style mobile forensic equipment which extracts basic information quickly enough for it to be put to a suspect in interview. These can be invaluable in obtaining an early indication of a guilty plea, therefore helping to minimise backlogs within the DFU. Future use of these devices is expected to increase, provided they can be utilised within the scope of the current regulatory and quality frameworks.

While both cloud storage and mobile forensics have applications beyond child protection, they also have the potential to play a significant role in such crimes; this is a potential source of digital evidence which is not currently being routinely or consistently exploited. It is also safe to say that in the future, investigators will need to consider a much wider array of device types; the Internet of Things (IoT), in-car systems, wearable technologies, and other such smart devices being only a few examples. IoT devices currently pose significant investigative challenges, as well as risks, Servida and Casey (2019).

In the future, such devices will likely become more commonplace, as will the expectation that forensic intelligence and evidence will be available from them. The forensic software and capabilities however need to catch up and keep pace with the technology. Acquisition of data from such devices is certainly possible, as evidenced in Findlay (2021), but it is far from routine or well-practiced. Technology offers wonderful possibilities, and with it, come potential new sources of intelligence and evidence which we must learn how to investigate.

Conclusion

Child protection and mobile technology are two of the key priorities within contemporary digital policing. Digital evidence can potentially interrelate with the cloud, and the challenges that cloud evidence presents. Technology changes quickly, evolving and developing at an incredible pace. With this comes new potential and possibilities for technology to be used in crimes.

There is an ever-moving game of 'catch-up' being played, between the developers of new devices and technologies and the ability to police and investigate crimes that involve such devices. New technology will always evolve and provide both opportunities and challenges. Front-line officers and investigators must ask the right questions and take the right actions at the scene and during interview. Such straightforward actions such as asking the owner of a seized mobile phone for the PIN or password to unlock their device really do make the digital forensic investigator's job easier, and thus typically result in better evidence being obtained.

Finally, guidance should always be available from the relevant specialists within the Digital Forensic, Cybercrime, and indeed other units, so never be afraid to ask for advice!

Evidence-based case study illustrating professional practice

The following case study is based on real events from a number of different murder cases. Relevant digital evidence from several cases has been combined together to create a hypothetical scenario that highlights how digital evidence can support or refute various lines of enquiry.

A 999 call was received in a force control room from the proprietor of a village shop, stating that his wife had been killed. He claimed that they had been attacked by an intruder, knocked unconscious, and when he came to, he found that the shop had been ransacked and his wife bludgeoned to death.

There was also a significant amount of cash missing from the shop's safe, when questioned, the husband stated he had been forced to unlock it before being knocked unconscious. The safe was fitted with a 5-minute countdown-timer security feature.

There was a wealth of evidence available at the scene to aid the investigation. The forensic strategy also included an assessment of possible digital evidence. As a result, digital technologies were identified and seized by the crime scene investigators for further examination. This included the electronic shop till, the premise's CCTV system and personal digital devices.

When later examined by the DFU, the electronic till indicated that the last time someone had been served was approximately 2 minutes before the 999 call was received. The customer was later identified via credit card details and when interviewed by a detective, the customer had not seen anyone when leaving the shop.

Further examination of the CCTV system revealed no sign of an intruder, although there were two blind spots. The CCTV did show the victim's husband briefly leaving and returning to the premises in between the 999 call being made and the police arriving. It was noted that the husband left carrying a black refuse bag and returned without it.

Examination of the personal digital devices of the victim and husband revealed significant information. Firstly, it became clear that the couple were, for all intents and purposes, living together but separated. Browser history records from the victim's laptop revealed she was frequenting dating websites and WhatsApp chats from the husband's smartphone indicated he was conducting an extra-marital affair. Although the black bag the husband left the shop with was never found, a large amount of cash was later located in the possession of the husband's lover.

Digital evidence was also recovered from the smart watches, and linked mobile phone's fitness apps, of both the victim and her husband. The logs from these sources revealed both the victim and her husband had significant elevated heart rates in the moments leading up to the victim's death, which could indicate signs of a struggle. The victim's time of death was effectively witnessed by her watch and smartphone, the fitness app logged and time-stamped the very moment that her pulse became zero. The husband's pulse continued to be elevated for some time after this moment, indicating that he may have been conscious and engaged in rigorous activity. The investigative team suggested that this was indicative of him ransacking the property to look as if the robbery had occurred.

Reflective question

With the rapid pace of technological development, and considering that digital forensic software and investigations are, by definition, most often reactive, how can we assure that we get best evidence, how do we know that we have acquired all of the data possible, and how do we know that we have seen everything that there is to see?

References

Association of Chief Police Officers. (2012). Good Practice Guide for Digital Evidence. [online]. http://library.college.police.uk/docs/acpo/digital-evidence-2012.pdf (accessed 9 January 2019).

Association of Police and Crime Commissioners & National Police Chiefs' Council. (2016). Policing Vision 2025. [online]. https://assets.college.police.uk/s3fs-public/policing_vision_2025.pdf (accessed 11 July 2024).

Cabinet Office. (2022). National Cyber Strategy 2022. [online]. www.gov.uk/government/publications/national-cyber-strategy-2022/national-cyber-security-strategy-2022 (accessed 4 July 2024).

College of Policing. (2024). News: Mobile App for Cyber and Digital Operations. [online]. www.college.police.uk/article/mobile-app-cyber-and-digital-operations (accessed 16 July 2024).

Europol. (2023). Dismantling Encrypted Criminal EncroChat Communications Leads to Over 6 500 Arrests and Close to EUR 900 Million Seized. [online]. www.europol.europa.eu/media-press/newsroom/news/dismantling-encrypted-criminal-encrochat-communications-leads-to-over-6-500-arrests-and-close-to-eur-900-million-seized (accessed 10 July 2024).

Findlay, B. (2021). A Forensically-Sound Methodology for Advanced Data Acquisition from Embedded Devices at-Scene. *Forensic Science International: Reports*, 3. [online]. https://doi.org/10.1016/j.fsir.2021.100188.

Forensic Science Regulator. (2023). Forensic Science Regulator: Code of Practice. [online]. www.gov.uk/government/publications/statutory-code-of-practice-for-forensic-science-activities/forensic-science-regulator-code-of-practice-accessible (accessed 4 July 2024).

Home Office. (2015). The Child Abuse Image Database (CAID). [online]. www.gov.uk/government/publications/child-abuse-image-database (accessed 9 January 2018).

Internet Watch Foundation. (2023). Sexual Abuse Imagery of Primary School Children 1,000 Per Cent Worse since Lockdown. [online]. www.iwf.org.uk/news-media/news/sexual-abuse-imagery-of-primary-school-children-1-000-per-cent-worse-since-lockdown/ (accessed 16 July 2024).

INTERPOL. (2018). International Child Exploitation Database. [online]. www.interpol.int/en/Crimes/Crimes-against-children/International-Child-Sexual-Exploitation-database (accessed 21 March 2019).

Ministry of Justice. (2020). The Code of Practice for Victims of Crime in England and Wales. [online]. www.gov.uk/government/publications/the-code-of-practice-for-victims-of-crime (accessed 11 July 2024).

National Police Chiefs' Council. (2024). Policing Vision 2030. [online]. www.npcc.police.uk/publications/policing-vision-2030/ (accessed 16 July 2024).

Office for National Statistics. (2022). Nature of Fraud and Computer Misuse in England and Wales: Year Ending March 2022. [online]. www.ons.gov.uk/peoplepopulationandcommunity/crimeandjustice/articles/natureoffraudandcomputermisuseinenglandandwales/yearendingmarch2022 (accessed 16 July 2024).

Office for National Statistics. (2024). Crime in England and Wales: Year Ending December 2023. [online]. www.ons.gov.uk/peoplepopulationandcommunity/crimeandjustice/bulletins/crimeinenglandandwales/yearendingdecember2023 (accessed 4 July 2024).

Pawlaszczyk, D., Friese, J., & Hummert, C. (2019). Alexa, Tell Me: A Forensic Examination of the Amazon Echo Dot 3rd Generation. *International Journal of Computer Sciences and Engineering*, 7(11), 20–29. https://doi.org/10.26438/ijcse/v7i11.2029.

Police and Criminal Evidence Act (1984). s.19. [online]. www.legislation.gov.uk/ukpga/1984/60/section/19 (accessed 10 July 2024).

Regulation of Investigatory Powers Act (2000). s.49. [online]. www.legislation.gov.uk/ukpga/2000/23/section/49 (accessed 10 July 2024).

Sachowski, J. (2018). *Digital Forensics and Investigations: People, Process, and Technologies to Defend the Enterprise*. Boca Raton, FL: CRC Press.

Servida, F., & Casey, E. (2019). IoT Forensic Challenges and Opportunities for Digital Traces. *Digital Investigation*, 28(supplement), S22–S29. https://doi.org/10.1016/j.diin.2019.01.012.

WePROTECT Global Alliance. (2016). Our Strategy to End the Sexual Exploitation of Children Online. [online]. www.weprotect.org/strategylaunch (accessed 9 January 2018).

12 Volunteers in policing

Colin Rogers

Introduction

Citizen participation in policing, as Bullock (2014) points out, has moved from focusing purely on re-establishing the principle of policing by consent and affirming the legitimacy of the police, to include more recent concerns around the wider themes of building capacity. In addition, the idea of using volunteers contributes to generating social capital and reviving structures of democracy. Social capital refers to social life that enables people to act together more effectively to pursue shared objectives, such as keeping the peace. It refers to social connections and the norms and trust that these generate (Putnam, 2000). It is valued for its potential to facilitate community action, especially through the solution of collective problems, including dealing with criminality (Halpern, 2007).

In this respect, the legitimacy of the police may be assisted by the recruitment of volunteers with wide-ranging backgrounds and characteristics which may better reflect those more recent of the community. Appeals to citizens and communities as a whole are at the heart of current policing ideas, especially in the pluralised world of policing which encourages volunteering. However, 'community' itself is a contested and complex idea that is portrayed differently according to its need. For example, the general term 'community' is portrayed as a positive image, homogeneous and consistent. 'Community' is often used to describe many ideas, including that of geographic location. Therefore, 'community' may best be understood not as a local area where people live, but as a network of social relationships that people have and maintain, which tie people together. The introduction of social media and networking has also challenged ideas of 'community' (Castells, 2010). Despite this, appeals to the community for volunteers to support police activity is an important one for the world of policing. Police volunteers now encompass a wide range of activities, but the one area most people seem to associate with volunteering in policing is that of the special constabulary.

DOI: 10.4324/9781003492948-13

Historical context

Special constables

The Anglo-Saxon period is identified as the context for the formal establishment of the idea of community involvement in crime control (Lee, 1901; Critchley, 1978). The Norman Conquest adapted the Anglo-Saxon arrangements into the Frankpledge system, which was communal, local and mutually beneficial for the community (Lee, 1901). Stead (1985) observes that this system was a distinct and workable model of social control. The model eventually evolved into a five-tier hierarchy of constables, each responsible for different aspects of governance and control. The statute of Westminster in 1285 rationalised the system and confirmed the duty and obligation of everyone to maintain the peace and if necessary arrest an offender. As society changed and became more industrialised episodes of unrest and extensive rioting took place. Newly developed policing systems were also utilised to deal with major disturbances. The use of voluntary groups was common, and this voluntary aspect is perhaps the best context in which to view the origins of the modern special constabulary.

Special constables have a long and varied history in England and Wales. Writing of their history, Radzinowicz (1974 [1956]) emphasises how during the eighteenth century constables were appointed for a special emergency and acted under the direction of a local magistrate. An act of 1801 allowed for special constables to be paid expenses and in 1803, under the threat of a French invasion, the government invoked magistrates to enlist trustworthy citizens for the role. In 1820, magistrates were allowed to appoint special constables not only in cases of public disorder but also as a preventative measure when they anticipated trouble. The idea of a permanent reserve force was clearly taking shape.

The enlistment of special constables therefore varied in proposition to the gravity of the emergency. In 1831 an act amended the laws relating to the appointment of special constables and preservation of the peace, an element which is still important today (Seth, 1961). The valuable, if not indispensable, nature of the services rendered by special constables, was witnessed in 1848, when chartists threatened to descend upon London. No fewer than 200 citizens enrolled themselves as special constables and in concert with regular officers of the Metropolitan Police prevented potential rioters advancing upon the capital (Lee, 1901). At the outbreak of the First World War in 1914, the special constabulary expanded significantly, with the Metropolitan Police Service alone beginning the process of recruiting 20,000 new special constables (Seth, 1961). During the Second World War, volunteer special constables continued to be recruited with many donating 2,500 to 3,000 hours a year, this was on top of their paid employment (Seth, 1961). In 2020 the special constabulary across England and Wales is reported as donating over 3 million hours (Association of Special Constabulary Officers, 2020).

While the idea of special constables can be traced to a statute passed in 1662, the Police Act 1964 is generally considered to be the Act that established the modern Special Constabulary.

It is worthy of note that like some of their regular police officer and staff colleagues, over the years a number of special constables have also made the ultimate sacrifice while volunteering their time supporting policing. Further information is available via the Digital UK Police Memorial (Police Arboretum Memorial Trust, 2019).

Current professional practice

Each force has its own Special Constabulary comprised of volunteers, who commit at least 4 hours per week to working with and supporting regular police officers. They wear similar uniforms and have similar equipment, when on duty, have the same powers as regular officers. 'Specials', as they are often referred to, are also subject to the same rules of conduct and disciplinary procedures as sworn officers. On recruitment, new 'specials' should study the special constables learning programme (SCLP), which should be successfully completed to various vocational levels including achievement of accompanied patrol status (APS) and qualified special constable (QSC).

In the past, 'specials' have been subject to some negativity and abuse; Seth (1961) discusses the views of some officers that special constables were a nuisance, special constables have also been labelled as 'hobby-bobbies'. Berry et al. (1998) discuss problems surrounding integration and communication between special constables and the regular police. However, special constables are representative of their community and have played a vital part in neighbourhood policing (Chapter 8). They also comprise an important component of plural policing. However, the idea of a volunteer 'special' police is much older than the Police Act of 1964, and this historical context is worthy of examination in order to understand the reasons behind the importance of the volunteer police officer's contemporary role. Generally speaking, a special constable's main role is to conduct local, intelligence-based patrols and to take part in crime prevention initiatives, often targeted at specific problem areas. In many forces, special constables are also involved in policing major incidents and events, and in providing operational support to regular officers. Depending upon their individual force, special constables generally engage in the following activities:

- conducting foot patrols,
- assisting at the scene of accidents or fires,
- enforcing road safety initiatives,
- conducting house-to-house enquiries,
- providing security at major events (such as sporting or carnivals),
- tackling anti-social behaviour,
- tackling alcohol-related incidents,
- spending time at local schools educating young people about crime reduction and community safety, and
- presenting evidence in court.

During the 2012 Olympic Games held in London, several thousand special constables from across police forces in England and Wales volunteered their time to assist the policing operation, in 2022 special constables supported policing for the funeral cortege for Queen Elizabeth II and in 2023 lined the route for the coronation of King Charles III. In 2024, 50 special constables were even deployed internationally to support the Paris Olympics (National Police Chiefs' Council, 2024).

The number of special constables has varied over time, with Bullock (2014) suggesting in post-war Britain it peaked in the 1950s at over 67,000. However, Gill and Mawby (1990) suggest that this had fallen to about 15,000 by 1980. One suggested reason for this reduction in numbers is the administrative removal of those less active members of the special constabulary. However, during the last decade, the number of special constables has continued a gradual decline until, by the mid-2000s, there was around 11,000. In 2024, the number of special constables in England and Wales was 6,118 (Home Office, 2024), a reduction of 28% from the 2023 figure of 8,545. Possible reasons for the decline are many, varied and intertwined but may include not insignificant numbers being recruited by the regular service, changes in the appeal of formal volunteering post-COVID-19, the general appeal and trust in policing among some communities. However, while special constables are generally the best-known form of police volunteering, there are other roles and functions carried out by volunteers.

Other forms of volunteers in policing

With a focus of involving citizens in policing, there are other roles for volunteers. The police service in England and Wales has increased the use of volunteers that are unpaid 'civilians', to work within the police organisation (National Police Improvement Agency, 2009). These are members of the public who had expressed an interest in working with the police service, undertaking various roles and responsibilities within the organisation; however, they are not sworn in special constables, have no police powers and are unwarranted.

Police support volunteers

Whereas special constables are officers with powers the same as a regular police officer, a police support volunteer is someone who donates time freely to perform tasks which are designed to enhance the work of the police and to provide additional support to local communities. Sometimes police support volunteers (PSVs) utilise their existing skills to aid policing, such as digital skills. As such, PSVs assist police officers and staff with various tasks enabling police officers to concentrate on core policing duties, this means more officers on the streets and improved community support. Maintaining a high police presence in communities will also help reduce crime, disorder and fear.

To become a PSV an applicant must usually satisfy the following criteria:

- Be aged 18 years or over.
- Be a British Citizen, a European Economic Area national or a commonwealth citizen, or a foreign national with no restrictions on your stay in the UK.
- Have a minimum of three years continuous residency in the UK (some roles requiring specific clearances require five years continuous residency), with less than twelve months spend abroad in the last three years (with some exceptions for those living on a UK military bases).

The Home Office (2024) report that in 2024, some 7,211 people are engaged as police support volunteers.

This approach is part of the concept of using volunteers within public services as a key feature of developing wider social capital, as an example, volunteers are increasingly becoming involved in running public libraries (Casselden et al., 2015) and other local provision of services.

Neighbourhood volunteers

Neighbourhood volunteers are also part of the police support volunteers' scheme in England and Wales. These volunteers assist when and where they can, as many enjoy the flexibility of supporting the police service and their local community. Depending on the hours donated by volunteers and the specific role, whether administrative or involving some sort of community engagement, volunteers work from police stations and others work on the street engaging with members of the public directly, engaging in community meetings, letter dropping, marking bikes, community speed or neighbourhood watch initiatives etc. Neighbourhood volunteers often work alongside neighbourhood police teams and other partner agencies.

Volunteer police cadet (VPC) leaders are also usually enrolled in policing as PSVs. The use of police cadets in England and Wales is not new, indeed, the idea can be traced back to well before the Second World War when young employees served as clerks and messengers (Commentary, 1966). The current scheme is now very different, seen as a youth volunteer organisation meeting weekly, cadet members are aged between 13 to 18 years of age, wear a uniform (although it is different between police forces) and study a formal programme of learning about policing while developing skills useful throughout life (Pepper & Rogers, 2022). Some forces also work in partnerships with primary schools to deliver a mini-police scheme for much younger people. The VPC scheme currently has in the region of 18,000 members (DeMarco & Bifulco, 2020). The main objectives of the scheme revolve around creating good citizens who support the police and the community. It is aimed at recruiting young people representing all aspects of society which it is believed will support the idea of police legitimacy within communities.

Student volunteering schemes for policing

Some police forces are also involved in partnerships with universities managing volunteering schemes for policing. Volunteers are typically undertaking degree qualifications in policing and related subject areas, with the schemes tending to run parallel with other police support volunteers' schemes. Student volunteers usually work with neighbourhood policing teams (NPTs) (Chapter 8), in many ways mirroring the role of PSVs. These volunteers work closely with the community and always under the supervision of members of the NPTs. As such they may be involved in a number of activities, such as leaflet drops or other crime prevention activities. These schemes enable students, who are often hoping to become full time police officers, to gain an insight into policing while managing a work/life balance while studying. This scheme is particularly useful given the current nature of police education and recruitment processes, although there are some areas of improvement required (Pepper et al., 2024).

Supporters of the use of volunteers in policing point to several main positive outcomes of encouraging such an approach. The first of these is the economic perspective of using volunteers.

Volunteers have been viewed as being cost effective, providing additional resources particularly in times of economic constraints. Acknowledging volunteers in policing are not a cost-free resource, their use can however save hundreds of thousands of pounds a year for the police service in England and Wales (Gravelle & Rogers, 2010; Pepper & Rogers, 2022).

The second positive aspect claimed for utilising volunteers is that it has been seen as a vehicle for improving the legitimacy of policing, with the idea that volunteers provide a hypothetical bridge joining regular officers and staff with communities. Additionally it is believed volunteers may be more representative of the community with their diverse skills and life experiences (Rogers & Pepper, 2022).

However, there has apparently been internal resentment to the increased use of volunteers in policing. While it has been reinforced that volunteers should complement rather than replace paid employees in current positions, staff unions in particular have expressed some concern regarding the use of volunteers for 'back office' or clerical functions.

In terms of how volunteers are regarded across policing, there is of course always the danger that volunteers will be exploited, with their good will being taken for granted. For example, many volunteers do not receive adequate training for their role. However, this is not confined to the police service in England and Wales (Rogers & Wintle, 2021). In particular there is some concern regarding the training and use of volunteers in the use of evidence-based practice.

Volunteers and evidence-based policing

Little published research exists exploring the effectiveness of transferring evidence-based policing (EBP) taught within volunteer policing programmes and training to enable its adoption and use in professional policing practice. This is particularly disappointing as it appears the police service has adopted this philosophy as a major policy for its regular police officers and a tool to be utilised across the service (Chapter 5).

Some senior leaders in policing have been involved in the development and delivery of an EBP input to newly appointed volunteers. This would be welcomed by Telep and Lum (2014), who identify how the receptivity of those in policing to EBP is likely to be influenced by the emphasis placed on it by executive leaders. The impact of first line leaders on the adoption of EBP is also crucial (Pepper et al., 2024), the importance of the support of the management is also highlighted by Fleming and Wingrove (2017). Savignac and Dunbar (2014) report similar findings across wider Canadian crime reduction initiatives, where the importance of the management team encouraging and supporting volunteers and others on the frontline was identified as crucial to the implementation of EBP approaches. Furthermore, while researching the adoption of EBP among police leaders in Canada, Kalyal (2020) identified that cultural resistance to the adoption of EBP could be overcome by communicating the benefits of its adoption across all staff and volunteers, not ignoring the ability of volunteers themselves to influence the behaviours of those they volunteer with (Schafer, 2009).

Therefore those supervising and leading volunteers need to understand and champion EBP. As this not only adds value as an authentic and practical perspective to EBP, but also demonstrates support from organisational leaders, while consolidating their vision of adopting an EBP approach to deal with future policing challenges. However, whether such approaches has influenced volunteering in policing requires much further research.

This move to engender a widespread adoption of EBP across policing practices is an important element embedded within the new educational entry routes for new police officers (Brown et al., 2018), but this does not appear to have been percolated towards volunteers in policing. This approach is important for a number of reasons, such as dealing with digital enabled crime, enabling officers and volunteers to deal with new challenges faced due to the changing landscape of policing. Such mainstream adoption of EBP by volunteers would enable them to better understand the benefits of research, being able to link this to their volunteer role requirements (Rojek et al., 2015). Additionally, Sherman (2013) acknowledges the benefits of reviewing international research to influence policing practices but continues to suggest that each police agency should develop their own research of what works within their policing environment. The evolution and use of the evidence-base for the policing profession is in some cases transferrable and benefits from both national and international research through the sharing of professional policing practice (Mitchell & Lewis, 2017). Mitchell and Lewis (2017) would argue that the police have an ethical obligation to their communities to use the best evidence-based practice. Such as the linking EBP to everyday local practices, in order to ensure its effective implementation, was highlighted by Sherman (1998).

Some commentators suggest that the way in which EBP is applied should not be limited to the traditional experimental approaches (Lumsden, 2017; Brown et al., 2018; Pepper et al., 2021), instead adopting the most appropriate and rigorous research approaches available, rather than focusing on just utilising the scientifically sound randomised controlled trials originally suggested by Sherman (1998). The benefits of utilising such alternate yet still rigorous methods of research, would enable volunteers for example, to better understand, explain to others, critically review, and apply a range of methods to inform and assist in solving policing problems. While Police officer's awareness and enthusiasm towards EBP seems to be affected by their previous education (Grieco, 2016; Telep, 2017), along with previous experiences of research (Telep, 2017), there is nothing comparable to volunteering this aspect of EBP within volunteers for policing.

Future developments

The College of Policing has highlighted developments and challenges that will affect policing in the future, and in particular the police workforce (College of Policing, 2020). The College of Policing (2020) highlight ten trends that will be the most impactive on policing over the next 20 years or so. These include rising inequality, expanding unregulated information space on line, changes to trust in public agencies and a more diverse population and workforce automation. As the demands for police response to incidents rises in both numbers and complexity, more and more specialists' departments may be introduced to deal with these challenges. This includes the recruitment and use of volunteers who have specialist skills such as the operation of commercial drones or certification within the maritime sector.

Cybercrime for example has increased substantially so that specialist units have been created to deal with this particular problem, staff being drawn away from uniform and preventative functions. This in turn leads to a shortage of highly visible police officers, and a lack of police officers to deal with other non-crime yet important issues. However, growth in the effective use of volunteers who have external workplace experience in aspects such as digital technologies can be used to assist in cyber investigations.

Whatever response the police provide for dealing with future demands upon the services it will have some impact upon the current workforce for policing in England and Wales. Over the past decade for example, driven by austerity measures, police forces have been attempting to rationalise their estates by selling off police buildings including police stations. Such behaviour may lead to a perception that the police are retreating from the community. Yet the police still need to provide a service function around public reassurance to improve public confidence and of course legitimacy and trust. Functions involving the maintenance of social order such as education in schools, could perhaps be dealt with by volunteers in policing. Consequently, more and more reliance will be made upon the use and abilities of volunteers in policing whether donating many hours a month on the frontline as a special constable, supporting a VPC scheme as a PSV or micro-volunteering utilising specialist skills one weekend a month. It is therefore important that volunteers are trained and adequately and empowered to enable them to deal with and resolve a variety of situations and problems that they will encounter, including an understanding of the evidence-based approach.

Conclusion

The use of volunteers in policing is not a new concept and will continue for the foreseeable future as the police workforce attempts to deal with an increasing number of complex and diverse situations including terrorist activity, serious organised crime, illegal drugs use and the many forms of cybercrime. Their use is not without some resistance and problems concerning workforce arrangements, in particular the attractiveness to potential volunteers of donating their time volunteering within policing.

In addition, tensions in police legitimacy and trust by the public have been major factors intensified by extensive media coverage, as well as official reports highlighting some inadequacies of current policing arrangements. It is important, therefore, that to maintain an efficient police service utilising our current policing model requires not only the support and involvement of all citizens, but particularly of those individuals who currently volunteer in one of the many roles now available. Volunteers are therefore a vital component of future policing in England and Wales. As the police workforce aligns itself to address complex challenges, involving technology, serious organised crime etc., and increasing demand for services in difficult economic conditions, the need for additional support becomes more important.

Resolving such issues and problems requires a different approach to traditional response reactive policing methods and will require a diverse police workforce which includes regular police officers, staff and the many volunteers, to engage in smarter policing, especially utilising evidence-based practices. Volunteers, in their various and diverse roles, can provide substantial support. However, for this to be achieved there needs to be a realisation that, for the purposes of alignment with regular police officers and other staff, a common approach to training and education which involves understanding the EBP needs to be considered. This in turn would support the current policing philosophy in this country, such as evidence-based practice, which it would appear, is deficient in the current structure of education for volunteers in the police in England and Wales.

> **Evidence-based case study illustrating professional practice**
>
> A local district in the police force area has suffered a number of domestic burglaries which has caused concern in the local community, distress to the victims as well as consuming much police time. The neighbourhood policing team (NPT), which includes special constables, for the area have been

tasked with reassuring the community and preventing further burglaries while the CID are actively investigating possible culprits.

Analysing the evidence and the modus operandi (MO) of the burglaries it is discovered that the majority of the burglaries are repeat offences, i.e. victims who have been burgled once had been re-burgled between 10–14 days after the original offence.

Carefully researching what has worked in other areas that have suffered similar problems, such as utilising the College of Policing Practice Bank, the team comes up with a plan.

- The team engages on a campaign of awareness, utilising police community support officers and special constables, to engage directly with residents the community, encouraging target hardening including the use of ring technology, other private CCTV applications, clear and visible signs indicating preventative measures in place, lights and extra locks on doors and windows.
- Accompanied by police support volunteers, volunteer police cadets engage in a supervised 'leaflet drop' to all households in the community.
- In addition, neighbourhood watch schemes are encouraged and supported during a local 'Police and Communities Together' (PACT) meeting chaired by a police officer from the NPT, creating a sense of guardianship among citizens to watch out for each other was undertaken, as well as patrolling the area whenever possible.

The result was a clear reduction in burglaries and other offences in the community area, the introduction of a neighbourhood watch scheme, and a general increase in support for policing. In addition, calls for police service decreased dramatically.

Reflective question

What other sources of information could you have utilised in order to provide evidence that would inform the policing actions in the evidence-based case study described?

References

Association of Special Constabulary Officers. (2020). Thinking about the Future – 2022. [online]. https://asco.police.uk/thinking-about-the-future/#:~:text=The%20UK%20has%20a%20long%20and%20proud%20history,year%20to%20support%20their%20local%20forces%20and%20communities (accessed 12 October 2024).

Berry, G., Izat, J., Mawby, R., Walley, L. & Wright, A. (1998). *Practical Police Management*. London: Police Review Publishing Company.

Bullock, K. (2014). *Citizens, Community and Crime Control*. Basingstoke: Palgrave Macmillan.

Brown, J., Belur, J., Tompson, L., McDowall, A., Hunter, G. & May, T. (2018). Extending the Remit of Evidence-Based Policing. *International Journal of Police Science & Management*, 20(1), 38–51. https://doi.org/10.1177/1461355717750173.

Casselden, B., Pickard, A.J. and McLeod, J., (2015), The Challenges Facing Public Libraries in the Big Society: The Role of Volunteers and the Issues that Surround Their Use in England. *Journal of Librarianship and Information Science*, 47(3), 187–203. https://doi.org/10.1177/0961000613518820.

Castells, M., (2010). *The Rise of the Network Society*, 2nd edition. Chichester: Wiley Blackwell.

College of Policing. (2020). Policing in England and Wales: Future Operating Environment 2040. [online]. https://assets.production.copweb.aws.college.police.uk/s3fs-public/2020-08/future-operating-environment-2040.pdf (accessed 18 September 2024).

Commentary. (1966). Commentary. *The Police Journal*, 39(1), 1–6. https://doi.org/10.1177/0032258X6603900101.

Critchley, T. (1978). *A History of Police in England and Wales 900–1966*. London: Constable.

DeMarco, J. & Bifulco, A. (2020). Shared Practice, Learning and Goals between Police and Young People: A Qualitative Analysis of the National Volunteer Police Cadets. *Policing*, 15(4), 2095–2110. https://doi.org/10.1093/police/paaa010.

Fleming, J. & Wingrove, J. (2017). 'We Would If We Could … but Not Sure If We Can': Implementing Evidence-based Practice: The Evidence-based Practice Agenda in the UK'. *Policing: A Journal of Policy and Practice*, 11(2), 202–213. https://doi.org/10.1093/police/pax006.

Gill, M. & Mawby, R. (1990). *A Special Constable: A Study of the Police Reserve*. Aldershot: Averbury.

Gravelle, J. & Rogers, C. (2010). The Economy of Policing – the Impact of the Volunteer. *Policing: A Journal of Policy and Practice*, 41(1), 56–63. https://doi.org/10.1093/police/pap016.

Grieco, J. (2016). Attitudinal Dimensions and Openness to Evidence-Based Policing: Perspectives of Academy Recruits. Dissertation, George Mason University. [online]. https://mars.gmu.edu/items/1ac37762-6843-4861-9ecd-11b0d16d0042 (accessed 12 October 2024).

Halpern, D, (2007). *Social Capital*. Cambridge: Polity Press.

Home Office. (2024). National Statistics, Police Workforce, England and Wales: 31 March 2024. [online]. www.gov.uk/government/statistics/police-workforce-england-and-wales-31-march-2024/police-workforce-england-and-wales-31-march-2024 (accessed 5 October 2024).

Kalyal, H. (2020). 'One Person's Evidence Is Another Person's Nonsense': Why Police Organizations Resist Evidence-Based Practices. *Policing: A Journal of Policy and Practice*, 14(4), 1151–1165. https://doi.org/10.1093/police/pay106.

Lee, W. (1901). *A History of Police in England*. London: Methuen.

Lumsden, K. (2017). Police Officer and Civilian Staff Receptivity to Research and Evidence-Based Policing in the UK: Providing a Contextual Understanding through Qualitative Interviews. *Policing: A Journal of Policy and Practice*, 11(2), 157–167. https://doi.org/10.1093/police/paw036.

Mitchell, R. & Lewis, S. (2017). Intention Is Not Method, Belief Is Not Evidence, Rank Is Not Proof: Ethical Policing Needs Evidence-Based Decision Making. *International*

Journal of Emergency Services, 6(3), 188–199. https://doi.org/10.1108/IJES-04-2017-0018.

National Police Chiefs' Council. (2024). News: 19 July. [online]. https://news.npcc.police.uk/releases/special-constables-confirmed-as-part-of-uk-support-package-for-paris2024 (accessed 10 October 2024)

National Police Improvement Agency. (2009). *Creating a Business Case*. London: NPIA.

Pepper, I., Brown, I. & Stubbs, P. (2021). A Degree of Recognition across Policing: Embedding a Degree Apprenticeship Encompassing Work-Based Research. *Journal of Work Applied Management*, 14(1). https://doi.org/10.1108/JWAM-12-2020-0056.

Pepper, I. & Rogers, C. (2022). Volunteer Police Cadet Leaders in England and Wales: Economic Benefits to Policing. *European Law Enforcement Research Bulletin*, 22, 117–129www.cepol.europa.eu/scientific-knowledge-and-research/european-law-enforcement-research-bulletin/european-law-enforcement-research-bulletin-previous-issues.

Pepper, I., Rogers, C. & Turner, J. (2024). The Adoption of Evidence-Based Policing: The Pivotal Role of First-Line Police Leaders across England and Wales. *International Journal of Emergency Services*, 13(1), 111–122. https://doi.org/10.1108/IJES-05-2023-0020.

Pepper, I., Rogers, C., Turner, J., Louis, N. & Williams, B. (2024). Enabling Student Employability through Volunteering: Insights from Police Volunteers Studying Professional Policing Degrees in Wales. *Higher Education, Skills and Work-based Learning*, 14(5), 1135–1148. https://doi.org/10.1108/HESWBL-09-2023-0253.

Police Arboretum Memorial Trust. (2019). UK Police Memorial. [online]. https://digital.ukpolicememorial.org/ (accessed 11 October 2024).

Putnam, R. (2000). *Bowling Alone: The Collapse and Revival of American Community*. New York: Simon & Schuster.

Radzinowicz, L. (1974 [1956]). *A History of English Criminal Law and its Administration from 1750, Vol. 3, Cross Currents in the Movement for the Reform of the Police*. London: Stevens and Sons.

Rogers, C. & Pepper, I. (2022). Volunteers in Policing: A Vehicle for Increased Representativeness in Policing?17 March. [online]. www.transformingsociety.co.uk/2022/03/15/volunteers-in-policing-a-vehicle-for-increased-representativeness/ (accessed 15 March 2022).

Rogers, C. & Wintle, E. (2021). To Serve Others and Do Good: An Examination of Volunteers in the New South Wales Police Force. *Salus Journal*, 9(1), 18–38. https://view.salusjournal.com/index.php/salusjournal/article/view/124.

Rojek, J., Martin, P., & Alpert, G. (2015). *Developing and Maintaining Police-Researcher Partnerships to Facilitate Research Use*. New York: Springer.

Savignac, J. & Dunbar, L. (2014). Guide on the Implementation of Evidence-Based Programs: What Do We Know so Far? [online]. www.publicsafety.gc.ca/cnt/rsrcs/pblctns/gd-mplmnttn-vdnc-prgrms/gd-mplmnttn-vdnc-prgrms-en.pdf (accessed 12 October 2024).

Schafer, J. (2009). Developing Effective Leadership in Policing: Perils, Pitfalls, and Paths Forward. *Policing: An International Journal*, 32(2), 238–260. https://doi.org/10.1108/13639510910958163.

Seth, R. (1961). *The Specials: The Story of the Special Constabulary*. London: Victor Gollancz.

Sherman, L. (1998). *Evidence-based policing: Ideas in American Policing*. Washington, DC: Police Foundation.

Sherman, L. (2013). The Rise of Evidence-Based Policing: Targeting, testing, and tracking. *Crime and Justice*, 42(1), 377–451https://doi.org/10.1086/670819.

Stead, P. (1985). *The Police of Britain*. London: Macmillan.

Telep, C. (2017). Police Officer Receptivity to Research and Evidence-Based Policing: Examining Variability Within and Across Agencies. *Crime & Delinquency*, 63(8), 976–999. https://doi.org/10.1177/0011128716642253.

Telep, C. & Lum, C. (2014). The Receptivity of Officers to Empirical Research and Evidence-Based Policing: An Examination of Survey Data From Three Agencies. *Police Quarterly*, 17(4), 359–385. https://doi.org/10.1177/1098611114548099.

13 An introduction to coaching and mentoring

David Taylor

Introduction

Professional dimensions and concepts in contemporary policing practices have been detailed in earlier chapters. Coaching and mentoring encompass important relationships and strategies that enable reflective processes and products to be expressed; in order to affect practice and, thereby develop human potential and the organisation (Law et al., 2007).

It is appropriate to consider whether the mentee is undergoing a coaching or mentoring programme as a 'means to an end' towards something defined by their organisation, or are they, as an individual, 'the end' in themselves? The answer may be a combination, and this interplay reflects how coaching and mentoring may meet the requirement for personal, professional and organisational goals.

This chapter introduces the reader to the history of mentoring and the complexity of defining coaching and mentoring due to the wide use of the terms within society. It seeks to clarify the roles across the police service and its use within initial training and manager development as two distinct areas of focus. This is to help identify what outcomes are required from these types of work-based schemes, and which of the coach/mentor role may be best applied to meet them. A generic coaching mentoring framework is given and there are links to reflective models for both roles. Whitmore's (1996) GROW model of communication is explained as a structure for coaches and mentors to work with. Five areas of change concerning the transitional learning of trainees/mentors are outlined to give some overview of where coaching and mentoring skills may be required. Mentor and mentee characteristics are discussed and the phases of developing someone from dependence to independence are explained.

History and context

Homer's *Odyssey* is often cited in mentoring literature; 'Mentor' was the name of the person who was chosen by Odysseus to guide his son Telemachus, while Odysseus fought in the Trojan wars (Wallace & Gravells, 2007). This situates the social phenomenon of mentoring in history. Often, this narrative has stimulated debate regarding the role and qualities a mentor should develop and apply in a mentoring relationship. In the eighteenth century, Carraccioli expressed his interest in the mentor's therapeutic effects upon the mentee and their holistic development (Clutterbuck et al., 2017). The nineteenth-century work of Fenelon developed the stories about Homer's 'Mentor', giving a narrative of someone who is both altruistic and generous (Garvey, 2017). While many descriptions of the term 'mentor' have been drawn from literature (Garvey, Stokes & Megginson, 2014), the concept of an older more experienced guide who supports and educates someone in their charge has endured – depending on who has required mentoring and for what purpose.

Mentoring is carried out in many parts of the world for a variety of reasons. It may be seen in skills development, managerial roles, leadership development, business and academic endeavours (Clutterbuck, 2014). There has been further development of mentoring in organisations and in literature across many disciplines over the last 30 years. Therefore, mentoring can be seen from different perspectives and can be a difficult concept to define because of this. However, Parsloe, Leedham and Newell (2017) identify that the term 'coaching' has been used more in the last two centuries. Predominantly in the areas of sport and performance, the coach is the more skilled and experienced person in the coaching relationship (Garvey et al., 2014).

The influence of business-management and academic models that seek to develop the performance and self-responsibility in employees has resulted in the development of coaching and mentoring roles and organisational learning. Universities have developed courses with professional qualifications, and this has led to evidence-based research in these fields of learning development (Parsloe et al., 2017). This creation of professional courses and governing bodies of coaching and mentoring reveal the depth and breadth of this development and how it is regarded. Clutterbuck et al. (2017) make the distinction that over time mentoring has moved from its naturalised ad-hoc state into a widespread phenomenon that affects society. An example of these wider social impacts can be seen in youth mentoring programmes (Eby, Rhodes & Allen, 2007) and other schemes that aim to support the rehabilitation of convicts and young offenders.

In the police service, the coaching of new officers has been a mainstay of initial police learning development programmes (IPLDPs) for several decades; this is a crucial step in developing the trainee constables' professional practice on patrol and full occupational competence, and an integral part of the current police constable entry routes (PCER). Mentoring is also utilised to support officers progressing to higher ranks and developing specialist skills. With the heavy responsibility and greater scrutiny of modern policing in the UK, there has been a development of recognised professional qualifications, ethical standards and the measurement of competence. This is evidenced in the ethical narrative of the Competency and Values Framework (College of Policing, 2024) and reflects the discourse of regarding policing as a profession.

The need for coaching and mentoring has arguably expanded. An example of this is where a training requirement is identified (whether in an individual or all those in a specific role), or where there may be a desire to support individuals in new, complex and pressured roles and processes. This may be directly or indirectly related to the development of performance and accountability. The College of Policing identifies several mentoring opportunities for police staff, including schemes such as Mentoring for all; Mentoring for chief officers; and the Women's Chief officer network (College of Policing 2024a). Given the important role of the police in society, it can be seen that police mentoring and coaching may impact on service to the public and how the police may be perceived in society.

A good question to ask when undertaking a coaching mentoring role or implementing a coaching mentoring programme is: What do 'we' mean by the terms coaching and mentoring?

Megginson and Clutterbuck (1995) refer to the process whereby an individual gives less formal support to another, to help them develop their knowledge, thinking and practical skills. Many reflective conversations are carried out between police colleagues, before and after an event occurs (the term 'event' is used to encompass any element of practice that concerns police practitioners). Collaborative learning can occur in these reflective conversations (Law et al. 2007). In this sense members of a police team may feel that they are being coached or mentored in a natural way. This can be a powerful part of a person's learning development and resonates with how individuals enter and develop within communities of practice (Lave & Wenger, 1991), such as an established policing team. However, this naturalness can also blur the lines of when coaching and mentoring occurs, or what may be effective or ineffective in a coaching or mentoring relationship in these circumstances.

Wallace and Gravells (2007) posit that mentoring is predominantly concerned with helping a person to move from one stage of learning to another and includes the skills of coaching and teaching. While coaching and mentoring share the purpose of developing the individual, Brockbank and McGill (2012) identify the 'performance coach', carries out observation, assessment and provides feedback to develop problem solving behaviours and increase performance - this can be identified in the police tutor's role as they coach new police officers. A key aspect of coaching may be the focus on completing tasks and developing performance over a short term, with the explicit use of targeted feedback (Clutterbuck, 2014).

While mentoring can have a broader focus over a longer-term and considers the potential of the mentee to holistically develop; collaborating to set the agenda according to their needs. Mentoring is more holistic in nature (Clutterbuck 2014) and the mentor may challenge, critique, support, listen and help their mentee to develop ideas, options, resources and networks with others.

Organisations may use other labels which may cause confusion and make the roles seem ambiguous. Very often what someone will term 'mentor' is a 'coach' and vice versa (Parsloe et al., 2017). This is an easy mistake to make as the two roles share characteristics (Garvey et al., 2014) and require similar qualities. However, the individual may require different types of support to others, at different stages of their potential progress.

The needs of the organisation and the mentee/trainee influence which of the two roles should be applied, for the best effect on their development. Each police role and departmental setting dictates specifically the qualities and characteristics that are emphasised and valued; (Garvey et al., 2014). It would seem that identifiable and measurable skills-performance would require some form of coaching. While more nuanced professional interpersonal management and leadership skills may require a mentoring relationship. Parsloe et al. (2017) make the pragmatic point that people in an organisation should know the definition of the coaching and mentoring roles that are most pertinent within their setting. This calls for clear and agreed aims and a consideration of the learner's needs. If a programme can express clearly identifiable goals, then the most appropriate characteristics of coaching or mentoring (Brockbank & McGill, 2012) can be identified and applied appropriately.

Mentoring and coaching in professional police practice

Helpfully, Morton-Cooper and Palmer (1993) identify three forms of mentoring relationships within policing. The first, classical, when the relationship forms naturally and is determined by the individuals involved; second, contract, where the relationship is largely defined by the organisation's goals; and finally, pseudo, where mentoring only seems to be done in appearance and within a short timescale (this may be where other forms of training and coaching may be carried out unwittingly under the title of mentoring). If a police force has an identified mentoring scheme where mentors and mentees are matched as to the needs of the individual and the organisation, this would indicate a contract relationship.

Finklestein and Poteet (2007) make the distinction between formal and informal mentoring programmes; formal programmes resemble the contractual one identified by Morton-Cooper and Palmer, and mentor and mentees are matched with some involvement by the organisation. Successful matching (in both coaching and mentoring) is reliant on the characteristics used to define participants and their needs, along with who decides what these are. However, if this matching is not done well, it can inhibit the chances of success. Staff numbers and unavailability limit the options for matching.

Clutterbuck (2014) discusses the merits of formal and informal mentoring; formal mentoring provides a clear purpose and support for mentors and mentees as they identify their outcomes; this type of programme offers more structure. Mentor training is usually involved in formal programmes, which may help identify the quality of the mentors prior to them forming mentor relationships. However formal programmes may recruit staff who feel pressured to become mentors in order to show certain skills. Alternatively, informal mentoring may not meet the aim of the organisation, although informal mentoring may last longer and feel more valued by those involved in the process (Clutterbuck, 2014).

Adapting Bruce-Foulds, Clark and Ray's (2017) distinctions between coaching and mentoring, the following explanations seek to clarify the matter for the policing environments. While concentrating on internal coaches and mentors in formal contracted schemes, it should be noted that there may still be some overlap between the roles in their settings and the type of guidance given by the mentee's/trainee's direct manager.

Coaching in practice

If the focus is to develop multiple skills that can be observed in practice, and incrementally developed with repetition, assessment and objective feedback within a set timescale, this would require a coaching relationship. There may be some responsibility for supporting the learner with listening skills and empathy, arranging materials and identifying opportunities for learning. However, this directed focus on performance (Brockbank & McGill, 2012) places the emphasis on coaching a trainee to develop specific skills and achieve levels of specific behavioural competencies; repetition, developmental discussion and assessment may be clearly identified in the behaviours of the relationship. The trainee therefore would perform, reflect and target areas of development towards this aim. This would infer that there may be a time limit to a completion date, whereby evidence is collated (perhaps physically within a portfolio or electronically online) to support achievement, or evidence where achievement has not occurred. This makes the relationship largely objective and quantifiable when measured against expectations.

The strengths to this approach are that the coaches are familiar with the structure and culture of their workplace (Parsloe et al., 2017) and can apply greater skill levels than external coaches. There is also a need to remain objective and be aware of the politics or relationships of the workplace, which may overshadow the opportunities for development at times.

Another consideration is how the internal coaches are recruited and by what means they are trained and supported in their extra role. Coaching on patrol/operational duties is intensive and tiring and concerns the entwined dual responsibility of worker and teacher. This can be intensified by the risk-aware nature of police work, which places pressure on the coach to decide when to coach and when to act in response to the needs of the public at any one time.

The reality of operational life influences when, where and how coaching can be done. For example, it would be very difficult for the coach to give feedback to a trainee in the middle of a sensitive incident, or at the scene of violent public disorder where the unfolding of events takes precedence. Emotions may run high for anyone in these circumstances and the UK police's Competency and Values Framework (College of Policing, 2024) identifies the importance of emotional awareness across professional roles. This can dictate the length and depth of coaching discussions.

Multiple skills and qualities are brought into play when carrying out live-coaching as the coach has to manage their trainee and themselves. Skills development may need to be addressed long after the heat or impact of an incident has occurred. This of course is not the same in all coaching relationships and some of these operational pressures may affect development to a greater or lesser extent. Coaching in the workplace may incorporate more exposure to external scrutiny, where the process and interplay of the relationship may be observed by the public and other officers already competent in their community of practice (Lave & Wenger, 1991).

Mentoring in practice

Alternatively, a mentoring relationship is where people may be matched over a longer time to help develop a less experienced person. They may not even be in contact with each other in the specific day-to-day workplace. This allows some freedom for discussion, confidentiality, guidance and a developmental dialogue with less immediate impacts. Rather than being concerned with detailed objectives in practice, the inexperienced person may be more concerned with richer outcomes over time, such as the judicious use of power and support within management, a growing confidence in leadership, developing networks in management and specialist environments, and developing their career (Parsloe et al., 2017). An example of where mentoring would help development in achieving these richer outcomes over time may be seen in the higher levels of the Competency and Values Framework (College of Policing, 2024).

The more experienced mentor may still use some form of coaching if it is required; however, this would not be the main role. The meetings may be more spaced apart, and contact could be by telephone and e-mail in between. The location of the meetings can be pre-arranged to suit both parties, which may be beneficial to confidentiality, depth and trust over time. Such a relationship allows the mentor to offer a safe forum to share knowledge and experience. Confidentiality may be required by both parties and they and the mentor scheme-supervisor may be the only ones who know it is being carried out. They can identify needs and provide impartial support, helping the mentee to develop by challenging them to self-manage as and where appropriate (Klasen & Clutterbuck, 2002).

Mentoring may be more subjective than the police coaching relationship. The strengths of this are that it may build strong relationships between generations and across the rank structure, while creating a sense of belonging to the wider police organisation, thus providing opportunities for inclusion and meeting the needs of diversity. However, this places a responsibility to identify the right mentors who can invest their time and efforts. The effectiveness of this would be enhanced with a clear mentoring policy, the organisational and staff 'buy-in' or visible sponsorship (Clutterbuck, 2014) to the process. With clear outcomes and intentions (Garvey et al., 2014). Requiring some form of dedicated programme-supervision to oversee and offer the participants guidance and support (Brockbank & McGill, 2012).

Influences on coaching and mentoring

It may be possible to identify which role needs to be applied by examining the relevance of the supporting individual to the trainee/mentee's day-to-day performance and their workplace. The more involved they are with the objective day-to-day performance and assessment of their candidate, the more they assume a coaching role; this may also be part of the manager's responsibility. The less involved they are, the more they may take up a mentoring identity.

A further consideration is the impact of police procedure and legislation such as the Police and Criminal Evidence Act (PACE), 1984. The operational coach trains the trainee to apply and adhere to these in their professional practice. Arguably, the mentoring relationship may not venture near this depending on what developmental concerns are being addressed. However, there may be other structures such as organisational policy and guidance from external governing bodies depending on the situation.

Garvey et al. (2014) also make the distinction that there is an emerging pattern of mentoring being reliant upon volunteerism. Whereas coaching may be a built-in part of someone's job description and therefore is paid work; the coach's performance may be judged by that of their trainee's development. This may be established in discussions between coaches, assessors and their managers, when discussing the development targets of the trainee. This in-line focus on performance emphasises how the trainee and coach share a focus on meeting organisational goals and the competence to meet them.

However, this is not necessarily part of a mentor's role, and they may only have contact with their mentees and possibly a mentor scheme supervisor. Garvey et al. (2014) make the point about the 'friendship' in these roles, identifying that while 'friendliness' is a good characteristic to have in a coaching relationship, an actual 'friendship' can be identified as an outcome of a mentoring one. 'Friendship' is not the sole domain of mentoring, however, and many police coaching relationships may build this, or not.

Clutterbuck (2014) discusses the possibility of the formal mentoring programme embedding a culture of mentoring, coaching and support in an organisation. Coaching and mentoring roles may change over time; once a new police officer has completed their initial development, it is not uncommon for their coaches to naturally become their mentors in an unofficial capacity. The same new officer may develop mentor-like relationships and help others. However, this development of roles hinges upon the nature of the relationships they are built on and the characteristics of the people involved.

Developing individuals

Police practitioners have vital responsibilities and need to develop important knowledge and skills. They may go through elements of change or 'transitional learning' (Daloz, 1986) where the developmental processes create new perspectives. Wallace and Gravells (2007) identify two key aspects of mentoring in lifelong learning; to enable the mentee to assimilate knowledge, and to help with the emotional changes such transitions may cause. Learning-transitions in the police require the development of cognitive, affective, and physical skills. However, very important intrapersonal, problem solving, and conflict management skills (Chapter 6) are key aspects of professional police work.

We can identify these areas of development when a police constable makes their first arrest. They need to be able to: know the law, consider their powers and apply them; there will be an emotional impact, possibly excitement, confidence, fear, anger or nervousness; they may have needed to physically restrain their suspect, thus incorporating other skills. When interviewing a suspect for a criminal offence, the officer has to negotiate the interview structure, review evidence and points of law, consider the suspect's viewpoint, challenge discrepancies and conflicting accounts. This can be a daunting experience although a fulfilling one.

A coach will be able to observe, guide and help the trainee to learn from their experience; this means the trainee's skills can then be developed over further arrests and investigations. Thus, helping them to develop their level of evidence-based practice and critical thinking as identified in the narrative of the Competency and Values Framework (College of Policing, 2024). However, as we can see in the case study, the emotional impact of the workplace can overshadow the development of other areas.

The transition of an experienced patrol officer to a supervisor demands a new set of learning requirements, building upon their existing experience and responding to new responsibilities to the public, their staff and the organisation. The Competency and Values Framework (College of Policing, 2024) sets out the expectations for behaviours in many of these changing roles. New responsibilities require development in knowledge, affective learning soft-skills, leadership and management. A mentoring approach may be applicable with regards to developing professional management in their practice over a longer period of time. A mentor may enable a safe space for them to discuss how to approach issues with their staff, other managers and members of the public.

Critically, positive and negative learning experiences help to shape our learning approaches and may obstruct or enable our capability to learn new things (Law et al., 2007). However, Lave and Wenger (1991) also identify that these varying experiences help us to move from the periphery of practice towards a more legitimate place within it. This reveals the important nature of the coach/mentor's role to navigate these experiences with their trainee/mentee and support the development of resilience.

Common to both roles in these circumstances is the emphasis on meaning-making with the trainee/mentee as they develop their practice; what meaning can trainees/mentees take from their experiences in order to help them develop. The coach may have more contact in practice environments to build upon this, by drawing meaning from everyday events through structured discussions. Kolb's experiential learning cycle (Kolb, 1984) and the later Gibbs cycle (Gibbs, 1988) enable a structured analysis of experiences, allowing collaborative verbal reflection to synthesise new learning and transfer it to further events and learning opportunities. Often used in coaching is the SMARTER model to focus objective target setting. For those required to perform to certain levels and requirements, the SMARTER model can offer more specific evidence of performance as it is timebound and has an element of evaluation.

The mentor and mentee may also consider the making of meanings in depth, probably less frequently and with more reliance on the mentee's recollections and motivations. This places more emphasis on the relationship, to create an environment of trust and confidentiality. Argyris and Schön's (1974) theory may be helpful; professional practice is developed by ascertaining what the mentee wanted to put in place yet had to adapt to what they actually used. Here the mentor and mentee can help create suggested interventions for the next time they work on something. Targeting specific needs or more general approaches and attitudes. This complexity can be addressed in some measure by the use of CPD (Continuing Professional Development) structures and opportunities. The College of Policing (2024b) offers online resources based upon the Gibbs cycle (Gibbs, 1988) that may enable the mentee to make sense of this complexity by providing a clearer expression of it in partnership with the mentor. However, another strategy is to apply the GROW model (Whitmore, 1996), which can be used as a less formal framework with the mentee/trainee to consider their:

- *Goal*
- *Reality* of the situation
- *Options* that are available
- *Will* to enact their choice of option.

Brockbank and McGill (2012) identify that it is useful for performance development with willing mentors/trainees; the framework can be used on short time periods, which would suit the coach, while it could be applied over months which would suit the pace of a mentoring relationship.

The possible movements of an individual within the structures of a policing organisation offer an opportunity to identify five areas where transitions may occur and require coaching and mentoring:

- *Initial entry to the police* – such as initial development in a response policing environment, which can be a fundamentally important part of a career, or, the early development of the officer entering via the Detective Degree Holder Entry Programme (DDHEP) or other direct entry pathways as they are introduced.
- *Situational* – if there are significant changes to practice within a policing role that affect established police practitioners. This could also apply to staff who are returning from absence, and these situations may shape more personal approaches depending on their needs.
- *Lateral* – into different areas of policing professional practice with different specialist functions, communities of practices and may be linked to work with outside agencies/stakeholders. This can be seen as an important development opportunity for specialising in new skill bases. Also, managers can be mentored in special areas and gain important feedback from those departments operating with the public. The police 'reverse mentoring scheme' echoes this ethos.
- *Ascending* – into different levels of leadership and management (promotion), with strategic responsibility. Where different skills are required to

manage police staff and to promote organisational values and apply policy and processes.
- *Cross-organisational* – where the transition is into another policing organisation/body with its own established and changing structures/processes and responses to local, cultural and national needs (such as recruitment/ assignment to a national policing unit countering terrorism) (Chapter 10). This may also be part of the multi-agency strategy that is commonly engaged with at practitioner and management levels, or indeed as mergers occur between forces.

Someone moving from one area of policing to another may identify with more than one of the five examples. An officer who is promoted to a leadership and management post in a specialist policing area may feel an ascendant transition into the higher rank and a lateral transition into the specialist area. The roles of the coach and mentor are to help enable and support these transitions which means their characteristics in the role are very important to success.

Characteristics of coach and mentor

The coach and mentor require characteristics to best enable their candidate's development. However, mentors may put obstacles in place if they are of particular mindsets and behaviours; either by being too rigid, egotistical or devious (Brockbank & McGill 2012). Darling (1984) categorised types of mentors who created obstacles, describing: Avoiders, who make themselves scarce; Dumpers, who throw the mentee into the deep end: Blockers, who refuse to meet the mentee's needs, by refusal, withholding support or by over-supervising; Destroyers, who may subtly undermine or overtly belittle the mentee. A mentee's responses may be to limit the amount of contact with their mentor or by possibly engaging only enough to get through the process. Certainly, a list of unwanted characteristics in the world of mentoring and coaching.

Many mistakes can also be made if one-sided personal agendas are strictly adhered to. Parsloe et al. (2017) identify the unique aspect of each mentee/ mentor relationship due to the unique qualities that comprise our individual make-up; positing that the mentor/coach interventions should accommodate personal differences and needs. Imposing a personal approach on a person rather than developing their approaches can stifle individual development and possibly limit their view of the opportunities that may result.

Assumptions about the other person, from both sides of the relationship, can effectively block the opportunities for development within the mentoring and coaching processes. Beliefs and values are powerful personal motivators, but they may differ between the coach/mentor and the trainee/mentee. The culture of the police, shaped by its history, social construct of law enforcement, practices, leaders and members, may produce assumptions about the other person in the relationship, which may be unfounded. During the coaching/mentoring process, there must be cognisance taken with regards to the protected characteristics identified in the Equality Act, 2010 (i.e. age, disability, gender reassignment, marriage and civil partnerships, pregnancy and maternity, race, religion or belief, sex and sexual orientation).

Brockbank and McGill (2012) regard the power imbalance of coaching and mentoring relationships. The coach or mentor may have power due to their rank or position; they also hold power with regards to their access to experience, knowledge and existing networks. This is what Garvey et al. (2014) term 'Legitimate' and 'Expert' power. In some cases, they hold the power of influence, as to whether the trainee/mentee will progress in the organisation at all.

Wallace and Gravells (2007) identify good mentoring qualities, which include the desire to help, to learn, be open-minded, have a perspective of 'giving' for success and have the experience of having been a mentee. Parsloe et al. (2017) contend that the mentor/coach should be aware of their own make-up and their motivations to better understand those of their mentees/trainees.

The mentoring process is a two-way relationship though, which requires the mentee/trainee to demonstrate specific characteristics to enable it to work effectively. These include respect, discretion, motivation and responsibility, open-mindedness and a willingness to be challenged and developed over the issues they identify. The mentor/coaching relationship may be undermined if the mentee/trainee does not engage and value it. Wallace and Gravells (2007) consider the impact of overconfident mentees/trainees or the ones who do not accept responsibility for their mistakes. Others, who solely elicit answers from their relationship without reflecting on their own development, may undermine the true opportunities offered to them.

The structure of the mentoring and coaching relationship

Mentoring and coaching processes should have an apparent entry point, phases of development and some form of exit. Fostering dialogue from the beginning and forming an appreciation of viewpoints and needs, provides a foundation for richer discussions and meanings as the relationship develops. Thereby diversity and inclusion are not just in the opportunity to partake in the process, but as an element of the relationship. Rich dialogue rests upon the rapport that is built up from the beginning (Wallace & Gravells, 2007) and is developed over time. This provides the opportunity for greater understanding and the identification of clearer avenues of support and guidance. Clarity between both parties at these early stages in the relationship provides a framework that may alleviate tensions and address the needs of both people as they progress. Thus, an expression of the potential, goals and limitations of both parties' involvement allows each to glimpse the ideas of the other and their expectations (Finklestein & Poteet, 2007). Both parties can enter into an agreement about how to proceed, which Wallace and Gravells (2007) term 'contracting'.

The first phase of development would see the mentee/trainer being dependent upon the mentor/coach and their expertise. Gradually the mentee/trainee would become less dependent, and the relationship would become more collaborative in its second phase. The final phase would be independence where the mentee/trainee develops from the collaborative to operate with more agency, still being observed or monitored by the coach/mentee. From this independent stage, an exit from the relationship can be negotiated, or imposed depending on the formal/informal nature of the role.

These frameworks may be highly structured in the case of coaching towards competencies and skills. Less so, if a mentoring relationship develops over time to encompass a breadth of holistic development. Irrespective of the timescales and linear appearance of these phases, development in multiple skills and qualities is complex and the phases should be negotiated according to need. The trainee/mentee may be dealing with varying areas of development, and it may not feel like a linear path from one phase to the other. Rather, it may feel like messy stratified layers of achievements and setbacks. Predetermined points to review the level of progression and re-organise the focus of it can help. Revisiting the initial contract can provide a good structure to focus on what was intended and how it needs to be adapted (Wallace & Gravells, 2007).

The independence of a mentee/trainee may be hard to quantify in certain relationships. The performance coach should be able to look at the recorded evidence from logged tasks and portfolio type records with which to make judgments and recommendations. However, the label of independence at the end of a coaching period may only be evidence that the trainee is safe to learn further, on their own. Rather than being independent in a fully more professional sense.

Independence in a mentoring relationship may not be clearly evidenced, as it relies on off-line mentee reflective processes. This may encourage a more subjective sense of independence expressed through confident and more collegiate discussion in this relationship. However, there may still be hard evidence to support and celebrate achievements in this process, such as an operational plan or project report. This may be assisted by periodical reviews and revisiting the original aims of the relationship as was set in the initial meeting. Comparing these reviews with how the mentee and mentor feel about the level and depth of development in the later stages, may provide something more substantial seeming from which to then go forward.

Conclusion

The chapter has sought to introduce the concepts of mentoring and coaching for the policing context. Given the amount of coaching and mentoring occurring in society, and the range of published work in existence, this chapter has merely introduced this process, considering some contextual situations for the police setting, rather than relying on conflicting definitions of both approaches. From the complexity of wider mentoring and coaching contexts a clear distinction has been drawn between the two roles. The distinction made here is not exclusive of the overlaps and similarities between these roles and others. However, it does seek to make it somewhat easier to understand in pragmatic terms, supported by voices of authority in coaching and mentoring theory.

Coaching and mentoring arguably develops professional identities or may undermine them if not conducted in congruence with their aim. Coaching can occur in many police work-settings, not just operational ones. Mentoring is not the sole domain of management; many police officers and staff within the service can benefit from this process of learning and development.

Whatever the terminology or scheme, both mentoring and coaching involve one person helping another to understand and develop as to their needs, within the frame of organisational requirements. It is a human and personal investment though, whatever the framework that it occurs in. As one Superintendent said at the end of a mentoring course, 'You realise after a while that despite all the things we have to do, it's all about people really'.

Evidence-based case study illustrating professional practice

Michael is a new police officer who is in the first two weeks of the tutored practice phase of his training. He works on patrol with an experienced police officer-coach. On being called to deal with a report of a non-suspicious sudden death, the coach takes the lead to role-model good practice, intending to reflect with Michael after the event in order to develop his learning from the experience. The bereaved relatives at the scene are very upset. Michael is polite and appears professional through the event as he observes and assists the coach, engaging with relatives and supporting them, securing and examining the evidence, liaising with others and accurately recording evidence as per his police force's procedures. Later, his coach reflects with Michael about the experience. However, Michael expresses some distress and appears shaken. He feels that despite the empathetic and professional manner displayed by the coach, the police approach felt limited and particularly callous once contact with the bereaved had ended and the deceased had been removed to a place of rest. Michael expected that more contact would be carried out to counsel the bereaved and that more visits to the relatives would be done. The reflective discussion takes much longer than the coach anticipated and focuses on the possible conflict of values between the trainee and the organisation. This emotional-learning experience takes the focus of development beyond the task that both coach and trainee worked on. It is an example of how workplace coaching can affect trainees and that mentoring skills may be required in shorter-term intensive coaching relationships. The issue of confidentiality arises in the workplace due to the personal nature of the effects on the trainee. The learning event reveals a developmental area that requires the coach to observe in the workplace again; this learning experience will require the creation of a clear record of evidence.

Reflective question

What are Michael's development needs and what skills will the coach have to use to support learning in this reflective discussion?

References

Argyris, C. & Schön, D. A. (1974). *Theory in Practice, Increasing Professional Effectiveness*. San Francisco, CA: Jossey Bass.

Brockbank, A. & McGill, I. (2012). *Facilitating Reflective Learning: Coaching, Mentoring and Supervision*, 2nd edition. London: Kogan Page.

Bruce-Foulds, C., Clark, G. & Ray, K. (2017). Coaching and Mentoring: What They Are and How They Are Used in Organisations. In E. Parsloe, M. Leedham & D. Newell (eds), *Coaching and Mentoring, Practical Techniques for Developing Learning and Performance*, 3rd ed. (pp. 225–242). London: Kogan Page.

Clutterbuck, D. (2014). *Everyone Needs a Mentor*, 5th edition. London: Chartered Institute of Personnel and Development.

Clutterbuck, D., Kochan, F., Lunsford, G., Dominguez, N. & Haddock-Millar, J. (eds). (2017). *The Sage Handbook of Mentoring*. London: Sage.

College of Policing. (2024). Competency and Values Framework (CVF). [online]. www.college.police.uk/career-learning/competency-and-values-framework (accessed 5 July 2024).

College of Policing. (2024a). Mentoring. [online]. www.college.police.uk/career-learning/support-for-career-development/mentoring (accessed 5 November 2024).

College of Policing. (2024b). Resources for Reflective Practice. [online] https://assets.college.police.uk/s3fs-public/2020-11/Resources_for_reflective_practice_v1_0.pdf (accessed 5 July 2024).

Daloz, L. (1986). *Effective Teaching and Mentoring: Realizing the Transformational Power of Adult Learning*. San Francisco, CA: Jossey-Bass.

Darling, L. A. W. (1984). What Do Nurses Want in a Mentor? *Journal of Nursing Administration*, 14(10), 42–44.

Eby, L. T., Rhodes, J. E. & Allen, T. D. (2007). Definition and Evolution of Mentoring. In T. D. Allen & L. T. Eby (eds), *The Blackwell Handbook of Mentoring: A Multiple Perspectives Approach*. Oxford: Blackwell.

Equality Act (2010). [online]. www.legislation.gov.uk/ukpga/2010/15/contents (accessed 22 October 2018).

Finklestein, L. M. & Poteet, M. L. (2007). Best Practices for Workplace Formal Mentoring Programs. In T. D. Allen & L. T. Eby (eds), *The Blackwell Handbook of Mentoring: A Multiple Perspectives Approach* (pp. 345–367). Oxford: Blackwell.

Garvey, R. (2017). Philosophical Origins of Mentoring: The Critical Narrative Analysis. In D. Clutterbuck et al. (eds), *The Sage Handbook of Mentoring* (pp. 15–22). London: Sage.

Garvey, R., Stokes, M. & Megginson, D. (2014). *Coaching and Mentoring, Theory and Practice*, 2nd edition. London: Sage.

Gibbs, G. (1988) *Learning by Doing: A Guide to Teaching and Learning Methods*. Oxford: Further Educational Unit Oxford Polytechnic.

Klasen, N. & Clutterbuck, D. (2002). *Implementing Mentoring Schemes. A Practical Guide to Successful Programs*. Oxford: Butterworth Heineman.

Kolb, D. A. (1984). *Experiential Learning: Experience as the Source of Learning and Development*. Upper Saddle River, NJ: Prentice Hall.

Lave, J. & Wenger, E., (1991) *Situated Learning: Legitimate Peripheral Participation*. Cambridge: Cambridge University Press.

Law, H., Ireland, S. & Hussain, Z. (2007). *The Psychology of Coaching Mentoring and Learning*. Chichester: Wiley and Sons.

Megginson, D. & Clutterbuck, D. (1995). Mentoring in Action: A Practical Guide for Managers. In S. Wallace & J. Gravells (eds), *Professional Development in the Lifelong Learning Sector. Mentoring*, 2nd edition. Exeter: Learning Matters.

Morton-Cooper, A. & Palmer, A. (1993). *Mentoring and Preceptorship*. Oxford: Blackwell Science.

Parsloe, E., Leedham, M. & Newell, D. (2017). *Coaching and Mentoring, Practical Techniques for Developing Learning and Performance*, 3rd ed. London: Kogan Page.

Police and Criminal Evidence Act (1984) (and Codes of Practice), c. 60. [online]. www.legislation.gov.uk/ukpga/1984/#60/contents (accessed 15 December 2019).

Wallace, S. & Gravells, J. (2007). *Professional Development in the Lifelong Learning Sector. Mentoring*, 2nd edition. Exeter: Learning Matters.

Whitmore, J. (1996). *Coaching for Performance*. London: Nicholas Brealey.

14 Leadership in policing

An international comparison

Ian Pepper, Rick Ruddell, Ross Wolf and Christopher D. O'Connor

Introduction

The nature of serving within policing, whether as a police officer, staff member or volunteer, requires the recruitment of individuals with strong interpersonal skills, leadership abilities, and the willingness to learn and develop to operate effectively regardless of rank or role. Leadership Standards established by the College of Policing (2023) set the benchmark for contemporary knowledge, understanding, skills, attitudes, behaviours and performance expected of those leading within policing across England and Wales.

These standards build upon what the College of Policing (2015) defined as leadership, the quality to identify what needs to be done and the ability to successfully complete it; this is something that those in policing are usually good at achieving. For example, the professional role profiles for response police officers describes the need to not only to be able to arrive at an incident and make decisions as to an appropriate response based on the threats present, risks and available resources, but also be able to take control as the lead organisation at the scene while liaising with supervision and other agencies (College of Policing, 2024). Police community support officers take the lead to work closely with key individuals and community bodies to support the vulnerable, promote community cohesion and tackle perennial problems such as anti-social behaviour (College of Policing, 2024). Whereas the Leadership Standards (College of Policing, 2023) identify how strategic leaders within the policing should take a leading role in managing critical incidents in line with legal and force requirements.

As part of their role, contemporary police leaders across all levels of the service are likely to experience the impact of transnational crime during their careers. Early in a policing career this could, for example, be on the frontline interacting with people who have been trafficked, making arrests for the importation of drugs or on the basis of an Interpol 'red notice', through to later in a policing career leading an investigation of crimes on the dark web, an extradition or leading a policing mission overseas. Neyroud (2011) highlights the importance of policing across international borders as a component of national security, along with significant international interest in police

DOI: 10.4324/9781003492948-15

leadership, with a particular emphasis on senior leaders from a number of countries including Canada and the USA, who may in the future take on demanding multi-faceted roles. In whichever context, the skills required for effective leadership, and the associated accountability for actions taken, are transferrable from local to global policing.

It is commonly suggested that 'every police officer is a leader'. The leadership standards for policing (College of Policing, 2023) support this view providing standards for everyone within policing, as regardless of whether a police officer, staff or volunteer, all are in some capacity involved in leadership. At whichever level of the police service an individual is working, the decisions made as a leader result in significant impact internally and/or externally. However, Sarver and Miller (2014) suggest there is no one prominent leadership style adopted within policing. It is therefore important to be aware of the context within which police leaders operate, understand the value of evidence-based approaches to decision making (Chapter 5), along with knowledge of a range of leadership styles and approaches which can be adopted and used to make ethically based decisions.

History and context

In 1819, a large-scale peaceful rally was organised in Manchester with tens of thousands of people attending. A team of volunteer magistrates, chaired by a stipendiary magistrate, William Hulton, were tasked with ensuring law and order for the event (Bates, 2018). Inexperienced at enforcing the law, the magistrates had several hundred special constables sworn in for the occasion along with the armed yeomanry and military placed at their disposal (Bates, 2018). Poorly informed decisions, perhaps with political bias, were made by the magistrates, who were not trained for such law enforcement situations. This led to the demonstrators being charged by the military on horseback with the resultant killing and injuring of hundreds. This event was instrumental in governmental democratic reform and the eventual establishment of a full-time and trained police service where the uniform purposefully did not resemble the red military tunics.

One of the core principles of contemporary policing, that of policing by consent, was written in the mid-1800s by two new police commissioners, Sir Charles Rowan (a military professional) and Sir Richard Mayne (a legal professional). The principle defines how the service polices not by fear but in co-operation with the public, where the police behave in a way which ensures the approval and respect of the communities they serve (Home Office, 2012). Pearson-Goff and Herrington (2014) describe some key characteristics expected of contemporary police leaders, which include honesty, integrity, trustworthiness and effective communication. Failing to achieve such characteristics, and many more, can do a great deal to damage the relationship between the police, the communities they serve and their recognition as a worthy profession. The Baroness Casey Review (2023) highlights how failures in leadership are undermining the ability to deliver a good service, as a result affecting the trust and confidence of the police within some communities.

While not approaching the loss of life in 19th century Manchester, police officials in Canada have also acted overzealously to legitimate political protests and public dissent. Three riots have been highlighted as failures in police leadership and provide insight into the relationships between the police and their political masters, including the Winnipeg General Strike (1919), the Regina Riot (1932) and the G20 protests in Toronto (2010). Although only three people died in these protests, hundreds were injured and over 1,000 unnecessary arrests were made; few of those protestors were ever sentenced. One of the most significant outcomes of these events was reducing police legitimacy with the public due to the display of such force (Beare & Des Rosiers, 2015).

The common theme underlying the General Strike, Regina Riot and the G20 protests was that political officials exercised inappropriate influence on the police services in the planning of their responses. One of the challenges of policing in a democracy is balancing political priorities and police independence (Roach, 2017). While political interference was a significant challenge for Canadian police leaders until the 1960s, it has waned since then, and although police services are more politically independent today, issues still emerge (Canadian Press, 2018). Although the fear of Bolshevism drove politicians to order violent police actions to quash the Winnipeg and Regina protests, the G20 protests in 2010 threatened the ambitions of politicians wanting to showcase an international event.

In a similar way, in cities throughout the United States (US) after the killing of George Floyd in May 2020, protesters faced off against police in violent clashes in midsized police departments and big-city forces where police officers nationwide may have been unprepared to handle the level of unrest (Barker, Baker & Watkins, 2021).

Like their predecessors, the challenge for today's executive officers, chiefs and commissioners is balancing the priorities of the politicians and administrative organisations who approve their agency's annual funding, while maintaining the rule of law and protecting the public with finite resources.

Models which can be adopted for leadership have moved on significantly since the fundamental principles suggested by Taylor (1911) of the prime focus being to ensure the maximum possible prosperity for the employer. McLean (2017) identifies that among a number of attributes, police leaders should be active listeners, resourceful, possess both integrity and direction, pay attention to detail and, as identified by Taylor (1911), leaders should value learning and development, to be successful engaging in formal education and ongoing on-the-job learning (Kratcoski, 2023). Leaders at all levels should be inclusive, taking responsibility to enhance the development of an inclusive workplace, eliminating discrimination, treating all fairly and championing a culture of inclusivity, extending this approach to all the communities served, ensuring everyone is treated with fairness and respect.

There are many and varied leadership models which can be adopted, these include:

- Authentic leaders are authentic in every sense (George, 2003). They are consistent and predictable, have high integrity, are trustworthy and self-disciplined, they do not like to compromise, leading based on their values.
- Empowering leaders motivate and inspire those in their charge by influencing and encouraging them as to their abilities, while sharing authority and the responsibility for making workplace decisions with those at the lowest levels of experience within the team where proficient decisions can be ensured (Amundsen & Martinsen, 2014; Hassan et al., 2013).
- Ethical leaders are honest and highly principled who make selfless decisions based on the needs of society as a whole (Hassan et al. 2013). They lead by example, model and champion high moral standards, integrity and ethical behaviour, encourage team members to respect equality, diversity and inclusion and champion the policing Code of Ethics.
- Situational leadership, focuses on achieving the task, often matching the task with the experiences of the leader and/or the team.
- Supportive leaders are approachable and empathetic, they create time to take an interest in, listen to and support individual team members along with supporting their overall wellbeing.
- Transformational leaders tend to be proactive, empowering individuals and motivating them to take on more challenging tasks while using their inherent ability to solve problems (Dobby et al. 2004)
- Transactional leaders tend to be more reactive, motivating others by using the concept of their preference for reward as opposed to sanction (Dobby et al., 2004). Vito, Higgins and Denney (2014) contend that transactional leaders monitor behaviour of those in their charge, encouraging involvement and rewarding the achievement of specific goals.
- Visionary leaders focus on the future of the team or organisation. They identify an opportunity when it occurs, then develop a clear vision which, being self-confident and persuasive communicators, they can set out as a clear vision for those in their charge and the standards expected of them.

In reality, leaders tend to adopt a blend of styles. Research found that among police chiefs across Texas, USA, there were a range of leadership styles were present, however transformational leaders were viewed as the most effective with those adopting such an approach appearing confident and open minded (Sarver & Miller, 2014), with a transformational leadership approach having a positive outcome on attitudes toward police work (Dobby et al., 2004). Although it must be acknowledged that in certain situations, such as a riot, a transactional 'command' approach may be required.

Current professional practice

Across England and Wales leadership standards set out the expected knowledge, understanding, skills, attitudes, behaviours and performance expected of leaders across policing (College of Policing, 2023). Strong leadership by all those leading in policing is crucial in setting the standards and culture which lead to an effective service (HMICFRS, 2024). Regardless of rank or role, police officer, staff or volunteer, the leadership standards establish benchmark expectations for leaders across five stages:

Stage 1   Foundation leadership.
Stage 2   First line leader.
Stage 3   Mid-level leader.
Stage 4   Senior leader.
Stage 5   Executive leader.

There are a range of leadership development opportunities available for leaders, engagement with which are worth making (HMICFRS, 2024), especially as part of a talent development strategy. For example, a police officer can seek promotion to police sergeant (who leads a team overseeing their daily tasks and taking responsibility for their welfare), then move to a mid-level leadership role as an inspector, senior leadership role as chief inspector, superintendent and chief superintendent. Those in senior leadership positions may then apply to join the ranks of the police force executive as an assistant chief constable, deputy chief constable and finally chief constable or commissioner of the Metropolitan Police Service.

There are slightly over 21,000 police sergeants across the 43 police forces in England and Wales (Home Office, 2024). Green, Lynch and Lynch (2015) describe how leadership by sergeants on the frontline of policing is critical to ensure the delivery of an effective service, with these first line leaders focusing their skills on dealing with the current task (Pearson-Goff and Herrington, 2014). The influence of first line leaders (such as sergeants) is significant. The contemporary police sergeant's role had expanded significantly with greater responsibility, more accountability for meeting performance targets and many more administrative tasks (Butterfield, Edwards and Woodall, 2005).

Opportunities for the development of sergeants include in force and on-the-job training. Sergeants are selected and developed for promotion through the four steps of the National Police Promotions Framework (NPPF):

1   demonstration of competence in current rank,
2   examination of law and procedure,
3   local selection process and matching to vacancies, and
4   temporary promotion for 12 months and work-based assessment leading to confirmation in rank.

There are also locally delivered continuing professional development (CPD) opportunities, such as the College of Policing first line leaders programme, although Pepper et al. (2024) highlight how first line leaders require not only the encouragement and support from senior leaders to attend CPD, but importantly the time made available to do so. During 2024 and 2025, a new approach to the selection and development of sergeants is being trialled, the Sergeant and

Inspector Promotion and Progression (SIPP) process, this being better aligned to Stages 2 and 3 of the leadership standards.

There are centrally delivered courses for aspiring senior leaders, such as the Senior Leadership Programme (SLP), Multi Agency Gold Incident Command (MAGIC) and Executive Leadership Programme (ELP). Smith (2015) discusses Direct Entry (DE) leadership initiatives for policing in England and Wales, highlighting how such talent management schemes have been adopted in other countries such as Hong Kong and the Netherlands. Since 2014 it has been possible to join policing in England and Wales in a strategic leadership role as a DE Superintendent, or later in an operational role as a DE Inspector. Recruitment to the DE superintendents scheme was 'paused' in 2020, followed by a 'pause' to recruitment for new DE Inspectors. Opinions continue to be divided as to the merits of such schemes and the ability to transfer business skills in to policing practice.

Case studies illustrating professional practice

In the 1980s, the police service commenced recruiting civilian staff (now called staff) in to some policing roles in order to release officer time for operational duties. At the time the Home Office (1988) described the requirement not only to recruit civilian staff but also to provide development and a career structure to enable progression to leadership roles. As such police officer and staff leaders can find themselves using their expertise to lead combined teams of police officers, staff and volunteers.

> **Reflection by a sergeant leading a team of police officers and a volunteer special constable**
>
> This example demonstrates how a first line leader acting in a transactional way meets the College of Policing (2023) Leadership Standards Stage 2: *Expectation 1, Leading a team acting in the public interest, to prioritise public service, cutting crime and improving the safety and wellbeing of the public.*
>
> As a police sergeant leading a team of police officers and volunteers, there have been some occasions where I had to take control of the situation and directly task officers to swiftly complete specific actions in order to ensure both their safety and that of the public.
>
> For example, I was responsible for a four-officer team and a special constable (SC) working a night shift in a busy town centre. One Saturday night a report came across the radio that a group of people were fighting outside of a night club. As I was nearby on foot, I responded along with two other police officers and the SC, one officer in a car with the SC and another on foot. Conscious of the need to first assess the incident, on my arrival the fight seemed to have ended but I could see someone lying on the floor bleeding. The first officer attending had arrived in the car and with the SC was trying to move people away from the person on the floor and at that

moment the second officer arrived. I immediately took control of the scene and using a transactional approach, I directed the second officer to check the person lying on the floor, while I communicated what was happening to the control room via the radio. I then helped the first officer and SC move people away from the incident, before stepping back and ascertaining the current situation, which had now calmed and an ambulance had arrived for the injured person. I later praised all involved for a job well done.

A first line leader leading a joint police staff and police officer team of crime scene investigators

This example demonstrates how a first line leader acts in a transformational way meeting the College of Policing Leadership Standards Stage 2: *Expectation 13, Managing wellbeing and resilience.*

As a civilian crime scene manager and first line supervisor, I lead forensic investigations at major crime scenes such as murders or serious assaults. Working in often very difficult situations, it was always important to support, consider the wellbeing and motivate the team of crime scene investigators (CSIs) who could be both police officers and police staff.

For example, while leading the recovery of photographic, forensic and fingerprint evidence at an outdoor murder scene involving two victims laid at the edge of a field during the winter, it swiftly became imperative not only to protect and preserve the evidence to make sure it was not lost, but it was also important to ensure both the physical and psychological wellbeing of the CSIs working within the scene. Therefore adopting a transformational approach, I empowered the CSIs to make decisions in relation to evidence recording, recovery and packaging at the scene, while I focused on scheduling regular breaks in warm and dry vehicles, and arranged supplies of hot food and drinks. I also made sure that I was prepared to actively listen to any of their concerns and address any issues they raised.

Policing is becoming ever more global, with crime crossing national boundaries both online and offline. The attributes of leaders within the police service are transferable not only within policing across England and Wales but internationally, here exploring police leadership across both Canada and the USA.

Police leadership across Canada

Canada has a fraction of the officers compared with the UK or USA. In 2023, there were 71,472 sworn officers and about 5% of them were senior officers holding the rank of inspector, lieutenant or higher (Statistics Canada, 2024a). These officers are working within about 160 police services ranging in size from small stand-alone operations employing fewer than ten officers to the Royal Canadian Mounted Police (RCMP), which is a federal police service employing about 19,000 officers; 600 (3%) of whom held the rank of Inspector or higher (RCMP, 2021). Most Canadian officers are employed by municipal police services, but there are also three provincial police services (Ontario, Quebec, and Newfoundland and Labrador), several Indigenous police services, and the RCMP, which contracts with municipalities, eight provinces and three northern territories to deliver police services.

The majority of senior officers stay with one department for their entire careers, however as across England and Wales, a number of them leave their career-long employers to serve as Chiefs and in other senior roles within different police services. If rising from the ranks into a Chief's position, the leader may stay in that role for several contracted terms, usually four or five years, but few individuals transferring in as a Chief stay more than one term.

As in England and Wales, senior officers have traditionally risen through the ranks and are promoted based on their seniority and operational career experiences, few had formal academic training. Instead, most participated in career development courses offered by their employers and facilitated by organisations such as the Canadian Association of Chiefs of Police; and about one-quarter of senior officers are members of that organisation. Since the 2000s an increasing number of senior officers have earned academic degrees. Accessing higher education has been facilitated by a growing number of academic programmes throughout the country that offer undergraduate and postgraduate degrees in policing. While few leadership positions formally require a degree, a growing number of police services are requiring that new officers have successfully completed an undergraduate diploma or degree.

Like their counterparts in other nations, senior police officers in Canada are expected to manage a rapidly evolving political, economic, demographic and social context and respond to those changes. There are increasing demands on their services in an era of declining budgets, increasing accountability and high public expectations. Movements like 'Black Lives Matter' and calls to defund the police have raised significant questions as to whether police leaders are equipped with the right skills to address complex societal problems. For example, in 2022 the 'Freedom Convoy', a group of truckers protesting vaccine mandates, descended on Canada's capital, Ottawa, and brought the downtown to a standstill. The Ottawa Police were ill-equipped to handle the protest, which lasted several weeks, and eventually the Emergencies Act was invoked for the first time in Canadian history to disperse the protesters.

Some of these challenges are distinctively Canadian, including policing the world's second largest nation – in terms of landmass – that is home to only 41 million people, and about three-quarters of them living within 150 kilometres of the US border. The police must provide services to the rest of the nation including rural, remote and isolated locations, and most rural RCMP detachments, for example, are thousands of kilometres away from their national headquarters.

Whereas, other challenges are also common to other wealthy, democratic nations. For example, Canada's crime-related problems include a growing prevalence of cyber-related offences and these crimes increased by 119% between 2018 and 2022 (Statistics Canada, 2024b). The Police Executive Research Forum (2018) discusses that technology is changing the nature of crime, and how it is investigated. One of the most significant challenges in responding to many of those offences is their origin in other nations, and investigators are expected to work with officials from those countries. Canadian police services, however, have generally been slow to respond to these changes and the Commissioner of the RCMP observes how the increasing demands of international investigations into crimes involving the internet require the RCMP to keep pace with the available investigative tools and resources (Tunney, 2018). The expectations of police leaders are changing along with increasing demands and a departure from their traditional roles, this will require new ways of thinking about and responding to crime. The changing context for policing has led to ongoing debates about the most appropriate role for the police (Police Executive Research Forum, 2018) and some scholars contend that the traditional approach to policing needs to be redesigned, reengineered or reinvented (Lum & Nagin, 2017; Millie & Bullock, 2012).

Kempa (2014) observes that debates over the role of the police often arise after economic transformations or contractions in the business cycle occur, as they lead to larger questions about the nature of government interventions, the definitions of public safety and the roles the police should play in maintaining order and public safety. Like in the USA, England and Wales, Canadian police services are still suffering from the effects of recession. The Covid pandemic has only exacerbated these challenges. In an era of austerity, one challenge for Canadian police leaders is resisting the demands of their government funders to pay for police services through user fees, fines (such as traffic violations) and the seizure of assets (Valiante, 2018; Canadian Constitution Foundation, 2016). The problem with this approach to bolstering resources is that the public begins to see the police as tax collectors rather than law enforcers and this may reduce their legitimacy and public support. US studies, for example, have shown that funding police operations through fines has a corrosive effect on police–community relationships (US Department of Justice, 2015).

There have also been a series of internal changes that are creating new challenges for police leaders. Most of these changes are related to personnel issues and include decreases in the number of individuals wanting to become police officers, the difficulty in recruiting a representative workforce, such as female officers and minority groups (including Canadians of Indigenous ancestry) and retaining these individuals. Police leaders are also expected to manage a growing proportion of new generation workers who have a different vision of policing than their predecessors and see policing as a job rather than a career. They are more likely than their older counterparts to advocate for a healthy work–life balance, and these officers can create friction with their older counterparts with their desire to have meaningful input into operational issues despite their inexperience. In order to manage such conflicting goals, forward-looking police leaders are key to implementing strategies to better engage new generations of officers (Batts, Smoot & Scrivner, 2012), continuing to identify a number of skills that should be developed by leaders including recognising global perspectives, being creative, adaptive and leading the implementation of new and innovative ideas so that they become embedded in policing (Batts, Smoot & Scrivner, 2012).

When Canadian police officers and civilian stakeholders were asked about the barriers to organisational reforms, they identified the following internal factors: resource limitations, organisational culture, resistance to change and police leadership (Duxbury et al., 2018). As almost all Canadian police services are being asked to 'do more with less', it is not surprising that resource limitations are considered a barrier to meaningful change. Moreover, many scholars have observed that the organisational culture of the police and resistance to change are intimately intertwined. More troubling is the finding that police leaders are considered an obstacle to reform rather than an asset.

Taken together, these internal and external environmental changes are placing considerable demands on police leadership in Canada. There is increasing evidence that the leadership efforts of senior officers from some organisations have fallen short and their conduct has harmed their organisations and the personnel working within them. A review of media accounts, for example, reveals that a growing number of police officers and civilian employees are suing Canadian police services as these agencies failed to provide workplaces free of bullying, harassment and sexual violence. Individual employees have sued police services across the country alleging discrimination and mistreatment.

Perhaps the most serious and widespread allegations of misconduct have been levelled against the RCMP and at least three class-action lawsuits, representing thousands of current and former employees, have been launched since 2010. The RCMP has acknowledged the problems within the agency, and a report written by the Civilian Review and Complaints Commission for the RCMP (2017) found that a culture of dysfunction existed in the agency and there was internal resistance to change that culture. According to the Commission, the dysfunctional organisational environment was due to shortcomings in senior leadership and their failure to foster a leadership culture. These problems were attributed to the agency's history, paramilitary origins and its culture. With respect to an absence of senior leadership, the Commission found that mid-level managers, responsible for fixing the organisation's culture, had a vested interest in maintaining the status quo and had little willingness to reduce workplace harassment and bullying. In terms of failing to foster a leadership culture, the Commission identified that promotion processes made things worse by rewarding self-promotion rather than leadership ability. As most officers rise through the ranks based on their operational knowledge and skills, they can lack the specialised knowledge that would enhance their leadership abilities and enable them to create a healthier and more productive workplace.

Police leadership across the United States

The USA has almost 18,000 police agencies which have the responsibility of enforcing the law, detecting crime and apprehension of criminals as the core requirements of their profession. Training for police officers on the frontline focuses on law enforcement, and less on keeping the peace or community service and partnerships. However, research indicates that community and public service by the police builds support and co-operation by working with citizens in non-punitive and supportive ways (Culbertson & Shin, 1989). This is exacerbated by contemporary records of both individual police officers, and entire police agencies, failing to serve the public (Schafer, 2008). The President's Task Force on 21st Century Policing (2015) discusses the divide in relationships between local policing and the communities they serve and protect. There is consequently a need for effective leadership in shaping modern police organisations to meet societal expectations of crime fighting and, likely more importantly, to make an effectual and long-lasting impact on community-level criminality.

The number of full-time sworn law enforcement officers in the USA has increased by about 7% (to approximately 787,500), while the population of the United States has increased by about 26% (to approximately 342 million). The latest federal data on police show that from 1996 to 2018, the number of full-time sworn officers per 1,000 US residents decreased from 2.50 to 2.41 (Gardner & Scott, 2022). The ratios of police officers to their community populations coupled with the small size of many police agencies in the nation create a situation where individual officers must provide substantial individual and organisational leadership, regardless of rank. Anderson, Gisborne and Holliday (2006) assert that all American police officers (this includes sheriff's deputies, constable offices, state police and other variations of 'police' in the United States) serve as leaders in their communities and consequently engage in some form of leadership in the performance of their duties, even among those with no obvious rank.

As in the UK, US police officers often work with extremely limited supervision and make countless high-discretion decisions every shift (Schafer, 2008; Engel, 2001). Police executive officers in the USA have been encouraged to motivate the development of leadership at all levels, recognising that split-second decision making and taking control of potentially dangerous or unpredictable situations is a form of leadership (Andreescu & Vito, 2010). Leadership development for police officers in the USA, therefore, is seen as taking a long view in that the profession must begin leadership training early in an officer's career, providing them with opportunities to learn through positive role modelling and mentorship. US police, for example, are trained to make life or death decisions on their own, without immediate supervisory influence. When confronted with a subject with a hand-gun (or other potentially deadly weapon), for example, unlike the UK, all US police officers are trained to make situational 'shoot or don't shoot' decisions without the need to rely on a superior officer for authority. Leadership for those in frontline positions therefore requires that these officers are appropriately trained to make good, legal and community-acceptable decisions on their own. Overall, according to Andreescu and Vito (2010), the literature on police leadership points to the importance of the relationship between senior police leaders and their followers.

The Federal Bureau for Investigation (FBI) delivers a leadership programme for local, municipal, state and federal police leaders with police agencies nominating supervisory personnel to attend the programme along with a small number of international police leaders. A research study focusing on police leaders attending this programme at the FBI National Academy found respondents indicated that effective leadership was limited by barriers, including finite resources, organisational structure, cultural opposition, external influences and internal agency politics, among others (Schafer, 2008). Participants in this study indicated that high-ranking police officials were key in developing and shaping the leadership and individual officer efficacy, providing positive leadership modelling behaviours for the entire agency (Schafer, 2008).

Andreescu and Vito (2010) studied police managers attending the Administrative Officers Course at the Southern Police Institute (AOC/SPI), a highly regarded police leadership school based on the FBI National Academy model. They found that managers who could reconcile conflict and reduce disorder, take on a leadership role, demonstrate consideration for the comfort and wellbeing of followers, integrate group members into the organisation and have the foresight to predict future outcomes accurately exemplified the most ideal behaviours of police managers. Krimmel and Lindermuth (2001) found that Pennsylvania city managers ranked police chiefs higher if they had previously managed a unionised police department, had at least some college credits or who were graduates of the FBI National Academy than those who did not possess such attributes.

While traditionally the authoritarian style of leadership was predominant in US policing agencies and associated organisations, as across the UK there has been a transition more recently to a transformational style of leadership, where police leaders encourage subordinates to make decisions and set their own goals (Wolf, 1998). Can, Hendy and Can (2017) identify three leadership dimensions that frontline officers perceive to be the most important in their immediate supervisors, providing clear communication, offering appropriate training and co-operation, and leading with fairness and honesty. However, styles vary greatly between US police departments and specific leaders, and conditions may cause leadership styles to change based on the situation (Sarver and Miller, 2014).

Future developments

The notion of evidence-based criminal justice interventions was first introduced in the 1990s and this concept has been gaining interest ever since. Evidence-based policing (EBP) originated with Sherman's (1998) contention that decisions about deploying the police ought to be based on the results of well-designed research. Police officers and researchers, he argued, should work together to take advantage of each other's respective knowledge, skills and experiences to increase police effectiveness and efficiency. EBP has gained considerable interest since that time, with Huey et al. (2018) observing that EBP has been established across Australia, New Zealand, Canada, the UK and USA with the sharing of research and practice across EBP events including conferences, workshops and accredited academic study. Information also being disseminated to researchers and practitioners using contemporary social media and peer-reviewed journals.

The movement to incorporate a greater number of police interventions based on the outcomes of research continues to gain pace, especially in jurisdictions where police services are expected to deliver the most cost-effective services. Martin and Mazerolle (2015) suggest that future police leaders will need to engage with the government and decision makers using such a tested evidence base to support their cases for enhanced financial and resource allocations. As the police service in England and Wales evolves its status as a profession, police leaders of the future also need to adopt the used of such an evidence base to inform and enable enhanced decision-making capacities resulting in better outcomes for both the service and the wider community they serve. The influence of first line leaders is pivotal in such wider adoption of EBP across the service (Pepper et al. 2024). The development and dissemination of authorised professional practice (APP) by the College of Policing also supports police leaders, while the 'What Works Centre' (College of Policing, 2017) assists in disseminating the best available evidence.

Internationally the interest and use of EBP to inform practice continues to grow. Huey et al. (2017) interviewed 29 senior police officers in Canada and all believed that operational decisions should be informed by scientific research, but they also observed that few police leadership programmes offered enough knowledge to adequately inform participants about the benefits of police research and EBP. Most of their respondents said that the best exposure to research occurred in formal academic programmes such as during postgraduate study, although some also received information about EBP from in-house personnel such as crime analysts, while others educated themselves about this approach. Given these findings the most effective way to expand EBP is to incorporate this information in formal academic programmes, provide a basic orientation to EBP in police training, expand this exposure in ongoing in-service officer training, and recruit officers who already have some knowledge about applying the findings from research to solve everyday problems (Huey et al., 2017).

Campbell and Kodz (2011) support the view that the evidence base for leadership within policing should continue to grow in order to support the varied and adaptable needs of contemporary policing. Martin and Mazerolle (2015) also support this lack of existing evidence for police leaders, while proposing that police leaders themselves need to recognise the current lack of evidence and champion its continued growth. This being supported by the College of Policing (2023) leadership standards, with stages calling for leaders to use the evidence-base to inform decision making. The College of Policing (2015) also identifies the importance of learning lessons on successful leadership, both nationally and internationally, from commercial businesses and public services outside of policing.

HMICFRS (2018) suggests that the police service should do more to both understand and develop the attributes and skills of its existing workforce, enabling the identification and development of future police leaders, all of whom have an impact on the professional recognition of the service. A prime example of this is the professional skills of leadership developed throughout their service as a police officers, staff or volunteers which are immense and should be recognised for their transferability not only within the organisation but beyond. Looking forward, such knowledge, understanding and skills should be recognised by an appropriate level of academic award which blends not only the practical skills of leadership, but also the academic underpinning knowledge and understanding of EBP to assist in identifying what works within leadership and why.

There is no doubt, however, that future senior police leaders have to balance a great deal of knowledge, skills and abilities to be effective. This includes not only adhering to the core principles of policing by consent displaying their honesty, integrity and trustworthiness, but also being visionary, open minded, resilient, inclusive and able to lead change, while being both politically astute and financially aware of the business of policing.

Conclusion

Police leaders are expected to lead a rapidly changing set of internal and external conditions where every government service expects more to be achieved with less. Moreover, these enhanced policing services must be delivered in an era of high public expectations and accountability driven by social media, the political environment, evolving social demographics (of the general public as well as within our police services) and the public's demands for immediate solutions to complex problems. Responding to these challenges places great demands on police leaders regardless of where they are employed, their rank, role or makeup of their agencies. While the expectations placed on leaders may vary, there is a common set of leadership skills and attributes these officers, staff and volunteers require in order to meet such expectations. The College of Policing (2023) have set out their expectations for leaders in policing across England and Wales through establishing leadership standards.

Contemporary police leaders, whether in England and Wales, USA or Canada, are learning that the approaches they used in the past are no longer completely effective in today's fast-paced and increasingly global policing environment, where effective leadership is critical in enhancing the professionalism of the service.

Although there seems to be general consensus on the value of a transformational approach (Wolf, 1998; Dobby et al., 2004; Vito et al., 2014), police leaders must be adept at adopting a blend of leadership styles most appropriate for dealing with the situation they face (Campbell and Kodz, 2011; Caless, 2011), while using the best evidence available to inform their decisions. Current and future leaders within the service need to continue to adopt and adapt their approaches to protect all of communities they serve.

> **Evidence-based case study illustrating leadership professional practice**
>
> Good leadership means championing good practice. Their role as the first line leader is essential in creating an inclusive environment, supporting staff wellbeing and enhancing policing for the general public. Good leaders should encourage and empower staff to be innovative and take the initiative, not only to resolve the problems faced but be creative and forward thinking.
>
> As an example, police officers and staff are recruited to work as tactical flight officers (TFOs) in one of 15 National Police Air Services (NPAS) regional bases means requiring the development of new knowledge and skills relating to aviation, aviation safety and helicopter operations, along with learning how to operate specialist equipment for policing such as the thermal imaging. Developing the competences and skills to work effectively in both day and night operations requires ability, commitment from the individual and the support of their leaders.
>
> A new recruit to one of the NPAS units highlighted to their leader how the requirement for the helicopter to land for refuelling while supporting an incident reduced its effectiveness and increased the time away from supporting the officers on the ground. Being innovative, the new TFO went on to identify that near one of the NPAS bases was a civil aviation academy which taught, qualified and certified operators in 'hot refuelling', which is where the aircraft can be refuelled while the main engine is running. Their leader acknowledged this and supported the TFO by seeking and negotiating for police force funding, then rearranged shifts so that a number of TFOs could attend the 'hot refuelling' course, become certified and as a result refuel the helicopter while the engine was running. This resulted in increased turn-around times from the helicopter landing to once again becoming airborne and returning to operations.
>
> The innovative approach of the TFO, with the empowerment of their first line leader in a transformational leadership style, increased the service offered to the public by one of the NPAS helicopter bases and its crews.

Reflective question

Reflect upon the challenges you could face as a sergeant leading a shift (06:00 to 14:00) of three officers, two police community support officers (PCSOs) and two marked vehicles, tasked with policing a small rural town of 9,000 inhabitants and the surrounding 100 square kilometres of predominantly farmland, road network and public footpaths.

Acknowledgement

We'd like to dedicate this chapter to our co-author and friend Rick Ruddell who passed away in January 2023. Rick was a prolific scholar, a wonderful colleague, and an all-around good guy. We are fortunate to have worked with and learned from him. His presence, insights and friendship are dearly missed.

References

Amundsen, S., and Martinsen, O, L. (2014). Empowering Leadership: construct clarification, conceptualization and validation of a new scale. *Leadership Quarterley*, 25 (3), 487–511. https://doi.org/10.1016/j.leaqua.2013.11.009.

Anderson, T. D., Gisborne, K. & Holliday, P. (2006). *Every Officer Is a Leader*, 2nd edition. Victoria: Trafford Publishing.

Andreescu, V. & Vito, G. F. (2010). An Exploratory Study on Ideal Leadership Behaviour: The Opinions of American Police Managers. *International Journal of Police Science & Management*, 12(4), 567–583. https://doi.org/10.1350/ijps.2010.12.4.20.

Barker, K., Baker, M., & Watkins, A. (2021). In City After City, Police Mishandled Black Lives Matter Protests. *The New York Times*, 20 March. [online]. www.nytimes.com/2021/03/20/us/protests-policing-george-floyd.html (accessed 16 July 2024).

Baroness Casey Review. (2023). Final Report: An independent review into the standards of behaviour and internal culture of the Metropolitan Police Service. [online]. www.met.police.uk/SysSiteAssets/media/downloads/met/about-us/baroness-casey-review/update-march-2023/baroness-casey-review-march-2023a.pdf (accessed 19 July 2024).

Bates, S. (2018). The Bloody Clash Which Changed Britain. *The Guardian*, 4 January. [online]. www.theguardian.com/news/2018/jan/04/peterloo-massacre-bloody-clash-that-changed-britain (accessed 22 July 2024).

Batts, A. W., Smoot, S. M. & Scrivner, E. (2012). *Police Leadership Challenges in a Changing World*. Cambridge, MA: Harvard Kennedy School.

Beare, M. E. & Des Rosiers, N. (2015). Introduction. In M. E. Beare, N. Des Rosiers & A. C. Deshman (eds), *Putting the State on Trial: The Policing of Protest During the G20 Summit* (pp. 3–22). Vancouver, BC: University of British Columbia Press.

Butterfield, R., Edwards, C. & Woodall, J. (2005). The New Public Management and Managerial Roles: The Case of the Police Sergeant. *British Journal of Management*, 16(4), 329–341. https://doi.org/10.1111/j.1467-8551.2005.00466.x.

Caless, B. (2011). *Policing at the Top: The Roles, Values and Attitudes of Chief Police Officers*. Bristol: Policy Press.

Campbell, I. & Kodz, J. (2011). *What Makes Great Police Leadership? What Research Can Tell Us About the Effectiveness of Different Leadership Styles, Competencies and Behaviours: A Rapid Evidence Review*. Bramshill: National Police Improvement Agency.

Can, S. H., Hendy, H. M. & Can, M. B. E. (2017). A Pilot Study to Develop the Police Transformational Leadership Scale (PTLS) and Examine Its Associations with Psychosocial Well-Being of Officers. *Journal of Police and Criminal Psychology*, 32, 105–113. https://doi.org/10.1007/s11896-016-9204-y.

Canadian Constitution Foundation. (2016). *Civil Forfeiture in Canada (2015–2016)*. Calgary, AB: Author.

Canadian Press. (2018). Coalition Avenir Quebec Candidate Called to Explain Allegation of 'Political Interference' in Policing. *National Post*, 2 September. [online]. https://na

tionalpost.com/news/politics/candidate-called-to-explain-allegation-of-political-interference-in-policing (accessed 12 December 2018).

Civilian Review and Complaints Commission for the RCMP. (2017). *Report into Workplace Harassment in the RCMP*. Ottawa, ON: Author.

College of Policing. (2015). *Leadership Review*. Ryton: College of Policing.

College of Policing. (2017). What Works Centre for Crime Reduction: Research. [online]. https://whatworks.college.police.uk/Research/Pages/default.aspx (accessed 25 November 2018).

College of Policing. (2023). Leadership Standards. [online]. www.college.police.uk/career-learning/leadership/leadership-standards (accessed 9 July 2024).

College of Policing. (2024). Professional Profile: Response Constable v1.0. [online]. https://profdev.college.police.uk/professional-profiles/profiles/job-families-sub-groups/ (accessed 8 July 2024).

Culbertson, H. M. & Shin, H. (1989). Police in America: A Study of Changing Institutional Roles as Viewed by Constituents. *Public Relations Research Annual*, 1, 155–174. [online]. https://login.ezproxy.net.ucf.edu/login?auth=shibb&url=https://search.ebscohost.com/login.aspx?direct=true&db=buh&AN=6433357&site=eds-live&scope=site (accessed 9 December 2018).

Dobby, J., Anscombe. J. & Tuffin. R. (2004). Police Leadership: Expectations and Impact. [online]. https://webarchive.nationalarchives.gov.uk/20110218140652/ http://rds.homeoffice.gov.uk/rds/pdfs04/rdsolr2004.pdf (accessed 17 November 2018).

Duxbury, L., Bennell, C., Halinski, M. & Murphy, S. (2018). Change or Be Changed: Diagnosing the Readiness to Change in the Canadian Police Sector. *Police Journal: Theory, Practice and Principles*, 91(4), 316–338. https://doi.org/10.1177/0032258X177403.

Engel, R. S. (2001). Supervisory Styles of Patrol Sergeants and Lieutenants. *Journal of Criminal Justice*, 29(1), 341–355. https://doi.org/10.1016/S0047-2352(01)00091-5.

Gardner, A. & Scott, K. (2022). Census of State and Local Law Enforcement Agencies, 2018 – Statistical Table. [online]. www.bjs.gov/index.cfm?ty=pbdetail&iid=6366 (accessed 15 July 2024).

George, W. (2003). *Authentic Leadership: Rediscovering the Secrets to Creating Lasting Value*. San Francisco, CA: Jossey-Bass.

Green, E., Lynch, R. & Lynch, S. (2015). *The Police Manager*, 7th edition. Abingdon: Routledge.

Hassan, S., Mahsud, R., Yukl, G. & Prussia, G. E. (2013). Ethical and empowering leadership and leader effectiveness. *Journal of Managerial Psychology*, 28(2), 133–146. https://doi.org/10.1108/02683941311300252.

HMICFRS. (2018). *PEEL: Police Leadership 2017 – A National Overview*. London: Her Majesty's Inspectorate of Constabulary and Fire & Rescue Services.

HMICFRS. (2024). State of Policing: The Annual Assessment of Policing in England and Wales 2023. [online]. https://hmicfrs.justiceinspectorates.gov.uk/publication-html/state-of-policing-the-annual-assessment-of-policing-in-england-and-wales-2023/ (accessed 22 July 2024).

Home Office. (1988). *Circular 105/1988: Civilian Staff in the Police Service*. London: Home Office.

Home Office. (2012). FOI Release: Definition of Policing by Consent. [online]. www.gov.uk/government/publications/policing-by-consent/definition-of-policing-by-consent (3 July 2024).

Home Office. (2024). Police Workforce, England and Wales: 31 March 2023. [online]. www.gov.uk/government/statistics/police-workforce-england-and-wales-31-march-2023/police-workforce-england-and-wales-31-march-2023 (accessed 9 July 2024).

Huey, L., Blaskovits, B., Bennell, C., Kalyal, H. & Walker, T. (2017). To What Extent Do Canadian Police Professionals Believe That Their Agencies Are 'Targeting, Testing, and Tracking' New Policing Strategies and Programs? *Police Practice and Research*, 18(6), 544–555. https://doi.org/10.1080/15614263.2017.1363968.

Huey, L., Kalyal, H., Peladeau, H. & Lindsay, F. (2018). 'If You're Gonna Make a Decision, You Should Understand the Rationale': Are Police Leadership Programs Preparing Canadian Police Leaders for Evidence-Based Policing? *Policing: A Journal of Policy and Practice*, 15(1), 197–207. https://doi.org/10.1093/police/pay086.

Kempa, M. (2014). *Understanding the Historical Relationship Between Economics and Change in Policing: A Policy Framework*. Ottawa, ON: Canadian Police College.

Kratcoski, P. (2023). Police Leadership: A Learning Experience. In A. D. Verma & K. Das (eds), *Police Leaders as Thinkers* (pp. 35–64). Cham: Springer. https://doi.org/10.1007/978-3-031-19700-0_3.

Krimmel, J. T. & Lindermuth, P. (2001). Police Chief Performance and Leadership Styles. *Police Quarterly*, 4(4), 469–483. https://doi.org/10.1177/109861101129197950.

Lum, C. & Nagin, D. S. (2017). Reinventing American Policing. *Crime and Justice*, 46(1), 339–393. https://doi.org/10.1086/688462.

Martin, P. & Mazerolle, L. (2015). Police Leadership in Fostering Evidence-Based Agency Reform. *Policing*, 10(1), 34–43. https://doi.org/10.1093/police/pav031.

McLean, K. (2017). 10 Essential Attributes of Effective Leaders. [online]. www.policechiefmagazine.org/10-essential-attributes-of-effective-leaders/?ref=08069055809254ebf8d1cc400043323a (accessed 16 December 2018).

Millie, A. & Bullock, K. (2012). Re-imagining Policing Post-austerity. *British Academy Review*, 19(1), 16–18.

Neyroud. P. (2011). *Review of Police Leadership and Training: Volume One*. London: Home Office.

Pearson-Goff, M. & Herrington, V. (2014). Police Leadership: A Systematic Review of the Literature. *Policing: A Journal of Policy and Practice*, 8(1), 14–26. https://doi.org/10.1093/police/pat027.

Pepper, I., Rogers, C. & Turner, J. (2024). The Adoption of Evidence-Based Policing: The Pivotal Role of First-Line Police Leaders across England and Wales. *International Journal of Emergency Services*, 13(1), 111–122. https://doi.org/10.1108/IJES-05-2023-0020.

Police Executive Research Forum. (2018). *The Changing Nature of Crime and Criminal Investigations*. Washington, DC: Author.

President's Task Force on 21st Century Policing. (2015). *Final Report of the President's Task Force on 21st Century Policing*. Washington, DC: Office of Community Oriented Policing Services.

RCMP. (2021). About the RCMP. [online]. www.rcmp-grc.gc.ca/en/about-rcmp (accessed 20 June 2024).

Roach, K. (2017). Police Government Relations and Police Independence. [online]. www.cepcsj.gouv.qc.ca/fileadmin/documents_client/recherche/Quebec_Police_Independence_pour_depot.pdf (accessed 12 December 2018).

Sarver, M. & Miller, H. (2014). Police Chief Leadership Styles and Effectiveness. *Policing: An International Journal of Police Strategies & Management*, 37(1), 126–143. https://doi.org/10.1108/PIJPSM-03-2013-0028.

Schafer, J. A. (2008). Developing Effective Leadership in Policing: Perils, Pitfalls, and Paths Forward. *Policing: An International Journal of Police Strategies & Management*, 32(2), 238–260. https://doi.org/10.1108/13639510910958163.

Sherman, L. W. (1998). *Evidence Based Policing*. Washington, DC: Police Foundation.

Smith, R. (2015). Talent management: Building the case for direct entry into leadership roles in British policing. *The Police Journal*, 88(2), 160–173. https://doi.org/10.1177/0032258X15579357.

Statistics Canada. (2024a). Police Personnel by Detailed Rank, Duties, and Gender. Table 35-10-0078-01. [online]. https://doi.org/10.25318/3510007801-eng (accessed 20 June 2024).

Statistics Canada. (2024b). Police-reported Cybercrime, by Cyber-related Violation, Canada. Table: 35-10-0001-01. [online]. https://doi.org/10.25318/3510000101-eng (accessed 26 June 2024).

Taylor, F. (1911). *The Principles of Scientific Management*. New York: Harper & Brothers.

Tunney, C. (2018). RCMP's Ability to Police Digital Realm 'Rapidly Declining' Commissioner Warned. *CBC News*, 24 September [online]. www.cbc.ca/news/politics/lucki-briefing-binde-cybercrime-1.4831340 (accessed 13 December 2018).

US Department of Justice. (2015). *Investigation of the Ferguson Police Department*. Washington, DC: Author.

Valiante, G. (2018). Montreal Eliminates Traffic and Parking Ticket Quota System. *The Globe and Mail*. [online]. www.theglobeandmail.com/news/national/montreal-eliminates-traffic-and-parking-ticket-quotas/article37674834/ (accessed 13 December 2018).

Vito, G., Higgins, G. & Denney, A. (2014). Transactional and Transformational Leadership. *Policing: An International Journal of Police Strategies & Management*, 37(4), 809–822. https://doi.org/10.1108/PIJPSM-01-2014-0008.

Wolf, R. A. (1998). Campus Safety Directors: A Leadership Frame Analysis. Dissertation, University of Central Florida. https://stars.library.ucf.edu/rtd/2585.

Index

Page numbers in *italics* denote figures, those in **bold** denote tables.

7 July 2005 London bombings (7/7) 170, 174, 182
9/11 168, 173, 177, 182

A (FC) and Others (FC) v Secretary of State for the Home Department (2004) 69
absolute rights 68
accompanied patrol status (APS) 203
accountability 11, 12, 13, 14, 66, 216, 230, 233, 236, 242
accurate misrepresentation 34
ACPO *see* Association of Chief Police Officers
active learning 27, 32
actus reus 50
Adlam, R. 35
adversarial model of justice 50, 56
age profile of police officers 150
aggression, controlled 101, 103
AI *see* artificial intelligence
Al-Qaeda 168
Alanov v Chief Constable of Sussex (2012) 75
alcohol use/dependency 138, 148
Alderson, J. 128, 130
algorithms 117, 118
Allport's Scale of Prejudice and Discrimination 16
Amman, Sudesh 180
Anderson Report (2017) 174, 178
Anderson, T. D. 239
Andreescu, V. 230
Angry Brigade 169
anomie 45
anti-social behaviour (ASB) 108–109, 132, 139
anti-terrorism 168, 177

Anti-Terrorism Branch (SO13) 169, 170
Anti-Terrorism, Crime and Security Act (2001) 69
antisemitism 171
appeal courts 51
Argyris, C. 27, 28, 222
Ariel, B. 86
Aristotle 32
arrest 68, 71; and equality and human rights 19–20; powers of 66, 70, 74–76, 78
artificial intelligence (AI): and crime prevention 58, 138; and neighbourhood policing 138; and police—community communication 107; and proactive policing 138; as problem-solving tool 118
Assistant Commissioner Special Operations 170
Association of Chief Police Officers (ACPO) 18, 127; Good Practice Guide for Digital Evidence 188
Association of Chief Police Officers, Terrorism and Allied Matters (ACPO-TAM) 174
Association of Police and Crime Commissioners & National Police Chiefs' Council 192
Attorney General 49
Attorney-General v MGN Limited and News Group Newspapers Ltd (2011) 68
attrition: domestic abuse (DA) 155, 156–160; rape and serious sexual offending (RASSO) 146–149
austerity measures 58–59, 130, 208, 237
Austin v Metropolitan Police Commissioner (2009) 72

Austin v The United Kingdom (2012) 72
Australia 2, 92, 116, 176, 241
authentic leaders 232
Authorised Professional Practice (APP) guidance 37, 241
authoritarian leadership 230

Bacon, M. 36, 37
Barends, E. 82, 89, 91, 92
Baroness Casey Review 3, 10, 26, 36, 37, 121, 230
Barrow-Grint, K. 155, 156, 159, 160
Basford, L. 135
Bayley, D. H. 101
beat meetings 134
Beccaria, Cesare 43
Becker, H. S. 46
behavioural chart 27
Bentham, Jeremy 43
Berry, G. 203
Betari's Box Framework 29
bias, unconscious 11, 14, 15
biological explanations for crime 44–45
Bittner, E. 101
black communities: policing of 10, 128; *see also* Brixton riots (1981)
Black Lives Matter 10, 236
Bletchley Park 176
Bluedorn, A. C. 158
body-worn video (BWV) 103
Bowers, K. 87
Braga, A. 117, 136
Brasher, K. 106
Brewster, N. 157
British Crime Survey (BCS) 128; *see also* Crime Survey for England and Wales
British Transport Police (BTP) 2
Brixton riots (1981) 10, 65, 66, 128
Brockbank, A. 216, 222, 224
Brodeur, J. P. 174–175, 176
'broken windows' theory 45, 114, 115
Brown, J. 90, 91
Brown, R. L. 149
Bruce-Foulds, C. 217
'Building Communities, Beating Crime' (White Paper, 2004) 129
Bulley, Nicola 99
Bullock, K. 121, 129, 204
Bush, George W. 177
Byard, R. 105

CAADA 157, 158
Cabinet Office, National Cyber Strategy 186–187
Campbell Collaboration 115
Campbell, I. 241
Can, M. B. E. 240
Can, S. H. 240
Canada 176, 207; evidenced-based policing (EBP) 241; Freedom Convoy protest (2022) 236; G20 protests, Toronto (2010) 231; police culture 238; police funding 236, 237; police leadership 230, 231, 235–238, 241; police officer numbers and retention 237; Regina Riot (1932) 231; Winnipeg General Strike (1919) 231
Canadian Association of Police Officers 236
'canteen culture' 18
Carraccioli, L-A. 215
case evidence 83; disclosure of 49
Casey, Baroness *see* Baroness Casey Review
Centre for Justice Innovation 157
Centre for the Protection of the National Infrastructure (CPNI) 179
Channel de-radicalisation programme 179, 180
character, personal 12
Charman, S. 102
Cherney, A. 116
Chicago Alternative Policing Strategy (CAPS) 128–129
Chicago School 45
chief constables 4, 48
child abuse: investigations 187, 190, 191, 192–193; number of cases 189
Child Abuse Image Database (CAID) 190
Child Exploitation and Online Protection (CEOP) 190
child protection 189, 197
child sexual abuse material (CSAM) 191, 192
Children and Young Persons Act (1933) 55
City of London Police 2
Civil Nuclear Constabulary (CNC) 2
Civilian Review and Complaints Commission for the RCMP 238
civilian staff: leadership roles 234, 235; *see also* police support volunteers (PSVs)
Clark, G. 217
Clarke, R. 113
classical criminology 43–44
Clerkenwell Prison explosion (1867) 169
Cloud computing 190, 193–194, 197
Clutterbuck, D. 215, 216, 217, 220
coaching 214–228; coach characteristics 223–224; collaboration relationship in 224–225; dependence of trainee 224;

250 *Index*

and friendship 220; GROW model of communication 214; history and context 214–217; independence of trainee 225; influences on 219–223; and learning transitions 220–221; live 218–219; meaning of term 216; and meaning-making 221–222; performance focus 218, 220; and police procedure and legislation 220; power imbalance in relationship 224; in professional police practice 217–219; SMARTER model 221; in supporting change of role 215–216; trainee characteristics 224; as training requirement 215; transitions that require 222–223
code of ethics 6, 12; *see also* College of Policing, Code of Ethics
Codes of Practice: Crown Prosecutors 49; Ethical Policing 13; National Intelligence Model (NIM) 136; Police and Criminal Evidence Act of (PACE) 65, 66–67, 73, 74–76; Victims of Crime (Victims' Code) 21, 56, 57, 196
Codes of Professional Conduct 13
Cohen, A. 46
Cohen, L. 135–136
Cold War 170, 176
collaboration: in coaching/mentoring relationship 224–225; inter-agency 58, 119–120, 132–133, 137; *see also* partnership working
College of Policing (CoP) 2, 3, 4, 5, 10, 26, 99, 101, 208, 216; Authorised Professional Practice (APP) guidance 37, 241; Code of Ethics 9, 12–14, 22, 29, 36, 102, 103, 105, 107; Competency and Values Framework (CVF) 2, 6, 29, 115, 117, 215, 218, 219, 221; CyberDigiTools app 195; definition of vulnerability 149; and evidenced-based policing (EBP) 83–84; first line leaders programme 233; and leadership standards 229, 230, 232–233, 234, 235, 241, 242; National Decision Model (NDM) 12, 13, 102–103, 104, 107; and neighbourhood policing 115, 131, 133, 134, 138; and procedural justice 46; and reflective practice 29; Serious Sexual Assault Investigators Development Programme (SSAIDP) 152, 154; What Works Centre *see* What Works Centre for Crime Reduction (WWCCR)
collegiate approach 89
Collier, P. 137

Commissioned Rehabilitative Service providers 54
Committee on Standards in Public Life 12
'common law' offences 50
communication: choice of language 16–17, 98, 99; coding/decoding of 99; face-to-face 99, 101; future developments 107; GROW model of 214, 222; historical context 98–100; interferences 99; misinterpretation 100; non-verbal 99, 100, 101, 105, 108; one to one 99; online 99; radio 107; sensitive, respectful and appropriate (SRA) model of 16; skills of 98, 100–102, 106–107, 108–109; stop, look, listen model 101; and technological advancements 107; telephone 99, 107; verbal 105, 108
community, idea of 201
community engagement 130, 133–134, 138
community intelligence 137
community and neighbourhood policing 4, 44, 45, 115, 116–118, 121, 127–144; and artificial intelligence (AI) 138; community engagement 130, 133–134, 138; and crime prevention 131; current professional practice 130–138; foot patrols 135–136; future developments 138–139; historical context 127–130; intelligence-led approach 129–130, 136–138; multi-agency and partnership working 132–133, 137; public meetings 134–135; staffing issues 138; student volunteers 206
community rehabilitation companies (CRCs) 54
Community Safety Partnerships (CSPs) 132, 134
Community Scrutiny Panels (CSPs) 74
community sentences 51, 53, 54
Competency and Values Framework (CVF) 2, 6, 29, 115, 117, 215, 218, 219, 221
confession evidence 65, 75
conflict management 103–107, 108, 220
consequence 12
CONTEST (Counter-Terrorism Strategy) 168, 173, 176–181; ALARP (as low as reasonably practicable) principle 177; Prevent 177, 179–181; Protect and Prepare 177, 178–179; Pursue 177, 178
continuing professional development (CPD) 151, 160, 222, 233
controlled aggression 101, 103

Cook, D. 157
coroners 47
Coroners and Justice Act (2009) 51
cost-of-living crisis 58
Council of Europe 67, 68, 69, 76
Counter Terrorism Advisory Officers 179
Counter Terrorism Command (SO15) 170, 174
Counter Terrorism Operations Centre 174
counter-terrorism 48, 168–185; Counter-Terrorism Strategy *see* CONTEST; future developments 181–182; historical context 168–181; intelligence 169; Joint Terrorism Analysis Centre (JTAC) 173–174; Regional Counter-Terrorism Units (RCTU) 174–176
Counter-Terrorism Policing (CPT) 174
Counterterrorism and Security Act (2015) 179–180
courage 13
Court of Appeal 51
court system *see* criminal courts
Covert Standards teams 192
COVID-19 pandemic 48, 49–50, 58, 189, 237
Cox, Jo 171
CPD *see* continuing professional development
CPNI (Centre for the Protection of the National Infrastructure) 179
CPS *see* Crown Prosecution Service
crime: biological explanations for 44–45; causes of 43–47; definition of 43; and environment 33, 45–46; fear of 128, 129, 137; 'hot' model of 44; new forms of 58; organised 58, 75, 175, 209; psychological explanations for 45; recorded, analysis of 129; and social upheaval 45–46; sociological explanations for 45–46; spatial pattern of 45; subcultural theory of 46; transnational 175, 229
Crime and Disorder Act (1998) 55, 132
crime prevention 42, 44, 45, 115, 116; AI-enhanced 58, 138; community-based approaches 44, 45, 129; digitalisation of 117; and evidence-based policing (EBP) 120; and foot patrols 135–136; use of intelligence in 129; and neighbourhood policing 131; and partnership working 132; and problem-solving 114, 116, 117; situational 44, 136; zero-tolerance approaches 45

crime reduction 116, 118; *see also* crime prevention; What Works Centre for Crime Reduction (WWCCR)
Crime Survey for England and Wales 154; *see also* British Crime Survey
criminal courts 47, 50–51, 58, 59
Criminal Injuries Compensation Authority 47
criminal justice 42; definition of 42; technological advances impact on 58
Criminal Justice Act (1991) 55
Criminal Justice Act (2003) 55
Criminal Justice and Court Services Act (2000) 54
Criminal Justice and Public Order Act 1994 (CJPOA) 65, 71, 73, 74, 77
criminal justice system 59–60; and children and young people 55–56; criminal courts 47, 50–51, 58, 59; Crown Prosecution Service (CPS) 47, 49–50, 57, 59, 156; current professional practice 47–51; future developments and contemporary challenges 58–59; penal system 52–55; police as institution within 47–48, 59; victims and 56–57
criminal law 43
Criminal Law Act (1967) 9
criminal liability 50
criminal offences: *actus reus* element 50; classification of 50–51; indictable offences 50; *mens rea* element 50; summary offences 50, 51; 'triable either way' 50
Criminal Procedure and Investigations Act (1996) 21, 49
Criminal Procedure Rules (2020) 51
criminal responsibility, age of 55
criminology 42–47, 59; classical 43–44; definition of 42; positivist 44–45
critical thinking 29, 92, 221
Crown Courts 50, 51
Crown Prosecution Service (CPS) 47, 49–50, 57, 59, 156
culture, organisational *see* police culture
custodial sentences 51, 52–53, 54, 55
CVF *see* Competency and Values Framework
Cyber Crime Units (CCUs) 192
cybercrime *see* digital (cyber) crime

Dahl, J. 115
Danielson, L. 27–28
Darling, L. A. W. 223

Darwin, Charles 44
Dau, P. 86
Davies, M. 53
Dawson, P. 89, 158
de Grazia, S. 158
de-radicalisation 179, 180
decision-making 98, 102–103, 108; conflict management 104–105; evidence and 92; life or death, US police 239–240; National Decision Model (NDM) 12, 13, 102–103, 104; and professional experience 89; records 103
Degree Holder Entry Programme (DHEP) 5, 37, 186
dementia 106–107
democracy 35
democratic deficit 32
Denhardt, R. B. 158
Denney, A. 232
deportation 71
descriptive studies 86
Detective Constable Entry Programme (DCEP) 5, 153
Detective Degree Holder Entry Programme (DDHEP) 222
detention 71
deterrence 52, 53
Dewey, J. 27, 36
DHEP(Degree Holder Entry Programme) 5, 37, 186
differential association theory 46
digital (cyber) crime 48, 58, 186–190, 196–197, 208, 237; cyber-dependent crime 186, 187; cyber-enabled crime 4, 186–187
Digital Forensic Units (DFU) 189, 192, 196
digital forensics 187, 188, 189–193, 195–196, 198–199; child abuse investigations 187, 190, 191, 192–193; ISO 17025 188, 189; mobile forensics 197
digital hygiene 194–195
Digital Media Investigator (DMI) teams 192
digital policing 117, 118, 186–200; current professional practice 190–196; future developments 196–197; historical context 187190
Digital UK Police Memorial 203
dignity 149
Direct Entry (DE) leadership initiatives 234
Director of Public Prosecutions 49
disclosure of evidence 49
discretion 32, 33–34, 119
discrimination 11, 15, 16–22, 66, 231, 238

disinformation, online 58
diversion interventions 46
diversity 8, 11, 14, 27, 208, 219, 224
diversity, equality and inclusion (DEI) 121, 232
Domestic Abuse Act (2022) 145
Domestic Abuse Commissioner 155
domestic abuse (DA) 57, 101, 119, 145, 146, 154–160, 161; 'absent-victim' prosecution 156; attrition 155, 156–160; definition of 145; Joint DA Action Plan 155; specialist domestic violence courts (SDVCs) 157; statistics 154–155; temporal sequencing and attrition 156, 158–160; victim withdrawal of complaints 156, 158, **159**, 159–160; vulnerability 154–156, 158, 160
domestic abuse risk assessments (DARA) 119
Domestic Abuse, Stalking and Harassment and Honour-based Violence (DASH) tool 155
domestic incidents 101, 102, 119
Domestic Violence, Crime and Victims Act (2004) 56, 57
dominance, responses to 16
Donnelly, D. 117
drug use/dependency 138
Duane, F. 106
Duggan, Mark 103
Dunn-Koczorowski, Oskar 171
Durkheim, E. 45

ECHR see European Convention on Human Rights and Fundamental Freedoms
Eck, J. 118
economic austerity 58–59, 130, 208, 237
economic values 12
ECtHR see European Court of Human Rights
education and training: Canadian senior police officers 236; and coaching/mentoring need 215; National Policing Curriculum (NPC) 2, 3, 107, 150; Policing Education Qualifications Framework (PEQF) 26, 65, 150; and rape and sexual offending cases 150–151, 151–154, 160; see also entry routes into policing
Egbert, S. 117, 118
Eliade, M. 158
Elphick, C. 118
EMMIE framework 87, 116–117

emotional intelligence 27
emotional labour 33
empathy 13, 101, 218
employment rights and legislation 11
empowering leadership 232
Enang, I. 149
Encrochat 188
Encrophone 188
entry routes into policing 2, 3, 4–6, 22, 215; Degree Holder Entry Programme (DHEP) 5, 37, 186; Detective Constable Entry Programme (DCEP) 5, 153; Detective Degree Holder Entry Programme (DDHEP) 222; leadership roles 234; Police Constable Degree Apprenticeship (PCDA) 5, 37, 186; Police Constable Entry Program (PCEP) 5, 150; Professional Policing Degree (PPD) 5
entry and search of property 66
environment and crime 44, 45–46
equal opportunities 11, 20
equality 8, 9, 11, 14, 19–20, 27, 232; general duties 19, 22
Equality Act (2010) 11, 14, 16, 17, 19, 20, 67, 224
Equality and Human Rights Commission 21
Esposito, E. 117, 118
ethical leadership 232
ethical/equality test 14–15
ethics/ethical behaviour 3–4, 8–23; current professional practice 11–22; historical context 8–11; and professional standards 30–31
European Convention on Human Rights and Fundamental Freedoms 1950 (ECHR) 65, 67–68, 70–71, 72
European Court of Human Rights (ECtHR) 68, 69–70, 74, 76, 78
Europol 182
evaluation of police practice 91
Everard, Sarah 36, 145, 155
evidence 82; confession 65, 75; digital *see* digital forensics; intelligence versus 175–176; *see also* case evidence; research evidence
evidence base 85–86, 87
evidence-based management 82, 89
evidence-based policing (EBP) 2–3, 26, 27, 30, 35, 36, 37, 47, 67, 82–97, 131; challenges associated with embedding 90–91; champions 88, 90, 92; coining of term 82, 84; and crime prevention 120; debate 87–88; definitions of 83–84; historical context 84–87; and leadership 88, 90, 240–242; and police powers 70, 78; and problem-solving 121–122; professional societies 92; research frameworks and 91–92; volunteers and 206–208, 209
evidence-based practice 4, 82, 84, 89, 132, 135
Executive (government), power of 66
Executive Leadership Programme (ELP) 234
experiential knowledge 89, 146
experiential learning 27, 32, 36, 221
expert opinions 86
extradition 71
Extreme Right Wing (XRW) 180–181

fair trial, right to 65, 72, 76
fairness 12, 13, 14, 98, 231; procedural 76, 149
far-right groups 171, 172, 174, 180–181
fear of crime 128, 129, 137
Federal Bureau of Investigation (FBI), leadership programme 240
Felson, M. 113, 135–136
Fenelon, F. 215
Fenian Campaign (1880s) 169
Fernanado, T. 105
Financial Investigation Units 192
Finkelstein, L. M. 217
firearms response 104
first line leaders (FLL) 88, 90, 131, 233–235, 241
Fishmongers Hall terrorist attack (2019) 180
'Five Eyes' partnership 176
Flannigan, R. 130
Fleming, J. 88, 89, 90, 207
Floyd, George 231
foot patrols 135–136
force, use of *see* use of force
Ford, D. A. 157
forensic investigation *see* digital forensics
Forensic Science Regulator 188, 189
Fox, Campbell and Hartley v United Kingdom (1990) 74
frames, awareness of 28–29
Frankpledge system 202
fraud, cyber-related 187, 188–189
Freedom of Assembly and Association 67, 68, 74
Freedom Convoy group 236
Freedom of Expression 67, 68

Freud, Sigmund 45
friendship, and coaching/mentoring relationship 220
full occupational competence (FOC) 3
funding 130, 236, 237
Funke v France (1993) 76
Fyfe, N. 87

G20 protests, Toronto (2010) 231
Gallie, W. B. 32
gang-related culture 46
Garvey, R. 220, 224
Gaza—Israel conflict 171–172
GCHQ *see* Government Communications Headquarters
General Equality Duties 19, 22
genetic explanations for criminal behaviour 45
Get Safe Online 190
Gibbons, S. 122
Gibb's Reflective Cycle 29, 221, 222
Gibraltar 2
Gill, M. 204
Gillan and Quinton v The United Kingdom (2010) 72
Gisborne, K. 239
Gladstone Report (1895) 53
globalisation 4
Goldstein Awards 113, 121
Goldstein, H. 82, 122, 128
Good Friday Agreement (1998) 170
Gorbachev, Mikhail 175
Gordievsky, Oleg 175
Government Code and Cypher School (GC & CS) 176
Government Communications Headquarters (GCHQ) 168, 176
Graef, R. 102
Gravells, J. 216, 224
Green, E. 233
GROW model of communication 214, 222
Guantánamo Bay detention facility 177–178
Gurvitch, G. 158

Hamas 171, 172
Hambley, O. 135
Hanrahan, K. 88
Hanway, P. 135
Hassard, J. 159
hate crime 21, 171
'Hate Crime Action Plan' (2016) 171
Hendy, H. M. 240
'Herbert Protocol' 120

Herrington, V. 230
Hester, M. 157
Hi-Tech Crime Units (HTCUs) 189, 192
hierarchical structure within policing 36, 38
Higgins, G. 232
'high' policing 174, 175, 176
Hillen, P. 37
Hillsborough disaster (1989) 10, 36
Hizballah 172
HM Inspectorate of Constabulary and Fire & Rescue Services (HMICFRS) 22, 26, 36, 37, 47, 98, 116, 155, 242
HM Inspectorate of Constabulary (HMIC) 105, 115, 130, 131, 137
HM Inspectorate of Probation 54
Hobbes, Thomas 66
Hohl, K. 149
Holliday, P. 239
Home Office 1, 4, 10, 48, 133, 234; Rape Review (2022) 146; Strategy Plan 2004—2008 129; Vulnerability Knowledge and Practice Programme (VKPP) 145
home security technology 114
Homer's 'Mentor' 214, 215
honesty 12, 13, 230, 242
'hot offenders' 44
'hot products' 44
hot spot policing 44, 93–94, 114, 115, 117, 135–136, 137
'hot victims' 44
'hue and cry' 98, 127
Huey, L. 241
Hughes, J. 30–31
Hulton, William 230
human rights 19–20, 35, 65, 67–73, 177
Human Rights Act 1998 (HRA) 8, 9, 11, 21, 65, 66, **67**, 67, 68–69, 72, 78
Hunter, G. 89, 90

I v DPP (2001) 68
impartiality 9
imprisonment *see* prison sentences
in groups 15
inclusion 8, 27, 219, 224, 231, 232
Inclusive Britain paper 74
independence: mentee/trainee 225; political, of police 231
Independent Office for Police Conduct (IOPC) 3, 10, 29, 37
independent patrol status (IPS) 3
Independent Police Complaints Commission (IPCC) 101, 104

independent sexual violence advisors (ISVAs) 148
indictable offences 50
inequality, social 46, 208
information 82
infrastructure, safeguarding of 179
initial police learning development programmes (IPLDPs) 215
Innes, M. 129, 135
innocence, presumption of 76
inspectors, Direct Entry 234
institutional racism 10, 66
integrity 12, 13, 230, 231, 232, 242
intelligence 175; actionable 176; counter-terrorism 169; neighbourhood policing and use of 129–130, 136–138; sharing of 176, 178; signals (SIGINT) 176; versus evidence 175–176
Intelligence and Security Committee, *What Needs to Change?* report 174
intelligence-based explanations for criminal behaviour 45
intelligence-led policing (ILP) 129, 137
inter-agency collaboration 58, 119–120, 132–133, 137
international terrorism 174
international/transnational crime 175, 229
Internet 186, 190, 191, 193, 237
Internet of Things (IoT) 197
Internet Watch Foundation (IWF) 189, 190
INTERPOL 190; 'red notice' 229
intersectionality, and victims of rape and serious sexual offending (RASSO) 149–151
intuition 89
Ioannou, M. 158
IOPC *see* Independent Office for Police Conduct
IPCC *see* Independent Police Complaints Commission
Ireland v The United Kingdom (1978) 68
Irish dissident terrorism 169, 170, 174
Irish Republican Army (IRA) 169, 170
Islamic extremism 171, 179–181
ISO 17025 188, 189
Israel—Gaza conflict 171–172

Jackson v Attorney General (2005) 66
James, A. 137
Jersey 2
Joint DA Action Plan 155
Joint Terrorism Analysis Centre (JTAC) 173–174
Judiciary, power of 66
juries 51
Just Stop Oil protests 65
justice: adversarial model of 50, 56; organisational 154; procedural 46, 151; reparative 52; restorative 52, 57
justices of the peace *see* magistrates

Kalyal, H. 207
Khan, Usman 180
Kinsella, E. A. 27, 28, 29
Kirby, S. 120, 121
knife crime 77
knowing-in-action 28, 30
knowledge 26, 27, 35, 36, 37, 82, 92; experiential 89, 146; tacit 28; 'Technical Rationality' model of 28
Koch, S. 106
Kodz, J. 241
Koehle, G. 88
Koerner, S. 29–30
Kolb, D. A. 221
Krameddine, Y. 100
Krimmel, J. T. 240

labelling theory 46
Langer, L. 82
language use 16–17, 98, 99
Lave, J. 221
Lawrence, Stephen 10, 21, 36
Laycock, G. 85, 92
leadership 12, 229–247; attributes 231; authentic 232; authoritarian 240; Canadian police 230, 231, 235–238, 241; civilian staff 234, 235; current professional practice 232–240; development opportunities 233–234; empowering 232; ethical 232; and evidence-based policing (EBP) 88, 90, 240–242; failures in 230–231; first line leaders 88, 90, 131, 233–235, 241; future development 240–242; history and context 230–232; police sergeants 233–234, 234–235; and problem-oriented policing (POP) 120–121; situational 120, 232; standards *see* leadership standards; supportive 232; transactional 120, 232, 234–234; transformational 120, 232, 235, 240, 242, 243; US police 230, 232, 239–240; visionary 232
leadership standards 229, 230, 232–233, 234, 235, 241, 242; Stage 1: Foundation leadership 233; Stage 2: First line leader 233; Stage 3: Mid-level leader 233;

Stage 4: Senior leader 233; Stage 5: Executive leader 233
learning: active 27, 32; experiential 27, 32, 36, 221; lifelong 220; transitions 220–221
learning culture 36
learning organisation 28, 37, 38
Leedham, M. 215
legal obligations 30, 31, 32, 33, 34, 37
legitimacy of police 46, 48, 70, 84, 98, 133, 145, 201, 205, 206, 208, 209, 231, 237
Lewis, S. 207
liberty: deprivation of 70, 71; right to 65, 68, 70–73, 74, 75, 78
lifelong learning 220
limited rights 68
Lindermuth, P. 240
listening 101, 102
Lister, S. 133
Litvinenko, Alexander 181
Lloyd, Tony, Baron Lloyd of Berwick 170
local criminal justice boards (LCJBs) 132
Lombroso, C. 44–45
London Rape Reviews, Metropolitan Police Service (MPS) 147, 148
London terrorist attacks: bombings July 2005 (7/7) 170, 174, 182; Fishmongers Hall (2019) 180; London Bridge (2017) 178; Streatham (2020) 180
'low' policing 174, 175, 176
Lum, C. 207
Lumsden, K. 88
Lynch, R. 233
Lynch, S. 233

Machiavelli, N. 12
MacIntyre, A. 33, 35
Macpherson, W. 10, 21
MacVean, A. 30
magistrates 51, 202
magistrates courts 50, 51
Mair, Thomas 171
Management of Sexual or Violent Offenders (MOSOVO) teams 192
Manchester Arena bombing (2017) 176, 178
Manchester rally (1819) 230
Manning, P. 35
Martin, P. 241
Maryland Scientific Methods Scale (SMS) 84, 85
Mastrofski, S. 101
Mawby, R. 204
Mayne, Sir Richard 8, 230
Mayor's Office for Policing and Crime (MOPAC) 4, 147

Mazerolle, L. 241
McCallum, Ken 181
McCann v The United Kingdom (1995) 68
McGill, I. 216, 222, 224
McKay, H. 45
McLean, K. 231
Me Too movement 10
meaning-making, trainee/mentee 221–222
media: relationships with 99; *see also* social media
Megginson, D. 216
Menezes, Jean Charles de 103
mens rea 50
mental health issues 119, 120, 138, 147, 148
mentoring 214–228; classical relationship in 217; collaborative relationship in 224–225; contract relationship in 217, 224, 225; dependence of mentee 224; formal 217; and friendship 220; GROW model of communication 214, 222; history and context 214–217; independence of mentee 225; influences on 219–223; informal 217; and learning transitions 220–221; and lifelong learning 220; meaning of term 216; and meaning-making 221–222; mentee characteristics 224; mentor characteristics 223–224; and police procedure and legislation 220; power imbalance in relationship 224; in professional police practice 217–219; pseudo relationship in 217; reverse 222; in supporting change of role 215–216; as training requirement 215; transitions that require 222–223; volunteerism 220
Merton, R. 45–46
Metropolitan Police Service (MPS) 2, 3, 4, 26, 48; Anti-Terrorism Branch (SO13) (Bomb Squad) 169, 170; Counter Terrorism Command (SO15) 170, 174; London Rape Reviews 147, 148; Special Branch 169, 170, 174; special constables 202
MI5 (Security Service) 169–170, 173, 174, 179, 182–183
MI6 (Secret Intelligence Service) 169, 175, 182–183
Miller, H. 230
miners' strikes (1980s) 65
Ministry of Defence Police (MDP) 2
misconduct 26; investigating complaints of 29; Royal Canadian Mounted Police (RCMP) 238

Index

misogyny 10, 26
missing persons 119, 120
Mitchell, R. 207
mobile technology 176, 187–188, 196–197; see also smartphones
Montesquieu, Baron de 66
moral agents/agency 32–33, 34, 35, 37–38
moral obligations 30, 31–32, 34, 35, 37
moral purpose 31
moralistic behaviour/decision-making 10
Morton-Cooper, A. 217
Mugari, I. 117
Multi Agency Gold Incident Command (MAGIC) course 234
multi-agency public protection arrangements (MAPPA) 55, 132, 192
multi-agency working see inter-agency collaboration
Murray v The United Kingdom (1996) 76
Myhill, A. 14

Nambiar, V. 118
National Counter Terrorism Security Office (NaCTSO) 2, 179
National Crime Agency (NCA) 2
National Cyber Security Centre (NCSC) 190
National Cyber Strategy 186–187
National Decision Model (NDM) 12, 13, 102–103, 104, 107
National Disclosure Improvement Plan (2018) 49
National Intelligence Model (NIM) 44, 129, 136, 137–138; codes of practice 136
National Investigators Exam (NIE) 5
National Police Air Service (NPAS) 2
National Police Chiefs' Council (NPCC) 4, 83, 138, 139, 145, 192; Terrorism Committee 170
National Police Promotions Framework (NPPF) 233
National Policing Curriculum (NPC) 2, 3, 107, 150
National Probation Service for England and Wales 54
National Protective Security Authority (NPSA) 179
National Reassurance Policing Programme (NRPP) 129
National Security Act (2023) 181
neighbourhood policing see community and neighbourhood policing
Neighbourhood Policing Programme 129–130

neighbourhood policing teams (NPTs) 130, 209
neighbourhood volunteers 205
Neighbourhood Watch schemes 44
neurophysiological explanations for criminal behaviour 45
New Zealand 92, 176, 241
Newell, D. 215
Newton, A. 90
Neyroud, P. 84, 229–230
NIM see National Intelligence Model
non-verbal communication 99, 100, 101, 105, 108
Northern Ireland 2, 170, 174
NPAS (National Police Air Service) 2
NPC see National Policing Curriculum
NPCC see National Police Chiefs' Council
NPPF (National Police Promotions Framework) 233
NPSA (National Protective Security Authority) 179
NRPP (National Reassurance Policing Programme) 129
Nutley, S. 88

oath of office 9–10
Obioha, E. 117
objectivity 12, 13
O'Brien, D. 114
offences see criminal offences
Offender Management Act (2007) 54
Offender Rehabilitation Act (2014) 54
offensive weapons 73, 77
Office for National Statistics (ONS) 154, 156, 188–189
officer in the case (OIC) 51
Official Secrets Acts 181
O'Hara v United Kingdom (2002) 76
Omand, Sir David 173
Omerta 188
Online Abuse Teams (OATs) 192
Online Child Abuse (Investigation) Teams (OCAT/OCAIT) 192
online child sexual abuse (OCSA) 118
Online Child Sexual Exploitation Teams (OCSEs) 192
online communication 99
online disinformation 58
online presence, police officers and staff presence on 194–195
ONS see Office for National Statistics
Open Source Intelligence (OSINT) teams 192
openness 13

Operation Hotton: Learning Report (IOPC) 10
Operation Soteria Bluestone 146, 150, 151, 154, 160
Operation Swamp 81 66
Operation Yewtree 190
O'Reilly, C. 117
organisational culture *see* police culture
organisational justice theory 154
organised crime 58, 75, 175, 209
out groups 15

PACE *see* Police and Criminal Evidence Act 1984
Paedophile Online Investigation Teams (POLITs) 192
Palmer, A. 217
Palmer, I. 2–3
Parliament, law-making power of 66, 69
Parole Board 47
Parsloe, E. 215, 217, 223, 224
partnership working 114; and crime prevention 132; and neighbourhood policing 132–133, 137; and problem-oriented policing (POP) 119–120, 122, 123
pattern recognition 118
PCCs *see* police and crime commissioners (PCCs)
PCDA (Police Constable Degree Apprenticeship) 5, 37, 186
PCSOs *see* police community support officers
PCEP (Police Constable Entry Programme) 5, 150
PCER (Police Constable Entry Routes) 2, 3, 4, 22, 215,
peaceful protest, right to 67, 78
Pearson-Goff, M. 230
Pease, K. 89, 91
PEEL (police effectiveness, efficiency and legitimacy) assessments 98, 131
Peel, Sir Robert 3, 8
'Peelian Principles' 3, 9, 127
penal system 52–57
penology 52
Pepper, I. 88, 90, 233
PEQF *see* Policing Education Qualifications Framework
personality, and criminal behaviour 45
Petersen, K. 86
PFCCs (police, fire and crime commissioners) 48
Philby, Kim 175

phronesis (practical wisdom) 32
Piaget, J. 27
Pickin v British Railways Board (1974) 66
Polanyi, M. 27, 28
police: and CPS relationship 49–49; 'gatekeeping' role of 48; as institution within criminal justice system 47–48, 59; role as public authority 65–81; and Victims' Code 57
Police Act (1964) 202
Police Act (1996) 9–10
police caution 77
police community support officers (PCSOs) 1, 130, 138, 229
Police and Community Together (PACT) meetings 134–135
Police (Complaints and Misconduct) Regulations (2020) 3
Police Conduct Regulations (2020) 14
Police Constable Degree Apprenticeship (PCDA) 5, 37, 176, 186
police constable entry routes *see* entry routes into policing
police and crime commissioners (PCCs) 4, 48, 130
Police and Criminal Evidence Act 1984 (PACE) 11, 20, 21, 65, 66, 67, 69, 70, 71, 72, 73, 74–76, 77, 177, 220; Codes of Practice 65, 66–67, 73, 74–76, 194
police culture 18; Canada 238; 'canteen culture' 18; change in 3, 121; conservatism 133; resistance to change 238
Police Executive Research Forum 237
police, fire and crime commissioners (PFCCs) 48
Police Foundation 138
police legitimacy 46, 48, 70, 84, 98, 133, 145, 201, 205, 206, 208, 209, 231, 237
police oath/attestation 9–10
police powers 65, 66–67, 69–70, 77–78; arrest 66, 70, 74–76, 78; and evidence-based policing (EBP) 70, 78; extraction of confession evidence 65, 75; proportionality in exercise of 70, 78; stop and search *see* stop and search powers
Police Reform Act (2002) 9, 10, 130
Police Reform and Social Responsibility Act (2011) 48, 130, 133–134
Police Scotland 2
Police Service of Northern Ireland (PSNI) 2
Police Staff Council Joint Circular 54 14

police support volunteers (PSVs) 1, 130, 204–206
policing by consent 8–9, 132, 201, 230, 242
Policing and Crime Act (2017) 48
Policing Education Qualifications Framework (PEQF) 26, 65, 150
'Policing Pledge' 130
policing principles 3–4, 9, 13; *see also* 'Peelian Principles'
Policing Protocol (2011) 32
Policing Uplift Programme (2019) 150, 153
Policing Vision (2025) 192
Policing Vision (2030) 139, 192–193
policing workforce 1–2; age profile of officers 150; numbers 130, 138, 150, 237, 239; percentage comparison of roles 1; Policing Uplift Programme (2019) 150, 153; retention issues 133, 150, 237; *see also* civilian staff; volunteers in policing
political independence 231
political policing 175
political values 12
Port, Stephen 10
positional asphyxia 105
positional duties 30, 31, 32, 33, 34, 37
positivist criminology 44–45
Poteet, M. L. 217
poverty 138
power: of branches of state 66; in coaching/mentoring relationship 224; *see also* police powers
PPD (Professional Policing Degree) 5
PPST (public and personal safety training) 104
practical wisdom (*phronesis*) 32
predictive policing 117, 118
prejudice 11, 14, 15, 16, 66
preventative policing *see* crime prevention
Prevention of Terrorism Act (2005) 69
Prevention of Terrorism (Temporary Provisions) Act (1974) 170
'Principles of Public Life' 12
prison overcrowding 53, 58
prison population 53
prison sentences 51, 52–53, 54, 55
prison service 47, 52–54, 59
'prison works' movement 53
privacy, invasion of 196
privacy settings, social media 194–195
private and family life, right to 8, 72
proactive policing 19, 115, 116, 121, 128, 129, 131, 138
Probation of Offenders Act (1907) 54

probation service 47, 52, 54–55, 57, 58, 59, 132
Probation Trusts 54
problem analysis triangle (PAT) 114
Problem Solving and Demand Reduction Programme (PSDRP) 120–121
problem-oriented policing (POP) 44, 82, 112, 115, 128, 129, 137; embedding 118–119, 122–123; future developments 121, 121–122; historical context 112–115; and leadership 120–121; in neighbourhoods and communities 116–117; and partnership working 119–120, 122, 123
problem-solving 44, 112, 113, 115, 116, 119, 129, 136, 137, 138, 220; and artificial intelligence (AI) 118; and crime prevention 114, 116, 117; and diversity, equality and inclusion (DEI) 121; and evidence-based policing (EBP) 121–122
procedural fairness 76, 149
procedural justice 46, 151
Professional Policing Degree (PPD) 5
professional practice, and reflective practice 28–29
professional standards 29, 30, 33, 34; and ethical behaviour 30–31; and positional duties and legal obligations 30, 31, 32, 33, 34; and reflective practice 26–27, 30, 31–32, 37
prohibited articles 72
'Project Rich Picture' 179
proportionality, doctrine of 70, 78
proscribed organisations 172, 180, 181
Prosecution of Offences Act (1985) 49
prosecutions: police-led 48; *see also* Crown Prosecution Service (CPS)
protected characteristics 16, 20, 67, 223–224protest, right to peaceful 67, 78
protest-related stop and search powers 73–74, 77–78
PSVs *see* police support volunteers
psychological explanations for criminal behaviour 45
public authority, role of police as 65–81
public meetings 134–135
public order, disruption of 68
Public Order Act (1986) 18, 65, 67
Public Order Act (2023) 65, 72, 73–74, 77
public and personal safety training (PPST) 104
public service 13
Punch, M. 2

punishment 51; purpose of 52; reductivist strategies 52; retributivist strategies 52, 53

qualified rights 68
qualitative research 87, 88, 91
Quality Assurance Agency (QAA) 5–6
Quinton, P. 14

R (Roberts) v Commissioner of the Metropolitan Police (2012) 73
Raaijmakers, N. 160
racism 18; institutional 10, 66
radicalisation 179–180, 181, 187
radio communication 107
Radzinowicz, L. 202
randomised controlled trials (RCTs) 84, 85, 86, 91
rank structure 35–36
rape and serious sexual offending (RASSO) 57, 145, 146–154, 160, 161–162; attrition 146–149; consent issues 146; contextual and situational aspects of vulnerability 149–151; first responders 150; intersectionality and victims of 149–151; learning and development opportunities for officers dealing with 150–151, 151–154, 160; National Operating Model (NOM) for 146; Operation Soteria Bluestone 146, 150, 151, 154, 160; person–specific aspects of vulnerability 149, 151; victim credibility 146, 148; victim withdrawal of complaints 148; victimisation and victim typologies 147, 149; vulnerability 146–151, 161–162; well-being of officers dealing with 153–154
rapid evidence assessments (REAs) 131
rational choice theory (RCT) 43–44, 114
Ray, K. 217
reactive policing model 115, 120, 121, 127, 128, 129, 209
Reagan, Ronald 175
reasonable doubt 50
reasonable suspicion, requirement of 66–67, 68, 72, 73, 74, 75
'reassurance gap' 129
'reassurance policing' 129
recorded crime, analysis of 129
records, decision-making 103
reductivist penal strategies 52
reflecting-in-action 28, 30
reflective organisations 35
reflective practice 19, 26–41, 89; and current professional policing practice 29–36; future developments 36–37; historical context 27–29; and professional practice 28–29; and professional standards 26–27, 30, 31–32, 37
reflective practitioners 27, 28–29; as moral agents 33, 34, 35, 37–38
reform/rehabilitation of offenders 51, 52, 53, 54, 55
Regina Riot (1932), Canada 231
Regional Counter-Terrorism Intelligence Units (CTIU) 174
Regional Counter-Terrorism Units (RCTU) 174–176
Regulation of Investigatory Powers Act 2000 (RIPA) 194
Reiner, R. 32
religious values 12
'religious wave' of terrorism 168, 171, 173, 176
reoffending 53
reparative justice 52
research 82; practitioners' co-production of 90; qualitative 87, 88, 91; rigour of 85, 86; validity of 85, 92
research evidence 83, 84; fallibility of 92; hierarchy of 84, 85–86, 86, 92; measuring and/or valuing 85–87, 91–92; professional experience as source of 89; quality of 85, 86; use of in contemporary professional policing 88–92
research methodologies 91, 92, 93, 208
research questions 91
researchers, status of 90–91
respect 12, 13, 14, 149, 231
response policing 119
responsibility, criminal, age of 55
responsibility-taking 29, 33
restorative justice 52, 57
retention of police officers 133, 150, 237
retributivist penal strategies 52, 53
Rhodes, A. 29
Rhodes, R. 88, 89
Right Care, Right Person (RCRP) initiative 102, 119–120
Riot Act (1715) 98
riots/rioting 65, 66, 67, 103, 105, 128
Roach, J. 89, 91
roads policing 119
Robinson, A. 157
Rogers, C. 90, 120
Rossmo, D. 118
routine activity theory (RAT) 43–44, 113–114, 136

Rowan, Sir Charles 8, 230
Rowe, M. 34
Royal Canadian Mounted Police (RCMP) 236, 237, 238
Royal Gibraltar Police 2
rule of law 12, 47, 177, 231
Rury, J. 36
Russia: state terrorism 181, 182–183; *see also* Soviet Union
Ryle, G. 27

Sachowski, J. 187
Salisbury poisonings (2018) 181, 182–183
SARA (scanning, analysis, response and assessment) framework 112–113, 116, 117, 122–123, 128, 137
Sarver, M. 230
Saunders Enquiry (2023) 176
Saunders v The United Kingdom (1997) 76
Scarman, L. G. 10, 66, 71, 128, 130
Schön, D. 27, 28, 29, 30, 222
'science of policing' 84
Scotland 2, 170, 174
Scott, M. 120, 121
Secret Intelligence Service *see* MI6
Secret Service Bureau 168–169
Secretary of State for the Home Department v JJ and Others (2007) 70
Security Service *see* MI5
Selby-Fell, H. 90
selflessness 13
Senior Leadership Programme (SLP) 234
sensitive, respectful and appropriate (SRA) model of communication 16
sentences 51; community 51, 53, 54; custodial/prison 51, 52–53, 54, 55; young offender 55
Sentencing Council 51
September 11 terrorist attacks (9/11) (2001) 168, 173, 177, 182
Sergeant and Inspector Promotion and Progression (SIPP) process 234
sergeants, leadership 233–234, 234–235
Serious Organised Crime and Police Act (2005) 75
Serious Sexual Assault Investigators Development Programme (SSAIDP) 152, 154
Serious Violence Reduction Orders (SVROs) 77
Seth, R. 203
Sex Offender Management Units (SOMUS) 192

sexual offences 57; *see also* rape and serious sexual offending (RASSO)
Shaw, C. 45
Shawcross, W. 177, 179, 180, 181
Sheptycki, J. W. E. 90–91
Sherman, L. 2, 82, 83, 84, 87, 207, 208, 240
Sidebottom, A 113, 115
'signal crimes' 129
signals intelligence (SIGINT) 176
Signori, R. 132
silence, right to 75, 76–77
Silverstone, P. 100
Simmons, A. J. 30
Singh, S. 118
situational crime prevention 44, 136
situational leadership 120, 232
Sklansky, D. A. 34
Skripal, Sergei and Yulia 182
smart home technologies 193, 194
SMARTER model in coaching 221
smartphones 187–188; applications 107
Smith, R. 234
SO13 *see* Anti-Terrorism Branch
SO15 *see* Counter Terrorism Command
social capital 201, 205
social contract theory 66, 70, 73
social disorganisation 45
social inequality 46, 208
social learning theory 46
social media 99, 107, 118, 193, 201, 242; police officers and staff presence on 194–195; privacy settings 194–195
social upheaval and crime 45–46
Society for Evidence Based Policing 92
sociological explanations for criminal behaviour 45–46
Socrates 12
Southern Police Institute (SPI), Administrative Officers Course 240
Soviet Union 175
Sparrow, M. 87, 88
spatial pattern of crime 45
Special Branch 169, 170, 174
Special Branch Regional Intelligence Centres (SB RIC) 174
special constables learning programme (SCLP) 203
special constables (SC) 1, 130, 138, 201, 202–204
Special Irish Branch 169
specialist domestic violence courts (SDVCs) 157
Staller, M. S. 29–30

262 Index

standards *see* leadership standards; professional standards
Stanko, E. (Betsy) 89, 90
state-sponsored terrorism 181–182, 182–183
Statement of Common Purpose and Values for the Police Service 3–4, 18
States of Jersey Police 2
status frustration 46
Statute of Westminster (1285) 202
'statutory' offences 50
Stead, P. 202
stereotyping 11, 14, 15, 16, 66
stigmatisation of offenders 46
Stockdale, K. 91
stop and search powers 15, 34, 65, 66–67, 71–74, 78; and Criminal Justice and Public Order Act (CJPOA) 73; protest-related 73–74, 77–78; and Public Order Act (2023) 73–74, 77; and right to liberty 71–73; safeguarding against misuse of 74
strain theory 45–46
Strategic Policing Requirement, and violence against women and girls (VAWG) 145
Strategic Review of Policing in England and Wales (Police Foundation, 2022) 138
Streatham terrorist attack (2020) 180
student volunteering schemes for policing 206
Sturgess, Dawn 182
subcultural theory of crime 46
summary offences 50
superintendents, Direct Entry 234
supportive leadership 232
Supreme Court 51
Sutherland, E. 46
Synott, J. 158
systematic reviews 85, 86, 117
Szewzuk, Michal 171

tacit knowledge 28
target hardening 44, 114, 115
tasers 104, 105
Taylor, F. 231
technical rationality 28
technological advancements 48; and communication 107; impact on criminal justice 58; *see also* artificial intelligence (AI); mobile technology
Telep, C. 207
telephone communication 99, 107

temporal sequencing 156, 158–160
terrorism 68, 69; definitions of 170–171; domestic 174; far-right 171, 172, 174, 180–181; international 174; Irish dissident 169, 170, 174; Islamic-based 171, 179–181; new 168, 176; proscribed organisations 172, 180, 181; 'religious wave' of 168, 171, 173, 176, 181; state-sponsored 181–182, 182–183; threat levels 173–174; *see also* anti-terrorism; counter-terrorism
Terrorism Act (2000) 170–171, 172
Thatcher, Margaret 175
Thomas, K. 114
Tilley Awards 113, 121
Tilley, N. 85, 92, 116
time: culture and differing perspectives on 158; cyclical conception of 159; linear concept of 158; theories of 156, 158–159
training *see* education and training
transactional leadership 120, 232, 234–235
transformational leadership 120, 232, 235, 240, 242, 243
transnational crime 175, 229
trial: accused's silence at 77; release pending 71; right to 71; right to fair trial 65, 72, 76
True, J. 119
trust in police 4, 8, 12, 13, 14, 36, 37, 38, 208, 209, 230
trustworthiness 230, 232, 242
Tuffin, R. 114

UK/USA Communication Intelligence Agreement (1946) 176
unconscious bias 11, 14, 15
Unit Beat Policing scheme 127
United States (USA): community policing 128–129; evidenced–based policing (EBP) 241; Federal Bureau of Investigation (FBI) 240; Guantánamo Bay detention facility 177–178; life or death decision-making by police 239–240; police funding 237; police leadership 230, 232, 239–240; police officer numbers 239; police violence 99; President's Task Force on 21st Century Policing (2015) 239; protest policing 231; right to silence 76; September 11 terrorist attacks (2001) 168, 173; and UK Communication Intelligence Agreement (1946) 176; War on Terror 168, 173, 177

use of force 103, 104, 105; aftercare 105; continuum 105, 108; reasonable 9, 68

validity of research 85, 92
values 11–12, 15, 29, 31
VAWG see violence against women and girls
Veltri, G. A. 87
vetting 26
Victim Personal Statement Scheme 7
Victim Support (charity) 56
victim-blaming 57
victimology, rape 147
victims 56–57; 'hot' 44; 'special measures' help 56–57; support/entitlements 21, 56–57; vulnerability/difference and selection of 21–22
Victims' Code 21, 56, 57, 196
Victims' Commissioner 57
Victims and Prisoners Act (2024) 56, 57
'video' doorbells 114
Villiers, P. 35
violence against women and girls (VAWG) 4, 10, 48, 119, 122, 145–146; and Strategic Policing Requirement 145; Strategic Threat and Risk Assessment (STRA) 145; vulnerability and 145, 160; see also domestic abuse (DA); rape and serious sexual offending (RASSO)
Violent and Sex Offender Register (ViSOR) 192
virtual court hearings 58
visibility 132, 133, 134, 135, 139
visionary leadership 232
Vito, G. F. 232, 240
volunteer police cadet (VPC) leaders 205
volunteers in policing 201–213; cost effectiveness 206; current professional practice 203–206; and evidence–based policing (EBP) 206–208, 209; future developments 208–209; historical context 202–203; internal resentment towards 206; and legitimacy of policing 206; neighbourhood volunteers 205; police support volunteers (PSV) 1, 130, 204–206; special constables (SC) 1, 130,
138, 201, 202–204; student volunteering schemes 206
vulnerability 160, 161; definitions of 149, 150; domestic abuse (DA) 154–156, 158, 160; rape and serious sexual offending (RASSO) 146–151, 161–162; violence against women and girls (VAWG) 145, 160
Vulnerability Knowledge and Practice Programme (VKPP) 145
vulnerable communities 132

Waddington, P. A. J. 18, 31, 35
Wallace, S. 216, 224
War on Terror 168, 173, 177
Weisburd, D. 84
Wenger, E. 221
WePROTECT Global Alliance 190
Westley, W. 99
What Works Centre for Crime Reduction (WWCCR) 85, 89, 131, 241; Manning cost-benefit tool (MCBT) 116; Toolkit 86, 87, 116–117
Whitmore, J. 214
Williams, E. 35, 90, 160
Williamson, T. 127
Willis, J. 101
Wilson, J. Q. 100
Wilson, P. 87
Wingrove, J. 207
Winnipeg General Strike (1919), Canada 231
Wood, D. 92
Wood, D. A. 35
Woolmington v DPP (1935) 76
workforce *see* policing workforce

Yesberg, J. 133
Youth Courts 55
Youth Justice Board (YJB) 55–56
youth justice system 55–56
youth mentoring programmes 215
youth offending teams (YOTs) 56
Youth Rehabilitation Orders 55

zero-tolerance policing 45

For Product Safety Concerns and Information please contact our EU representative GPSR@taylorandfrancis.com Taylor & Francis Verlag GmbH, Kaufingerstraße 24, 80331 München, Germany